# THE SCHOOLS
# OUR CHILDREN
# DESERVE

ALSO BY ALFIE KOHN

*No Contest: The Case Against Competition*

*The Brighter Side of Human Nature:*
*Altruism and Empathy in Everyday Life*

*You Know What They Say . . . :*
*The Truth About Popular Beliefs*

*Punished by Rewards: The Trouble with*
*Gold Stars, Incentive Plans, A's, Praise, and Other Bribes*

*Beyond Discipline:*
*From Compliance to Community*

EDITOR:
*Education, Inc.:*
*Turning Learning into a Business*

*What to Look For in a Classroom . . . and Other Essays*

# The Schools Our Children Deserve

## MOVING BEYOND TRADITIONAL CLASSROOMS AND "TOUGHER STANDARDS"

*Alfie Kohn*

HOUGHTON MIFFLIN COMPANY

*Boston    New York*

1999

For information about permission to reproduce selections from
this book, write to Permissions, Houghton Mifflin Company,
215 Park Avenue South, New York, New York 10003.

Library of Congress Cataloging-in-Publication Data
Kohn, Alfie.
The schools our children deserve : moving
beyond traditional classrooms and "tougher
standards" / Alfie Kohn.
p.    cm.
Includes bibliographical references (p.    ) and index.
ISBN 0-395-94039-7
1. School improvement programs — United States.
2. Education — Aims and objectives — United States.
3. Educational change — United States.   I. Title.
LB2822.82.K65   1999
371.2'00973 — dc21      99-31122
CIP

Printed in the United States of America

QUM  10  9  8  7  6  5  4  3  2  1

# CONTENTS

# THE SCHOOLS
# OUR CHILDREN
# DESERVE

# ❧ 1 ❧
# FORWARD . . .
# INTO THE PAST

*Abigail is given plenty of worksheets to complete in class as well as a substantial amount of homework. She studies to get good grades, and her school is proud of its high standardized test scores. Outstanding students are publicly recognized by the use of honor rolls, awards assemblies, and bumper stickers. Abigail's teacher, a charismatic lecturer, is clearly in control of the class: students raise their hands and wait patiently to be recognized. The teacher prepares detailed lesson plans well ahead of time, uses the latest textbooks, and gives regular quizzes to make sure kids stay on track.*

WHAT'S WRONG with this picture? Just about everything.

The features of our children's classrooms that we find the most reassuring—largely because we recognize them from our own days in school—typically turn out to be those least likely to help students become effective and enthusiastic learners. That dilemma is at the heart of education reform—or at least at the heart of this book. On the relatively rare occasions when nontraditional kinds of instruction show up in classrooms, many of us become nervous if not openly hostile. "Hey, when I was in school the teacher was in front of the room, teaching us what we needed to know about addition and adverbs and atoms. We paid attention and studied hard if we knew what was good for us. And it worked!"

Or did it? Never mind all those kids who gave up on school and came to think of themselves as stupid. The more interesting question is whether those of us who were successful students "achieved this success by memorizing an enormous number of words without necessarily understanding them or caring about them."[1] Is it possible that we are not really as well educated as we'd like to think? Might we have spent a good chunk of our childhoods doing stuff that was exactly as pointless as we suspected it was at the time?

It's not easy to acknowledge these possibilities, which may help to explain the aggressive nostalgia that is loose in the land. Any number of people subscribe to the Listerine theory of education: the old ways may be distasteful, but they're effective. Doubtless, this belief is reassuring; unfortunately, it's also wrong. Traditional schooling turns out to be as unproductive as it is unappealing. Thus, we ought to be demanding *non*-traditional classrooms for our kids, and supporting teachers who know enough to reject the siren call of "back to basics." We ought to be asking why our children aren't spending more time thinking about ideas and playing a more active role in the process of learning. In such an environment, they're not only more likely to be engaged with what they're doing but also to do it better.

Parents have rarely been invited to consider this point of view, which is why schools continue operating in pretty much the same way, using pretty much the same set of assumptions and practices, as the decades roll by. In this chapter, I'll try to explain what traditional schooling is, then make the case that it's still the dominant model in American education and explain why this is so. After that, I'll turn to a more recent, and closely related, phenomenon: the widespread call to raise "standards" that has come to dominate discussions about school reform. Once we understand more about the support for traditional teaching and for Tougher Standards — arguably the two dominant forces in our educational system — we'll be ready to analyze them critically and explore alternatives that may make more sense for our children.

## Two Models of Schooling

Let us begin by acknowledging that there are as many ways of teaching as there are teachers. Anyone who attempts to apply a single set of labels to all educators will be omitting some details and ignoring some complications — not unlike someone who describes politicians in terms of how far they are to the left or right. Still, it isn't entirely inaccurate to classify some classrooms and schools, some people and proposals, as tilting toward a philosophy that is more traditional or conservative as opposed to nontraditional or progressive. The former might be called the Old School of education, which of course is not a building but a state of mind — and ultimately a statement about the mind.

When asked what they think schools ought to look like, some back-to-basics proponents cite the importance of "obedience to authority" and list certain favored classroom practices: "Students sit together (usually in rows) and everyone follows the same lesson. Missing are . . . clusters of youngsters working at a pace and on a topic of their own choosing. In basics classrooms, lines of responsibility are very clear; everyone knows his or her task and recognizes who is in charge." The idea is to have students memorize facts and definitions, to make sure that skills are "drilled into" them. Even in social studies, as one principal explains, "We are much more concerned about teaching where Miami is than about Miami's problem with Cubans."[2] Not all traditionalists would go quite that far, but most would agree that schooling amounts to the transmission of a body of knowledge from the teacher (who has it) to the child (who doesn't), a process that relies on getting the child to listen to lectures, read textbooks, and, often, to practice skills by completing worksheets. Furthermore, "children should be behind their desks, not roaming around the room. Teachers should be at the head of the classrooms, drilling knowledge into their charges."[3]

In the Old School, reading lessons tend to teach specific sounds, such as long vowels, in isolation; math classes emphasize basic facts and calculations. Academic fields (math, English, history) are taught separately. Within each subject, big things are broken down into bits, which are then taught in a very specific sequence. The model also tends to include traditional grades, plenty of tests and quizzes, strict (punitive) discipline, competition, and lots of homework. Anything that deviates from this model is often reviled as a fad, with special scorn reserved for efforts to teach social skills or address students' feelings, to have students learn from one another, to use nontraditional ways of assessing what they can do, as well as to adopt bilingual education, a multicultural curriculum, or a structure that brings together students of different ages or abilities.

Nontraditional or progressive education is defined in part by its divergence from all of this. Here, the point of departure is that kids should be taken seriously. Because learning is regarded as an active process, learners are given an active role. Their questions help to shape the curriculum, and their capacity for thinking critically is honored even as it is honed. In such classrooms, facts and skills are important but not ends in themselves. Rather, they are more likely to be organized around broad themes, connected to real issues, and seen as part of the process of coming to understand ideas from the inside out. A classroom is a place where a community of learners—as opposed to a collection of discrete individuals—engages in discovery and invention, reflection and problem solving.

These aspects of progressive education (and many others, to be discussed in chapter 8) have been around for a very long time—so long, in fact, that they may actually define the more traditional approach. For centuries, children learned by doing at least as much as by listening. Hands-on activities sometimes took place in the context of a mentor-apprentice relationship and sometimes in a one-room schoolhouse with plenty of cooperative learning among kids of different ages. Many aspects of the Old School, meanwhile, really aren't so old: "The isolated-skills approach to learning," for example, "was, in fact, an innovation that started in the 1920s."[4]

What we may as well continue to call the traditional approach (if only to avoid confusion) represents an uneasy blend of behaviorist psychology and conservative social philosophy. The former, associated with such men as B. F. Skinner and Edward L. Thorndike (who never met a test he didn't like), is based on the idea that people, like other organisms, do only what they have been reinforced for doing. "All behavior is ultimately initiated by the external environment,"[5] as the behaviorists see it — and anything other than behavior, anything that isn't observable, either isn't worth our time or doesn't really exist. Learning is just the acquisition of very specific skills and bits of knowledge, a process that is linear, incremental, measurable. It says the learner should progress from step to step in a predictable sequence, interrupted by frequent testing and reinforcement, with each step getting progressively more challenging.

It's a straight shot from a theory like that to a reliance on worksheets, lectures, and standardized tests. On the other hand, not all proponents of worksheets, lectures, and standardized tests consider themselves behaviorists. In some cases, traditional educational practices are justified in terms of philosophical or religious beliefs. There is no single seminal figure responsible for an emphasis on order and obedience in the classroom, but the idea that education should consist of transmitting a body of information is today promoted most visibly by E. D. Hirsch, Jr., a man best known for specifying what facts every first-grader, second-grader, third-grader, and so on ought to know.

In the case of progressive education, it can safely be said that two twentieth-century individuals, John Dewey and Jean Piaget, have shaped the way we think of this movement. Dewey (1859–1952) was a philosopher who disdained the capital-letter abstractions of Truth and Meaning, preferring to see these ideas in the context of real human purposes. Thinking, he argued, is something that emerges from our shared experiences and activities: it is what we do that animates what we know. Dewey was also interested in democracy as a way of living, not just as a form of government. In applying these ideas to education, he made the case that schools shouldn't be about handing down a collection of static truths to the next generation but about responding to the needs and interests of the students themselves. When you do that, he maintained, you won't have to bribe, threaten, or otherwise artificially induce them to learn (as is routinely done in traditional classrooms).

Jean Piaget (1896–1980), a Swiss psychologist, demonstrated that the way children think is qualitatively different from the way adults think and argued that a child's way of thinking progresses through a series of distinct stages. Later in his life, he began to analyze the nature of learning, describing it as a two-way relationship between a person and the environment. All of us develop theories or perspectives through which we understand everything we encounter, yet those theories are themselves revised on the basis of our experience. Even very young children play an active role in making sense of things, "constructing" reality rather than just acquiring knowledge.

•

These two basic approaches rarely show up in pure form, with schools being completely traditional or nontraditional. The defining features of traditional education don't always appear together, or at least not with equal emphasis. Some decidedly Old School teachers assign essays as well as worksheets; others downplay rote memorization. Likewise, some progressive classrooms emphasize individual discovery more than cooperation among students. Even from a theoretical perspective, what appears at a distance to be a unified school of thought turns out, as you approach it, to be more like a teeming collection of factions that accept some common principles but loudly disagree about a good many others.

Still, those common principles are worth exploring. There is a very real contrast between behaviorism and "constructivism," the latter having grown out of Piaget's investigations. The things that teachers do can usefully be described as more consistent with one theory of learning or the other. Likewise, there is a marked difference between classrooms that are relatively authoritarian or "teacher-centered" and those that are more "learner-centered,"[6] in which students play a role in making decisions. It's therefore worth thinking about the philosophy that predominates in the schools to which we send our kids.

## Back *to Basics? When Did We Leave?*

Proponents of traditional education often complain that the model they favor is on the wane. They're apt to describe themselves as a brave minority under siege, fighting an uphill battle for old-fashioned methods that have been driven out of the schools by an educational establishment united in its desire for radical change.[7]

Such claims are understandable as a political strategy; it's always rhetorically advantageous to position yourself as outside the establishment and to describe whatever you oppose as "fashionable." To those of us who spend time in real schools, though, claims about the dominance of progressive teaching represent an inversion of the truth so audacious as to be downright comical. As we slip into a new century, traditional education is alive and well and—as I see it—damaging a whole new generation of students. If this isn't always obvious, it may be because we rarely think about how many aspects of education could be different but aren't. What we take for granted as being necessary features of the school experience are actually reflections of one kind of schooling—the traditional kind.[8]

Consider: Just as we did, our kids spend most of their time in school with children their own age. Most high school instruction is still divided into 45- or 50-minute periods. Students still have very little to say about what they will do and how they will learn. Good behavior or meritorious academic performance, as determined unilaterally by adults, is still rewarded; deviations are still punished. Grades are still handed out; awards assemblies are still held. Students are still "tracked," particularly in the older grades, so that some take honors and advanced placement courses while others get "basic" this and "remedial" that. Kids may be permitted to learn in groups periodically, but at the end of the day eyes must still be kept on one's own paper. Even from a purely physical standpoint, schools today look much as they did decades ago.[9]

Education, like other social institutions, is said to go through pendulum-like swings, from left to right and back again.[10] We are now living through what will surely be classified as a particularly conservative, even reactionary, era in American education. But the extent of experimentation with alternative models even during the more progressive periods has been exaggerated. As the educational historian Larry Cuban has argued, "Basic ways of schooling children have been remarkably durable over the last hundred years." His review of "almost 7,000 different classroom accounts and results from studies in numerous settings revealed the persistent occurrence of teacher-centered practices since the turn of the century."[11] (We used to copy facts from the World Book; today, our kids download them from the Web. So much for the educational revolution.) Most of the nontraditional practices I will describe later exist as "isolated examples," which are "tolerated only occasionally as alternatives for special groups of students," notes another scholar.[12] And from yet a third source: "Most teaching in U.S. classrooms is rather didactic. Teachers and students spend most of their time with lectures, or formal recitations, or worksheets, or some combination thereof."[13]

Shortly before his death, Dewey reflected sadly on how little of his vision had ever made it into the schools, how the changes that did occur were merely "atmospheric" and hadn't "really penetrated and permeated the foundations of the educational institution." The "fundamental authoritarianism" of that institution, he remarked, had remained intact.[14] Other observers have agreed, with one historian writing, "One cannot understand the history of education in the United States during the twentieth century unless one realizes that Edward K. Thorndike won and John Dewey lost."[15]

Nor is this just a matter of speculation. In 1979, John Goodlad conducted what is still regarded as one of the most comprehensive studies of American classrooms, visiting more than a thousand in all. He found virtually nothing but traditional instruction all over the country: the overwhelming majority of classrooms were "almost entirely teacher dominated with respect to seating, grouping, content, materials, use of space, time utilization, and learning activities." Moreover, "teachers out-talked the entire class of students by a ratio of three to one," and when students did get to talk, it was usually to give a factual answer to a teacher's question.[16]

Since then, very little has changed. One writer estimates that reform efforts in the 1980s affected maybe one school in a hundred.[17] Goodlad's subsequent visits to schools around the country (like my own, I might add) have turned up precious little evidence that the Old School has lost ground — outside a few oases of nontraditional education. In 1999, Goodlad wrote, "Although progressive views have enjoyed sufficient visibility to bring down on them and their adherents barrages of negative rhetoric, they have managed to create only isolated islands of practice. . . . Most teachers adhere closely to a view of school as they experienced it as students and so perpetuate the traditional."[18]

In many places, things are actually moving backward. Take "the children's garden," which is the translation of *Kindergarten*. In many places, it has been "turned into a first-grade readiness program," with "whole-class, teacher-directed instruction, formal reading instruction, written assignments out of workbooks, and frequent grading." This is being done to five-year-olds despite the nearly unanimous view among early childhood specialists that it's a horrible idea.[19] One kindergarten teacher who has begun drilling her children on vocabulary words remarked that "they can play and take naps at home. They are here to learn."[20] Indeed, the back-to-basics movement has been defined in part as an effort to ensure that "teaching methods intended for high-school students were imposed on first graders."[21]

But pity the high school students for whom these methods were originally intended. While some younger children have so far been spared this stultifying approach to schooling, few teenagers are so lucky. There has been "a dearth of experience with progressive education at the secondary school level anywhere in the country, even in private or suburban schools* that [have] had a tradition of progressive schooling on the elementary level."[22]

At all age levels, "traditional mathematics teaching . . . is still the norm in our nation's schools," one researcher reported in 1999.[23] The emphasis on traditional techniques and basic skills in that subject stands out even more sharply when U.S. teachers are compared to their peers in other countries, such as Japan (see pp. 226–27). Moreover, "from 40% (elementary) to 69% (high school) of [U.S.] math teachers indicated that they rely on a textbook for *more than 80% of their teaching,* and most math teachers (at least 60%) reported that their instruction is 'very [similar]' or 'quite similar' to textbook tests."[24] In science teaching, meanwhile, hands-on activities have become more popular, but lecturing and textbooks continue to dominate here, too.[25]

If there is one area where nontraditional schooling has had some impact, it has been the teaching of reading and writing in the early grades. But the idea that old-fashioned methods have been abandoned in favor of the more progressive approach known as Whole Language (see chapter 9) is patently false. In a large national survey published in 1998,[26] 99 percent of randomly selected kindergarten, first-grade, and second-grade teachers said they were committed to the idea that phonics instruction is important, if not essential. This means either that Whole Language isn't as rampant as has been claimed or that it doesn't exclude the teaching of phonics. The latter, as we'll see later, is definitely true. But the former explanation also seems accurate, judging by a closer reading of that survey.[27] Indeed, one expert estimated that only about 5 percent of American primary-grade teachers could be described as really following the philosophy of Whole Language.[28]

Even that low number may be dropping as conservative opponents succeed in convincing public officials to back their position with the force of law. Educators from coast to coast "have been faced with increasingly prescriptive mandates [regarding] the way children are taught to read."[29] For example, in just two years, 1996 and 1997, state legislators across the country introduced sixty-seven phonics bills. To date, at least ten

---

* The difference between an elite high school and a run-of-the-mill high school is that in the former a small number of students listen intently to the teacher while in the latter a large number of students are supposed to be listening intently to the teacher.

states have enacted such laws, a result of lobbying by some of the very people who ordinarily denounce the encroachment of Big Government.[30] In California, politicians have even succeeded in requiring people who train teachers to take what is basically a phonics loyalty oath.[31] Thus, whatever popularity Whole Language manages to earn may be undone by people outside the field of education who won't allow it to be used.

This reflects a pattern that extends beyond how children are taught to read. Even where mild, tentative efforts have been made to change how students are taught and tested, many of these reforms subsequently get rolled back. Look at the way students and schools are evaluated: a definitive survey published in 1997 reported that politicians across the country have "pushed to set aside innovative approaches to assessment and to return to commercially available, norm-referenced tests."[32] Look at the middle school movement, a long-overdue attempt to turn the hell that is junior high school into a more supportive, developmentally appropriate place for young adolescents. Today, that movement is on the defensive as champions of the Old School succeed in their quest for ever-tougher standards, more testing, and a return to high school–style instruction.[33] And look at the entire state of California, which in the 1990s has put the French counterrevolution to shame with its reversals of attempts to reform how reading is taught, how math is taught, and how learning is assessed.[34]

Overall, Larry Cuban concluded in the fall of 1998, "The traditionalists have won. New math and whole-language reading are in retreat. Today there are more phonics, more multiplication tables, more tests. There is a consensus between the public and officials that the basic, traditional model is the one to pursue."[35]

## Poor Teaching for Poor Kids

One place where traditional teaching rules with a vengeance is in "urban" or "inner-city" schools, which are generally euphemisms for those attended by children of color from low-income families. In 1977, one writer observed that "the ghetto has been a hotbed for the basics." It was still true twenty years later: "The highly traditional techniques of instruction are prevalent among lower-status groups." Now, however, minority children are also more likely than their peers to spend time taking multiple-choice standardized tests and to be taught a low-level curriculum designed around those tests — all in the name of "raising standards," of course.[36]

Some people may favor subjecting poor African-American and Latino children to "teaching styles that stress drill, practice, and other mind-numbing strategies" because they assume that "such children lack ability."[37] Others swear that they simply have the best interests of these kids at heart when they make them fill in blanks and even chant answers in unison. Lately, this kind of prescription for inner-city schools has been endorsed by a number of mainstream journalists and politicians. One reporter, writing in the *Atlantic Monthly* in 1998, endorsed a packaged drill-and-skill program called Success for All that is "used almost exclusively in poor schools," remarking that it may be "punitive to local school boards, principals, and teachers — but they had it coming."[38] (He doesn't say what the children have done to deserve it.) The mayor of Jersey City, New Jersey, also waxed enthusiastic about a pedagogical approach that relies on "constant drill and repetition." In his words, "It's not that hard to give answers if someone just told you. They memorize back and know and get used to a lot of A's on quizzes." So would he send his own kids to the kind of school he is advocating for those who are poor and black? Well, no. " 'Those schools are best for certain children,' he said."[39]

The question is not whether inner-city schools are in trouble. The question is whether they're in trouble because they're insufficiently traditional or overly devoted to higher-level thinking. If the problem lies elsewhere, then more emphasis on basic skills is unlikely to make things better. Indeed, given what the research says about that approach (see Appendix A), we may be witnessing an example of destroying these schools in order to save them. Dorothy Strickland, an African-American educator, has remarked that "skills-based instruction, the type to which most children of color are subjected, tends to foster low-level uniformity and subvert academic potential."[40] Thus, the more they fill in worksheets on command, the further they fall behind affluent kids who are less tightly controlled and more likely to get lessons that help them understand ideas.

"What the academic achievement gap may really be telling us," suggests Mano Singham of Case Western Reserve University, "is that, while the symptoms of the education system's ills are more clearly visible in the black community than in the white, there are fundamental problems with the way education is delivered to *all* students"[41] — beginning, perhaps, with the metaphor of education as something that is "delivered" to passive recipients. Even if we attribute only the best of intentions to those who insist on an industrial-strength version of Old School methods for disadvantaged youngsters, this recommendation reflects the assumption that when things get really bad, when the need is greatest, nothing works as well as traditional methods. As long as that assumption persists, alternative ways of teaching will rarely be used even if the evidence supports their value for all children.

## Explaining Educational Déjà Vu

I have taken the time to demonstrate the continued traditionalism of American schools for two reasons. First, to look at all this evidence together is to understand the absurdity of claims that progressivism runs rampant in our educational system. Second, many traditionalists insist that our schools are failing. Let's assume, despite some data to the contrary (coming up in a few pages), that here they have a point. In that case, we'll be better able to understand why there's a problem if we begin with a truthful account of what's really going on in our schools. If, as the evidence indicates, anything that might reasonably be called progressive is actually a rarity in American education, it becomes rather difficult to blame our problems (real or alleged) on these progressive practices. Indeed, the facts have the effect of turning the argument on its head: if students aren't learning effectively, it may be *because of* the persistence of traditional beliefs and practices—a hypothesis supported by a considerable body of evidence, as we'll see.

Of course, this possibility just raises another question: if traditional education hasn't succeeded on its merits, why is it still around? Broadly speaking, there are two answers. First, the tried-and-false methods have attracted a loyal constituency that acts to thwart reform efforts; and second, nontraditional education is very difficult to do well and sustain. We'll consider the first reason now and come back to the second one later in the book.

Without a doubt, traditionalists continue to be remarkably successful at disseminating their models and methods and at persuading the public of their value. The trick here is to figure out how this happens without resorting to the equivalent of their own bizarre conspiracy theories about a monolithic "educationist" establishment. This much is quite clear: conservatives of different stripes have fought hard, and usually successfully, to retain back-to-basics, skills-oriented education. For starters, this teacher-centered model follows naturally from seeing "the purpose of education [as mastering] a body of knowledge," and that view, in turn, is held with some fervor by "religious conservatives who look upon the Bible as the revealed truth."[42] E. D. Hirsch Jr.'s *Dictionary of Cultural Literacy,* which popularized what we might call the "bunch o' facts" approach to education, was enthusiastically endorsed in Phyllis Schlafly's Eagle Forum newsletter. "In a number of communities," meanwhile, support of direct phonics instruction and opposition to Whole Language "is one of the main organizing issues for the Christian Coalition."[43] And more secular conservatives lobby just as hard. In 1998 alone, the Direct Instruction model (see p. 213) was the subject of wildly enthusiastic articles in the *National Review, Policy Review* (published by the right-wing Heritage Foundation), and *Investors Business Daily.*

The Old School may owe a debt of gratitude to this alliance of social-religious and economic conservatives (who disagree on many other issues), but our search for explanations doesn't end here. Politicians and business leaders, only some of whom would identify themselves as conservative, tend to support the identical educational agenda — or at least are unlikely to oppose it. It's politically safe — and, if you've never really thought about the issues involved, apparently sensible — to come out in favor of a back-to-basics approach to education.

Then there are the mass media. More than a few reporters, columnists, and other writers vigorously support traditional education, sometimes turning news stories into barely disguised editorials lauding various aspects of the Old School and deriding anything progressive. But possibly even more influential are their less committed colleagues who accept the premises of traditional education without being aware of it, who casually ignore or write off some of the most promising, rigorous, and research-backed educational reforms. Articles about education that appear in U.S. newspapers and magazines, like depictions of classrooms in movies and on TV, reinforce traditional assumptions about how things should look (the teacher in front, holding forth) and how excellence is defined (knowing a set body of facts and skills).

Even many reporters who specialize in education are likely to accept standardized test scores as the sole basis for deciding whether a practice is effective or a school is in trouble. That such scores may be meaningless or worse (see chapter 4) literally hasn't occurred to these journalists, nor have they questioned other elements of the educational status quo. Thus, when a recent survey revealed that the men and women who make their living studying how children learn have some ideas that diverge from those of the general public, that finding wasn't presented by reporters as an invitation to rethink our assumptions about education. Rather, it was the experts who were simply assumed to be "out of touch."[44] In short, the result of a steady stream of articles about education that take so much of the Old School for granted, along with a relentless drumbeat of support by advocates, is that this model comes to be accepted by the rest of us, and it endures.

Of course, that model already enjoys the advantage of being familiar to us from our own days at school. We're reassured by signs of traditionalism—letter grades, spelling quizzes, heavy textbooks, a teacher in firm control of the classroom—and we're unnerved by their absence.* Our kids may hate school, but we accept that as a fact of life. Instead of demanding that our children get better than we got, it's as though our position was: "Listen, if it was bad enough for me, it's bad enough for my kids."

And what if our kids are lucky enough to have a teacher who does things differently and makes school exciting for them? Sure, we're glad to see them happy, but part of us wonders whether they're really learning anything. After all, "learning" is memorizing random facts and doing whatever you're told. You're not supposed to like it. And if we're mostly concerned to get our children into college, that process further strengthens the "conception of teaching as transmitting codified knowledge."[46] What's remarkable in light of all these factors is not that the Old School persists, but that there are any places where it doesn't.

## The Demand for Tougher Standards

"Motherhood" can be a code for keeping women out of the workplace, and apple pie is loaded with fat and sugar. These days, anyone looking for a cause without controversy would do better to come out in favor of higher standards for our schools. It's a safe bet that almost any audience will vigorously applaud such a sentiment, since it is widely agreed that our educational system is in deep trouble and that raising standards is the solution. On the other hand, whenever agreement is a bit too quick and consensus a little too broad, it's worth taking another look.

People who talk about educational "standards" use the term in different ways. Sometimes they're referring to guidelines for teaching, the implication being that we should change the nature of instruction—a horizontal shift, if you will. (In the case of the standards drafted by the National Council of Teachers of Mathematics [NCTM] in 1989, for example, the idea was to shift away from isolated facts and memorized procedures toward conceptual understanding and problem solving.) By contrast, when you hear someone say that we need to "raise standards," that

---

* In response to people who say that traditional schooling has "worked just fine" for decades, we might ask how long they "would continue to go to a doctor who says: 'I practice medicine exactly the same way today that I did thirty years ago—I haven't changed a thing. I don't hold with all that newfangled stuff.' "[45]

represents a vertical shift, a claim that students ought to know more, do more, perform better.

This can get confusing because discussions about standards sometimes are limited to only one of these meanings, sometimes flipflop between them, and sometimes involve an implicit appeal to one in order to press for the other. Most of the talk about standards today falls into the second category, and that is my primary concern here. Thus, in expressing doubts about this approach to educational reform, I don't mean to say that we shouldn't have any guidelines for what goes on in classrooms, and I don't mean that our current approaches shouldn't be changed. Indeed, the new standards that began to appear in the 1980s (including those from the NCTM) represent what I believe are significant improvements in thinking about how to teach various subjects. (Interestingly, those reforms are often opposed by some of the very people who argue most strenuously for ratcheting up the standards. You might say they want vertical movement without horizontal movement.)

Even the idea of vertical movement seems hard to argue against, at least in the abstract. Don't we want schools to be of high quality and students to be able to do many things? Of course. But the current demand for Tougher Standards, particularly by politicians and businesspeople, carries with it a bundle of assumptions about the proper role of schools, the nature and causes of failure, and the way students learn. A number of people (mostly educators) have come to view with concern, even alarm, these increasingly strident demands (mostly from noneducators) to raise standards. People from parents to presidents have begun to sound like cranky, ill-informed radio talk-show hosts, and almost anything can be done to students and to schools, no matter how ill considered, as long as it is done in the name of "raising standards" or "accountability."

Significantly, such buzzwords are favored by policymakers across the political spectrum. It's almost impossible to distinguish Democrats from Republicans on these issues—only those people with some understanding of how children learn from those who haven't a clue. The disagreement that plays itself out on boards of education and in state legislatures is pretty much limited to a clash between, on one side, the champions of Tougher Standards (a constituency that includes virtually all corporate groups, the president,[47] almost all the governors, and most education officials), and, on the other side, those on the extreme right wing, whose suspicion of anything involving the federal government leads them to oppose *national* standards or testing. (They, too, tend to endorse the idea of Tougher Standards but insist on local control.)[48] That's often the extent of public debate on the subject. Left out almost entirely is the point of view of the students themselves and the impact on their learning.

The dominant position is reflected in an endless series of reports on American schooling released by the Business Coalition for Education Reform, the Business Roundtable, the National Alliance of Business, the Committee for Economic Development, and other clusters of corporations. Rather like a party game in which players create sentences by randomly selecting an adjective from one list and a noun from another, these virtually interchangeable documents seem to consist mostly of different combinations of terms like "tough," "competitive," "world-class," "measurable," "accountability," "standards," "results," and "raising the bar." Also, almost all of them begin by solemnly announcing the arrival of the twenty-first century, in case we had forgotten.[49]

Jargon aside, there is good reason to oppose the disproportionate role that corporate executives have been granted in shaping our country's educational agenda. It isn't just a matter of whether they know enough but of what they're looking for. Ultimately, the *goals* of business are not the same as those of educators and parents. Corporations exist to provide a financial return to the people who own them: they are in business to make a profit. As individuals, those who work in (or even run) these companies may have other goals, too, when they turn their attention to public policy or education or anything else. But business *qua* business is concerned principally about its own bottom line. Thus, when business thinks about schools, its agenda is driven by what will maximize its profitability, not necessarily by what is in the best interest of students.[50] Any overlap between these two goals would be purely accidental—and, in practice, turns out to be minimal. What maximizes corporate profit often does not benefit children, and vice versa. To a significant extent, the push for Tougher Standards is about the former more than the latter.[51]

That's why it's so disturbing that the government tends to ride in business's wake, issuing reports that contain remarkably similar language, essentially the same recommendations, and the identical objectives.[52] Many of our elected officials have virtually handed the keys to our schools over to corporate interests. Presidential commissions on education are commonly chaired by the executives of large companies. "We must tell the business community that, if it wants better employees and higher profits, it must be involved in what the schools teach and how they teach it," announced James B. Hunt, Jr., the Democratic governor of North Carolina.[53] In March 1996, the Republican governor of Wisconsin, Tommy Thompson, joined IBM in hosting the prestigious National Education Summit at its suburban New York headquarters to talk about the need for higher standards—and, to no one's astonishment, the importance of technology in schools. Most of the country's governors attended, and each was invited to bring along a corporate chieftain. (Imagine the likelihood of a summit on the future of American business management to which the nation's governors were invited to bring along a schoolteacher.)

Corporate and government reports on education also look very similar to (and sometimes even borrow from) analyses by teachers' unions, notably the American Federation of Teachers. Both the AFT and *Education Week*, the newspaper of record in the field, publish annual reports that grade the states on their standards and expose those that fail to measure up.[54] The difference between these documents and a report by, say, the National Rifle Association that assigns low ratings to legislators who are not sufficiently pro-gun is that in the latter case everyone realizes that the ratings reflect a very particular, very debatable point of view. Yet business, government, and labor in this country have all pretty much accepted and adopted the same approach to school reform (if "reform" is really the right word). So too for the leading newspapers and magazines, regardless of whether they are generally regarded as liberal or conservative on other issues.[55]

This remarkable consensus around Tougher Standards is closely connected to the perpetuation of Old School styles of teaching mentioned earlier. Holding schools "accountable" for meeting "standards" usually means requiring them to live up to conventional measures of student performance, and traditional kinds of instruction are most closely geared to — and thus perpetuated by — these measures. The dominant philosophy of fixing schools consists of saying, in effect, that "what we're doing is OK, we just need to do it harder, longer, stronger, louder, meaner, and we'll have a better country."[56] Thus, it isn't unusual to hear corporate groups (or, once again, the leadership of the American Federation of Teachers)[57] emphasizing the need to prepare students for the challenges of the future — and then calling for a renewed emphasis on the methods of the past.

## Are Our Schools Failing?

The most obvious reason that people talk about the need to raise standards is that they believe current standards are too low and that our schools are doing a terrible job. Indeed, studies are released with numbing regularity that purport to show how little our kids know, how many questions they get wrong, how poorly they stack up against students in other countries, and how things are getting worse every year. It may be surprising, then, to learn that the people who follow this research for a living disagree vigorously about what the studies actually show.[58] Rarely are newspaper readers given any hint that many of these reports may be highly misleading and that their conclusions may be wildly exaggerated.

At the very least, the results will vary, depending on which age group is being tested, with which exam, and in what subject. Often, for example, people claiming that our educational system is in trouble note that SAT scores are lower today than they once were. But this tells us almost nothing about the quality of high schools and their students. Rather, it tells us about the characteristics of the group of students who chose to take the test in a given year — or in a given state. "The SAT is useless for evaluating changes in academic performance, and any educator, journalist, or politician who uses SAT results as an index of change in educational achievement does so in ignorance or for reasons that must be considered suspect."[59]

A more logical place to look for answers may be the National Assessment of Educational Progress (NAEP), set up by the federal government to serve as "the nation's report card" by periodically testing students who are nine, thirteen, and seventeen years old. The results have been used to support various theories, but the inescapable conclusion is that there has been very little change over the last couple of decades, and most of the change that has occurred has been for the better. The most recent results available at this writing — from 1998 in reading and from 1996 in math and science — show that nine-year-olds and thirteen-year-olds did better in all three subjects than children in the early 1970s, when the tests were introduced. Seventeen-year-olds, meanwhile, were down a bit in science and up a bit in math and reading. The shifts in most cases have not been terribly significant, but it is noteworthy that of these nine comparisons (three age groups in three subjects), eight of them show some improvement.[60]

When critics who pound the lectern about declining scores are given statistics showing that our schools are actually doing about as well as ever, they don't miss a beat. "Well, doing as well as we used to do just isn't good enough!" they declare — presumably to distract us from the fact that their original claims were baseless. Or they may change the subject to international comparisons. Here, the results depend on the subject matter and the students' age. A 1992 examination of the reading literacy of 93,000 nine-year-olds around the world found that U.S. students had the second-highest average score of the thirty-two participating countries. The average U.S. score (547) was 22 points behind the top country's and 164 points ahead of the bottom country's.[61]

Strangely, the results of that exam got a lot less press coverage in the United States than did a comparison of math results from the Third International Mathematics and Science Study (TIMSS). Even there, not as much attention was paid to the elementary school level, where the performance of U.S. students was exemplary, as to the upper grade levels, where U.S. students lagged. But aside from some serious questions about the way the TIMSS research was conducted,[62] we should also be wary of focusing on how U.S. students rank against those from other countries, regardless of the results. A nation's position on a list tells us nothing about the quality of its schools. If, for example, all the countries did reasonably well, there would be no shame (and, perhaps, no statistical significance) to being at the bottom. If all the countries did poorly, there would be no glory to being at the top. Headlines about how "our" schools are doing compared to "theirs" are based on the premise that what matters is *relative* performance, which suggests that we're less concerned with the quality of education than with whether we can chant, "We're Number One!"[63]

Apart from the specific tests, claims about our failing schools often seem a little suspicious for several reasons. First, just about every generation, going back more than a century, has sounded remarkably similar alarms about how the educational system is falling apart—and some of them have been sounded during periods now regarded as the golden age of education.[64] Second, it's worth noticing that the schools are blamed (without any real evidence) when the economy sputters,[65] but when the economy hums along splendidly the schools never get the credit. Moreover, the Tougher Standards movement, ushered in amid charges that our economy was being dragged down by the schools, has persisted and proliferated even after the economy recovered. It's hard not to suspect that economic circumstances were merely an excuse for getting tough with students and teachers.

Lending credence to that suspicion, some warnings about the mediocrity of our schools are issued for reasons that clearly have little to do with the objective state of education. In the late 1950s, dire pronouncements about a crisis in U.S. science education were provoked not by any measurement of students' progress but by the Soviet launch of Sputnik. In 1983, the Reagan administration released a report ("A Nation at Risk") that used near-apocalyptic language to describe the state of our schools—a claim that just happened to set the stage for the conservative agenda being proposed. These days, some of the loudest critics of our schools are people whose real agenda is to privatize American education. More and more, public schools are under attack "not just because they are deemed ineffective but because they are public."[66]

Any announcement that our schools are inadequate finds a sympathetic audience since, for many of us, the way things are can never measure up to the way they used to be. The present, with its sharply etched flaws, can never compare to the lovely picture of the past preserved by our memories, with most of the problems having been airbrushed away. This bias is worth keeping in mind whenever people shake their heads in disgust about "these kids today" and how poorly they compare to students in the old days. More specifically, many of us are apt to "compare our own relatively homogeneous, even segregated, school experiences," where plenty of students we never met "either dropped out of school or were tracked into custodial, nonacademic programs," with a system that tries to serve a more diverse population.[67]

Yet another cause for skepticism: all the talk about how our educational system is faring assumes that the status of an entire country's schools can be summarized by a single number. This is like looking at an average pollution statistic for the United States to determine the cleanliness of "American air." In fact, our top states do as well on international tests as the top countries; our bottom states are down there with the lowest countries.[68] Clearly, some U.S. schools are in real trouble by any measure: they are typically underfunded,[69] and their students may worry more about surviving to adulthood than about passing an exam. A pair of educational researchers concluded not long ago that "on the whole, the American school system is in far better shape than the critics would have us believe"—but, at the same time, "*some* American schools are terrible places . . . because those schools lack resources and must contend with some of society's worst social problems."[70]

Finally, it is assumed that the standardized test scores used to draw all these conclusions are valid indicators of the quality of education. (That we routinely ignore this basic premise is itself enough to give one pause about the schools we attended.) You or I could design a test in half an hour that would be failed by most of the children, and even the adults, who took it. Then we could hold a press conference to fulminate about the ignorance of those kids and the Crisis of Our Schools. But until it is clear what was on the test, how reasonable and appropriate its content, such an announcement would deserve to be ignored. My guess, though, is that it would be on the front page of almost every newspaper in the country the next morning.

This concern is not hypothetical. Many of the specific tests being used to generate speeches and articles about the desperate plight of American education—and on which our children are being judged individually, by the way—are seriously deficient: students should not be taking them, and, in any case, we should not be taking them very seriously. As I'll argue later, most of these tests don't look for a deep understanding of ideas; they just measure how well students have memorized a bunch of words or facts, or how well they can apply fixed formulas about triangles or verbs. But most critics don't bother to defend these tests. They aren't even familiar with them. All they see is that a particular score is down, and that's enough to start up the rhetoric about failing schools and falling standards. There is something unsatisfying, and even misconceived, about the whole debate between these educational Chicken Littles and those who challenge them. If the tests turn out to have an extremely limited value, we may be wasting our time arguing about the scores.

•

We are not wasting our time, however, if we ask whether students are learning effectively by more meaningful criteria. The story is told that John Dewey, while visiting a classroom one day, asked the students what they might find if they dug a hole in the earth. Nobody answered. He asked a second time and again was met with silence. Finally, the teacher suggested that Professor Dewey had asked the wrong question. "What is the state of the center of the earth?" she asked her class, and all the students chorused, "Igneous fusion."[71]

As long as standardized tests avoid asking the "wrong" question, lots of students can and do answer them correctly. But even the most able are tripped up by unexpected challenges—those that require thinking in novel ways, connecting apparently disparate facts, or distinguishing between things that appear to be the same. Only when they are not expected to understand what they are doing does their performance seem satisfactory. This problem was identified as long ago as the 1840s and as recently as the latest assessment of students' understanding of mathematical principles.[72]

In his book *The Unschooled Mind*, Howard Gardner of Harvard University explains how years of schooling fail to challenge the naive beliefs about the world that most of us form even before we set foot in kindergarten. We've learned plenty of new words and skills since then, but our knowledge is "fragile": ask a probing question in almost any subject, and even those of us who are considered well educated will likely reveal the same basic misconceptions we started with.[73] In Emily Dickinson's lovely phrase, we have "the facts, but not the phosphorescence of thought."[74]

So doesn't this suggest that our schools really are failing—indeed, that they're even more wretched than the conventional wisdom has it? Actually, the problems I am talking about are fundamentally different from those usually mentioned. Conventional methods of measuring success, notably standardized tests, aren't merely uninformative about the educational issues that matter: they prevent us from understanding what is really going on and what to do about it. Complaints about low or dropping test scores are often based on misinformation, but the point is that this way of framing the issue will likely leave us with a very different prescription for our schools than if we focused on what is lacking in students' understanding. We'll end up "focusing on nonexistent problems while perhaps ignoring the real ones."[75] We'll end up, in short, with a call for Tougher Standards.[76]

## Five Fatal Flaws

Back in 1959, the education critic John Holt became concerned about the way some people were already starting to talk about improving education. "One ironical consequence of the drive for so-called higher standards in schools," he remarked, "is that the children are too busy to think."[77] His implication is that higher standards and better thinking are not only different ideas in theory but may be opposites in practice — an idea that will seem surprising, even confusing, to a lot of people. But I think Holt has been proved right over the ensuing four decades. Specifically, I would contend that the Tougher Standards movement is fundamentally misguided in five separate respects. Each of the next five chapters will be devoted to one of these problems.

First, this approach proceeds from the assumption — one so widely shared as to be largely taken for granted — that students ought to be thinking constantly about improving their performance. This focus on results turns out to be remarkably simplistic, particularly when one considers the psychological issues involved. A *preoccupation with achievement* is not only different from, but often detrimental to, a focus on learning.

Second, as I've already noted, the Tougher Standards movement tends to favor *Old-School teaching,* the sort of instruction that treats kids as though they were inert objects, that prepares a concoction called "basic skills" or "core knowledge" and then tries to pour it down children's throats. This model might be described as outdated were it not for the fact that, frankly, it never worked all that well. Modern cognitive science just explains more systematically why it has always come up short.

Third, this movement is *wedded to standardized testing.* "Excellence" and "higher standards" typically mean higher test scores, and that is what schools are pressed to produce. Indeed, much of the discussion about education today is arrested at the level of "Test scores are low;

make them go up." All the limits of, and problems with, such testing amount to a serious indictment of the version of school reform that relies on these tests.

Fourth, the Tougher Standards movement usually consists of *imposing specific requirements and trying to coerce improvement* by specifying exactly what must be taught and learned — that is, by mandating a particular kind of education. Even if we set aside the first three concerns — a very problematic set of beliefs about achievement, teaching, and measurement, respectively — we should be wary of the assumption that the way one changes education is simply to compel teachers and students to do things differently.

Finally, weaving its way through many of these ideas is an implicit assumption about what it means to improve, about the nature of "rigor" or "challenge." That assumption can be summarized in three words: *harder is better.* This reductive (and really rather silly) premise is the basis for judging teachers, textbooks, and tests; it lurks behind complaints about "dumbing down" education and strident calls to "raise the bar." Its first cousin is the idea that if something isn't working very well — say, requiring students to do homework of dubious value — then insisting on more of the same will surely solve the problem.

After exploring each of these shaky foundations of the move toward Tougher Standards, we'll look at what can replace the Old School as well as how we might rethink the whole idea of education.

· *Part One* ·

# TOUGHER
# STANDARDS
## *Versus*
# BETTER
# EDUCATION

Teaching requires the consent of students, and discontent will not be chased away by the exercise of power.

—John Nicholls, 1993

# ☙ 2 ☙

# GETTING
# MOTIVATION WRONG
## The Costs of Overemphasizing
## Achievement

IF WE WANT to talk about schools in a way that matters, we have to talk about the people in schools. In fact, we have to make a habit of seeing things from the perspective of that student sitting right over there. You see her? She's playing with her hair and wondering why the clock stops moving during math class. Meaningful educational reform requires us to understand her point of view: Can she connect at any level with what she just read? Does she have any reason for wanting to connect with it? What's her goal when she opens a book? If she puts any effort into her writing, is it because she gets a kick out of finding the right words, because she wants to please her mom, or because she's afraid of looking lame?

I don't want to mention any names, but some social scientists specializing in education may as well be crunching numbers about *E. coli* or the electromagnetic spectrum. Even those who conduct research on motivation sometimes forget to ask students "what sorts of subject matter and what associated teaching methods make sense to them."[1] Likewise, some teachers are "more interested in what they're teaching than in what students are learning,"[2] more focused on the subject matter than on the kids.

These distinctions are not idle or incidental. They are not platitudes about the Importance of Children lifted from a soothing after-dinner speech. For anyone who cares about education, these are the issues that matter the most. They have the power to turn our beliefs and practices inside out, as we're about to see. Does it matter whether your child studied last night? Yes; but what may matter even more is *why* he did so (or didn't). Does it make any difference whether your child did well on a test? Sure; but what will be even more important over the long haul is *why* she thinks she did well—that is, how she accounts for her success. It is the student's point of view—specifically, a psychologically informed understanding of that point of view—that determines whether real learning will happen and keep happening. As any number of studies have found, a child's "thoughts and emotions while performing an action are more important in determining subsequent engagement than the actual outcome of that action."[3]

The failure to understand this is the first distinguishing feature of those who march behind the banner of Tougher Standards. I refer especially to the people who sit on Mount Olympus, where no children live, and insist that students be made to learn. They like to talk about motivating kids, as though motivation could be imposed from the outside. They are fixated on observable, testable behaviors (such as correctly pronouncing the words on a page) while ignoring the people who are doing the behaving (and whether they care about, or understand, those words). They may even set up a dichotomy whereby we are supposed to choose between being committed to Excellence, on the one hand, and just being worried about how students "feel" about what they're doing, on the other.

The fact is, unless we attend to how students feel about what they're doing, it's less likely that they will become excellent learners. All those demands to raise standards aren't just disrespectful of kids; ultimately, they're unlikely to succeed even on their own terms. This chapter explains why.

## *What Versus How Well*

When he was the mayor of New York City, beginning in the late 1970s, Ed Koch was famous for wandering through the streets and asking passersby, "How'm I doin'?" This affectation he evidently regarded as endearing—as opposed to, say, neurotic. Getting students to ask this same question umpteen times a day seems to be a major purpose of our educational system. Indeed, the dominant version of contemporary educational reform consists of leaning on students, teachers, administrators, and parents until they focus ever more intently on results.

What could possibly be wrong with results? To answer this question, we first have to recognize that for people to think about *how well* they're doing is not at all the same as thinking about *what* they're doing.[4] These represent two very different mind-sets for parents, students, and educators. Imagine two parents, for example, both of whose children mention that they wrote an essay in school that day. One parent wants to know how good the essay was and asks what the teacher said about it. The other parent asks about the essay itself and the process of writing it: Why did you choose that topic? Did your opinion about the subject change while you were writing? How did you decide what to include in the opening paragraph?

Or imagine a student who comes home from school announcing that "she had a great day because she got an A, did better than her best friend, or . . . won the spelling bee." These accomplishments reflect a very different set of goals than those held by a student who says "she had a great day because she finally mastered long division, read a wonderful story about India, or tried to solve a really difficult problem."[5] One of these children regards learning as a means (to a grade or a victory or just to being able to say she was successful). The other regards learning as an end.

Teachers and administrators, too, may promote one mind-set more than the other. Consider a school that constantly emphasizes the importance of performance! results! achievement! success! A child who has absorbed that message may find it difficult to get swept away with the process of creating a poem, trying to build a working telescope, or figuring out why fighting always seems to be breaking out in the Balkans. He may be so concerned about the results that he's not all that concerned about the activity that produces those results.

As students move from elementary to middle or junior high school, there is an especially marked, and often irreversible, shift from trying to figure things out to trying to be high achievers[6] — although it isn't unusual to find even young children being led to think less about making sense of what they're doing and more about how successful they've been at doing it. The two goals aren't mutually exclusive, of course, but in practice they feel different and lead to different kinds of behaviors.[7] Without even knowing how well a student actually did at a task or how smart she is supposed to be, we can tell a lot just from knowing whether she is more concerned about layers of learning or levels of achievement.

Like most people, I think it matters how effectively students are learning. It's appropriate to sit down with them every so often to figure out how successful they (and their teachers) have been. But when we get carried away with results, we wind up, paradoxically, with results that are less than ideal. Surprising as it may seem, the evidence suggests that our long-term goals for children and schools are less likely to be realized when teachers, parents, and the students themselves become preoccupied with standards and achievement.

# The Costs of Overemphasizing Achievement

Let's be clear about exactly what is wrong with encouraging students to put "how well they're doing" ahead of "what they're doing." An impressive and growing body of research suggests that this emphasis (1) undermines students' interest in learning, (2) makes failure seem overwhelming, (3) leads students to avoid challenging themselves, (4) reduces the quality of learning, and (5) invites students to think about how smart they are instead of how hard they tried. Any one of these five consequences should be cause for concern; together, they make it abundantly clear that the conventional wisdom about schooling has to be rethought.

**Interest.** When students are constantly encouraged to think about how well they're performing, the first likely casualty is their attitude toward learning. They may come to view the tasks themselves—the stories and science projects and math problems—as stuff they're supposed to do better at, not stuff they're excited about exploring. Or, as Carol Dweck, one of the leading researchers in this field, once put it, "Performance goals may well create the very conditions that have been found to undermine intrinsic interest."[8]

We can immediately see that the kind of student who is "learning-oriented"—the student whose goal is to understand and who is thinking about *what* she is doing—is likely to enjoy school. But the flip side is that her classmate, who is mostly concerned with being a top performer, is probably a lot less eager. Research and experience teach us that when "performance-oriented instructional strategies" are used, such as emphasizing the importance of good grades and high test scores, students tend to value reading less.[9]

That doesn't mean they won't read. Indeed, some performance-driven or competitive students may persevere at a task when they've been told they have to do well. But a genuine interest in the task—or excitement about the whole idea of learning—often begins to evaporate as soon as achievement becomes the main point. Assuming it's important to us that our children become lifelong learners, we have good reason to be concerned if too much attention to boosting achievement during school can make the whole idea of learning seem like a chore.

**Reaction to Failure.** No one succeeds all the time, and no one can learn very effectively without making mistakes and bumping up against limits. It's extremely important, therefore, to encourage a healthy and resilient attitude toward failure. As a rule, that is exactly what students tend to have if their main goal is to learn: when they do something incorrectly, they figure out what went wrong and how to fix it. Their mood is generally positive and their attitude is optimistic.

Not so for the kids who are mostly concerned about how well they're doing, who believe (often because they have been told explicitly) that the point is to succeed—or even to do better than everyone else. They seem to be fine as long as they're succeeding, but as soon as they hit a bump they may regard themselves as failures and act as though they're helpless to do anything about it. They are "always vulnerable to becoming overwhelmed by a failure experience," so that a momentary stumble can seem to cancel out all their past successes.[10] *When the point isn't to figure things out but to prove how good you are, it's often hard to cope with being told you're not so good.*

Consider the student who falls apart when he gets a 92 instead of his usual 100. We've all seen such kids. We may even have such a kid or have been such a kid. The problem is that no matter how familiar we are with such a reaction, we invariably analyze what's going on incorrectly. Consistent with our whole society's tendency to ignore the bigger picture, we usually see it as a problem with the individual and conclude that such students are just too hard on themselves. But the distinction between "what I'm doing" and "how well I'm doing" can let us see what is going on here through a new lens. Instead of blaming the student's anxiety or depression on his psychological makeup, we begin to realize that a systemic demand for high achievement may have led him to become debilitated when he fails—even if the failure is only relative. The important point isn't what level of performance qualifies as failure (a 92 vs. a 40, say); it's the perceived pressure not to fail. That can have a particularly harmful impact on high-achieving and high-ability students.[11]

Thus, reassuring such a student that "a 92 is still very good" or that we're sure he'll "do better next time" doesn't just miss the point—it makes things worse by underscoring yet again that success is all that counts. We may intend to be supportive and helpful, but in fact we've managed to drive home the message that the point of school isn't to explore ideas, it's to do well. Similarly, it really doesn't help to give students easier tasks so they can "experience success" and feel more confident, or to provide them with lots of positive feedback.[12] None of this gets at what is really going on, which is emphasizing the level of achievement to the exclusion of learning.

**Avoidance of Challenge.** If the point is to succeed rather than to stretch one's thinking or discover new ideas, it is completely logical for a student to want to do whatever is easiest. That, after all, will maximize the probability of success—or at least minimize the probability of failure.

Again we have a new explanation for a familiar phenomenon: we've all seen children cut corners and do as little as they can get away with. But perhaps we shouldn't assume it's just because they're lazy—another explanation based on the characteristics of individuals, which happens to be extremely convenient for adults because it implies that only the child has to be fixed. Perhaps "performance goals work against the pursuit of challenge."[13]

A number of researchers have tested this hypothesis. Typically, a bunch of kids are told they're going to be given a task, such as recognizing patterns or rearranging letters. Some are informed that this is a test, that it will count for a grade, or that they're going to be told how well they've done or videotaped so their performance can be evaluated. The others, meanwhile, are encouraged to think of this as an opportunity to learn rather than to do well. Then each student is allowed to choose how hard a version of the task he or she wants to try. The result is always the same: those who have been told it's "an opportunity to learn" are more willing to challenge themselves than those who had been led to think about how well they'd do.[14]

It doesn't seem to matter how old the children are. It doesn't even matter how secure they may be about their abilities. Those led to think about the level of their achievement probably won't reach beyond their comfort zone to see what they're capable of doing or learning. When you place enough stress on results, research shows that even the most confident students will actively steer toward easier tasks.[15] In fact, some of them will be so determined to perform well that they'll take the next logical step to cut corners: a 1998 study confirmed that the more schools emphasize grades, honor rolls, and other indicators of performance, the more likely students are to cheat, even if they know it's wrong.[16]

Sometimes the pressure comes from school, and sometimes it comes from home. While very few parents would tell their kids to copy answers or even to stick to tasks they can do easily, their priorities come through clearly enough. A study of 501 mothers of elementary school students found that those moms for whom achievement mattered most were more likely to want their children to choose projects "that would involve a minimum of struggle and likely result in success" rather than those "where they'll learn a lot of new things but also make a lot of mistakes."[17]

And the kids get the message. They're not being lazy so much as rational. They're adapting to an environment where results, not intellectual exploration, are what count. They're saying to us, "Hey, *you* told me the point here is to achieve, to get A's, to bring home a bumper sticker about how successful I am! Well, I'm not stupid: the easier the task, the more likely it is that I'll be able to give you what you want. So don't blame me when I try to find the least challenging thing to do and end up not learning anything." Once students start to think this way, it's hard for them to stop: even when they're not being evaluated, they may have gotten into the habit of picking easy things to do so they'll appear smart. The pressure to perform has left its mark.[18] If they've internalized the imperative to get good grades, they'll still be looking for the easiest possible courses when they get to college.[19]

It's not hard to tell whether we've created such a mind-set for any given group of students. All we have to do is watch for signs that they're more interested in getting the right answer than in figuring out why this answer may be better than that one. All we have to do is watch for students zipping through an assignment as though speed mattered most. ("Done!") All we have to do is give them something ridiculously simple to do and watch how they respond. If they seem relieved and happy, something is seriously amiss. If, however, they seem disappointed — "Ah, this is too easy. This is no fun. Where's the challenge?" — then we've done something right, either in the attitudes we've taught them at home[20] or the norms and structures we've set up at school.

In putting the emphasis on "we," I think of how Peter Scholtes, a management consultant, answers executives who want to know what they should do with "all the deadwood" in their companies. Scholtes likes to reply that the real question is what their organizations have done to kill all those live trees. The problem, in other words, isn't with the individuals, their effort or attitude, so much as with the system in which they find themselves. With students, too, the irony is almost palpable when parents and teachers and school reformers complain bitterly about how kids today just want to take the easy way out — while simultaneously emphasizing performance and results so as to lead predictably to that very outcome.

**Quality of Learning.** The goal of some students is to acquire new skills, to find out about the world, to understand what they're doing. When they pick up a book, they're thinking about what they're reading, not about how well they're reading it. Paradoxically, these students who have put success out of their minds are likely to be successful. They process information more deeply, review things they didn't understand the first time, make connections between what they're doing now and what they learned earlier, and use more strategies to make sense of the ideas they're encountering. All of this has been demonstrated empirically.[21]

What about the students who have been led to focus on results? How well do they do? That depends on what we mean by "how well." Students who think about nothing but producing the right answer, scoring well on a test, or getting an A may adopt the kinds of study habits that generate more right answers and high test scores and good grades.[22] (I say "may" because some students just become demoralized or demotivated and give up.)

If, however, our top priority is for kids to think widely and deeply and explore ideas thoughtfully—that is, if we're more interested in excellence than in high grades and test scores—then the news isn't good. In this sense, *students who have been led to focus on how well they're doing tend not to do very well.* One facet of excellence is the ability to transfer understanding—that is, to take something you've learned over here and apply it to a new task or question over there. In 1985, as a group of eighth-graders were about to begin a week-long unit in science class, two researchers asked them some questions designed to determine whether they were more interested in understanding or in success. When the unit was over, the students were tested on their ability to transfer their new knowledge. Regardless of whether their earlier test scores had been high or low, the success-oriented students simply did not do as well as those who were more oriented toward learning.[23]

Of course, that's just one study. But a dozen years later another researcher looked for other experiments that had addressed this same basic question to see whether the two goals had different effects on how successful students actually were. He dug up two dozen such studies that used a variety of different tasks to measure achievement, from reading comprehension tests to collages, from anagrams to computer simulations. Using a statistical technique known as meta-analysis, he combined them into one giant, powerful experiment and ultimately reached this simple conclusion: "Learning goals will lead to better task outcomes than will performance goals." This result was especially true of older students and with tasks that were relatively complicated. The more that real thinking was required, the worse the results for kids who were concerned about high achievement.[24]

Again, it may be possible to get good grades, at least in the short run, by focusing on performance. It may be that reading, practicing, or memorizing only what's likely to be on the test—and covering that material in a cursory way—can sometimes help students do well on the test itself. But does this prove that it "works" to focus on how well one is doing? Or does it reveal how little grades and tests really tell us and instead point up what's wrong with the disproportionate emphasis on achievement that suffuses our schools?

In the long run, even these less meaningful measures of achievement like grades and tests may be adversely affected by too much attention to performance. Remember the study showing that success-oriented mothers wanted their children to avoid unnecessary challenges? Two other groups of researchers went a step further, looking at whether a parent's perspective affected how well students actually learned. In the first study, conducted in Vermont, fifth-grade children and their parents were interviewed, and special attention was paid to moms and dads who either punished their kids for bad grades or rewarded them for good grades. Both practices, it turned out, "were associated with lower grades and poorer achievement scores" as well as "less motivation, pleasure, and persistence in doing their work in school." (In fact, rewarding seemed to be even more harmful than punishing.) In the second study, conducted in California, researchers were interested in how much mothers of nine-year-olds valued their kids' "curiosity, mastery, and exposure to new experiences" in school — as opposed to valuing achievement to the point of pushing their kids (by emphasizing the importance of doing well, giving rewards for good grades, or removing privileges for bad grades). Once again it turned out that the children whose parents stressed success were less interested in learning and, as a result, were *less likely to do well in school.*[25] The more that achievement was the parents' chief concern, the lower was the kids' achievement.

So what might explain this intriguing, even disturbing, tendency for too much emphasis on results — at home or at school — to undermine exactly what we'd like to promote? We've already come across some possible answers: this mind-set, remember, can produce students who have no particular interest in learning new ways of thinking, who may fall apart when they make a mistake, and who will probably avoid challenging themselves unnecessarily. If any of these things happens, then the quality of learning would logically be expected to suffer as well.[26] We might add to that list yet another research finding: students who are concerned about doing well, especially in comparison to their classmates, are relatively unlikely to ask for help when they need it.[27] When they do ask for help, moreover, it's likely because they've given up and just want to know the answer — as opposed to asking for clues so they can solve the problem on their own.[28]

There is one more explanation, which can also be considered the fifth consequence of placing more emphasis on "how well" than on "what." It's important enough to deserve a section of its own.

## *Think You're Smart? Think Again*

Imagine that your child comes home from school today with a score of 100 on a quiz. For the time being, let's put aside the question of how sensible it is for teachers to rely on traditional quizzes, requiring students to memorize certain facts so their performance can be reduced to a number or letter. Let's just consider whether you regard this 100 as good news. If you're like most parents, it would never occur to you not to be delighted. No one has ever given you any other way to look at it.

Until now. The fact is that a number of different lines of research "converge on one point: success or failure per se might be less important than a child's perception of the *causes* of the success or failure."[29] Thus, what matters more than the score is why your child thinks she got it.

Consider what some of those reasons may be. One possibility is *effort:* she tried hard, studied, did all she could to learn the material. A second possibility is *ability:* if you asked her how she got 100, she might reply, "Well, I guess I'm just smart." (Even if she doesn't say it out loud, she might think it's true.) Yet another answer is *luck:* she believes she guessed correctly or was just having a good day. Finally, she may explain the result in terms of the level of *difficulty* of the task—in this case, the test was easy.

Notice that these same four reasons could be used by another kid— not yours, of course—to make sense of his grade of 23 on the same quiz: I didn't try hard; I'm just stupid; it was bad luck; the test was hard. This basic framework for understanding success and failure was developed a generation ago by a psychologist named Bernard Weiner, and it has generated a flood of research. If you think about it, the four factors can be classified in several different ways. Two of the four (ability and effort) are features of the student herself; the other two (luck and difficulty) are external. Ability and maybe even task difficulty are relatively stable factors; the other two may vary from one moment to the next. One variable (effort) she can control; the other three she can't.

After I lay all this out for educators during a speech or workshop, I ask them to make a value judgment: Which of these four explanations for doing well (or poorly) do you favor? Which would you like to see your students use to account for their performance? (Take a moment here to make your own choice.) The answer is almost always unanimous, regardless of politics, positions on various educational controversies, or knowledge about psychological research. Traditionalists and progressives, kindergarten teachers and high school principals and professors—nearly everyone votes for effort. It bodes well for the future when kids attribute a score of 100 to how carefully they prepared for the test. Likewise, those who attribute a 23 to *not* preparing for the test "tend to perceive failure as surmountable and will often show heightened persistence or improved performance in the face of negative evaluation."[30] It makes perfect sense.

So here's the punch line: *When kids are led to focus on how well they are performing in school, they tend to explain their performance not by how hard they tried but by how smart they are.* A student with a performance focus—How am I doing? Am I improving fast enough? Are my grades high enough? Do I know the right answers?—is likely to interpret the answer to all these questions "in terms of how much ability [he or she has] and whether or not this ability is adequate to achieve success," as Dweck and a colleague have explained.[31] In a study of academically advanced students, for example, the more emphasis that teachers put on getting good grades, avoiding mistakes, and keeping up with everyone else, the more the students tended to attribute poor performance to lack of ability or to how hard the tasks were—that is, to factors outside their control.[32] When students are constantly made to think about how well they are doing, they are apt to explain the outcome in terms of who they are rather than how hard they tried.

This is clearly not a productive way for kids to look at things, regardless of whether they have been successful or unsuccessful.[33] Research demonstrates that adolescents who explain how well they're doing on the basis of ability tend to think less deeply and carefully about what they're learning than do those who appeal to the idea of effort.[34] Similarly, elementary school students who attribute failure to ability are likely to be poorer readers.[35] And if children are encouraged to think of themselves as "smart" when they succeed, doing poorly on a subsequent task will bring down their achievement even though it doesn't trip up other kids.[36] Thus, if focusing on how well one is doing is counterproductive, as we saw before, it may be partly because of the way it induces students to think about the reasons for how well they're doing (and what that says about how smart they are).

There are several theories about why explaining results in terms of one's intelligence—and construing intelligence as basically unchangeable[37]—is so destructive.[38] First, if a student believes he screwed up because he's just not smart enough, the implication is that he can't be successful. In a pattern that can begin as early as first grade, he will come to expect failure,[39] which creates a self-fulfilling prophecy: a posture of helplessness makes him throw up his hands and do exactly as poorly as he feared. The problem here is with my brain, he figures, so what's the point of trying? And so he stops.

Second, he may become preoccupied with, and upset by, the idea of his own incompetence—to the point that it distracts him from what he's doing, thus bringing down his achievement even further. Like the student who thinks too much about being successful, the one who attributes the results to ability tends "to be debilitated by failure."[40]

Finally, if he is sufficiently worried about his intelligence, he may deliberately avoid studying so he can point to that fact as the only reason he failed. Ironically, his concern with his own ability may lead him to take defensive measures that allow him to believe his ability isn't so low after all. ("Hey, if I *had* studied. . . .")[41] The student who brags right before a test about how little he did to prepare is not only providing himself with an excuse for failure but an explanation for success: if he aces the test, it's obviously because he's smart. "Those with performance goals . . . viewed effort and ability as inversely related"[42]: only dumb kids need to study. All of this makes it less likely that such a student will apply himself — or, as already noted, ask for help — which is another reason that thinking in terms of ability is so counterproductive.

So what leads students to attribute success or failure to ability rather than to effort? Gender apparently plays a role, with a number of studies suggesting that girls are more likely than boys to believe that results reflect intelligence, particularly in fields like math and science. Culture is also relevant: as more and more commentators are noticing, the Japanese tend to attribute results to effort, whereas Americans think in terms of ability.[43] But beyond gender and culture, the unfortunate tendency for students to think about how well they're doing as a function of how smart or stupid they happen to be is partly due to the exaggerated emphasis placed on how well they're doing in the first place.

The upshot of all this is that beliefs about intelligence, and about the causes of one's own success and failure, matter a lot. They often make more of a difference than how confident students are, how successful they are, or what they're truly capable of doing. If, like the cheerleaders for Tougher Standards, we look only at the test scores and grades, we end up overlooking how students make sense of those results. And if we get kids thinking too much about how to do better, they may end up making sense of those results in the least constructive way.

## *Making a Bad Thing Worse*

Having explored how an emphasis on achievement can backfire, we're now ready to consider the possibility that some versions of this mind-set are worse than others. If we were determined, for some perverse reason, to maximize the harm of this whole focus on achievement, we could simply do any of the following three things: (1) increase the pressure on students, (2) set them against one another in some kind of contest, or (3) dare them not to fail.

The first of these is fairly straightforward. People of all ages need to have some say about what they're doing, to feel "self-determining."[44] "When children believe that they can exert control over success in school, they perform better on cognitive tasks. And, when children succeed in school, they are more likely to view school performance as a controllable outcome."[45] Turning performance into something that feels coerced interrupts this constructive cycle and exacerbates the damage. It's bad enough to get kids thinking mostly about how well they're doing; it's worse to get them thinking about how well they've *got* to be doing. To look at school from the student's point of view is to understand "the importance of keeping the pressure off."[46]

The second way of increasing the destructive potential of a performance orientation is to get students thinking not just about how well they're doing, but how well they're doing *compared to everyone else.* Learning doesn't stand a chance when the point is to keep up with, or triumph over, other students. Now we're two steps away from where we should be. The idea isn't for students to understand or even for them to perform well. The idea is for them to win.

The difference between learning and achievement is hard enough to grasp; the difference between doing well and doing better than others is especially confusing in a society so obsessed with being Number One that the ideas of excellence and winning have been thoroughly conflated. Witness all the talk about how schools and organizations need to become more "competitive"—as though that was synonymous with "quality." (Not only is it not synonymous; it's often not even compatible.) I have discussed this topic at length elsewhere[47] and will resist the temptation to belabor the point here. Still, it's worth pointing out that some of the analysis and evidence already cited in this chapter have either incorporated competition into the concept of high performance or have found that competition is the most destructive way to define performance.

If we want our children to "develop or exercise their powers as fully as possible or to accomplish as much as they can," said the late educational psychologist John Nicholls, then "it would be irrational for us to promote competitive or publicly evaluative educational environments."[48] Thus, letter and number grades are bad enough, but grading students on a curve, or ranking them against one another, is an abomination. Standardized testing (as we'll see later) is a major impediment to improving schools, but "norm-referenced" tests, where students are compared not to a standard but to one another, is counterproductive in the extreme. Awards assemblies, spelling bees and similar contests, "Who can tell me . . . ?" questions asked of the whole class (where the point is to be the first with the right answer), posted charts of students' relative standing — all of these practices exact a terrible price even from the students who win. Winners and losers alike are made to think they're competent and valuable only to the extent that they've defeated others. Winners and losers alike come to distrust and resent their peers, since the central lesson of all competition is that other people are obstacles to their own success. Winners and losers alike are apt to lose interest in the learning itself and to learn less effectively.

The research supporting these claims is there for anyone who cares to find it. These studies show quite clearly that

- students who have come to equate success with doing better than others are more likely to think in a "surface-level" way,[49]
- students are more likely to attribute the results of a competition to factors outside their control (compared with how they explain non-competitive success or failure),[50]
- a competitive learning environment causes students to dislike school and show less interest in a given subject,[51]
- people of different abilities tend to learn more effectively on a range of tasks when they're able to cooperate with one another than when they're trying to defeat one another,[52]

and so on and so on. If competition were a consumer product rather than an ideology, it would have been banned long ago.

To say this is not to imply that we think kids are equally good at everything.[53] Rather, it means that we understand the difference between quality and victory. As a parent, I'm naturally interested in, though I hope not obsessed with, how successfully my daughter is learning. But it is neither legitimate nor helpful for me to want to know how she's doing compared to everyone else in class — and frankly, I have no business asking. Some reference point, of course, is required to gauge her progress, and I expect that experience with many other students over the years indirectly contributes to an educator's judgment about whether there's any reason for me to be concerned about my daughter. But that's very different from wanting to rank the students in a given class.* It may be unrealistic to ignore the differences between them, but it is positively utopian to think we can emphasize competitive performance while still valuing learning.

---

* I once met an elementary school teacher who said that when parents insist on such comparisons, she confides to them, "You know, [your child] is the best in the class!" Then, after a pause, she muses, "Of course, this is the dumbest class I've ever had." Apart from its wit, her answer nicely points up just how useless such rankings really are.

Thus far, I've mentioned two ways in which making students preoccupied with how well they're doing can be made even more harmful: by increasing control and by introducing competition. The third method of making things worse is by emphasizing failure rather than success. In the last few years, some psychologists have been arguing that there are actually two kinds of performance orientation, one where the point is to show how good you are and the other where the point is to show how bad you're not. They contend that the latter is the worst possible goal. People who are put in the position of trying to escape failure may work hard and get things done, but they're especially likely to fall victim to everything discussed in this chapter: they lose interest in what they're doing, go out of their way to avoid difficult tasks, get thrown for a loop when they do fail, and attribute that failure to a lack of ability.[54]

While trying to escape failure is a particularly unproductive goal for a student, perhaps we should pause to reflect on how the experience of actually failing is also bad news. Wanting to help kids learn to deal with failure in a healthy way is not an argument for making them fail more often than necessary. Subjecting children to unusually difficult assignments, concepts beyond their grasp, very tough grading, and other gratuitous causes of failure simply is not a sensible strategy. It shouldn't be necessary to point this out, but there are actually people walking around — some of whom come into contact with children on a regular basis — who talk like this: "Once upon a time . . . you passed or you failed. You made the team or you didn't. If you fell short, if your ego was bruised by getting a D or by seeing your name on the cut list, then you buckled down and you made it next time and felt good about yourself. . . . Failure can be a terrific motivator."[55]

It is difficult to imagine a point of view more at variance with everything we know about motivation and learning. While it can be useful, even necessary, to give students some feedback on their efforts, teachers who cover a student's paper with corrections often aren't upholding high standards so much as a chilly sort of perfectionism that ignores its real effects on real people. Look at it from the student's point of view. Does he say to himself, "Well, it appears that this essay on which I worked so hard is a worthless piece of trash and that I can't write a single sentence that the teacher likes. But, gosh darn it, this failure is just going to motivate me to try even harder next time and reach excellence!"?

We may want children to rebound from failure, but wanting does not automatically make it true. For students to do serious thinking, they have to "feel confident in their ability to make sense of problematic situations," one researcher explains.[56] And the source of that confidence? "To a large extent," writes another psychologist, "perceived competence comes from success experiences."[57] Doing well doesn't guarantee that one will have that faith in oneself (especially if the success is attributed to inborn ability), and having faith in oneself doesn't guarantee high levels of achievement.[58] But the experience of screwing up is a poorer bet by orders of magnitude.

When children fail at a task, the most likely result, all things being equal,[59] is that they'll expect to do poorly on similar tasks in the future,[60] and this expectation, as we've seen, can set a self-fulfilling prophecy into motion. Thus, because failure can engender a feeling of incompetence (if not helplessness), future levels of achievement are compromised. Indeed, a bundle of research suggests that kids who fail at something are less likely to succeed the next time—even if they're perfectly capable of completing the second task.[61]

Moreover, repeated or unexpected or especially significant failure can lead to those other consequences we keep coming across: avoiding challenging tasks,[62] losing interest in the task,[63] and thinking in terms of ability rather than effort.[64] Even those students who really do buckle down and try harder when they fail—the supposed success stories of traditional methods—may be doing so out of an anxious, compulsive pressure to feel better about themselves rather than because they enjoy learning.[65] They may manage to understand what they're reading today, but they may not want to read tomorrow.

## Grade Expectations

It's hard to use the phrase "anxious, compulsive pressure" in the context of schooling without immediately thinking about the ritual of grading. The emphasis on doing well most commonly takes the form of report cards: not only do they specify exactly how well students are doing (in the opinion of the teacher, at least), but the anticipation of good or bad grades serves to create precisely the kind of exaggerated focus on achievement that is so destructive.

As parents, of course, we have a right to monitor our own children's academic progress to get a sense of how they're doing in school. In chapter 10, I'll discuss some ways that such information can be provided without doing damage in the process. But before weighing these alternatives, we have to understand how traditional grades and report cards are not only unhelpful but destructive.

Take it from a teacher: "If I were asked to enumerate ten educational stupidities, the giving of grades would head the list. . . . If I can't give a child a better reason for studying than a grade on a report card, I ought to lock my desk and go home and stay there." So wrote Dorothy De Zouche, a junior high school teacher in Missouri, in an article published in February . . . of 1945.[66] Even earlier, numerous essays and studies had been published in education journals contending that grades "divert attention from education itself" and otherwise prove counterproductive.[67] Since then, of course, evidence has continued to accumulate.

The first problem with grades is simple: they don't provide accurate and reliable information about how students are doing. A grade of B in English tells you nothing about what your child can do, what she understands, where she needs help. Moreover, the basis for that grade is as subjective as the result is uninformative. A teacher can meticulously record scores for one test or assignment after another, eventually calculating averages down to a hundredth of a percentage point, but that doesn't change the arbitrariness of each individual mark. Even the score on a math test is largely a reflection of how the test was written: what skills the teacher decided to assess, what kinds of questions happened to be left out, and how many points each section was "worth." Moreover, research has long been available to confirm what all of us know: any given assignment may well be given two different grades by two equally qualified teachers. It may even be given two different grades by a single teacher who reads it at two different times.[68] In short, what grades offer is spurious precision—a subjective rating masquerading as an objective evaluation.[69]

Apart from its dubious accuracy in reporting the quality of student achievement, how do traditional grades affect the quality of student achievement? To a large extent, that depends on what you mean by "achievement." If you're just talking about getting students to hand in an assignment, one study showed that threatening to deduct points from their final grade can increase the probability that they'll comply.[70] If you take graduate students (who have presumably been trained for many years to accept the importance of grades) and suddenly tell them that they'll automatically receive a B for the class, then they won't work as hard—as measured by the amount they memorize for the final exam.[71]

As far as I can tell, that pretty much exhausts the research that finds positive achievement effects from the use of grades: they're confined to the temporary retention of facts or low-level skills. More surprising and significant, however, are the results of a range of other studies:

- When the curriculum was engaging—in this case, involving hands-on, interactive learning activities at the junior high school level—

students who weren't graded at all did just as well on a proficiency exam as those who were.[72]

- Students who had attended elementary schools where no grades were given did just as well in junior high school as a carefully matched sample of students who had received traditional report cards for six years.[73]

- Fifth-graders told they would be graded on how well they learned a social studies lesson had more trouble understanding the main point of the text than did those who were told that no grades would be involved. Even on a measure of rote recall, the graded group remembered fewer facts a week later.[74]

- Three different studies, all with older elementary students, found that the children given numerical grades for their performance on a series of word games and other tasks proved to be significantly less creative than those who received qualitative feedback but no grades. The more creative the task, the worse the performance of the students who knew they were going to be graded. Providing students with comments in addition to a grade didn't help: the highest achievement occurred only when comments were given *instead of* numerical scores.[75]

- College students, asked to read a scientific article, were told either that they would be tested on it for a grade or that they wouldn't be tested but would be asked to teach the content to another student. The two groups did equally well at memorizing facts, but the graded group didn't do nearly as well on a measure of conceptual learning.[76]

- High school students who tended to think about current events in terms of what they'd need to know for a grade were less knowledgeable than their peers, even after taking other variables into account.[77]

These negative effects of giving students grades (and leading them to focus on getting as high a grade as possible) are actually quite predictable. Again we see the relevance of distinguishing between a student who is thinking about what she's doing and a student who is thinking about how well she's doing: grades create a counterproductive shift toward the latter. Recall that the first casualty of this shift is one's attitude toward learning. Thus, we shouldn't be surprised to discover that some of the studies mentioned above—the fifth-grade social studies lesson, the comparison of grades with comments, and the comparison of grades with teaching a peer—found that *interest, like achievement, is usually lower when students are working for a grade.* Other studies have found exactly the same thing,[78] and the effect has been confirmed not only in the United States but in Iran, Israel, and Japan. In fact, I'm not aware of any research investigating this question that has failed to find students who lose interest in the learning itself as a result of being graded.

While it's not impossible for a student to be concerned about getting high marks and also to like what he's doing, the practical reality is that these two ways of thinking generally pull in opposite directions. Some research has explicitly demonstrated that a grade orientation and a learning orientation are inversely related.[79] Hence the timeless question from the back row: "Do we have to know this?" Hence the concern that "learning will cease as soon as grades are no longer given—at graduation."[80] Furthermore, echoing what we've seen to be true about a preoccupation with achievement more generally, studies have shown that students of all ages who are thinking about grades will probably pick the easiest possible task if given a choice: the more pressure to get an A, the less inclination to truly challenge oneself.[81]

In sum, researchers have found that traditional grades are likely to lead to three separate results: less impressive learning, less interest in learning, and less desire to do challenging learning. Moreover, a school's use of letter or number grades (just like its use of standardized tests) may encourage a fact-oriented curriculum since that sort of knowledge is easier to score.[82] In any case, grades certainly don't "encourage teachers to help students improve, because only the students are blamed when they fail to learn."[83] Grading, in other words, relieves educators from having to rethink what and how they are teaching. It's always the kid who is said to have "earned" an A or an F.

How a teacher feels about this topic will tell you quite a bit about his or her whole value system. Some teachers like grades, defend them, and assume they're necessary to "motivate" students. In my experience, these tend to be the most traditional teachers. They often keep intricate records of students' marks. They talk about how hard students have to "work" for a good grade in their classes and take pride in how they are upholding high standards.* They periodically warn students that they're "going to have to know this for the test" as a way of compelling them to pay attention or do the assigned readings—and they may even use surprise quizzes for that purpose.[84]

---

* Because they unwittingly create a climate that is not conducive to intellectual exploration, one might argue that these Old School teachers are actually undermining genuinely high standards of learning.

Other teachers, however, don't need the artificial inducement of grades to get students interested and don't like what grades do to their relationships with students—namely, make them adversaries instead of allies. Consider this lament by a fictional teacher:

> I'm getting tired of running a classroom in which everything we do revolves around grades. I'm tired of being suspicious when students give me compliments, wondering whether or not they are just trying to raise their grade. I'm tired of spending so much time and energy grading your papers, when there are probably a dozen more productive and enjoyable ways for all of us to handle the evaluation of papers. I'm tired of hearing you ask me "Does this count?" And, heaven knows, I'm certainly tired of all those little arguments and disagreements we get into concerning marks which take so much fun out of the teaching and the learning.[85]

Most parents, meanwhile, have simply accepted grades as a fact of life; they've rarely (if ever) been invited to question the simplistic axiom that high grades are good and low grades are bad. Even those moms and dads who would never dream of paying their children for A's still hope for and welcome that scarlet letter. But as surprising as it may be to hear, and as difficult as it may be to accept, the available research suggests that celebrating a good report card helps to shift children's goals in an unproductive direction. When our kids work hard in the hopes of getting an A, we ought to be concerned—at least, if we value the quality of their thinking or their desire to think. As Martin Covington, a psychologist at the University of California at Berkeley, has written, "Parents often fear the wrong thing. Far from being worried if their children do not enter the frenzied rat race for grades, they should start worrying when their children do. All too often the result is not excellence but self-doubt, anger, and a decline in true task involvement."[86]

Notice that this argument for the abolition of traditional grades isn't based on the observation that some kids won't get A's and, as a result, will have their feelings hurt. Rather, it is based on the observation that almost all kids will come to accept that the point of going to school is to get A's and, as a result, their learning will be hurt. The more we stay focused on our long-term goals for our kids, the more we'll do everything in our power to help them forget about grades so they can become excited about ideas. At the same time, we'll join other parents and teachers in an effort to get rid of grades entirely, replacing them with more meaningful and less damaging forms of assessment (more about which in the final chapter).

Unfortunately, rather than thinking about what grades do to the way kids look at learning, many people have become preoccupied with superficial questions concerning the criteria for grading. For example, we tend to respect a "fair" teacher who offers in advance a detailed list of what must be done in exchange for a C, a B, or an A. This is fine as far as it goes, but it overlooks the far more significant respects in which "such schooling is unfair." As John Nicholls pointed out, it "prepares students to pass other people's tests without strengthening their capacity to set their own assignment in collaboration with their fellows. The concern with grades can blind them to the triviality of the questions they address" in this safe and predictable ritual of seeing assignments as something that must be completed in order to receive a particular grade in return.[87]

More disturbing yet are people who, rather than calling attention to the number of students who have become fixated on grades, make a fuss about too many students' allegedly getting A's. All the dire warnings about "grade inflation" are usually based on one of two premises. The first is that if teachers aren't sufficiently stingy with top grades, students won't be motivated. The limited research on this question, looking at the achievement effects of more or less stringent grading policies, fails to offer convincing support for this belief.[88]

The other reason some people become so exercised over the possibility of grade inflation has to do with the role that grades play, particularly in high school and college, in sorting and selecting students. This, of course, represents a reason for assessing learning that is altogether different from providing information that will help all students succeed. As a rule, the more that grades are used to decide who is better than whom, the more people will worry about making sure that the number of good grades is kept in check. A few years ago, for example, several elite colleges announced new policies to "encourag[e] professors to grade more harshly," the goal being "to provide graduate schools and employers with a way to compare students."[89]

The same thing often goes on in high schools, which not only rate their students but often rank them against one another — either explicitly, on the basis of their grade-point averages, or by grading them on a curve in individual classes[90] — thereby adding all the destructive features of competition to the problems with grading itself. The fear is that if more and more students receive A's, pretty soon grades won't mean anything.[91] To this we might respond, "Good! Then perhaps schools can begin to emphasize learning."

## Grades: The Long View

As soon as schools come to see themselves as personnel agencies, it's fair to ask whether they sort students effectively—and, specifically, how reliably grades can predict later-life success. The answer is, Not very. Researchers have tried to quantify the extent to which different variables contribute to such measures of occupational performance as income, job satisfaction, and ratings of effectiveness at work. It turns out that even *college* grades and test scores tell you very little about how those things will turn out: in statistical terms, they account for less than 3 percent of the variance.[92]

Likewise, a 1997 study of physicians found that applicants to medical school who were given special consideration—that is, those who were admitted as a result of an affirmative action policy or some other criteria even though their undergraduate grades and standardized test scores were relatively unimpressive—did indeed get lower grades in medical school. But these students did just as well as their peers once they started working in hospitals and then went on to pursue careers indistinguishable from the careers of those who were allegedly better qualified. When this study was published, it was cited as an argument for affirmative action, but it is at least as significant as evidence of how little grades and test scores mean with respect to ultimate success.[93] Indeed, William Glasser went so far as to suggest that some people may become successful "more in spite of grades than because of them."[94]

Both because of their failure to predict occupational outcomes and because they interfere with learning during school, the authors of a major study of grading recommended that employers ignore students' grade-point averages when hiring[95]—precisely the opposite of what is typically urged by proponents of Tougher Standards, who want to make grades matter even more so that students will feel compelled to "work harder." The latter view reflects a failure to understand the difference between harder and better—or, for that matter, between working and learning. It reflects a naive belief that one can get meaningful results from coercion. And, to bring this discussion full circle, it reflects an ignorance of the destructive effects of getting students to become preoccupied with how well (as opposed to what) they're doing.

# ❧ 3 ❧
# GETTING TEACHING AND LEARNING WRONG
## Traditional Education and Its Victims

THE TROUBLE with the Tougher Standards movement isn't limited to its failure to understand the costs of overemphasizing achievement. The movement is also vulnerable because of how it *defines* achievement. The vast majority of policymakers have accepted a dubious set of assumptions about what good teaching and learning are all about. Their pedagogy, in other words, is as faulty as their psychology.

In most states, to stand for educational excellence is to issue a list that begins: "All students will be able to . . ." Even before we discuss those expectations, two features of this whole enterprise are noteworthy. First, these standards are uniform. Second, the standards are highly specific, often consisting of hundreds of detailed items.

Many of us, once we think about it, will be uncomfortable with the first premise—that is, the implicit assumption that all students need the same amount of time to reach a certain goal. It's one thing to say that everyone should be able to do such-and-such by the time he or she graduates from high school; it's something else to dictate that every student must be able to do such-and-such by the end of second grade. The latter requirement fails to understand that kids develop at different rates—and that this is perfectly acceptable. The result of grade-by-grade standards, with their willful disregard of individual differences, is that some children will be branded as failures because they don't learn as quickly as their peers.

As for the specificity of standards, it is widely assumed these days that rigor is equivalent to narrowness. We are living at a time when such objectives as wanting students to learn how to write persuasively or solve problems effectively are dismissed as "mushy." Instead, the Tougher Standards contingent demands—and has often succeeded in backing with the force of law—long lists of facts and skills that students must acquire. In some places, these standards are listed explicitly; elsewhere they can be inferred from the test questions that all students are supposed to be able to answer. Thus, all fourth-graders may be required to know about "the increasing ethnic polarization of the Iberian peninsula circa 1350–1500,"[1] while high school biology students must know whether the tissue that conducts organic food throughout a vascular plant is composed of cambium, xylem, phloem, or epidermal cells.[2]

Given this view of schooling, it is refreshing and a little startling to recall a recent comment by Harold Howe II, former U.S. commissioner of education. Asked what a set of national standards should be like if we had to adopt them, he summarized half a century of wisdom in one short sentence: "They should be as vague as possible."[3] His point was that the more precise the requirements, the less responsive educators can be to what distinguishes one circumstance from another, and your child from mine. In other words, the specificity problem and the uniformity problem are related.

The real flaw of setting narrow standards, however, runs even deeper. It concerns the basic model of instruction that underlies most talk about achievement and accountability. That model overlaps with what I have called the Old School of education, in which someone hands down lists of definitions and dates, announces that this is what all kids ought to know, and specifies how much of it they ought to know at each age. The premise here is that the more facts students acquire, the better educated they are. The more single-mindedly this mission is pursued, the higher the quality of the school.

Of course, this doctrine has been an integral part of traditional education long before it became popular to include the word "standards" in every sentence on the subject. It is a doctrine that recalls the motto of the fictional university in the movie *Animal House:* "Knowledge Is Good." But when we turn a parody into a philosophy, we beg several important questions: Knowledge about how many different things? Knowledge acquired in what way and for what purpose? Knowledge acquisition at the expense of what other intellectual activities? The "bunch o' facts" model of education turns out to be connected to a series of other assumptions about teaching and learning. Many of them are widely taken on faith. All of them are worth questioning.

## *"Emphasize the Basics"*

Those who sermonize about the need to raise standards often proceed, in the next breath, to call for a return to the "basics." Indeed, this term holds a certain appeal for most people. But the question isn't whether we're for or against the basics; it's how we define them. If traditionalists mean that a lot more time should be spent on reading, writing, and arithmetic than on other subjects, plenty of people might object to neglecting art, science, social studies, and so on. If, however, they mean that more attention should be paid to the foundations of each subject, then the question becomes: What constitutes the foundations? Are we to assume that "skills taught directly by rote methods are basic while skills taught in other ways are not"?[4] And what is most fundamental about learning to write: remembering how to spell words correctly or developing a feel for how certain words will affect a reader? What is at the heart of math: memorizing procedures for computation or getting a sense of how quantities are related to each other so that one can estimate intelligently?

Traditionalists often use "the basics" to refer to little more than the mechanics of the "three R's," and they assume these are what kids primarily need and lack. Indeed, everyone has an anecdote, intended either to horrify or entertain, about a store clerk who couldn't add, a teenager who thought Oregon was in Europe, or a writer who couldn't make his tenses agrees. But a group of scholars from the University of Illinois point out that when you look at studies rather than stories, "There is considerable converging evidence that by sixth grade, children have some success at mastering basic skills of reading, writing, and arithmetic."[5]

However, the same authors continue, "there are also disturbing signs that many students lack a firm conceptual grasp of the goal of the activities in which they engage."[6] And a good case can be made that this deeper understanding is ultimately more important. A growing number of educational theorists over the last couple of decades have made the point that facts come and go, while what endures, what we really require, is the ability to look up facts, to interpret them, to connect one with another, and to analyze their importance. Like the adage "Give someone a fish, he eats for a day; teach him to fish, he eats for a lifetime," it is the capacity to acquire and use information that matters more than the information itself.

To this extent, parents ought to be concerned if a substantial part of their children's education consists of learning the state capitals, the multiplication table, the names of the explorers of the New World, or the parts of speech. It's not that these pieces of information are harmful in themselves; it's that the time spent learning them is time not spent doing other things — like thinking.

To this argument, the Old School rejoins that "learning how to learn" is an abstraction; you need to have stuff to work on, facts to analyze, a storehouse of knowledge on which to reflect. But no one argues that kids should be taught to think about nothing, that facts ought to be omitted so that only higher intellectual processes can be used. Frankly, it's not clear how we would go about teaching that way even if it seemed like a good idea. Whenever we think, it's about something. Indeed, as we'll see later, the rebellion against the Old School is founded on the need for more context, more connection to real questions. The argument here is about how much time should be spent memorizing facts and practicing skills — and about whether these activities should be treated as ends in themselves rather than as means for understanding the world.

I have no objection to teaching kids about the Magna Carta or even to having them know approximately when it was written. But if they don't have a feeling for why it was written, how it was received, why it matters when it was written; if they don't have an opinion about its contents; if it's taught in such a way that they have no reason to care about any of this — then what's the point? To prepare them for an appearance on *Jeopardy!*? As the philosopher Alfred North Whitehead observed long ago, "A merely well-informed man is the most useless bore on God's earth." "Scraps of information," he added, are only worth something if they are put to use or at least "thrown into fresh combinations."[7]

## *"Thinking Comes Later"*

If Old Schoolers are forced to acknowledge that understanding is ultimately more important than rote recall, they promptly fall back on a claim that appears to be a "no-brainer." One reason their method of teaching continues to be so prevalent is that it's based on a proposition that seems hard to dispute: the basics must come first. You want kids to read for understanding? First they have to learn how to read. You want them to pursue interesting mathematical problems? First they've got to know how to add, subtract, multiply, and divide. One fifth-grade math teacher speaks for millions of other Americans: "It's important at the elementary level to stress the basics. I don't have time for all the fancy stuff — problem solving and estimating. Kids have to first learn how to do computation. Even then, you have to keep pounding it into their heads. Later on, at the junior high level, it'll start to make sense to them."[8] Of course, someone who has actually spent time in a junior high school might frown at that last sentence (a premise critical to the whole argument, incidentally), since for some odd reason the stuff still doesn't make much sense to them, even after more years of pounding. But the teacher's premise seems no more controversial than the proposition that you've got to walk before you can run. Everyone accepts that starting with the basics is just plain common sense.

Everyone, that is, except those who have actually studied the subject.

In fact, this formulation doesn't reflect an immutable truth about learning. It reflects a particular model of learning, *behaviorism*, which has lost credibility among experts even as it retains a stranglehold on the popular consciousness. Two facts about this doctrine should immediately give us pause. One is that it is all about predicting and producing *behaviors*. "Because there is no place in the model for *understanding*, it is not surprising that behaviorist training rarely produces it."[9] Second, the objective is to produce the "correct" behaviors: in the purest form of this approach, the teacher breaks "learning down into such small steps that errors are not experienced."[10] As I'll argue shortly, no one can learn effectively, particularly in a way that involves serious thinking, if the primary purpose is to get the right answer.

But let's forget about the baggage carried by behaviorism and just look at the contention that kids must focus on the basics before they attempt all the "fancy stuff." In the real world, the result is that the fancy stuff is often put off forever. The traditional curriculum keeps moving students from one isolated fact or skill to the next: the assignments get harder but not more meaningful. Thus, the claim that learning the basics prepares kids for what comes later turns out to be a kind of con: as high school seniors, they're still memorizing and practicing the basics—just different basics.[11]

Even traditional educators who don't see this outcome as desirable are unwittingly selling their students short. Just as there are real questions about the conventional sequence of courses—biology to chemistry to physics, for example[12]—so there are good reasons to challenge the belief that within a given course students must begin by covering basic skills and only later engage in more ambitious kinds of learning that require thinking. Back in the 1920s, Whitehead declared that "it is not true that the easier subjects should precede the harder. On the contrary, some of the hardest must come first because nature so dictates, and because they are essential to life."[13]

Cognitive and educational psychologists have gradually come to realize the truth of this apparently paradoxical position. The consensus of these experts was summarized by Lauren Resnick at the University of Pittsburgh, herself one of the leading authorities in the field, and she is worth quoting at length:

> The most important single message of modern research on the nature of thinking is that the kinds of activities traditionally associated with thinking are not limited to advanced levels of development. Instead, these activities are an intimate part of even elementary levels of reading, mathematics, and other branches of learning—when learning is proceeding well. In fact, the term "higher order" skills is probably itself fundamentally misleading, for it suggests that another set of skills, presumably called "lower order," needs to come first. This assumption—that there is a sequence from lower level activities that do not require much independent thinking or judgment to higher level ones that do—colors much educational theory and practice. Implicitly at least, it justifies long years of drill on the "basics" before thinking and problem solving are demanded. Cognitive research on the nature of basic skills such as reading and mathematics provides a fundamental challenge to this assumption. Indeed, research suggests that failure to cultivate aspects of thinking [that are part of] higher order skills may be the source of major learning difficulties even in elementary school.[14]

Examples of how the best teachers act on this finding will be offered later. Now I just want to emphasize the limits of the behavioral prescription for teaching. Two problems quickly become apparent if you think about how you learned to drive a car. First, the process wasn't incremental, with expertise developing in tiny, evenly spaced steps. Rather, there were probably leaps of improvement so that everything came together one day and you were suddenly driving more proficiently than you had earlier. This is equally true of intellectual growth, which "does not take place in small, linear increments but is better described as occurring in qualitative and uneven shifts in understanding."[15]

The second feature of learning to drive is that you mastered the activity as a whole; you didn't work on separate skills and then put them together later. If someone asked, you could have named some of those skills—applying the right amount of pressure to the accelerator, judging distances, knowing when to glance in the rearview mirror, and so on—but real driving can't be reduced to those parts, and it isn't learned by concentrating on them in sequence. You practiced the individual skills in the context of the act of driving.

Another example speaks to this last point. With the exception of trained musicians, few of us can sing a note followed immediately by the fourth tone of its scale (say, a C and then an F). Or can we? In isolation it is impossibly hard, but embedded in a meaningful context it is remarkably easy. Just sing the first two notes of the song "Tonight" from *West Side Story*.[16] In academics, too, we learn most readily, most naturally, most effectively, when we start with the big picture—precisely when the basics *don't* come first.[17]

This is what underlies the approach known as "Whole Language" (see chapter 9): it's not that children shouldn't learn phonics, but that phonics shouldn't be the point of departure. The point of departure is the story, and kids master the reading and writing skills necessary to follow or tell that story. It's just not true that one must learn to read before being able to read for understanding; it makes a lot more sense to learn to read *by* reading for understanding. Precisely the same thing may be said of math: wise educators don't teach addition and subtraction as prerequisites for pursuing interesting problems; they teach these skills *through* interesting problems, for instance, the need to figure out how many grapes each child can take so there will be enough for everyone. "Students can do more advanced concepts even if they don't have all the basic skills"[18]—and they can most effectively learn those skills if they're invited from the beginning to think in a sophisticated way about the underlying concepts.

I remember talking with a woman at a reading conference who sounded a lot like that fifth-grade math teacher quoted earlier. When I disputed her contention that the basics had to come first, she said, "Well, you need facts in life." I asked where knowing facts is more important than knowing how to think (or knowing which facts are most relevant), and her answer was "College." That would be true only at a pretty poor college, I replied, to which she played her discussion-ending trump card: "Well, that's life!"

That—or a comparable invocation of the "real world"—is frequently the Old School's last refuge, its way of dismissing reform and reformers. A history professor recalled that her own education was "rote learning, boring details, tedious routines, to be sure, but school—and life—is like that."[19] (Maybe Santayana was wrong: it is those who don't realize that the past could be otherwise who are condemned to repeat it. Or make their children repeat it.) The reasonable reply, it seems to me, is that nothing could be less "realistic" than the staples of a traditional education,[20] including having to learn skills outside a practical context.

# "Facts Must Be Memorized"

The Old School not only emphasizes basic facts but often requires students to learn many of them "by heart." One justification is that memorizing is useful in its own right, a way of training the mind. To the best of my knowledge, there is no evidence to support this belief. Committing things to memory may train you to be a better memorizer, but there is absolutely no reason to think that it provides any real cognitive benefits. Stuffing facts into your head doesn't help you think better; indeed, the time spent stuffing is time *not* spent analyzing or inventing or communicating, making distinctions or drawing connections.

The other justification is that this information has to be inside your head to be useful. Yet as a rule, observes William Glasser, "the world says look it up, don't rely on your memory." He adds, "I would hate to drive over a bridge, work in a building, or fly in an airplane designed by engineers who depended only upon memory."[21] In most situations, information doesn't have to be locked in cranial storage—and most information simply can't be just because there's so much of it.

But let's acknowledge that there are situations where there isn't time to look up facts. Even so, that doesn't mean the best way of getting them into one's head is to sit down and learn them by rote. That, as the psychologist Ellen Langer points out, is basically "a strategy for taking in material that has no personal meaning."[22] The very fact that you have to make an effort to memorize it suggests something artificial about the whole business. More to the point, deliberately committing things to memory usually doesn't work very well—at least not for long. After decades of studying the question, Joseph Novak, professor of science education at Cornell University, has concluded, "Knowledge acquired by rote learning will not be assimilated . . . into a cognitive structure."[23]

Think about it: how much do you still remember of what you had to memorize in school? (What's a gerund? What's the capital of North Dakota? What's the formula for finding the volume of a sphere?) Even the high-achieving students in traditional classrooms typically report that what they've been taught vanishes after a short time.[24] But if a certain fact or skill is so important that we want students to carry it inside their heads, we ought to listen to what experts on learning like David Perkins have to say: "Over and over again, studies have demonstrated that we memorize best when we analyze what we are learning, find patterns in it, and relate it to knowledge we already have. In other words, when we think about it."[25]

And, one might add, when we use it. The word processing commands

I use when I type are burned into my memory simply because I call on them almost every day, not because I tried to memorize them. The latter is like pushing a boulder uphill: it rolls back down because it doesn't need to be there.

# *"Skills Require Drills"*

Closely related to memorizing facts is practicing skills. Driven by a theory of learning no more sophisticated than the old saw "practice makes perfect," children are made to do something over and over and over, to "attain efficiency in outward doing without the use of intelligence," in John Dewey's words.[26] Clearly, this factory-like approach is so unappealing that many students come to hate school, so there had better be a compelling pedagogical justification for it.

There isn't. In the Old School classroom, six-year-olds are handed worksheets and told to fill in the missing letters in one word after another (as in: w_ste of t_me). Sixteen-year-olds are shown a two-variable equation on the blackboard and then given umpteen more just like it to do on their own. Such instruction requires very little of the instructor — which is why it's most common "in places where teachers are poorly trained"[27] — and it offers very little to students. Indeed, the completed assignments reflect very little of students. Even proud parents who collect every memento of their children's years in school have no reason to save these sterile worksheets.

Kids who are variously called "at-risk," "low-achievers," or "slow learners" usually "suffer most from a proficiency-driven curriculum because they are consigned indefinitely to dull and repetitive skills instruction that does not enable them to grasp underlying concepts."[28] Drilling isn't teaching. If I don't understand how to do something, making me do it repeatedly is just going to make me feel dumber or angrier. Yet students who are already struggling are those most likely to be forced to do this kind of stuff.[29]

Even when students already have the skill in question, drills are of dubious value. "Thinking does not develop and cannot be perfected through mere practice," Constance Kamii, a leading mathematics educator, has written.[30] The Old School isn't about developing understanding but about producing the right answer — perhaps with a standardized test in mind. If it turns out that the technique known wryly as "drill 'n kill" does raise test scores, that's an invitation to reevaluate the superficiality of those tests, not a reason to continue using this technique.[31]

As with knowing certain facts by memory, there are times when it is useful for a skill to be automatic—looking at the squiggles on a page and understanding the words they represent, for example. But that, again, isn't an argument for a particular method of teaching. Just as deliberately memorizing facts isn't the best way to learn something by heart, so worksheets don't offer the best way to acquire a skill. Moreover, practicing some things until you can almost do them in your sleep often interferes with flexibility and innovation. What can be done without thinking usually is done without thinking, and that locks us into patterns and procedures that are less than ideal.[32]

## *"The Point Is to Get the Right Answer"*

Memorizing facts and practicing skills are based on the idea that answers and strategies are either correct or incorrect—and, more important, that schooling is mostly about training students to produce the correct ones. Once again, Dewey got to the heart of the issue: "The zeal for 'answers' is the explanation of much of the zeal for rigid and mechanical methods."[33]

This is another example of how thoroughly the traditionalists have triumphed: we've been conditioned to accept as an obvious truth—rather than one particular model of schooling—the idea that learning is a process of getting things right, and thus that the "good" students get more right than the "bad" ones. A child produces the right answer and everyone is happy; on to the next problem, the next topic, the next grade. A child gets the wrong answer, and whether the adult's response is harsh or friendly, the goal will be to get her to produce the right answer tomorrow. (Although we may try to soften the blow by saying, "No, but you're very close!" the message is clear: all that matters is proximity to the correct response.)[34]

The discussions teachers conduct are often fishing expeditions: they're not invitations to reflect deeply on complicated issues but attempts to elicit the right answer. Even in English or social studies classes, where the questions appear to be more open-ended, students inspect the teacher's face to see how nearly their responses approximate what's expected. I see this in classrooms all over the country. In a Chicago public school, a second-grade teacher asks about the concept of tolerance. She pleasantly acknowledges a variety of answers until she hears the one she wants, at which point she nods vigorously, exclaims, "Say that again!" and writes only that comment on the board. In a Seattle private school, the atmosphere is informal and the level is advanced, but the approach isn't all that different: the high school history teacher asks what makes a society "civilized," then gently tries to pull the right answers from students rather than inviting a real exchange of ideas. In a Minneapolis kindergarten class, the art projects pasted to the wall are virtually identical, suggesting that there is one right answer even to the question "How do you make a pumpkin?"

Some students—only some—will figure out how to say what the teacher wants to hear, how to fill in the bubble that the standardized test scoring machines will count as correct. These students will receive colorful stickers and trophies and A's; their papers will be proudly pushpinned to the bulletin boards, and they will eventually be admitted to expensive colleges. But all the kids will learn that school is like a factory where the point is to produce error-free widgets, to perform well, to play the game. "Knowing the right answer requires no decisions, carries no risks, and makes no demands," says Eleanor Duckworth of Harvard. "It is automatic. It is thoughtless." And when children's ideas, rather than being taken seriously, are "simply scanned for correspondence to what the teacher want[s]," well, then it isn't too hard to figure out "what happens to children's curiosity and resourcefulness later in their childhood."[35]

That rumbling you hear in the distance is the right wing readying its invocation of the dreaded charge of relativism. "What?! Are you saying there aren't any right answers? That eight plus three can be ten if you say so? That one scientific or historical theory is as valid as the next?" No, no, and again, no. What I am saying is if we want kids to be thinkers, we have to encourage (and help) them to think—and that means spending most of their time in most subject areas on questions that don't lend themselves to single-word answers that are either right or wrong. There should be fewer questions like "What was the name of the town where the characters in this story lived?" and more questions like "Why do you think the characters in this story never left the town where they lived?" There should be less time defining words like "nationalism" and more time discussing what the world would be like if there were no countries.

Notice two things about this recommendation. First, it's not relativistic because there are better and worse ways of answering these questions (and students get a much richer education, incidentally, if they participate in devising those criteria). Second, to answer these questions well, kids need to have some facts and skills. But the facts and skills are acquired in the context of answering meaningful, engaging questions. They are not acquired purely for the purpose of coughing up the right answers to dull, testlike questions. It's the same pattern we saw with remembering facts and again with acquiring skills: even to the extent we want kids to have the correct information, we don't do it by making them seek out correct information all day.

"Knowing is a process, not a product," said the distinguished educator Jerome Bruner,[36] and when we get that backward—when teachers or parents lead students to believe their task is to produce right answers— those students are less inclined to talk with one another, to try out possibilities, to play with ideas. They may get the answer because they've memorized a fact or a formula, but with no understanding of why or under what conditions it's true. Plenty of students score well on standardized tests because they can come up with the correct responses even though they have only the dimmest sense of what they're doing or why (see pp. 20–21, 173–74).

The limits of focusing on right answers are apparent even in math, where right answers unquestionably exist. Having received a decent elementary school education, I can tell you how to divide one fraction by another: flip over the second fraction and then multiply them. But don't ask me why it's done that way. I have no idea. I was given a bunch of tricks whose purpose was to yield the right answers—not to help me understand. The two are completely different in theory, different in practice, and often different in results. My test scores were super, but my grasp of mathematical principles was superficial.

What it comes down to is that not all right answers are equal: some reflect mindless, short-term memorization, and others reflect something more. Not all wrong answers are equal, either: some reflect sloppiness, and others reflect a complete lack of understanding. (Thus the response "No, but you're very close!" is also pretty silly: a child may be off by only one digit but have no idea what she's doing.) These distinctions, critical to learning, are lost if the only criterion is whether a child's answers matches the one at the back of the book (or in the teacher's head).

In a right-answer environment, moreover, such as a classroom where teachers are under pressure to raise standards (read: test scores), there is less openness to thoughtful but unconventional responses. There is less concern with how students arrived at their answers, whether right or wrong. "Posing narrow questions for which one seeks a singular answer denies teachers the opportunity to peer into students' minds"[37] and thus to help them learn most effectively. Indeed, Jean Piaget's vital contribution to our understanding of how children learn was based on studying the qualitatively different errors they make at different stages of development.[38]

Any of these reasons may explain why there is less emphasis on right answers in other countries, such as Japan.[39] It's always instructive, and often quite surprising, to find that the things we take for granted—the foundations of traditional American education, for example—aren't necessarily present throughout the world. It's also illuminating to realize that, even to the extent we regard schooling as preparation for adult life (or, more narrowly, for work), the traditional methods and assumptions may not make much sense. While we adults often need to find the right answer, there are more occasions in a given week when we will wrestle with questions such as "What would be a better way to do this?" "Which of the possible explanations for this problem seems most relevant?" "How do I cope with my child's latest crisis?" and "What does it mean to lead a good life?" Not only are there no cut-and-dried answers to these queries, but twelve or more years of being trained to look for such answers may well put us at a disadvantage.

## *"Get to the Civil War by Thanksgiving"*

One of the most distinctive features of American education is the expectation that a great many things will be "covered" as quickly as possible in order to maximize the number of topics about which students will presumably be knowledgeable. Teaching sometimes resembles a caricature of American tourists in Europe: there are only $x$ days to see $y$ countries, so the rental car screeches to a stop in front of a famous ruin, the family jumps out and snaps pictures, and the children are herded back into the car. Those who protest that they didn't really see anything are told not to worry: "You'll see it when we get home."[40] It's like checking off items on a list: we can say we saw all these places even if we don't really know what any of them are like. Same with school: if it's Tuesday, this must be a preposition.

What drives such teaching is the imposition of a long list of standards along with demands that students and teachers be held accountable for covering all of them, however superficially. Linda Darling-Hammond, a researcher who has studied this topic extensively, observed that "many existing standards documents do not encourage teaching for understanding. . . . They outline hundreds of bits of information for students to acquire at various grade levels in each subject area, creating expectations for content coverage that render impossible the in-depth study students need to understand and apply ideas."[41]

The more such expectations are created, the greater the probability that teachers will rely on textbooks, which invariably include a little bit of everything and a thoughtful treatment of nothing. (It can safely be said that any course consisting mostly of reading a textbook, chapter by chapter, is a course worth avoiding.)* In turn, the teacher's use of textbooks and the state's lists of standards reflect a certain philosophy of learning — namely, that education consists of accumulating a bunch o' facts.[43]

The problem with covering so many things, of course, is that you can only scratch the surface of each. It takes time to write a decent story or essay; you need to invent and polish and then let it sit for a while and come back to it later. It takes time for a young child to figure out why only some objects float, for an older student to figure out why only some countries got involved in World War I, for a reader of any age to savor the sweetness of fine prose. Some kids can get the right answer to a math problem quickly, but it takes time to understand how someone else managed to get the same answer using a radically different method. It takes time to design, set up, and carry out a clever experiment that will tell you what you really want to know. It takes time to learn.

That's why parents who would like to see school move beyond the realm of the superficial should get very nervous if too much territory is being covered over the course of a year, or a week, in their children's classrooms. Experts in cognitive psychology overwhelmingly oppose — and even crusade against — the tendency to march double-time through a set curriculum. Howard Gardner and his colleagues refer to coverage as the single greatest enemy of understanding.[44] Fred Newmann, at the University of Wisconsin, contends that real thinking is "persistently undermined by the effort to transmit information on countless topics to ensure that children possess basic (cultural, scientific, mathematical, economic, and civic) 'literacy' "[45] — which is a reasonably good summary of the traditional model of education. An emphasis on "basic literacy" is death to depth.[46]

The piquant irony, though, is that exposing students to fact after fact doesn't just prevent them from thinking well: it also gets in the way of learning the facts. Traditional education fails, therefore, even on its own terms. "Most of the time," Newmann continues, "students receive only superficial exposure to countless items of knowledge that low-achieving students rarely learn and that high-achieving students remember only

---

* This doesn't mean that textbooks have no legitimate uses. They can be excellent references, like dictionaries, to be consulted when students need to check a fact. They can be used self-referentially, to spur a discussion about the content of textbooks and the consequences of relying on them. The cleverest use I've ever seen for a science textbook was in a fourth-grade classroom in New York where various quantities of books were stacked with rulers leaning against them so that students could systematically investigate the effect of dropping marbles down these inclined planes.[42]

long enough to succeed on tests."[47] Instead of seeing the pattern here, instead of realizing how our system of teaching (and our demands for Tougher Standards) are to blame, we accuse the slow kids of not trying hard enough and congratulate the quick kids for doing so well.

As though it were not enough to say that understanding is undermined and even the facts are not retained, consider that this style of teaching also trains students to value doing lots of stuff even if they don't get much out of it, a mindset that may linger throughout their lives.[48] (Could the Americans' tour of Europe reflect the American education that preceded it?) Moreover, it views as dispensable the students who need more time to understand something, since the pressure to move on to the next topic is so strong. (Apart from the fact that schooling is conceived of as a competitive event, it's interesting that the race is to the swift, not to the reflective.) Finally, it discourages active student involvement in learning. In her study of American high schools, Linda McNeil of Rice University found that teachers believed "the pace of the lecture was critical to covering the course [material] adequately. To maintain that pace, student talk had to be kept to a minimum."[49] As we'll see, student talk is critical to learning — yet another explanation of why learning suffers in traditional classrooms and in districts obsessed with standards.

## "Bring Your Own Containers"

"I want you to teach my kid the basics even if you have to pound them into her head," a sixth-grade teacher in the state of Washington was commanded by a student's father not long ago. Whatever we may think of his preference for "the basics," it is the metaphor of pounding (which, you may recall, was also used by the math teacher quoted on pp. 50–51) that is ultimately more pervasive and pernicious. It suggests that we can make students learn by the sheer force of didactic instruction, by having the teacher write on the blackboard while disgorging information that students are supposed to lap up and copy down.

The teacher tells; the students listen. And when they aren't listening, they're reading things like textbooks in order to absorb information. Then come the quizzes, compulsory recitations, and other ways of proving that they indeed remember what they were told. All of this adds up to a system, an approach to teaching, that lends itself to a variety of colorful labels. Critics in the field of education call it "chalk 'n talk," "stand and deliver," "the sage on the stage" (or, from the student's point of view, "sit 'n git"). Dewey said these methods reflect a "static, cold-storage ideal of knowledge."[50] The great Brazilian teacher Paulo Freire called it the "banking" concept of education: facts are deposited in students' heads and then withdrawn on demand.[51] It's also been referred to as the "jug and mug" model: stuff is poured from the big container into the little ones.

Remarkably similar metaphors are used by people who are not at all critical of this approach and sometimes aren't even aware they're using metaphors. Education has been described as the "delivery of instruction" or the "transfer of information." More testing of students has been demanded (in this case by the governor of Wisconsin) on the grounds that otherwise "we don't know what went into their heads."[52] Perhaps the most memorable illustration of this model appeared in one of those tidbits in the *Reader's Digest* that are designed to induce mild chuckles. The item described a sign on a high school bulletin board: "FREE. Every Monday through Friday. Knowledge. Bring your own containers."[53]

If you think of education as transferring or transmitting a bunch o' facts, it also makes sense to think of children as little more than empty vessels into which that knowledge is poured. This is the premise of all the Old School methods discussed in this chapter. The "transmission" model is found in first-grade classrooms devoted to the systematic teaching of phonics and in high school honors classes where teachers slap transparencies on the overhead projector and lecture endlessly about Romantic poets or genetic codes. As a rule, the more that standardized tests are used (and their results emphasized), the more we can expect schools to adopt this approach to teaching students of all ages.

Here is one more example of how a defining doctrine of traditional education not only persists in our classrooms but has come to be confused with education itself. Why this happens isn't all that hard to understand. First of all, most of us have sat and listened to teachers lecture at us year after year, so we naturally think that's what teaching is all about. Second, there's a kind of commonsense plausibility to this model: if we've never had the opportunity to think about how learning happens, it's reasonable to assume that a teacher, who presumably is more knowledgeable than his students, would simply tell them what he knows.

When I was teaching, it never dawned on me to question this view. There was a stretch of seven years, for example, when I took great pleasure in teaching an intensive course on existentialism to high school students. In between terms, I fine-tuned the reading list and perfected the lectures, looking forward to the next year when I could teach it again — rather as one might tinker with a new car in the garage before proudly driving it around. It wasn't until years later that I began to realize just how little I understood of education. The idea of a teacher with a ready-made course just waiting to be taught makes about as much sense as a single person with a ready-made marriage who needs nothing more than a partner to share it with.

Eventually I came to understand that a course is created for and with a particular group of students. "Teaching is not essentially performance," Bill Ayers remarked. "It is not the delivery of the goods. Teaching is an interactive practice that begins and ends with 'seeing' the student."[54] I didn't know that, so I ended up seeing only my reading list and lecture notes. Because I was trying to find the most efficient way of giving students the knowledge and skills that I already had, I was treating them as interchangeable receptacles.

That isn't what people are, however, and it isn't how they learn. As a later chapter will describe, even infants are active meaning-makers. By the time a child toddles into a classroom, he is already buzzing with beliefs and ideas and questions. He encounters new facts and theories in light of what (and how) he already thinks. If he is just given new facts — without an opportunity to assimilate them, think them through, and use them — he'll probably forget them. If he is just told about new theories, he probably won't really understand them and will just shake them off and continue thinking the way he did before.

I used to assume I was a good teacher because I knew what I was talking about, I enjoyed what I was talking about, and I was a good talker. The problem was that I thought teaching was about talking, so I did way too much of it. I wasn't familiar with the cognitive research demonstrating that "knowledge cannot be given directly to students."[55] Precisely because I was successful in conventional terms, I had no reason to question them. It would have been deeply disconcerting to realize that I hadn't the foggiest understanding of how learning takes place. That recognition would have forced me to consider the possibility that I wasn't nearly as good as I thought I was, that my skill at organizing and presenting information didn't mean that I was a qualified teacher.[56]

Had someone asked me at the time, I would have conceded, and perhaps made a wry joke about, the fact that my students would probably forget most of what they had learned in class. I might have rationalized this as a fact of life or a sign of deficiency in the students. But one very good book on the subject observes that it's not really accurate to complain that students forget what they learned. Why? Because they never really "learned" it in the first place. They were just taught it.[57]

Such statements, of course, are so much red meat to Old School partisans, who vociferously defend the transmission model and attack anything offered in its place (often by reducing all the alternatives to cartoon-like versions of touchy-feely experiences). The possibility that children might bring their minds to school, rather than their "own containers," provokes traditionalists to such fury that it makes you wonder about the source of their visceral attachment to the idea that learning is just a transfer of information.[58]

In fairness, though, calling the transmission model into question makes a lot of people uncomfortable. It challenges the cynical teacher, who insists he "taught a good lesson even if the kids didn't learn it"—as if this weren't a contradiction in terms.[59] It challenges the compassionate teacher, who wants to make things easier for a struggling student and just says, "Here, this is how you do it." It challenges the principal who comes in to observe a teacher and, seeing that she's not "standing up in front of the room giving a lecture," offers to come back on a day when she's "really teaching."[60]

And it challenges parents. If we want our kids to be superb learners, then we'll have to take the customary assumptions about what makes a good teacher and turn them upside down. We will be less excited about having our children assigned to someone who is a charismatic lecturer, someone who makes information interesting as he pours it in. A great teacher isn't necessarily more patient or proficient at getting information across; he is more likely to understand that getting information across isn't his primary job. What matters isn't how well he holds students' attention so much as whether he knows enough to stop being the center of attention. Thus, the common parental question "Yes, but is my child really learning anything?" ought to be asked mostly about classrooms characterized by lectures and textbooks and quizzes and worksheets— and an implicit model of teaching as transmission.

## "Don't Do Something—Sit There"

Howard Gardner has a nice line: he says if we ask our kids what they did in school today and they reply "Nothing," they're probably right. They didn't do anything because traditional schooling is *"done to* students."[61] There are a thousand signs of this. One is boredom, which we parents either shrug off as a natural response to school or mistakenly attribute to the assignments' being too easy. It doesn't occur to us to wonder with Dewey whether each child has to "leave his mind behind because there is no way to use it in the school."[62] Another, even more specific, symptom is the tendency to use the indefinite pronoun when talking about a book

—as in, "They say on page 65 that . . ." When the author disappears into "they," you can bet that kids haven't been helped to recognize (much less wrestle with) the particular point of view being offered. They haven't been encouraged to see books as a source of ideas that can be challenged.

If I had to describe the student in the Old School with a single word, it would be "passive." He or she is an empty bin, a receiver of other people's ideas. Underlying the transmission version of teaching is (once again) the behaviorist view of learning, which, you will recall, sees humans as essentially passive responders to the environment rather than active thinkers and meaning-makers. Behaviorism is consistent not only with a particular kind of pedagogy ("Take out your worksheets, boys and girls") but also with a situation where the curriculum is fixed and the students have little to say about the process or the content. They are supposed to sit there and do what they're told, finish the assignment, study for the test, memorize the right answers that someone else decided they have to know. Other people prepare the meal for students, feed it to them, and then oversee their digestion of it.[63] When the digestion is finished,* we judge the whole process, not on the basis of how deeply children have understood or how keen they are to know more, but in terms of their grades and test scores. The good kids comply; the smart kids get the highest numbers and the lowest letters.

It doesn't take a suspicious mind to conclude that relegating children to such a passive role — treating them as objects, really — suggests a basic lack of respect. That's certainly what strikes me every time I peek into traditional classrooms. These adults basically don't trust that kids turned loose on arithmetic problems could ever find their way to the right answer without being handed a step-by-step procedure. They don't believe that kids can do justice to controversial issues in social studies and complicated themes in literature; they must be told what's what. (By the same token, it's assumed that kids are incapable of deciding what kind of classroom environment they want to have and must instead be rewarded and threatened into meeting the teacher's specific expectations for how to behave.)[64]

E. D. Hirsch, Jr., perhaps the most prominent contemporary spokesman for the Old School, comes close to conceding all this: "What children remember remains uncontrolled, contingent, and largely irrelevant to definite and responsible learning goals." (For "responsible" read "approved by Hirsch.") Thus, "whenever there is an absence of explicit fo-

---

* Perhaps it's time to abandon this particular metaphor.

cus and definite goals—that is, whenever there is an absence of 'traditional' schooling—there is also an absence of secure and universal learning. Process-outcome research has shown that what children bring away from naturalistic, 'integrated' learning is likely to be highly variable and uncertain."[65] Actually, I agree with his last point. It's true: in nontraditional classrooms such as I will describe later, we can't be completely sure what kids will end up learning. However, precisely the same thing is true of traditional classrooms, where we can be sure only of what those teachers are teaching. Hirsch seems to think that by controlling every detail of what students do, by spoon-feeding them facts, the uncertainty inherent to the process of education—indeed, the uncertainty of dealing with *Homo sapiens*—can be eliminated and learning can be guaranteed.

But surely we know better. Students can't be compelled to learn, only invited and encouraged and helped. At least nontraditional educators acknowledge that reality. They begin with the premise that kids deserve respect for their ability to learn. Kids can be trusted to discover remarkable things precisely when we ease up with the "explicit focus and definite goals"—particularly when that focus is through the wrong end of a telescope. Furthermore, consider from a purely practical perspective how self-defeating is the pinched sensibility that demands passive pupils. They're not learning much? Look at how you're treating them! The more that traditional methods fail, the more they are prescribed; their failure is blamed on the nature of children instead of on certain beliefs about children and the creaky techniques still used to teach them.

The evidence suggests that "little learning is retained when it is learned on command," as Piaget pithily put it.[66] Meaningful learning will more often take place in a classroom that does *not* operate according to the principles I have been describing here. Helping students become active learners isn't just more respectful; it works better.* But before exploring how to do this, we should be sure we really want children who aren't passive, who think for themselves and ask sharp, unsettling questions. "The notion that all children could and should be inventors of their own theories, critics of other people's ideas, analyzers of evidence, and makers of their own personal marks on this most complex world"—this, says Deborah Meier, is "an idea with revolutionary implications."[67] For some adults, the status quo is a great deal more appealing.

---

* A review of research on the relative effectiveness of traditional versus progressive education can be found in Appendix A.

# "*Give It to Them in Bits and Pieces*"

If "passive" describes the student in traditional American classrooms, "fragmented" describes their learning experience. A number of different flaws turn out to represent varied facets of this basic problem.

**One kind of learning is separated from another.** Sharp lines are drawn between academic and nonacademic pursuits. Activities that help kids become good learners are seen as quite different from activities that help them become good people. A traditional education emphasizes the former, perhaps because its advocates see academics as more important than anything else[68] or perhaps because they see academics as the only proper mission of schools. But notice the underlying premise here—that it's possible to separate these different kinds of learning in order to address one without the other.

To be sure, a school can eliminate any scheduled opportunities to build social skills, teach values, or address problems that kids are having with their teachers or their peers or their feelings. But this approach is short-sighted because it's impossible to erect a wall between the intellectual part of ourselves and the rest of who we are. Even when she's multiplying numbers, a child remains a whole and complex person with a unique perspective, someone defined by her expectations and fears and desires. We can try to ignore all that during school hours, but that doesn't make it go away. No reminders to "Pay attention!" will stop her from thinking about why her best friend isn't talking to her today. No narrowing of the curriculum will prevent her from seeing a math problem through the filter of her interests and concerns. In fact, shoving these things aside will likely make it even harder for her to develop a proficiency at the very academic tasks that are supposed to be the only items on the agenda.

Moreover, there is no such thing as a value-free classroom. The only questions are what the values will be and whether they will be explicit or implicit. The Old School, for example, firmly rejects cooperative learning, in which kids can experience the value of doing things together. We're informed that this isn't what school is supposed to be about, that students should interact on their own time. (The more traditional a classroom, the less the children's time there can be said to be their own.) But preventing them from sitting together and helping one another doesn't avoid teaching values. It just teaches a different value—namely, that learning is something you have to do by yourself.

That certain practices can be effective at simultaneously promoting— or undermining—intellectual, social, and moral growth reminds us that different kinds of learning are so connected that it's hard to say where one leaves off and the other begins. Put plainly, pure academics doesn't exist, and pretending otherwise creates a fragmented school experience and a study in missed opportunities.

**One subject is separated from another.** We've been trained to think that intellectual exploration naturally occurs in separate disciplines: history is over here and English is over there; this is a matter for physics teachers and that's a matter for chemistry teachers. But there is nothing inherent in the idea of knowledge that requires it to be divided up this way: the current arrangement is actually just a function of convenience and academic politics. Indeed, some areas of study that we take for granted today, such as psychology, didn't even exist as distinct disciplines a little more than a century ago.

Pursue a subject (say, ancient Greece) or an interesting question (Is it more natural for human beings to help or hurt one another?), and you end up having to draw from a wide range of disciplines. Starting from the subject or the question makes so much sense that it can soon become a habit. It also points up how artificial and confining it is to study just literature, then biology, then math—examining only those issues that allegedly fall within the limits of each field.

But traditionalists not only see nothing wrong with this approach, they like to assert (with no logic or evidence) that an excellent education *demands* the separation of disciplines and the creation of distinct standards for each one.[69] In reality, the effect of this is twofold. First, when standards are created by people in separate subject areas, each group unaware of what others are doing, the scope of the combined requirements is ludicrously unrealistic. Researchers have calculated that for high school students to meet all the current standards being proposed, it "would require as much classroom time as has historically resulted in a master's or professional degree."[70] Second, students are denied a coherent educational program when they are presented with standards in separate disciplines. Instead, their schooling is marked by what Whitehead called "the fatal disconnection of subjects."[71] That disconnection is easiest to see, and hardest to justify, in the traditional high school schedule, where students have no sooner begun discussing *The Brothers Karamazov* than a bell signals that it's time to stop and move on to binomial equations down the hall. But even without this ridiculous regimentation, the walls erected between the subjects themselves are of questionable value. Even when an elementary school teacher says, "OK, boys and girls, let's put away our science books and take out our math books," we ought to realize this is not the only way of learning, let alone the best way.

**One task is separated from another.** First the idea of learning is split into academic and nonacademic, then academic learning is split into separate disciplines. But the Old School isn't satisfied: now each discipline must be divided into separate tasks, discrete units, individual lessons that coincide with measurable objectives (for example, mastering capitalization). Parts are rarely connected, and if they're intended to be in the service of a larger objective, it's usually lost on the student.

Each skill is something unto itself: students don't learn multiplication as a tool for figuring out how large a room is; they're just taught how to multiply. Then, later, they're taught geometry. Indeed, math textbooks may even "treat two-digit subtraction with regrouping as a skill distinct from two-digit subtraction without regrouping," in effect separating problems like 37–21 from problems like 37–28.[72]

Or take language. You and I learn what words mean by reading them in books or hearing them in conversation. We make sense of them in a context, or we look them up because we want to understand the ideas they express. But the Old School hands out vocabulary lists to learn: one word after another, with no relationship among them (except that they're all going to be on Friday's quiz) and no connection to broader ideas. Spelling is its own subject, separate from reading and writing. In other fields it's much the same: learning consists of mastering a chain of isolated facts.

All of this reflects, again, the enduring legacy of behaviorism. It's not just a curious teaching style at work here but a tacit view of knowledge as a collection of separate skills, a belief that any whole can be reduced to its parts.[73] The curriculum amounts to a series of individual, microlevel tasks, each taught and then tested. If kids learn one word after another, it's assumed that by the end they'll know how to write; if they're taught a list of events in sequence, they're supposed to understand history. In reality, such fragmentation produces an incoherent curriculum that is hard for even the "good" students to really understand, much less to care about.[74] And "raising standards," so that they have to learn even more words and events, only makes things worse.

**Learning is separated from doing.** Closely connected to divorcing facts from each other and from context is the tendency to divorce them from life as it's actually lived. Traditional education "assume[s] a separation between knowing and doing," with the result that students at best just "acquire algorithms, routines, and decontextualized definitions that they cannot use and that, therefore, lie inert."[75] Too often our kids are taught *about* scientific principles rather than *doing* science; they memorize the parts of speech rather than *using* them to tell a story.

All of us understand that this makes no sense with certain activities.

We wouldn't dream of sending our children to a piano teacher who simply lectured to them for an hour every week about tempo and tone. If you want to learn how to play the piano, you've got to play the piano. But it isn't all that different with reading, writing, math, science, and other academic subjects, all of which to some extent require learning by doing.[76] If that's news to us, it's probably because all we know is how we ourselves were taught.

**One student is separated from another.** Fragmentation extends to the way children themselves are treated. First, they will almost certainly be separated by age—a technique borrowed from Prussia in the mid-nineteenth century to improve the efficiency of instruction. (To get a sense of how contrived this arrangement is, just ask yourself when you last spent time only with people who are exactly as old as you are.)[77] Second, in each classroom, they may be separated again on the basis of how adept they are at academic tasks, a practice known as ability grouping.[78] Finally, even if we look at a roomful of students who were born in the same year or who are supposed to be at the same level, there is little opportunity for them to create a sense of community in the Old School.

As Jesse Goodman of Indiana University explains, when students are cut off from their peers, they don't even have the consolation of being treated as individuals. Under the traditional model of instruction, students

> spend the vast majority of their school day working at individual desks in single rows, answering questions and problems in separate workbooks or worksheets, individually taking tests, and asking questions related to their individual concerns in order to finish prescribed schoolwork. In this sense, individualized instruction has little to do with developing the individuality of students, that is, with responding to each child's unique learning style, recognizing and giving voice to the personal knowledge base that each student brings to school, and consciously promoting each child's originality, creativity, thoughtfulness, and efficacy. Rather, as practiced in most schools, individualized education refers to an instructional design that separates each child's learning from that of his or her classmates and focuses on his or her particular achievement in standardized curriculum content.[79]

•

Anyone who is interested could show how all these ways of dividing up what is taught—and who is taught—are legacies of an influential tradition in Western philosophy in which thinking is split from feeling, mind from body, theory from practice—after which we are expected to choose up sides and embrace one option in each duality to the exclusion of the other. But whatever its roots, the results are hard to miss. Linda Darling-Hammond has remarked that "if we taught babies to talk as most skills are taught in school, they would memorize lists of sounds in a predetermined order and practice them alone in a closet."[80] (The only thing saving us from this scenario is that the back-to-basics approach hasn't been extended to infancy. Yet.)

When we take a step back and look at the traditional model as a whole —the fragmentation and enforced passivity, the reliance on basics and postponement of thinking, the memorization of facts and rehearsal of skills and the emphasis on transmitting right answers—the effects on the quality of students' learning aren't encouraging. But beyond achievement, we also have to consider how kids come to regard what they're doing, the impact on their continuing motivation to learn. Of course, not all students will react the same way to anything. But, as a rule, it's hard to deny that their excitement about learning is almost visibly drained away by the Old School approach.

"Hooked on phonics" is a joke. Who gets hooked on the *cr* sound? Likewise, "we've discouraged so many kids from science that there is hardly anyone left. The attitude has been 'Let them eat facts.' It's no wonder they lose interest."[81] Overall, enough memorization of vocabulary words, enough dittos filled with naked numbers—and pretty soon rooms full of curious children are turned into so many antsy clockwatchers, turned off to English, to science, to school, to learning. But rather than identifying the source of the problem, many adults have an annoying habit of blaming the student. As Dewey put it, if a child was "engaged in physical truancy, or in the mental truancy of mind-wandering and finally built up an emotional revulsion against the subject, he was held to be at fault. No question was raised as to whether the trouble might lie in the subject-matter or in the way in which it was offered."[82]

Traditional teachers have a tendency to see "minimal student efforts as evidence of limits of student abilities"[83]—or simply of a paucity of motivation—according to one study of high schools. As a teacher complained to another researcher, "The kids here are where the problem is today. There's nothing wrong with the curriculum. If I could just get people who wanted to learn, I would teach and everything would be wonderful."[84] Teachers with this attitude quickly find themselves relying on artificial inducements, bribing students with A's or threatening them with F's in a desperate effort to "motivate" them to do what they understandably have little interest in doing. (Sadly, these carrots and sticks then further reduce their interest in the learning itself.)

Looking at the long-term impact of traditional teaching and the push for Tougher Standards, then, we are finally left with Dewey's timeless and troubling question: "What avail is it to win prescribed amounts of information about geography and history, to win ability to read and write, if in the process the individual loses his own soul: loses his appreciation of things worth while, of the values to which these things are relative; if he loses desire to apply what he has learned and, above all, loses the ability to extract meaning from his future experiences as they occur?"[85]

# ❧ 4 ❧

# GETTING
# EVALUATION WRONG
# The Case Against Standardized
# Testing

## How Little Test Scores Mean

NOT LONG AGO, I am told, a widely respected middle school teacher in Wisconsin, famous for helping students design their own innovative learning projects, stood up at a community meeting and announced that he "used to be" a good teacher. These days, he explained, he just handed out textbooks and quizzed his students on what they had memorized. The reason was very simple. He and his colleagues were increasingly being held accountable for raising test scores. The kind of wide-ranging and enthusiastic exploration of ideas that once characterized his classroom could no longer survive when the emphasis was on preparing students to take a standardized examination. Because the purveyors of Tougher Standards had won, the students had lost.

I don't know how many teachers across the country would identify with this story—either because they have already thrown up their hands, as this man did, or because they struggle every Monday morning to try to avoid his fate. But I do know this: the issue of standardized testing is not reserved for bureaucrats and specialists. All of us with children need to make it our business to understand just how much harm these tests are doing. They are not an inevitable part of "life" or even a necessary part of school; they are a relatively recent invention that gets in the way of our kids' learning. Their impact is deep, direct, and personal. Every time we judge a school on the basis of a standardized test score—indeed, every time we permit our children to participate in these mass testing programs —we unwittingly help to make our schools just a little bit worse.

In case I am being too subtle here, let me state clearly that I think standardized testing is a very bad thing, and the more familiar you become with it, the more appalled you are likely to be. I am not talking about the kind of tests invented by individual teachers for their classes but about those prepared by giant companies and taken by thousands of students across schools, districts, and even states. Similarly, I am not primarily interested in the tests used for admission to college, like the SAT—although there is plenty wrong with these exams, too.[1] Of more immediate concern are those that begin much earlier, tests used all over the country, like the Iowa and Comprehensive Test of Basic Skills (ITBS and CTBS) and the Metropolitan, Stanford, and California Achievement Tests, as well as those developed for use in just one state, such as the ISAT in Illinois, the TAAS in Texas, the MEAP in Michigan, and so on.

The case against exams like these "may be as intellectually and ethically rigorous as any argument made about social policy in the past 20 years," says one writer, "but such testing continues to dominate the education system. . . . We are a nation of standardized-testing junkies."[2] Estimates of how many times students in the United States sit down to take these tests every year vary from 40 million to 400 million. It is clear, though, that no other nation in the world does anything like this to its children.[3] Yet despite requirements for some students to take several standardized tests a year,[4] and although even young children are routinely subjected to these tests[5] (in the face of explicit appeals by experts to stop), the trend, incredibly, is for even more testing.

In some cases, this trend reflects a deliberate strategy, part of an educational philosophy based on getting students to memorize a bunch of basic facts and skills. Standardized tests generally go hand-in-hand with that kind of teaching—and with a system of carrot-and-stick control to mandate that kind of teaching. In other cases, the use of such tests reflects no particular endorsement of a style of instruction or testing—only a vague desire to hold schools accountable coupled with a total ignorance of other ways of achieving that goal. For example, civil rights groups and sympathetic judges who are understandably outraged by disparities among school systems in the same state (or even county) may uncritically use standardized tests to indicate how much progress has been made to "close the gap" between black and white neighborhoods or poor and rich districts—all the while apparently unaware of how much harm they are doing by legitimating and perpetuating a reliance on such testing.

Standardized tests persist and proliferate for other reasons, too. First, they are enormously profitable for the corporations that prepare and grade them. (More often than not, these companies simultaneously sell teaching materials designed to raise scores on their own tests.) Second, they appeal to school systems because they're efficient, and the worst tests are usually the most efficient. It is fast, easy, and therefore relatively inexpensive[6] to administer a multiple-choice exam that arrives from somewhere else and is sent back to be graded by a machine at lightning speed. There is little incentive to replace these tests with more meaningful forms of assessment that require human beings to evaluate the quality of students' accomplishments. In the words of Norman Frederiksen, a specialist in the measurement of learning with the Educational Testing Service, "Efficient tests tend to drive out less efficient tests, leaving many important abilities untested—and untaught."[7]

Anyone trying to account for the popularity of standardized tests may also want to consider our cultural penchant for attaching numbers to things. One writer has called it a "prosaic mentality": a preoccupation with that which can be seen and measured.[8] Any aspect of learning (or life) that resists being reduced to numbers is regarded as vaguely suspicious. By contrast, anything that appears in numerical form seems reassuringly scientific; if the numbers are getting larger over time, we must be making progress. Concepts like intrinsic motivation and intellectual exploration are hard for the prosaic mind to grasp, whereas test scores, like sales figures or votes, can be calculated and charted and used to define success and failure. The more tests we make kids take, the more precise our knowledge about who has learned well, who has taught well, which districts are in trouble, and even which schools (in this brave new world of for-profit education) will survive another day.

In a broad sense, it is easier to measure efficiency than effectiveness, easier to rate how well we are doing something than to ask if what we are doing makes sense. But the heirs of Descartes and Bacon, Skinner and Taylor, rarely make such distinctions. More to the point, they fail to see how the process of coming to understand ideas in a classroom is not always linear or quantifiable. Contrary to virtually every discussion of education by the Tougher Standards contingent, meaningful learning does not proceed along a single dimension in such a way that we can nail down the extent of improvement. In fact, as Linda McNeil has observed, "Measurable outcomes may be the least significant results of learning."[9] (That sentence ought to be printed out in 36-point Helvetica and hung in the office of every person in the country involved with school reform.) To talk about what happens in schools as moving forward or backward in specifiable degrees is not only simplistic, in the sense that it fails to capture what is actually going on; it is destructive, because it can change what is going on for the worse. Once teachers and students are compelled to focus only on what lends itself to quantification, such as the number of grammatical errors in a composition or the number of state capitals memorized, the process of thinking has been severely compromised.

If it is worth reflecting critically on our infatuation with numbers, it is at least as important to examine our assumptions about standardized tests in particular. Such tests are commonly justified on the basis of providing us with objective information about teaching and learning, but the precise score assigned to a student or school is meaningless until we know the content of the test and whether it is a valid measure of learning. Similarly, you can call these tests "objective" in the sense that they are scored by machines, but it was people who wrote the questions (which may be biased or murky or stupid) and people who decided to include them on the exam. As one writer put it, "Judgment was used in the choice of items and that judgment decided which bubble would count and which would not, and hence what the score would be. The people exercising the judgment are too far out of the picture to have faces and personalities, so it is easy to act as if they do not exist."[10]

Beyond the test-makers, we need to look at the test-takers. Those scientific-sounding results are actually the product of rows of real students scrunched into desks, frantically filling in bubbles. As soon as we focus on this human part of the testing process, the significance of the scores becomes dubious. For example, test anxiety has grown into a subfield of educational psychology, and its prevalence means that the tests that produce this reaction are not giving us a good picture of what many students really know and can do. The more a test is made to "count"—in terms of being the basis for promoting or retaining students, for funding or closing down schools—the more that anxiety is likely to rise and *the less valid the scores become.*

Then there are the students who don't take the tests seriously. A friend of mine remembers neatly filling in those ovals with his pencil in such a way that they made a picture of a Christmas tree. (He was assigned to a low-level class as a result, since his score on a single test was all the evidence anyone needed to judge his capabilities.) Even those test-takers who are not quite so creative may just guess wildly, fill in ovals randomly, or otherwise blow off the whole exercise, understandably regarding it as a waste of time. In short, it may be that a good proportion of students either couldn't care less about the tests, on the one hand, or care so much that they choke, on the other. Either way, their scores aren't very meaningful. Anyone who can relate to these descriptions of what goes through the minds of real students on test day ought to think twice before celebrating a high score, complaining about a low one, or using standardized tests to judge schools.

Can tests be reliable indicators despite these factors? Perhaps, but it is an open secret among educators that much of what the scores are indicating is just the socioeconomic status of the students who take them. One educator suggests we should save everyone a lot of time and money by eliminating standardized tests, since we could get the same results by asking a single question: "How much money does your mom make? . . . OK, you're on the bottom."[11] (In the case of the SATs, the scores reflect not only family income [see pp. 262–63n1, par.4] but also the proportion of the eligible population that actually took the test.) The larger point is that "a ranking of states, districts, or schools by test scores is too crude a measure to offer any insight about the quality of education" because other factors, having nothing to do with instruction, contribute significantly to those scores.[12]

## The Worst Kind of Testing

Some standardized tests aren't this bad. They're worse. I have in mind the tests that by design "provide little or no information about . . . what the individual can do. They tell that one student is more or less proficient than another, but do not tell how proficient either of them is with respect to the subject matter tasks involved."[13] Those are the words of a psychologist named Robert Glaser, who many years ago coined the term "norm-referenced" to describe this kind of test and contrasted it with a "criterion-referenced" test, which *does* compare each individual to a given standard. Believe it or not, the majority of states today rely on norm-referenced tests,[14] that is, tests that aren't intended to find out how much students know. These tests were created only to find out how well your child does compared to every other child taking the test, which is usually reported as a percentile.

Think for a moment about the implications of this fact. No matter how many students take the test, no matter how well or poorly they were taught, no matter how difficult the questions are, the pattern of results is guaranteed to be the same: exactly 10 percent of those who take the test will score in the top 10 percent, and half will always fall below the median. That's not because our schools are failing; that's because of what "median" means. A good score on a norm-referenced test means "better than other people," but we don't even know how much better. It could be that everyone's actual scores are all pretty similar, in which case the distinctions between them are meaningless — rather like saying I'm the tallest person on my block even though I'm only half an inch taller than the shortest person on my block.

More important, even if the top 10 percent did a lot better than the bottom 10 percent, that still doesn't tell us anything at all about how well they did in absolute terms, such as how many questions they got right. Maybe everyone did reasonably well; maybe everyone blew it. We don't know. Norm-referenced tests aren't meant to tell us how well a student did or how much of a body of knowledge was effectively learned. To use them for that purpose is, in the words of a leading authority on the subject, "like measuring temperature with a tablespoon."[15] Yet they *are* used for exactly that purpose all across the United States.[16]

We've already bumped up against some of these same criticisms in the context of surveys that rank students from different countries. Exactly the same points apply to ranking schools or districts or states. A reasonably informed person would not care how her child's school did compared to other schools in the area; a reasonably conscientious journalist would not dream of publishing something so meaningless and misleading. The only thing that should count is how many questions on a test were answered correctly (assuming they measured important knowledge). By the same token, the news that your state moved up this year from thirty-seventh in the country to eighteenth says nothing about whether its schools are really improving: for all you know, the schools in your state are in worse shape than they were last year, but those in other states slid even further.[17]

Even that doesn't tell the whole story. When specialists sit down to design a norm-referenced test, they're not interested in making sure the questions cover what is most important for students to know. Rather, their goal is to include questions that some test-takers—not all of them, and not none of them—will get right. They don't want everyone to do well. Furthermore, they want each question to be answered correctly by the same students who get most of the other questions right. The ultimate objective, remember, is not to evaluate how well the students were taught but to separate them, to get a range of scores. If a certain question is included in a trial test and almost everyone gets it right—or, for that matter, if almost no one gets it right—that question will likely be tossed out. Whether it is reasonable for kids to get it right is completely irrelevant. Moreover, the questions that "too many" students will answer correctly are probably those that deal with the content teachers have been emphasizing in class because they thought it was important. So norm-referenced tests are likely to include a lot of trivial stuff that isn't emphasized in school because that helps to distinguish one student from another.[18]

Given that scores from norm-referenced tests are widely regarded as if they said something meaningful about how our children (and their schools) are doing, they are not only dumb but dangerous. And the harm ramifies through the whole system in a variety of ways. First, these tests contribute to the already pathological competitiveness of our culture, which leads us to regard others as obstacles to our own success—with all the suspicion, envy, self-doubt, and hostility that rivalry entails. The process of assigning children to percentiles helps to ensure that schooling is more about triumphing over everyone else than about learning.

Second, because every distribution of scores will contain a bottom, it will always appear that some kids are doing terribly. That, in turn, reinforces a sense that the schools are failing. Worse, it contributes to the insidious assumption that some children just can't learn—especially if the same kids always seem to fall below the median. (This conclusion, based on a misunderstanding of statistics, is then defended as "just being realistic.") Parents and teachers may come to believe this falsehood, and so too may the kids themselves. They may figure: no matter how much I improve, everyone else will probably get better too, and I'm always going to be at the bottom. Thus, why bother trying? Conversely, a very successful student, trained to believe that rankings are what matter, may be confident of remaining at the top and therefore have no reason to do as well as possible. (Remember: excellence and victory are two completely different goals.) For both groups, it is difficult to imagine a more powerful demotivator than norm-referenced testing.

One more disturbing consequence: teachers and administrators who are determined to outsmart the test—or who are under significant pressure to bring up their school's rank—may try to adjust the curriculum in order to bolster their students' scores. (More about this later.) But if the tests emphasize relatively unimportant knowledge that's designed for sorting, then "teaching to the test" isn't going to improve the quality of education. It may have exactly the opposite effect.

Even though they suffer from the more general problems with standardized testing, criterion-based exams make more sense than the norm-referenced kind. At least they're set up so everyone theoretically could do very well (or very badly); it's not a zero-sum game. But in practice these tests may be treated as though they *were* norm-referenced. This can happen if parents or students aren't helped to understand that a score of 80 percent refers to the proportion of questions answered correctly, leaving them to assume that it refers to a score better than 80 percent of the other test-takers.[19] Worse yet, criterion-referenced tests may be turned *into* the norm-referenced kind if newspapers publish charts showing how every school or district ranks on the same test, thus calling attention to what is least significant. (One expert on testing suggests that if newspapers insist on publishing such a chart, they should at least run it where it belongs, in the sports section.)[20]

Still, the main point is that when the tests themselves have been designed specifically as sorting devices, the harm is damn near inescapable. It is a point that almost everyone should be able to understand, yet our children continue to be subjected to tests like the ITBS that are both destructive and ridiculously ill suited to the purposes for which they are used. And they will continue to be used — and the scores will continue to be published — until you and I stop responding to the results by saying, "Ninety-fifth percentile! That's terrific!" or "Bottom quartile? What went wrong?" and start responding to such numbers by saying, "Wait a minute. What difference does that make? Do they think we're idiots?"

## What the Tests Test

Even standardized tests that are criterion- rather than norm-referenced tend to be contrived exercises that tell us very little about the intellectual capabilities that matter most. What they primarily seem to be measuring is how much a student has crammed into his short-term memory. Lauren Resnick concedes that some standardized tests contain "isolated items that test students' critical thinking and reasoning knowledge," but she explains that they nevertheless fail to offer students the opportunity "to carry out extended analyses, to solve open-ended problems, or to display command of complex relationships, although these abilities are at the heart of higher-order competence."[21]

Resnick points out that what generally passes for a test of reading comprehension is a series of separate questions about short passages on random topics. These questions "rarely examine how students interrelate parts of the text and do not require justifications that support the interpretations"; indeed, the whole point is the "quick finding of answers rather than reflective interpretation." Tests of writing, meanwhile, are positively laughable: they are about memorizing the mechanics of grammar and punctuation, often requiring that students correct mistakes in isolated sentences. To state the obvious, "Recognizing other people's errors and choosing the correct alternatives are not the same processes as those needed to produce good written language."[22]

In mathematics, the story is much the same. An analysis of the most widely used standardized math tests found that only 3 percent of the questions required "high level conceptual knowledge" and only 5 percent tested "high level thinking skills such as problem solving and reasoning."[23] Typically, the tests aim to make sure that students have memorized a series of procedures, not that they understand what they are doing. They also end up measuring knowledge of arbitrary conventions (such as the accepted way of writing a ratio or knowing that "<" means "less than") more than a capacity for logical thinking.[24] Even those parts of math tests that have names like "Concepts and Applications" are "still given in multiple-choice format, are computational in nature, and test for knowledge of basic skills through the use of traditional algorithms."[25] As for science, the parts of standardized examinations devoted to this subject often amount to nothing more than a vocabulary test. Multiple-choice questions that focus on "excruciatingly boring material" fail to judge students' capacity to think and wind up driving away potential future scientists, according to the president of the National Academy of Sciences.[26]

The point here is not that standardized tests are too hard or too easy. The problem is not the difficulty level, per se, but that they are geared to a different, less sophisticated kind of knowledge. And the more this is so, the more teaching comes to imitate these tests as teachers are steered away from helping kids learn how to think. Indeed, the students who ace these tests are often those who are least interested in learning and most superficially engaged in what they are doing. This is not just my opinion: studies of elementary, middle school, and high school students have all found *a statistical association between high scores on standardized tests and relatively shallow thinking.* Not only are these examinations not about deep understanding—they seem to be about its opposite.[27]

Perhaps this is why, as Piaget pointed out years ago, "anyone can confirm how little the grading that results from examinations corresponds to the final useful work of people in life."[28] But never mind their inability to predict what students will be able to do later; they don't even capture what students can do today. In fact, we could say that such tests fail in two directions at once. On the one hand, they overestimate what some students know: those who score well often understand very little of the subject in question. They may be able to find a synonym or antonym for a word without being able to use it properly in a sentence. Older students may have memorized the steps of comparing the areas of two geometric figures without really understanding geometry at all. Younger children may be able to correctly "write 8 next to a picture of eight ice cream cones" while continuing to believe that eight of them spread out are more than eight crowded together.[29] Students may even be able to "psych out" the test itself by ascertaining which kinds of answers are usually incorrect or what the writers of the test are looking for.

On the other hand, standardized tests underestimate what other students know because, as any teacher can tell you, very talented kids often get low scores. It is true in writing—"countless cases of magnificent student writers whose work was labeled as 'not proficient' because it did not follow the step-by-step sequence of what the test scorers (many of whom are not educators, by the way) think good expository writing should look like."[30] It is true in reading: a first-grade teacher in Ohio, frustrated that an excellent reader was being placed in a remedial class because he didn't perform well on a standardized test, showed an administrator the books this boy could read as well as an entire book he had written. This evidence was brushed aside and she was told just to look at the test scores. As she recalls the conversation, "When I pointed out that there wasn't even any reading on this so-called reading-readiness test, well then [the administrator] said maybe that was the problem — that I should spend more time getting them ready to read rather than having the kids read."[31]

What we have here is a double indictment of standardized testing. "Pupils who read widely and with good comprehension may be undervalued, while pupils who perform well on isolated skill tests but who can't or don't care to read are lulled into complacency."[32] The same is true in math. One group of researchers described a fifth-grader who flawlessly marched through the steps of subtracting $2\frac{5}{6}$ from $3\frac{1}{3}$, ending up quite correctly with $\frac{3}{6}$ and then reducing that to $\frac{1}{2}$. But successfully performing this final reduction doesn't mean he understood that the two fractions were equivalent. In fact, he remarked in an interview that $\frac{1}{2}$ was larger than $\frac{3}{6}$ because "the denominator is smaller so the pieces are larger."

Meanwhile, one of his classmates, whose answer had been marked wrong because it hadn't been expressed in the correct terms, clearly understood the underlying concepts. Intrigued, the researchers then proceeded to interview a number of fifth-graders about another topic, division, and discovered that 41 percent had memorized the process without really grasping the idea, whereas 11 percent understood the concept but made minor errors that resulted in getting the wrong answers. A standardized test therefore would have misclassified more than half of these students.[33]

As disturbing as all of this may be, we can dig even deeper, looking not only at the specific questions that appear on such tests but at the format and nature of the tests themselves. It is the very features of standardized testing we take for granted that ultimately undermine their usefulness:

- These tests ignore the most important characteristics of a good learner, to say nothing of a good person. Bill Ayers, an educator, offers his list: "Standardized tests can't measure initiative, creativity, imagination, conceptual thinking, curiosity, effort, irony, judgment, commitment, nuance, good will, ethical reflection, or a host of other valuable dispositions and attributes. What they can measure and count are isolated skills, specific facts and functions, the least interesting and least significant aspects of learning."[34]

- Behaviorist psychology rears its unattractive head yet again. These tests are predicated on the predilection for breaking things down into their components and offering them in a prescribed sequence: a, then b, then c, then d, and so forth: facts before thinking, skills before content, this skill before that one. I've already argued that this model is deficient and that it is the underpinning of traditional teaching. The point now is merely that standardized testing is very much an example of the same paradigm, an example of what one critic has called "the application of twentieth century statistics to nineteenth century psychology."[35]

- These tests care only about whether the student got the right answer. To point this out is not to claim that there is no such thing as a right answer; it is to observe once again that right answers don't necessarily signal understanding and wrong answers don't necessarily signal the absence of understanding. Standardized tests ignore the process by which students arrive at an answer, so a miss is as good as a mile and a minor calculation error is interchangeable with a major failure of reasoning.

  The right-answer focus of standardized testing also means that all the problems were chosen precisely because they have unambiguously correct solutions, with definite criteria for determining what those solutions are and a clear technique for getting there. The only thing wrong with these problems is that they bear no resemblance to most problems in the natural and social sciences that occupy people in the real world.[36]

- These tests are frequently dominated by multiple-choice questions, a format that is inherently limited and limiting. Multiple-choice tests were practically unheard-of before the middle of the twentieth century. Today, almost all states (with only a handful of notable exceptions) rely on them to a significant extent to judge kids and schools. At this writing, twenty-nine states use at least one test that consists exclusively of multiple-choice questions.[37] By contrast, this form of testing is unusual in other countries.[38]

  "I don't think there's any way to build a multiple-choice question that allows students to show what they can do with what they know," says Roger Farr, a professor of education at Indiana University[39]—a statement all the more remarkable given that Farr personally helped to write a number of standardized tests. The reasons should be obvious. Students aren't allowed to generate a response; all they can do is recognize one by picking it out of four or five answers generated by someone else. They can't even explain their reasons for choosing the answer they did. Obviously they have to do some sort of remembering, calculating, or thinking to figure out the answer, but other sorts of mental operations (such as organizing information or constructing an argument) are pretty much excluded by the format. No matter how clever or tricky the questions, a multiple-choice test simply "does not measure the same cognitive skills as are measured by similar problems in free-response form," as one expert explained in a now-classic article. The difference between the two formats (which is to say, the limits of multiple-choice questions) really shows up when the idea is to measure "complex cognitive problem-solving skills."[40] This doesn't mean that an essay test is necessarily a valid measure of important things; it just means that a multiple-choice test necessarily isn't.[41]

- These tests are timed. Standardized tests—at least the nationally used norm-referenced variety—put a premium on speed as opposed to creativity or even thoroughness. It's not that one small part of the test has to be done in a set amount of time, indicating that the ability to do things quickly and under pressure is one of many valued attributes. Rather, the whole test must be taken under the gun, indicating that this ability is prized above others. (In the case of young children, standardized tests also seem to be evaluating the capacity to sit still for an extended period of time.)

- These tests are given to individuals, not to groups, and helping one another is regarded as a serious offense. Not only is there no measure of the capacity to cooperate effectively, or even to assimilate other people's ideas into your own, but they communicate precisely the opposite message: only what you can do alone is of any value. "We have been so convinced of the notion that intellect is an isolated, individual quality that we utterly lack the procedures or the psychometrics to study students' performances in group situations," as Dennie Wolf and her colleagues put it.[42]

- The content of these tests is kept secret. Given their nature, this is hardly surprising, but look at it this way: What does it say about an approach to assessing learning that it can be done only by playing "Gotcha!"? Tests "that continually keep students in the dark are built upon procedures with roots in premodern traditions of legal proceedings and religious inquisitions."[43] Apart from raising stress levels, the kind of evaluation where students aren't allowed to know in advance what they'll be asked to do suggests a heavy emphasis on memorization. It also has the practical effect of preventing teachers from reviewing the test with students after it's over and using it as a learning tool.

•

Put these last few points together and you have a scenario that is not merely disagreeable but ludicrously contrived. After all, how many jobs demand that employees come up with the right answer on the spot, from memory, while the clock is ticking? (I can think of one or two, but they are the exceptions that prove the rule.) How often are we forbidden to ask coworkers for help or to depend on a larger organization for support —even in a society that worships self-sufficiency? And when someone is going to judge the quality of your work, whether you are a sculptor, a lifeguard, a financial analyst, a housekeeper, a professor, a refrigerator repairman, a reporter, or a therapist, how common is it for you to be given a secret pencil-and-paper exam? Isn't it far more likely that the evaluator will look at examples of what you've already done or perhaps watch you perform your normal tasks? To be consistent, those educational critics who indignantly insist that schools should be doing more to prepare students for the real world ought to be manning the barricades to demand an end to these artificial exercises called standardized tests.

Of course, anyone who reads through this list may be inclined to wonder, "Well, how could you have a standardized test that *wasn't* concerned only with right answers or wasn't secret or timed or whatever?" Indeed, you probably couldn't. But here is a very different question: How could you devise a way of figuring out how well students are learning, or schools are teaching, that didn't have these features? As we'll see in the final chapter, this question does have an answer. But it's critical that we frame the issue in these broader terms, that this becomes our point of departure, because only then are we free to look beyond—and solve the problems created by—standardized tests.

## Raising the Scores, Ruining the Schools

Lately, some opponents of standardized testing have invoked a bucolic saying: "You don't fatten a steer by weighing it." The point, of course, is that merely measuring something, such as students' learning, doesn't in itself lead to any change in what is being measured. This is true as far as it goes, but the metaphor is poorly chosen[44] because it implies that testing has no impact on education. The reality is that it almost always does have an impact, increasingly by design. Unfortunately, the impact is usually negative.

Consider the messages that standardized testing communicates to children about the nature of learning. Because a premium is placed on remembering facts in many of these tests, students may come to think that this is what really matters—and they may even come to develop a "quiz show" view of intelligence that confuses being smart with knowing a lot of stuff. Because the tests are timed, students may be encouraged to see intelligence as a function of how quickly people can do things. Because the tests often rely on a multiple-choice format, students may infer "that a right or wrong answer is available for all questions and problems" in life and "that someone else already knows the answer to [all these questions], so original interpretations are not expected; the task is to find or guess the right answer, rather than to engage in interpretive activity."[45]

If we're looking for more direct harms, we could just tally up the time students and teachers waste actually taking these tests. But where our kids really pay the price is with what comes before and because of the tests. "It is the hours spent practicing types of questions that might appear on the tests and the days denying students enrichment options that are truly meaningful that make proficiency tests so harmful and invasive," as one educator put it.[46] In schools around the country, the content and style of teaching are being placed in the service of the tests. Teachers often feel obliged to set aside other subjects for weeks at a time in order to teach test-taking skills. Sometimes the tests hijack the entire curriculum as schools are transformed into giant test-prep centers. When students will be judged on the basis of a multiple-choice test, teachers may use multiple-choice activities beforehand. It is not uncommon to find instruction "in the same format as the test rather than [in a form] used in the real world. For example, teachers reported giving up essay tests because they are inefficient in preparing students for multiple-choice tests."[47] The assignments (in class and to take home) may change as well. It's not unusual to hear of schools where teachers are required to use multiple-choice formats in their teaching.[48] This has aptly been called the "dumbing down" of instruction, although curiously not by the conservative critics with whom that phrase is normally associated.

More striking, either because they think it is best for their students or because they have a gun to their heads, teachers will dispense with poetry and focus on prose, breeze through the Depression and linger on the Cold War, cut back on social studies to make room for more math—depending on what they think will be emphasized on the tests. They may even put all instruction on hold and spend time giving practice tests.

The defenders of standardized testing don't try to deny that it forces schools to reconfigure the curriculum; indeed, they cheerfully acknowledge this. "There's nothing wrong with teaching to the test. That is what education is all about," declared Robert V. Antonucci, the former commissioner of education for Massachusetts.[49] An article in the *American School Board Journal* prefers the euphemism "curriculum alignment" and insists that it's paying off . . . as measured exclusively by test scores![50]

It is a relatively new idea—that tests should be used not only to measure but to mandate—but in scarcely a generation it has come to be taken for granted. Sometimes it is done deliberately, perhaps because it offers policymakers "one of the few levers on the curriculum that [they] can control."[51] Other times, educators and parents simply realize that a test emphasizes isolated facts rather than critical thinking and figure the curriculum had better be retooled accordingly. Either way, the tail of testing is now wagging the educational dog.

You'd think that when officials sit down to formulate an education policy, they would begin by agreeing on some broad outlines of what students ought to know and be able to do, and only then address the question of measuring how successfully this is happening. The reality, though, often seems to be exactly the opposite: "What can be measured reliably and validly becomes what is important to know," as critics of one state's reform efforts observed.[52] It's rather like the old joke about the fellow who was looking around for his lost keys one night, explaining to a passerby that he was searching the sidewalk right near a streetlight not because that was where he dropped them but because "the light is better here."

A more indirect effect of the same mentality can be glimpsed in Ohio, where the pressure to boost proficiency test scores has led to changes in how teachers of children from age 9 to 14 are certified by the state. Teachers have been forced to specialize in only two content areas (such as math and science), which means that the kind of departmentalization that has created such a fragmented educational experience in high school may now happen, thanks to testing pressures, as early as fourth grade.[53]

In some states, as the following chapter will explain, officials have turned up the heat by creating "high-stakes" testing programs. But even without this added pressure, it's virtually inevitable that teachers will feel pressured to change what they do. As one principal in Virginia put it, "We know what's being tested. So now we know what we have to teach."[54]

In fact, when teachers from forty-eight schools around the country were surveyed a few years ago, nearly all "reported spending substantial time (a week or more) giving students worksheets that review test content, giving students practice with the item formats likely to be on the test, and directly teaching test-taking strategies."[55] And teachers understand the costs of doing this. In another survey, 60 percent of the math teachers and 63 percent of the science teachers described the "negative effects of a testing program on curriculum or student learning," citing the "narrowing and fragmenting of the curriculum" among other consequences.[56]

We've already seen some illustrations of the limits of these tests. If students get higher scores on math exams for memorizing techniques than for understanding concepts, which do you think teachers will emphasize? If a teacher sees first-graders being penalized for having spent time reading rather than being drilled on reading-readiness skills, what direction will her class take the following year? Teachers all over the country struggle with variations of this dilemma, worrying not only about their own jobs but about the short-term price their students may have to pay for more authentic learning. The choices are grim: either the teachers capitulate, or they struggle courageously to resist this, or they find another career.[57]

I remember visiting a school in Illinois a few years ago where the battle had already been lost. The district was under a court order to bring up its test scores and had bought a packaged program called "Success for All" to do just that (see p. 300n53). The result resembled a factory more than a place of learning, with children being exhorted to succeed and perform and achieve. (By contrast, words like "curiosity," "discovery," and "exploration" were nowhere to be seen or heard.) In room after room I saw children correcting punctuation, answering plot questions about story fragments, and completing worksheets full of multiplication problems and those all-too-familiar analogy questions.

Of course I hadn't seen the school earlier, so I can't say for sure that its patron saint was John Dewey before it became Stanley Kaplan. In other places, though, the shift is visible to the naked eye:

- As ITBS testing gets closer, sixth-grade science at a school in Arizona mutates from hands-on learning to textbooks and dittos — and the total time allocated to science is sharply curtailed (and, for a while, completely eliminated) to make more time for tested subjects.
- In a Texas high school, classes are shortened in favor of a daily test-prep period; in other schools, weekly learning objectives are explic-

itly chosen to boost performance on the Texas Assessment of Academic Skills. Teachers can remember a time before they had to engage in "daylong TAAS drilling."

- During the spring, many Illinois teachers "stop introducing new material to review and practice for the state-mandated achievement tests and the Iowa Test of Basic Skills" — a process that begins earlier and lasts longer with each passing year. Thus, "the demands for improved grade and test outcomes seem to slow instruction."
- In New Jersey, many schools now focus "less on in-depth writing and more on the quick essays demanded on the [new statewide proficiency] tests. . . . In what some fear will actually lead to a dumbing down of writing, many schools now emphasize a five-paragraph essay format that they believe satisfies test graders."
- In North Carolina, social studies, science, and other subjects not being tested are shortchanged in favor of a "forced march through the state's Standard Course of Study" in reading, writing, and math.
- In a Maryland school, where a banner reads (all too accurately) "We're nuts about the CAT [California Achievement Test]," second-graders are given extensive test-taking instruction and fifth-graders are held back from music class to practice their commas.
- "Schools have virtually suspended their normal curriculums to administer practice tests" for a new three-day exam administered to all fourth-graders in New York. "Almost every class, from kindergarten on up, is filled with exercises in spelling and grammar."[58]

And so it goes. "Everywhere we turned," one group of educators reported in 1998, "we heard stories of teachers who were being told, in the name of 'raising standards,' that they could no longer teach reading using the best of children's literature but instead must fill their classrooms and their days with worksheets, exercises, and drills." The result in any given classroom was that "children who had been excited about books, reading with each other, and talking to each other were now struggling to categorize lists of words."[59]

In some classes, of course, it was never otherwise. The very raison d'être of high school advanced placement (AP) courses, for example, has always been to prepare students for a test. (There has been much discussion about who gets to take these classes[60] but very little about their basic purpose and high-powered drill-and-skill method of instruction.) One writer suggests that teachers ought to just issue a formal declaration of surrender to the Educational Testing Service and be done with it.[61]

Even in classes less noticeably ravaged by the imperatives of test preparation, there are hidden costs—opportunities missed, intellectual roads not taken. For one thing, teachers are less likely to work together in teams.[62] For another, in each classroom, "the most engaging questions kids bring up spontaneously—'teachable moments'—become annoyances."[63] Excitement about learning pulls in one direction; covering the material that will be on the test pulls in the other. No wonder elementary school teachers in one state overwhelmingly denounced the effects of a new testing program, saying in a recent survey that "morale has sunk, practice tests are soaking up teaching time, and students are more anxious about school than ever before."[64]

Sometimes teachers feel they must depart from teaching testable facts in testlike fashion . . . in order to impart advice about test-taking, per se. The first thing to be said about using school for this purpose is that it is an egregious waste of our children's time—although the fault lies not with the teachers who do it but with the tests themselves and those who pay inordinate attention to the results. Second, it is educationally "harmful if students transfer [these test-taking tactics] to other classroom activities."[65] We don't want kids to get in the habit of skimming a book, looking for facts they might be asked on a test, instead of really thinking about and responding to what they're reading.

Third, even if clever strategies (for example, skipping to the questions first, then going back to the passage to find the answers) are effective, this means that, to some extent at least, a high test score reflects not knowledge or intelligence but good test-taking skills. If one can be successful by engaging in what some have called "legal cheating"—if we can indeed raise students' scores by teaching them tricks or by cramming them full of carefully chosen information at the last minute—this should be seen not as an endorsement of such methods but as a devastating revelation about how little these tests are really telling us.

Linda Darling-Hammond offers this analogy: Suppose it has been decided that hospital standards must be raised, so all patients must now have their temperatures taken on a regular basis. Shortly before the thermometers are inserted, the doctors run around giving out huge doses of aspirin and lots of cold drinks. Remarkably, then, it turns out that no one is running a fever! The quality of hospital care is at an all-time high![66] What is really going on, of course, is completely different from providing good health care and assessing it accurately—just as teaching to the test is completely different from providing good instruction and assessing it accurately. "By focusing on improving test scores," two researchers warn, "only test scores, and not schools themselves, will improve."[67]

Notice that scores typically plummet whenever a state or district decides to administer a new test. (And the headlines read: Our schools are failing! Our students are ignorant!) After a few years, the scores begin to rise as students and teachers get used to the test. (And the headlines read: Our schools are improving! Tougher standards are effective!)[68] Another kind of evidence comes from stories like the one about a junior high school in New Jersey where an intensive test-prep effort succeeded in producing the highest scores in the area — after which one third of the students required remedial classes when they got to high school.[69] They weren't helped to learn; they were helped to get good scores, which did them no good and may even have done them considerable harm.

What all this means can be summarized in a sentence: *At best, high test scores for a given school or district are probably meaningless; at worst, they're actually bad news because of the kind of teaching that was done to produce those scores.*

To talk about the kind of teaching that was done is to talk about the kind of teaching that was not done. The first thing to go in a school or district where these tests matter a lot is a more vibrant, integrated, active, effective kind of instruction. A Cambridge, Massachusetts, teacher of seventh- and eighth-grade students[70] can tick off exactly what she's had to sacrifice in order to prepare her students for that state's new test. Class meetings to build community, learn democratic skills, and solve problems together? No time. The flexibility to depart from the lesson plan and discuss important current events? Forget it; today's news won't be on the exam. A while back, this teacher had devised a remarkable unit in which every student picked an activity that he or she cared about and then proceeded to become an expert in it. Each subject, from baking to ballet, was researched intensively, described in a detailed report, and taught to the rest of the class. The idea was to hone research and writing skills as well as to help each student feel like an expert in something and to heighten everyone's appreciation for the craft involved in activities they may not have thought much about. In short, it was the kind of academic experience that people look back on years later as a highlight of their time in school. But now her students won't have the chance: "Because we have so much content material to cover, I don't have the time to do it," this teacher says ruefully. "I mean, I've got to do the Industrial Revolution because it's going to be on the test."

One leading educational organization has noted that "ironically, the calls for excellence in education that have produced widespread reliance on standardized testing may have had the opposite effect — mediocrity."[71] But it's important to point out that this effect shows up in some areas more than others. The noted high school reformer Ted Sizer recalls a conversation he once had with a top school official who was "proposing to test the kids until they begged for mercy." It turned out, you may not be surprised to learn, that this administrator sent his own kids to private schools where standardized tests were exceedingly rare if they were used at all and, incidentally, where excellence meant an emphasis on discovery rather than a "back-to-basics" mentality.[72]

The point isn't that this official was caught in a political faux pas for pulling his children out of the public schools he was supposed to be defending. Rather, he seemed to think the traditional approach to education, including a heavy diet of standardized testing, is for other people's children—and, as it turns out, particularly for children of color. Even apart from charges that some standardized tests are biased against minorities because of their content,[73] such tests—with all the implications for teaching they carry—are more likely to be used and emphasized in schools with higher percentages of minority students.[74] The result is that even people who are understandably desperate to improve inner-city schools wind up making the problem worse when they cause reform efforts to be framed in terms of improving standardized test scores.

Indeed, the whole conversation about improving education in this country has been narrowed by the use of these tests. The more that scores are emphasized, as Sherman Dorn at the University of South Florida has pointed out, the less we discuss the proper goals of schooling. Now it's just a matter of finding the most efficient means for what has become the de facto goal: doing better on tests. Furthermore, we tend to stop using (or developing) other ways for evaluating classroom practices and student learning: "As long as a school or teacher has adequate test scores, what happens in the classroom is irrelevant," Dorn remarks. Similarly, poor test scores are viewed as indicators that change is needed, "no matter what happens in the classroom."[75]

For a parent, the implications of all this are straightforward. In the words of Gail Jones, a professor of education at the University of North Carolina, "The bottom line is, do you want to have a child who can take tests well or do you want to have a well-educated child?"[76]

# ❧ 5 ❧
# GETTING SCHOOL REFORM WRONG
## The Arrogance of Top-Down Coercion

### *Do It My Way . . . or Else*

THERE ARE basically two ways to change what happens in schools. The first might be called the support model, and the second, the demand model.[1] The support model begins with the premise that the role of teachers, administrators, parents, public officials, and the community at large is to help students act on their desire to make sense of the world. The school should guide and stimulate their interest in exploring what is unfamiliar, constructing meaning, and developing a competence at (and a passion for) playing with words and numbers and ideas. Improvement is seen as something that tends to follow when students are provided with stimulating, worthwhile tasks. Students are not just expected to take responsibility for their own learning but are actively assisted in doing so.

In the demand model, by contrast, those outside — and, figuratively speaking, above — the classroom decide what the people in it are required to do. Lists of specific achievement goals are imposed on teachers and students. The methods and metaphors of this process are often borrowed from the corporate world, with much talk of results, performance, accountability, and incentives. Children are even described as "workers" who have an obligation to do a better job. Schools represent an "investment" and must become more "competitive," the idea being that test scores in the United States ought to surpass those in other countries. Education is described as though it were a hybrid of an assembly line and a sports match.

The latter approach, of course, describes the Tougher Standards movement to a T. In fact, that movement is true to the historical roots of the word "standard," which originally referred to the place on the battlefield where the king issued orders to his army.[2] A cartoon published in the early 1990s nicely captured the current direction of school reform: the president is shown atop a tank, its weapon trained on a schoolchild sitting in a desk down below. The president bellows a single command: "LEARN!" This may be the sort of image that Elliot Eisner of Stanford University had in mind when he warned that

> the language of standards is by and large a limiting rather than a liberating language. . . . It distracts us from paying attention to the importance of building a culture of schooling that is genuinely intellectual in character, that values questions and ideas at least as much as getting right answers. . . . The challenge in teaching is to provide the conditions that will foster the growth of those personal characteristics that are socially important and, at the same time, personally satisfying to the student. The aim of education is not to train an army that marches to the same drummer, at the same pace, toward the same destination. Such an aim may be appropriate for totalitarian societies, but it is incompatible with democratic ideals.[3]

Not content with requiring that all students learn the same things, some people want them to learn the same things at the same time. Some even want this to happen across the whole country. Such standardization probably wouldn't enhance learning,[4] but it is the whole idea of imposed standards, not just the prospect of nationalizing them, that should give us pause. Let's face it: many of the people doing the imposing, even at the state or local level, know precious little about teaching and learning.[5] Of course we wouldn't expect most state legislators to be aware of the latest research on pedagogy, just as we wouldn't expect them to understand the latest research on kidney disease. The difference is that while few lawmakers would presume to tell physicians when to recommend dialysis, many think nothing of dictating a particular method of teaching children to read.*

The demand model doesn't make much sense for other reasons as well. "Nothing has brought pedagogical theory into greater disrepute than the belief that it is identified with handing out to teachers recipes and models to be followed in teaching." So said John Dewey when the twentieth century was new, and his point is still well taken.[6] Yet these pedagogical theorists share with legislators, curriculum publishers, and others a persistent belief in the feasibility of a "teacher-proof curriculum." This belief is not

---

* This kind of arrogance would be objectionable even if they didn't tend to mandate a particularly poor method, which they almost always do.

just insulting to teachers but corrosive to the very enterprise of schooling, which becomes less like educating and more like training. In the words of two school reform experts, "The more the curriculum is specified and defined externally, the more the role of the teacher becomes that of the technician, expected to put into play decisions made by others outside the school. This is true whether the external source is the state department of education, a textbook company, or a standardized test. . . . How can we expect students to be problem solvers, thinkers, and decision makers when we do not expect the same of their teachers?"[7]

In fact, we can't expect it and we don't get it. Here is a study you may want to track down, photocopy, and mail to every school board member, education reporter, and state legislator in your area. Researchers at the University of Colorado asked a group of fourth-grade teachers to teach a specific task. About half of them were told that when they were finished, their students must "perform up to standards" and do well on a test. The other teachers were simply invited to "facilitate the children's learning." The result: students in the "standards" classrooms did not learn the task as well as those whose teachers felt less pressured.[8] A carefully controlled scientific experiment, then, confirms real-life experience: even on a traditional test, the demand model that practically defines contemporary education reform turns out to be counterproductive.

Telling teachers exactly what to do and then holding them "accountable" for the results[9] does not reflect a commitment to excellence. It reflects a commitment to an outmoded, top-down model of control that is reminiscent of Frederick Taylor's "scientific management" method for speeding up factory production.[10] Is it really surprising that this approach tends to backfire? The factory offers one of many examples outside education where people often rely on power to try to compel certain results. Those higher up in a hierarchy attempt to maximize efficiency by tightly controlling the actions of those down below. Unfortunately, we humans just don't respond very well when people do things *to* us rather than working *with* us.

That doesn't necessarily doom the whole concept of accountability. The idea can be valid and valuable if we define it as a sense of responsibility to oneself, to one another, and to the community—and if it's nested in a support model.[11] But these days teachers are held accountable for the wrong things (specifically, for producing higher standardized test scores) and in the wrong way. The word has come to be a euphemism for more control over what goes on in classrooms by people who aren't in classrooms, and it has approximately the same effect on learning that a noose has on breathing.

When teachers are told exactly what and how to teach, when they feel pressured to produce results, they in turn tend to pressure their students. That is exactly what another study found: teachers who felt controlled became more controlling, removing virtually any opportunities for students to direct their own learning.[12] (The same thing is on display every day in corporations: the middle managers who are most rigidly controlled by top executives tend to do the same to their subordinates.)[13] Since people don't do their best when they feel controlled, the results of the Colorado study make perfect sense: the more teachers are pressured to make their students perform, the less well they actually perform.

## Burnt at the High Stakes

Suppose you were a superintendent or a school board member or a state legislator. Suppose all these arguments and data just rolled off your back, and you remained determined to impose your version of standards on the schools, complete with an exaggerated emphasis on achievement and a traditional model of instruction. The chances are, you would use standardized tests to impose this agenda, and the chances are that this strategy would be pretty darned effective—providing that the people in the schools came to worry a lot about the test results. The question then becomes: How can you make sure they do so?

To begin with, you can order that such tests be given frequently, thus raising their visibility among teachers and students. Then you can see to it that the scores are published in the newspapers, preferably in a chart that encourages readers to see it as a way of comparing the quality of schools or districts. The prospect of looking bad may serve as a kind of "public shaming" and thereby pressure educators to do anything necessary to crank up their scores.

Best of all, though, you can create a structure to "motivate" educators to become more concerned about the tests. Here you would say, in effect, "Oh, so you don't care about these tests, huh? You think they're shallow and based on a simplistic approach to instruction? You'd rather pursue other kinds of learning? Well, we'll *force* you to care about them!" Students can be punished for low scores by being held back a year—or, in the case of "exit exams," prevented from graduating on the basis of a single test regardless of their academic records.[14] Teachers can be evaluated on the basis of their students' scores and then find their paychecks swollen or shrunk accordingly. Principals can be suspended or fired; their schools may receive bundles of money for high scores or, in extreme cases, be shut down or taken over by the state for low scores.

This collection of tactics, known as "high-stakes" testing, has spread like the plague it is. Unhappily, most of the discussion about it has tended to focus on the particulars of implementation, with people asking whether rewards are better than punishments, which specific strategies work best, or whether threats should be concentrated on teachers or students.[15] Rarely do we hear more substantive criticisms concerning the validity and effects of the tests themselves. (If the tests are norm-referenced, then we really don't have any legitimate basis for rewarding or punishing.) And rarely do we examine high-stakes testing in light of the misconceived view of human psychology that underlies it. Apart from the inherent problems of control, there are specific drawbacks to dangling something desirable (such as money) in front of people or threatening them with something unpleasant.

The use of punishments, even if referred to euphemistically as negative incentives, sanctions, or consequences, creates a climate of fear, and fear generates anger and resentment. It also leads people to switch into damage-control mode and act more cautiously. Human beings simply do not think creatively and reach for excellence when they perceive themselves to be threatened. The philosophy behind high-stakes testing has been deftly satirized by a sign in some offices and classrooms: THE BEATINGS WILL CONTINUE UNTIL MORALE IMPROVES. When teachers are deprived of job security or pay raises in an effort to make them perform better, they usually become demoralized rather than motivated.

What is true of sticks is ultimately true of carrots as well.[16] The simplistic call to reward excellence (or what passes for excellence in the minds of many observers) overlooks an enormous body of research and experience demonstrating that rewards are just a different way of controlling people. Moreover, rewards are based on a fundamental psychological misconception—namely, that there is a single entity called "motivation," something of which one can have a lot or a little. If this premise were true, then rewards and punishments might well make sense because they would presumably make someone's level of motivation go up. Unfortunately, the premise is false: there are different kinds of motivation, and the kind matters more than the amount.

Psychologists typically distinguish between "intrinsic motivation," a fancy term for finding something worth doing in its own right, and "extrinsic motivation," which means that you do one thing so that something else, outside the task, will happen. (Specifically, you'll receive a reward or escape a punishment.) It is quite clear—to everyone except a small group of orthodox behaviorists, at least—that these two kinds of motivation are qualitatively different. It is equally clear to most of us that intrinsic motivation is more desirable than extrinsic, and that no amount of the latter can make up for the absence of the former. Adults who consistently do excellent work, and students whose learning is most impressive, are usually those who love what they do, not those who see what they do as a tedious prerequisite for getting dollars or A's.

But the real revelation is not that extrinsic motivation is different or inferior; it's that it is corrosive: it tends to undermine intrinsic motivation. This is one of the most thoroughly replicated findings in the field of social psychology: *the more you reward people for doing something, the more they tend to lose interest in whatever they had to do to get the reward.* Thus, the intrinsic motivation that is so vital to quality—to say nothing of quality of life—often evaporates in the face of extrinsic incentives. More specifically, researchers have found that people's interest in a task ordinarily plummets when they are acutely aware of being evaluated on their performance—even if the evaluation is positive. "When subjects expect rewards for attaining a specified level of competence, the anticipation of performance evaluation interferes with intrinsic interest," one group of researchers concluded.[17] And when interest drops, so too does excellence.

Beyond these general hazards of carrot-and-stick psychology, high-stakes testing to hold schools accountable is profoundly unfair for several reasons. First, even assuming the tests themselves were valid measures of meaningful learning, low scores (in absolute and especially in relative terms) are to a large extent reflections of how educated and affluent the student's family is. To this extent, punishing people for those scores is cruel and pointless. Second, to the extent the scores do reflect school experience, that experience is hardly limited to the current year. Thus, it seems hard to justify holding a fourth-grade teacher accountable for her students' test scores when they reflect all that has happened to the children before they even got to her class.

Third, the fairest way of allocating money for education—considered common sense in some other countries—is to provide higher levels of support for the schools and districts that are in the most trouble. The high-stakes approach, to the extent it involves money, usually amounts to precisely the opposite basis for funding: give more to those already successful and less to those who really need it. Finally, because high-stakes strategies lead to teaching to the test, and because "teaching to the test can raise scores more dramatically than can instruction designed to improve achievement, the incentive system could reward the worst practices," as the noted researcher Lorrie Shepard points out.[18] It could also be based on distorted information, since test scores don't reflect achievement per se. (The more teachers end up teaching to the test, the less valid the tests become as measures of what students can do.)

The practical effects of high-stakes testing are no less appalling for being completely predictable. Teaching to the test—and all the ways it damages education—is obviously far more likely to take place in the crudest and most extreme way when the stakes are high. Indeed, when the carrot is appealing enough or the stick is aversive enough, people may do more than adjust the curriculum to assure the desired results. In a desperate effort to raise scores, educators are sometimes reduced to playing games. Some focus all their attention on the students who, they believe, are just shy of getting high scores, thereby slighting everyone else. Some flunk low achievers on the theory that they'll do better on the exam after repeating a grade and in the meantime won't bring down the average of those in the next grade.[19] Some try to assign such students to special education classes so they won't have to take the tests at all. And some cheat in more conventional ways: principals in numerous states have been accused of "excessive coaching" and even of altering students' answer sheets.

Far from being a constructive force, high-stakes testing makes teachers defensive as they try to show that low scores are not their fault. It sets them against each other and skews their priorities. David Berliner and Bruce Biddle recall how one state

> based high school mathematics teachers' annual raises on gains in their students' achievement scores. The next year some of the top teachers in the state resigned in disgust. Those who remained entered into intense competition with one another, which disrupted school programs and caused morale to drop throughout the state. (Among other things, some math teachers demanded that their schools restrict extracurricular activities, cancel school assemblies, and abolish out-of-school trips that might interfere with their instructional efforts.) The following year the incentive program was dropped.[20]

That story, at least, had a moderately happy ending, but often the program remains and the educators don't. High-stakes testing routinely drives good people out of the profession, and it is particularly hard to find qualified educators in those areas who will agree to take a position as principal. (The paradoxical result, once again, is that the Tougher Standards movement leads to lower standards.) One middle school principal in Kentucky says he has watched his colleagues "disappear from the ranks. No one wants to blame it on [high-stakes testing programs], but from my perspective as a practicing principal, many of them made it clear they weren't going to put up with unreasonable demands."[21] Or perhaps they refused to relinquish control over the curriculum to the faceless individuals who design the tests.

By the time they have a choice, students may react to more tests and threats in exactly the same way. According to a study jointly prepared by U.S. and Irish researchers, "Evidence from a number of countries indicates that the use of competency tests for graduation or retention results in increasing the student drop-out rate."[22] Some observers have begun to suspect that this is precisely the intent of these mandatory tests for graduation, which at this writing are used by almost half the states. Ironically, students who drop out are not necessarily the lowest achievers;[23] they may just be the kind of people who don't want any part of a school system that views them as dispensable or uses coercion to heighten their concern about test scores. Or maybe they sense that standardized testing doesn't exist for their benefit.

We come back to the contrast between a demand model and a support model. High-stakes testing must surely be the ultimate example of the former: impose tougher standards and accountability, use standardized tests, and try to manipulate everyone in sight by bribing and threatening them into raising scores. Apart from the disadvantages of this strategy, it has, as Linda Darling-Hammond summarizes the evidence, basically "failed wherever it has been tried."[24] Even when you judge by a standardized test (the NAEP), "States without high-stakes tests are showing more improvement than those with them."[25] And the evidence from other countries is similarly discouraging.[26]

But the response to all these cautionary data on the part of the Tougher Standards crowd is true to form: do it some more! Thus, when a new superintendent was installed in a Maryland school district several years ago —a man who said he didn't see how education is "any different from any other major business"[27]—his pledge was not to help students learn more effectively. It was to raise test scores. As a reporter describes it, "He carried out this pledge by removing student artwork that had graced the walls of the conference room adjacent to his office and replacing it with charts that showed the test performance of every school in the district, along with the principal's name."[28] Here is as fitting, and as poignant, an image as any for the prevailing version of school reform.

# ✺ 6 ✺
# GETTING
# IMPROVEMENT WRONG
## Confusing Harder
## with Better

### . . . and the Devil Take the Hindmost

ONE CONSEQUENCE of the push to raise standards is so basic, so predictable, and so egregious that it is difficult to believe how rarely it figures in discussions on the subject. You can read lengthy articles devoted to sneering at our educational system for "dumbing down" the curriculum—indeed, entire books harrumphing about the need to raise our expectations and settle for nothing less than excellence—and find not a single word about what we're supposed to do with the kids who can't measure up to these new standards.

It's not just speeches and editorials that neglect this question. Most states don't require and fund extra help for students likely to have trouble meeting tougher standards,[1] which is just what we would expect of the demand model: an insistence on improvement without a plan for giving educators what is necessary to support it. But if you don't happen to subscribe to *Educational Researcher,* you may have missed the following common-sense response to all the talk about higher expectations: "If students cannot now measure up to old, presumably less demanding standards, increased demands seem pointless."[2]

Never mind pointless: try "poisonous." Students who are already struggling are likely to become frustrated and eventually drop out. We've already been asked to apply the brutal logic of the marketplace to schools, as reflected in school choice and voucher proposals, where those that can't compete are deliberately doomed to extinction. But now, with demands for Tougher Standards without any plan to support those unlikely to meet them, we are being invited to subject children to the same economic principles, treating them like widgets on an assembly line that can simply be discarded if they don't measure up.

It's not an oversight, argues the educational historian David Labaree. "Most of the current strategies that fall under the heading of academic standards" are attempts to "create more losers in order to make space for the winners."[3] Notwithstanding the rhetoric about higher standards "for all students," those standards are essentially used as selection devices to privilege some over others. This movement is not only more about demanding than supporting; it is more about sorting than teaching.

But surely, you reply, this cannot be the conscious intent of most advocates of standards. Maybe not, but it's hard to dispute that this is the effect of what they're doing. Even if it seems ungenerous to accuse them of an undemocratic sensibility, it seems impossible to accept that the solution for families short on money or political clout is to set up new hoops for them to jump through in the name of educational excellence. The most charitable thing we can say about the demands for Tougher Standards is that they're based on a serious confusion about the source of the original problem.

## More of the Same

How might someone try to justify "raising the bar" without regard to the children who have trouble jumping that high? Possibly by blaming the kids themselves. This strategy, as it turns out, is at the heart of the current approach to school reform: Demand more effort and diligence and persistence on the part of individuals. Announce, as a government report did in 1992, that "it is the students who must learn more, and it is they who must do the work."[4] Declare, as the late Al Shanker did, that "most U.S. students don't achieve at very high levels because they don't work very hard."[5]

The implication here is that the traditional approach to education is basically sound; it's just that some slackers are goofing off. Students (and perhaps teachers) *could* be doing a fine job right now but have just decided not to. What is needed isn't a different structure, a better theory of learning, or more resources, but a swift kick in the butt—and more tests to make sure they live up to someone else's expectations. To focus on raising standards is, in effect, to ignore most aspects of the status quo and, therefore, to preserve them.

As evidence, consider that when proponents of Tougher Standards do suggest changes—beyond keeping the pressure on individuals to persevere, beyond carrots and sticks and exhortations to try harder—their prescription for educational reform is for more of the same. Give them more homework! Keep them in school even longer! Test them more often! Make them jump through more hoops to get a good grade — or even to pass! All of these prescriptions "would change schooling very little, if at all, for the majority of American students," according to George Wood, an education professor and high school principal. Their workload may increase, "but they would not find their daily tasks any more educational."[6] A teacher told Wood what these changes look like from the vantage point of the classroom: "The list of reforms was the most anti-student list we could imagine. More tests, more homework, more drill, more hours, more days. It's as if we are to just do more of what isn't working now. . . . What we feel these reforms really mean is to take control away from us and to turn the kids into little assembly-line products — none of us thinking or engaging, just doing what we are told."[7]

Nobody cites any research to prove that merely setting standards higher will help students learn better — presumably because no such research exists.[8] As for the specific examples of this philosophy, sometimes called "intensification," there are some data, and they don't look good.

**More time.** Take the idea that keeping students in school longer will lead to higher achievement. The theory may be plausible, but researchers who have tried to find a connection have often come up with "inconsistent and modest results." Schools that increase what is sometimes called "time on task" may or may not find a benefit, depending on "whether the time was needed or irrelevant, used appropriately or totally wasted"[9] and whether the test was at a low or high level.[10] A Stanford University study, meanwhile, compared four different reforms: peer tutoring, smaller classes, increased computer use, and an hour of additional instruction each day. "On a cost-effectiveness basis, the time intervention was found to rank at the bottom with respect to improving student performance in mathematics and third out of the four [in reading]."[11]

Another kind of evidence comes from a recent international comparison, which discovered that the United States "is above average . . . in the number of hours it devotes to mathematics and science instruction," even though student achievement (at least in the higher grades) is not. Adding still more time is unlikely to improve things, the study's authors concluded, at least if that "means more of the same thing that teachers are doing now."[12] Indeed, more time spent on traditional instruction would likely make students even more bored, more alienated, and more likely to drop out at the earliest opportunity.

Of course, *allocation* of time is often an important consideration. Most American high schools, for instance, are still using a century-old schedule that has never been shown to be conducive to learning. Longer periods to explore fewer things more deeply would seem logical,[13] but the movement for Tougher Standards, greater accountability, and more testing paradoxically makes that shift more difficult to achieve since it tends to emphasize exposing students to more facts more superficially. To talk about time on task isn't to explore a different philosophy of learning, which could be reflected in a different way of organizing the school day. It's interpreted as simply extending the school day, or year, or time for academic instruction. (In some parts of the country, the push for Tougher Standards has even led administrators to eliminate recess in elementary school.)[14]

In short, if students aren't learning effectively, the trouble may lie with whether the task was worth doing, how much say they had in deciding how to do it, whether they could collaborate with their peers or had to struggle alone, and dozens of other variables. How much simpler it is, though, to declare that the only thing wrong is that students haven't sat in school long enough.

**More homework.** Another example of intensification is the assignment of more, and possibly more difficult, homework. For some people, the premise here seems to be that we can relax (about the quality of our schools) if kids don't have time to relax. If they have lots of work to do every night, never mind what it is, then they must be learning. With this premise, it seems perfectly acceptable to assign substantial amounts of homework even to first-graders. "This is what's demanded to stay competitive in a global market," said one New Jersey principal with a shrug.[15]

In 1989 a researcher named Harris Cooper published what is still regarded as the definitive review of scientific data on this subject. He began by noting that, as is so often the case with educational research, the available studies looked mostly at the effects on achievement, not at how homework affected the way students felt about school, about learning, about themselves, or about their teachers. He concluded that the amount of time students spent on homework was related to achievement in high school (and, to a lesser extent, in junior high school) but was virtually irrelevant in elementary school. Even in high school, achievement was related to how much homework the students actually did, not to how much the teacher assigned. And there was no evidence that homework fostered responsibility or discipline.[16]

More recent research raises further doubts. For one thing, the amount of homework students had in high school physics courses was not related to how successful they were in physics when they got to college.[17] For another thing, when Cooper and his colleagues conducted a new study in

1998, they not only confirmed that doing more homework doesn't benefit younger children but found that the only benefit for older students was measured by the grades given to them by the same teachers who had assigned the homework! When they looked at another, less biased measure of achievement, they found that *homework didn't help at any age.* And they also discovered that in the lower grades, "more homework assigned by teachers may cause poorer attitudes in students."[18]

Homework provides another example of a debate that ignores what matters most. On one side are those who assert that homework is important and more homework is even better. On the other side are parents who object to often unmanageable assignments for students that interfere with sleep, family life, and psychological health. But neither position addresses what students are being asked to do or whether it's useful for helping them learn. In a series of lengthy interviews with high school students, one researcher found that most of them accepted the idea of doing homework in principle but often rebelled in practice, not because they were lazy but because the assignments amounted to pointless "busywork."[19]

In short, it only scratches the surface to ask whether students bring home something to do from school, and, if so, how much. Rather than demanding a rigid schoolwide "homework policy" or simply nagging their children to do what's assigned, parents ought to be asking about the philosophy of teaching reflected in the nature and purpose of those assignments.[20]

**More kids held back.** Should students be forced to repeat a year if they don't do as well as their peers? Here is the ultimate example of "more of the same": going through third grade all over again. This proposal appeals to the Tougher Standards crowd because of its intimations of getting tough with kids, demanding that they work harder on pain of being kept back a year. Promotion to the next grade level must be earned! No free lunches!

Even if what is called "retention" isn't intended as a punishment, it's likely to be experienced that way. Put yourself in the shoes of such a student and imagine how you would feel about yourself and about school. The premise, once again, is that the students themselves are to be "held accountable" — that is, blamed and made to suffer — if they don't have the skills deemed appropriate for their grade level.[21] The beauty of retention as a matter of policy is that it removes from us any obligation to examine what and how students are being taught; the responsibility is wholly theirs to try harder.

Interestingly, even those who firmly support this idea tend to feel a little different when it's their own kid who is being held back. (This suggests a possible slogan to rally around: *If it's not good enough for your child, it's not good enough for anyone's child.*) Historically speaking, automatic promotion from one grade to the next was relatively uncontroversial as long as it benefited the middle class. At least one scholar has drawn the gloomy conclusion that research and logic about the effects of retention are unlikely to have much of an impact on policy, since it is really issues of class and ideology that will determine whether kids get held back.[22]

That conclusion is supported by the fact that "retaining students has become a more popular practice during the very time period that research has revealed its negative effects on those retained."[23] The most comprehensive review of the available evidence finds that "few practices in education have such overwhelmingly negative research findings arrayed against them. . . . It would be difficult to find a more pernicious practice." Students who have to repeat a grade are much more likely to drop out of school years later than if they hadn't been held back. "At-risk students who are promoted achieve at the same or higher levels than comparable at-risk students who have been retained and . . . effects measured long-term [are] more strongly negative than those measured short-term." The authors observe that advocates of retention may "acknowledge some potential harm to a child's self-esteem but hold that achievement gains are more important than this potential risk." Yet the data suggest that retention is even more harmful to achievement than it is to a student's self-concept or attitude toward school.[24]

This doesn't mean that automatically promoting children without paying any attention to their problems is the logical alternative. Kids who need help should get it: special arrangements for tutoring make sense and may turn out to be less expensive than having the child repeat a grade. Better yet, teachers ought to work together, and with parents, to consider how they've been teaching. (The opposite of retention, we might say, isn't social promotion but the willingness to look for deficiencies in the instruction instead of just in the learner.) A more ambitious structural change, whose advantages go far beyond the question of retention versus promotion, is known as multiage or nongraded teaching, where children of different ages are combined in a single classroom, and where a child who is struggling is more likely to get the help she needs. Even some elementary schools unwilling to question the practice of segregating children by age have begun letting teachers stay with a class over two or more years, a reform known as "looping." If someone has to be retained, perhaps it should be the teacher.[25]

•

Well before the most recent round of international comparisons in school performance, it had become commonplace to cite the success of Japan's educational system—and to attribute it to the relentless effort of its students. Their kids study; our kids loaf. Their schools have high expectations; ours have a watered-down curriculum where anything goes. But does this really explain the putative superiority of Japanese academic performance? Hardly. In fact, the reality is precisely the opposite of what American traditionalists would have us believe.

- **Tracking:** The practice of separating students by alleged ability is a mainstay of U.S. education, and efforts to reverse this process are fiercely denounced for lowering standards. Yet there is virtually no tracking, no separation of high and low, fast and slow, in Japanese schools through the ninth grade.[26]
- **Retention:** Japanese students are almost never held back a grade.[27]
- **Testing:** "Elementary achievement is high because Japanese teachers are free from the pressure to teach to standardized tests"—a freedom won back in the 1960s, when the Japanese teachers' union prevented the Ministry of Education from implementing a national achievement test.[28] (As already noted, Japan is not unusual in this respect; we are. Presumably, then, anyone who complains about how poorly U.S. students are doing compared to other students around the world would be in the forefront of the opposition to national and state testing.)
- **Role of academics:** While many Japanese students compete for university admission by cramming for an all-important exam they will take during high school, the elementary school years are marked by a very progressive, student-centered approach. Free play is a significant part of the school day for younger children, and teachers work with them to create a sense of community in the classroom so that everyone feels included and all participate in making decisions. While intellectual growth is important, the emphasis is on "the whole child."[29]
- **Type of instruction:** Teaching in Japanese elementary schools is the very opposite of the back-to-basics style favored by American traditionalists. Students learn through guided reflection and discussion far more than from direct instruction. Particularly in math and science, the emphasis is on active, student-directed problem-solving and exploration rather than rote memorization and drill. Learning is rarely referred to—or treated as—"work."[30] For what they're worth, international tests show that Japanese elementary school students score very high in just such an environment.[31]

It is not uncommon to hear Japanese teachers invoke the name of John Dewey in explaining what they are trying to do (suggesting an interesting parallel with the late American management guru W. Edwards Deming, who is far more celebrated and influential in Japan than in his native land). Dewey's work can be seen as one long, systematic, decisive refutation of the Tougher Standards movement in all its particulars. "When a child feels that his work is a task, it is only under compunction that he gives himself to it," Dewey wrote in 1913. "At every let-up of external pressure his attention, released from constraint, flies to what interests him."[32] The greater the pressure on students to achieve—or on teachers to raise standards—the less engaged students become with what they are doing. And the worse things get, the more this brand of reform demands further emphasis on exactly what made them worse.

## Harder Is Better

I'll tell you something I've noticed from visiting a lot of American schools: the more traditional the teacher, the grimmer the mood. These classrooms don't always resemble Dickensian factories, mind you, but if you watch the kids' faces (or the teachers'), the phrase "joy of discovery" probably won't leap to mind. And here's the interesting part: the people who defend the Old School usually don't deny that this is true, and they don't even seem to mind. Sometimes they actually take a perverse pride in presiding over (or sending their kids to) this bleak house because for them that constitutes proof that real education is happening. No pain, no gain. Cooperative learning, for example, is immediately suspect. As one conservative columnist put it, "Learning takes work and cooperative learning takes the work right out of learning."[33] No need to look at the data to see whether kids tend to grasp ideas better in such a classroom: if they're not sweating, how productive can it be? Case closed.

Does this mean that the Old School endures because of a Protestant ethic of self-denial, fear of pleasure, redemption through suffering? I don't know; you decide. What intrigues me is the snug fit between this surprisingly common (though rarely articulated) assumption and traditional ways of teaching. The busywork that kids are given is sometimes rationalized on the theory that if they hate it, it must be good for them. Interestingly, children in skills-oriented classrooms are likely "to perceive that what they are doing is *work* that they have to do" rather than "learning."[34]

I've also noticed that teachers in such classrooms are especially likely to offer rewards—stickers, grades, pizza, praise—to students who successfully complete their "work." A series of studies found that many parents and other adults "perceived academic tasks as 'work' and evidently assumed that interest in schoolwork, which they deemed to be uninteresting, boring, and repetitive, may be increased by reward."[35] Is that because few members of our species would ever do this stuff without being offered some goody—or because the same sensibility that says education is bitter medicine also says that motivation must be supplied from outside, that human beings lack any natural desire to do things that are worthwhile? Cause and effect may be hard to pin down, but these three things occur together with striking regularity: the view that the quality of an education is directly proportional to its unpleasantness, the reliance on traditional course content and teaching styles, and the use of rewards (along with the belief in their inevitability).

And here's something else that follows from this worldview: if learning is always hard work, then the harder it is, the better it must be. Therefore the main thing wrong with schools today is that kids get off too easy. It's a small step from defining improvement as making them do more of the same stuff to defining improvement as doing more difficult stuff.

Now, the first and most obvious response is that assignments and tests can be too difficult just as they can be too easy. If the latter can leave students insufficiently challenged, the former can make them feel stupid, which, in turn, can lead them to feel alienated, to lose interest in the subject matter,[36] and sometimes to misbehave. (It's usually less threatening for kids to be seen as incorrigible than as inadequate.) Anyone can ask students questions that are laughably easy or impossibly difficult. "The trick," said Jerome Bruner, "is to find the medium questions that can be answered and that take you somewhere."[37] In short, maximum difficulty isn't the same as optimal difficulty.*

But let's delve a little deeper. Maybe the question isn't whether harder is always better so much as why we focus so much attention on the whole question of difficulty. Dewey reminded us that the value of what students do "resides in its connection with a stimulation of greater *thoughtfulness*, not in the greater strain it imposes"[39]—an observation I find myself returning to again and again. If you were making a list of what counts in

---

* One technique for finding just the right level of challenge for each student is so simple that few of us think of it: let the student choose. As long as the classroom doesn't overemphasize performance, doesn't lead students to think mostly about getting good grades or doing better than others, children will generally seek out tasks that are just beyond what they're able to do easily.[38]

education—that is, the criteria to use in judging whether students will benefit from what they are doing—the task's difficulty level would be only one factor among many and almost certainly not the most important. To judge schools by how demanding they are is rather like judging an opera on the basis of how many notes are hard for the singers to hit. In other words, it leaves out most of what matters.

Here's what follows from this recognition: if tests or homework assignments consist of factual recall questions, it really doesn't make all that much difference whether there are twenty-five tough questions or ten easy ones. A textbook does not become a more appropriate teaching tool just because it is intended for a higher grade level. Some parents indignantly complain that their kids are bored and can complete the worksheets without breaking a sweat. They ought to be complaining that the teacher is relying on worksheets at all. The point is, we have to look at the whole method of instruction, the underlying theory of learning, rather than just quibbling about how hard the assignment is.

One reason the Old School curriculum fits perfectly with the philosophy of prizing hard work is that it *creates* hard work—often unnecessarily. It's more difficult to learn to read if you work on individual letters than if you try to make sense of interesting stories. It's more exhausting to memorize a list of scientific vocabulary words than it is to learn scientific concepts by devising your own experiment. If kids are going to be forced to learn facts without context and skills without meaning, it's certainly handy to have an ideology that values difficulty for its own sake. Without a doubt, learning often requires sustained attention and effort. But there's a vital difference between that which is rigorous and that which is merely onerous.

If that distinction is missed by some parents and teachers, it is systematically ignored by the purveyors of Tougher Standards. Recently, my own state began to phase in a test that students will have to pass before receiving a high school diploma. It requires them to know a considerable amount about topics like the Ming Dynasty, the Mongol invasion of Europe, Germany's disunity until 1871, and the colonial possessions of Portugal in 1700. It obliges them to write extended essays (under pressure) based on six difficult literary excerpts, to be conversant in the language of trigonometry, to explain aquatic food chains, vectors, jigs, density, astrolabes, DNA sequences—and on and on, until their number two pencils have been ground into stubs.

Several questions come to mind here. First, how many adults could pass this test? How many high school teachers possess the requisite stock of information outside their own subjects? How many college professors, for that matter, or business executives, or state legislators could confidently write an essay about Mayan agricultural practices or divergent plate boundaries? Consider (Deborah) Meier's Mandate: *No student should be expected to meet an academic requirement that a cross section of successful adults in the community cannot.* (Or Kohn's Corollary to Meier's Mandate: All persons given to pious rhetoric about the need to "raise standards" and produce "world-class academic performance for the twenty-first century" not only should be required to take these exams themselves but must agree to have their scores published in the newspaper.) We ought to be asking about each fact or skill "why it matters and who cares," says Meier, rather than just generating "lists of 465 skills, facts, and concepts multiplied by the number of disciplines academia can invent."[40]

Actually, there are two separate problems here. The first—brought home by the question How many of us could meet these standards?—is the assumption that the ideal difficulty level is always "extremely high" —as opposed to "moderate" or "variable, depending on the circumstances." After new proficiency exams were failed by a significant proportion of students in Nevada, Alabama, and Virginia, education officials in all three states responded by making the tests even harder the following year. The commissioner of education for Colorado offered some insight into the sensibility underlying such decisions: "Unless you get bad results," he declared, "it is highly doubtful you have done anything useful with your tests. Low scores have become synonymous with good tests."[41] Such is the logic on which the Tougher Standards movement has been built.*

The second question, beyond whether we could meet the standards being demanded of students, is How many of us *need* to know this stuff— not just on the basis of job requirements but as a reflection of what it means to be well educated? Do these facts and skills reflect what we honor, what matters to us about schooling and human life? Often, the standards being rammed into our children's classrooms are not merely unreasonable but irrelevant; it is the kinds of things students are being forced to learn and the approach to learning itself that don't ring true. The tests that result—for students and sometimes for teachers[43]—are

---

* Meier has pointed out that this kind of thinking inevitably results in the view that standards are sufficiently difficult only if it is impossible for everyone to meet them. If all students manage to achieve something, this is often taken as prima facie evidence that our standards are too low, which means that talk of "excellence" and "setting the bar higher" signifies almost by definition that some students must fail. Once again, the point is to sort more than to teach.[42]

not just ridiculously difficult but simply ridiculous. It is time for us to look for more sensible alternatives—better ways of understanding the sources of achievement, better ways of teaching, and better ways of evaluating the success of students and schools.

## · Part Two ·
# FOR THE
# LOVE
# *of*
# LEARNING

Our tutors never stop bawling into our ears, as though they were pouring water into a funnel; and our task is only to repeat what has been told us. I should like the tutor to correct this practice, and right from the start, according to the capacity of the mind he has in hand, to begin putting it through its paces, making it taste things, choose them, and discern them by itself; sometimes clearing the way for [the pupil], sometimes letting him clear his own way. I don't want [the tutor] to think and talk alone, I want him to listen to his pupil speaking in his turn.

—Montaigne, 1580

Teaching is mostly listening, and learning is mostly telling.

—Deborah Meier, 1995

# STARTING FROM
# SCRATCH

## *What's the Point?*

MOST OF US send our kids off to school each weekday morning without giving much thought to the reasons we do so. If asked, we might say that going to school is just what kids do, much as adults go to work. Besides, the law requires it. But why do we as a society want our kids to be educated? What's the point of having them learn? These questions are not merely academic, nor are the answers self-evident. Indeed, the rationale for educating children has a direct bearing on what they'll actually do in the classroom — and on the practical question of what we can do to help them become enthusiastic and excellent learners.

Immediately, the matter of overall purpose splinters into smaller questions. For example, should schools be devoted chiefly to academics? To judge by the tests given to students, that seems to be the only function we think schools should perform. But some people emphatically disagree. For example, Nel Noddings, professor emeritus at Stanford University, urges us to reject "the deadly notion that the schools' first priority should be intellectual development." She argues that "the main aim of education should be to produce competent, caring, loving, and lovable people."[1]

Other educators are content to restrict schools to the intellectual realm but insist that the focus should be not merely on what students learn, but on how strong their desire is to keep learning. It isn't just about how many skills they acquire but about whether they want to acquire still more. Perhaps, as Seymour Sarason says, "the overarching purpose of schooling is to stimulate, capitalize on, and sustain the kind of motivation, intellectual curiosity, awe, and wonder that a child possesses when he or she begins schooling."[2]

Even someone who feels safer just asking schools to promote students' intellectual capabilities will have to decide which capabilities are relevant. Is the point to transmit knowledge to students or to help them become reflective people? Do we define an educated person as someone who knows a lot of stuff or someone who's a good thinker? Most of us would answer "Both" to each question, but we don't all strike the same balance between the two ends of the continuum. Clearly, our children's days are going to be spent differently if we're primarily concerned that they've memorized a list of what everyone their age is supposed to know, as opposed to if we believe that "the purpose of education is not primarily to help children know more; rather, it is to help children become better able to think, care, imagine, understand, and adapt—to become autonomous learners."[3]

Those of us who are attracted to the latter formulation should be aware that when schools were invented, they weren't set up for anything so ambitious. They were designed to teach children routine skills and to "facilitate the memorization of important texts, principally religious ones," with which everyone was already acquainted. Schools weren't meant to help students "interpret unfamiliar texts, create material others would want and need to read, construct convincing arguments, develop original solutions to technical or social problems."[4] Thus, when people today say that education should not just prepare students "to do things [but to] decide what is worth doing,"[5] or when they ask our schools to "help children make fuller, deeper, and more accurate sense of their experiences,"[6] the implication is that we'll have to commit ourselves to remaking education. As it stands, traditional practices, such as direct instruction, fact-based tests, and a quest for the right answer are more consistent with the original conception of schools, whose catechisms "sought to produce believers rather than thinkers."[7]

That last distinction raises the question of whether we see schools as places where cultural knowledge is transmitted to a new generation in order to preserve important institutions, or as places where a new generation learns the skills and dispositions necessary to *evaluate* those institutions. Again, it's more a continuum than an either-or, but the point on that continuum we identify as ideal makes all the difference. Are we more inclined to want schools to turn out kids who accept or who question, who conserve traditions or who create new ones? We can side with Émile Durkheim, who said schools should "exert pressure upon [the student] in order that he may learn proper consideration for others, respect for customs and conventions, the need for work, etc."[8]—or we can cast our lot with Jean Piaget, who believed that "the principal goal of education is to create men and women who are capable of doing new things, not simply of repeating what other generations have done—men and women who are creative, inventive and discoverers, [who] have minds which can be critical, can verify [rather than] accept everything they are offered."[9]

One way of splitting the difference on this dispute is to pursue the latter goal with a select group of students (who are deemed capable of being creative) while doing something less challenging with everyone else. Woodrow Wilson, during his tenure as president of Princeton University, stood before a roomful of high school teachers and announced, "We want one class of persons to have a liberal education, and we want another class of persons, a very much larger class of necessity in every society, to forgo the privilege of a liberal education and fit themselves to perform specific difficult manual tasks."[10] This, of course, raises yet another basic question: Do we want schools to be about "sorting people out, the presumed abler from the less able" or "educating *all* children, generously and without qualification"?[11]

Our country has been of two minds about this matter almost since its founding. Today, the only thing more common than rhetoric about how "everyone can learn" and the importance of "high expectations for all students" is a set of practices that belie those sentiments — practices such as tracking children into very different kinds of classrooms. Few people today are as crude (or candid) as Wilson was, but his notion of the purpose of schools is alive and well and on display whenever some children are pointed toward algebra and others toward "consumer math."

Interestingly, many latter-day Wilsonians share with their critics a focus on what will happen after students graduate. The "sorters" are thinking about preparing children for very different kinds of futures, but the more egalitarian may also be concerned about what comes later. Rather provocatively, Dewey insisted that education should be seen as "a process of living and not a preparation for future living."[12] To take children seriously is to value them for who they are right now rather than seeing them as just adults-in-the-making. However, Dewey's colleague William Kilpatrick believed that it is legitimate to attend to both. Ideally, he said, education "prepares best for life [when] at the same time it constitutes the present worthy life itself."[13]

The words "best" and "worthy" in Kilpatrick's comment signal that there may be better and worse ways of conceiving of schooling in either the present *or* the future tense. The same is true of another fundamental distinction: Do we send our kids to school for the benefits they will derive personally or for the benefits their education will ultimately bring about for our society? Most people will be tempted to say, "Both," but again, we shouldn't be content to let it go at that. What matters is the nature of the benefits we're talking about for either the individual student or for the society.

Let's assume that we think schools should be seen as providing some public benefit. One of the great fault lines running through discussions about education creates two camps that might be labeled "education for democracy" and "education for profits." The former says that schools should be equipping students with the skills they'll need to sustain (or, possibly, to create) a democratic society. The latter, in its purest form, says that schools should be preparing students to be productive workers in order to sustain a booming economy.

In practice, however, the economic justification for schooling often goes hand in hand with the Wilsonian vision of separating the privileged from the peons, creating a pool of adequately skilled laborers who will do their part to increase the profitability of corporations. Here, the emphasis is on transmitting basic skills as well as good "work habits" — that is, training students to show up on time, do what they're told, and get used to being measured and goaded by rewards and punishments. In the early 1900s, there was much talk about the need to set up schools to resemble factories, partly because that was thought to be the most efficient way of organizing any enterprise and partly because that would prepare students to take their place in real factories.[14]

"In the twentieth century's ongoing debate about the purposes of education, business interests have prevailed," one writer concludes. The triumph of this agenda effectively "whittles the purpose of schooling down to an almost sinister notion of making good little workers for future employment."[15] This rationale is consistent with all the talk we hear today about Tougher Standards and accountability, the huge role played by standardized testing, the references to education as an "investment," and the prevalent idea that our students must be Number One, outscoring their counterparts in other countries today so that "our" corporations can triumph over their overseas rivals tomorrow. Marveling that "Democrats and Republicans are saying rather similar things about education," a front-page story in the *New York Times* in the fall of 1998 explained, "One reason there seems to be such a consensus on education is that the economic rationale for schooling has triumphed."[16]

The idea that we send our children to school to raise the gross national product (much less the value of General Motors stock) strikes some people as disturbing, if not outrageous. They argue that students' own interests should take precedence when we think about the point of education and when we plan the details of what and how they are taught. But even here we find a lack of agreement about which of "the students' own interests" matter most. On the one hand, there are humanistic goals: helping children become contented and fulfilled, helping them grow into adults with a deeper understanding of themselves and the world around them. On the other hand, there are more utilitarian goals, such as helping children grow into adults with a lot of money.

In the late 1950s, Erich Fromm wrote a striking sentence: "Few parents," he declared, "have the courage and independence to care more for their children's happiness than for their 'success.' "[17] Forty years later, an educational historian named David Labaree argued that the financial success of each child vis-à-vis his fellows has become the driving force of American education — eclipsing not only happiness and other humanistic goals but also the *public* rationales for schooling. Those who are busy arguing whether we should think about education in terms of "what it can do for democracy [as opposed to] the economy" may be missing the more fundamental shift, which is toward asking "what it can do for me." This transformation, Labaree contends, has turned our school systems into "a vast public subsidy for private ambition," "an arena for zero-sum competition filled with self-interested actors seeking opportunities for gaining educational distinctions at the expense of each other." In the process, the substance of education takes a backseat to the credentials it provides.[18]

Depending on whether we think schools should be promoting individual or social goals, and whether we primarily value humanistic or economic values, we find ourselves with four possible agendas for education (see Table 1). Once again, it's possible to pursue more than one at a

*Table 1: The Purpose of Schools*

|  | PRIVATE | PUBLIC |
|---|---|---|
| HUMANISTIC | Enhancing personal fulfillment | Building a democratic society |
| ECONOMIC | Maximizing competitive financial success | Increasing corporate profits |

time, but it's not at all clear that we can dedicate our schools to all of these goals.[19] My own vision of schooling, which necessarily informs this entire book, is defined by a concern for both the fulfillment of each child and the creation of a more democratic society. As for the other objectives discussed here, I believe school should be about more than just academics, more about producing thinkers than walking repositories of knowledge, more about creating an ethic of questioning than of preserving the status quo, more about teaching and learning than sorting and selecting, and more about honoring the needs and interests of the child in the present but without overlooking legitimate, humanistic concerns about the future.

Your goals and mine may not be exactly the same. But to the extent they do overlap, the relevant question for us is this: How well do concrete school practices—all the things that take place in classrooms throughout the country on a given Thursday morning—reflect the commitments we share? Traditional teaching, the kind familiar to most of us from our own days in school, is well matched to the goals many of us would identify as the least ambitious, the least appealing, the least worthy of our children. To that extent, the Old School has worn out its welcome.

## Goals and Memories

While beliefs about the ultimate purpose of schooling exert an invisible influence on real educational decisions, that influence is usually indirect. Let's make the discussion more personal. Whenever I give a talk to a group of parents or a workshop for teachers, I like to begin by asking these questions: How would you like your children—or, in the case of educators, the students you teach—to turn out? What are your long-term goals for them? What word or phrase best describes what you want them to be like after they're grown up and gone?

The answers that come back are strikingly similar, whether they come from parents or teachers, whether the students in question are toddlers or teenagers, whether the school in question is public or private, and whether the community is urban, suburban, or rural. Wherever I go, people say they want their kids to be happy and fulfilled, successful and productive, ethical and decent, independent and self-reliant, but also caring and compassionate—and (to continue the alliteration) confident, curious, creative, critical thinkers, and good communicators. Also, someone invariably expresses the hope that his or her child will always keep learning, and wanting to learn, even after leaving school. (If you sneaked into the bedroom of a random elementary school teacher at three in the morning and yelled, "Quick! What's your long-term goal for the students you teach?" a bleary voice would probably reply, "Uh, lifelong learners." This phrase has become something of a cliché in educational circles, but it is a goal commonly shared by parents and teachers whether they use those words or not.)

Several things about the list as a whole strike me as interesting. First, it's very rare for people in any neighborhood to say that a top goal is to have their children make lots of money. Second, most of the items (proposed by teachers as well as parents) reach beyond intellectual characteristics and deal with the kind of human beings kids will become—their character and psychological state. Third, even when intellectual features are mentioned, they tend to be broad dispositions such as "curious" and "creative" and "critical." No one has ever said, "What's most important to me is that my kid will be able to convert a fraction into a decimal" or "will know the difference between a simile and a metaphor." In my experience, when people are asked to reflect on their long-term goals for children, no one thinks in terms of possessing a storehouse of facts.

This last observation raises a troubling question: Are school practices in sync with the long-term goals shared by most parents and teachers? Logically speaking, there are only three possibilities: either schools are (a) helping children to turn out the way we hope, (b) doing things that are mostly irrelevant to our objectives, or (c) making it less likely that they'll acquire the characteristics we regard as most important. I believe the effects of traditional schooling typically include some of (b) and a lot of (c). There's a disconnect between our goals and our practices, a clash between what we ultimately desire for our kids and the kind of education they actually receive. We say we want one thing, but we're really doing another—or at least allowing another to be done.

Sometimes the clash isn't just between long-term goals and everyday practices but between long-term and short-term goals. We want kids to be independent thinkers eventually, but for now we ignore that because we want them to know long division by the end of the year. We want them to love learning, but we set that aside because right now it's more important to us that they bring up their grade-point averages.

You ask: Can't we have it all? I answer: It depends. If we focus on traditional short-term goals (such as knowing this fact by that deadline or getting good grades), it is entirely possible that the long-term goals will not be met. If we teach too many topics over the course of a year, then a deep understanding of meaty ideas may be impossible. If school is based on the "bunch o' facts" model for long enough, our children may be less likely to develop the skills and dispositions of critical thinking. If kids are drilled incessantly on separate letters and then separate words, it may be unrealistic to expect them to be avid readers for life. If they get the message that the point of going to school is to snag as many A's as possible, then, as we've seen, the depth of their understanding and their motivation to learn will suffer.[20]

The good news, on the other hand, is that if we start with the long-term goals and teach in such a way as to promote them, students may end up remembering more facts and acquiring more skills to boot. Thus, even relatively superficial short-term goals may not require us to abandon what we really care about over the long run — and may not require the kind of traditional teaching that ultimately proves so problematic. As the data reviewed in Appendix A suggest, progressive education not only produces major gains on measures of thinking and motivation but may help (or at least probably won't hurt) the lower-level competencies that are measured by standardized tests.

A former high school English teacher[21] told me that at the beginning of the year, he would lay out his (short-term) objectives, which were for his students to be able to write clear, well-structured essays, to take pleasure in self-expression, to do sustained, independent research, and to participate constructively in discussions. It's hard to imagine anyone objecting to these goals, which is why it's noteworthy that he was best able to meet them by teaching in a nontraditional way: he rarely lectured, had them spend more time with fewer books, created the opportunities for frequent collaboration, and didn't grade their individual assignments.

The moral is that we need to reflect on, and periodically revisit, our long-term goals — and to evaluate what happens in school in light of those goals. In the meantime, it's possible that remembering what happened to us when we were in school can put those short-term objectives in perspective. Harvey Daniels and his colleagues, who work with the Chicago public schools, find that many parents initially parrot the "superficial received wisdom" about Tougher Standards and basic skills. These off-the-cuff comments are consistent with national polls showing wide support for a "reactionary, back-to-basics agenda." But when parents "stop to think seriously about their own student experience, the vast majority want something very different and better for their children."

In workshops, Daniels asks everyone to think privately about, then scribble down, and finally describe to someone sitting nearby, a couple of key experiences he or she had in school: a memory of learning to read, a time when writing went especially well, a moment that stands out as particularly awful. The lessons that emerge from these recollections, it turns out, are that "rote grammar instruction does not improve writing, writers should choose their own topics, collaboration improves the quality of texts," and so on. In other words, once they reflect on their own schooling, most parents realize they "don't want their children to endure the same deadening seat work, passive memorization, lockstep assignments, demoralizing grading practices, and hurtful discipline" that they themselves did.[22]

So: ask parents about the future (their long-term goals for their kids) and remind them about the past (their own experiences as students). Then add to that the best research available in the present, and you find that all three point away from traditional kinds of teaching—and toward something better. Most of us can remember glimpsing that something better, even if only rarely, so the question is whether we want it to be the rule or the exception for our children. Wouldn't we like them to have better schools than we had?

## Beyond Achievement

Virtually any ambitious goal for our children will require us to rethink the set of psychological assumptions—or perhaps I should say the disregard of psychological factors—that characterize the Tougher Standards movement. Recall from chapter 2 that a serious disservice is done to students when they are led to become so preoccupied with how well they're doing that they end up becoming less engaged with what they're doing. How do we set about reversing this? To start with, parents will do well to reconsider how they talk with their children about school. As a rule, it's better to ask, "So what did you figure out in class today?" "What did you learn that was surprising?" "How did you manage to solve that tricky problem?" "How do *you* think the Civil War started?"—as opposed to "How'd you do on that test?" "How come you only got a C in math?" "Are you going to make the honor roll this term?"

Ultimately, though, we may have to concern ourselves with what's actually happening in school and not merely with how we talk about it. Let's put the question this way: If chapter 2 explained the effects of getting students to think constantly about how well they're doing, what are the causes of this phenomenon? Many of us are inclined to think in terms of the personality of the individual students.[23] To be sure, there are differences among kids, but what appears to matter more is their environment, the structure and culture of the school.[24] So what specific practices in schools lead kids to focus on their performance? Make your own list and you'll probably come up with some of the same items I've heard from people all over the country who were asked this question:

- Grades.
- Variations on grades that increase their impact, such as privileges made contingent on a high grade-point average, honor rolls and societies, and weighted grades (where some classes count for more than others).
- Standardized tests, especially when the scores are published.
- Academic contests and other instances of competition.
- Frequent evaluations of student performance, particularly when done publicly.
- Rewards ranging from gold stars to scholarships.
- The segregation of students by performance or alleged ability, including tracking and special enrichments for those labeled "gifted and talented."
- The current criteria for (and sometimes mistaken beliefs about) college admission.
- The kind of teaching that values error-free assignments and right answers more than real thinking.

It comes down to this: all of us who are bothered by the effects of overemphasizing achievement—namely, the prospect of kids trying to take the easy way out, thinking superficially, and losing interest in learning—will view this as a "hit list." Collectively, these items describe an antilearning environment—reason enough for us to work to eliminate (and, in the meantime, deemphasize) as many of these practices as possible. The consequences of a preoccupation with performance are quite clear; the question is whether we're willing to follow that analysis where it leads.

One place it leads is to the recognition that the problem with tests is not limited to their content. Rather, the harm comes from paying too much attention to the results. Even the most unbiased, carefully constructed, "authentic" measure of what students know is likely to be worrisome, psychologically speaking, if too big a deal is made about how they performed, thus leading them (and their teachers) to think less about learning and more about test outcomes. This point is overlooked even by some of the most incisive critics of standardized testing and traditional instruction.[25]

Another disconcerting implication of this whole analysis is that we're obliged to rethink the very idea of motivation. Getting students to become preoccupied with how well they're doing is typically achieved by techniques intended to "motivate" them. These include giving students rewards for good performance — or, in what seems almost a parody of Skinnerian psychology, giving them one reward (like money) for having received another reward (a good grade)! This practice is so patently destructive that you can almost watch kids' interest in learning fade before your eyes. Yet some of the parents who do this are obviously bright, thoughtful, and well intentioned. How is this possible?

Two simple and almost universally shared beliefs about motivation may account for the use of such gimmicks. Belief number one, which is so elementary that no one even thinks about it, is that it's possible to motivate someone else, such as your child. The truth is that doing so is impossible, unnecessary, and undesirable. Let's take these in order. First, while you can often make someone else do something — in effect buying a behavior with a bribe or a threat — you can never make him or her *want* to do something, which is what "motivation" means. The best you can do is create the kind of setting and offer the kind of tasks that will tap and nourish people's own motivation.

Second, such motivation is natural. I don't think I've ever met a child who wasn't motivated to figure things out, to find the answers to personally relevant questions. However, I've met (and taught) plenty of kids who aren't motivated to sit quietly and listen to someone else talk or to memorize the definitions of a list of words. That lack of interest doesn't suggest an absence of motivation (to be remedied with carrots and sticks) but a problem with the model of instruction or with the curriculum. Anyone who has been around young children knows that it's hard to stop them from learning, almost impossible to curb their natural motivation. They persist in asking questions about things we take for granted. They want to apply their new reading skills to every sign in sight, from highway billboards to restaurant menus.

"A passion for learning . . . isn't something you have to inspire [kids] with; it's something you have to keep from extinguishing," as Deborah Meier has remarked.[26] Unhappily, it often does get extinguished. At least in the United States, research has repeatedly found that this enthusiasm for learning declines sharply by the time kids are well along in elementary school.[27] Even so, it's not helpful to see our task as "motivating" such kids. Rather, our short-term obligation is to help revive or resuscitate what used to come naturally, and our long-term obligation is to figure out (and change) what's going on in schools that's contributing to this decline.

Finally, even if it were possible to provide motivation from outside, it's not a good idea. Think for a moment about the arrogance of setting out to motivate a child. It should be clear that this is an exercise in control and therefore likely to boomerang, if only because humans hate to be controlled. Once the issue is framed as "how to motivate" someone, it is quite likely that the usual techniques of control—namely, rewards and punishments—will be used.

One popular myth about motivation, then, is that it can be done to others. The other, even more basic misconception is one we encountered while looking at high-stakes testing—the idea that there's a thing called motivation, a single substance that people possess to a certain degree. The reality, remember, is that there are qualitatively different types of motivation. What determines how effectively students will learn isn't how motivated they are. It's how they are motivated. The type of motivation referred to as "extrinsic"—which we find, for example, when kids are led to read books so they can get some goodie—turns out to be not merely ineffective but counterproductive. It tends to reduce "intrinsic" motivation—that is, an interest in reading itself.[28] Thus, when things go badly for kids at school, it "is just as likely the result of [their] being *overmotivated,* but for the wrong reasons, as it is of not being motivated at all," in the words of Martin Covington.[29]

This basic point—that all motivation isn't created equal—goes a long way toward explaining those data demonstrating that giving (and emphasizing) grades is such a mistake. Recall the three key consequences of grading: less interest in learning, less proficiency at learning, and less desire to challenge oneself (pp. 41–43). None of these findings seems so counterintuitive once you stop thinking of motivation as something that comes in only one flavor.

Even apart from how more of one kind of motivation can mean less of another, the simple fact that there are different kinds can change the way you look at kids in school. Say you walk into a classroom and find everyone in the middle of doing an assignment. All the kids are busy and "on task," as some educators like to say. But don't leave without asking a few kids what they're doing[30]—*and why*. If the most common answer is "Because Mr. Riley told us to" or "Because it's going to be on the test," then something here may be terribly wrong just below the surface. The kind of answers we hope to hear sound more like this: "Because I just don't get why the character in this story told her friend to go away!" or "Because we're trying to figure out a better lunch schedule for all the classes. You want to see what we've come up with?" Both sets of answers may indicate that students are motivated. But the kinds of motivation are altogether different—and so are the long-term effects.

# The Secret of Success

Understanding how certain features of schooling are likely to do more harm than good may be a prerequisite for constructive change. If extrinsic motivators—and, more broadly, an excessive concern with bottom-line results—are apt to blow up in our faces, that can help us focus our efforts as parents or teachers. But what, other than removing barriers, can help to foster a learning orientation? How do we get kids to act on their desire to figure things out? How do we help them to become more interested in what they're doing?

Part of the answer concerns what (and how) they're being taught, which is the subject of the following chapter. If we want kids to learn for the right reasons, then the content and method of the instruction become directly relevant. In fact, there's some preliminary evidence that an instructional program explicitly geared to helping students develop a "learning orientation" can make a difference with those who are falling behind[31]—a particularly welcome finding, given that most interventions for "at-risk" populations are geared to bringing up test scores or otherwise increasing the pressure to achieve at higher levels.

But let's take a step back. Chapter 2 amounted to an invitation to reconsider the whole idea of achievement, to reflect on how we want our kids to think about school. It didn't argue that success doesn't matter but rather that success can't be sought directly. In effect, it pointed to the conclusion that *high achievement is a by-product.* Now we're ready to ask: A by-product of what? And the answer is: Of interest.[32]

This will not come as a surprise to—nor require much change from—those of us who believe schools should be promoting students' desire to continue learning, or those of us who number lifelong curiosity among our long-term goals for our children, or those of us who understand that the most profound sort of motivation is intrinsic. But what about people who don't see interest in learning as an end in itself and care only about achievement? In its main policy statement, for example, the 1996 National Education Summit of the nation's governors asserted that "the only reason to undertake change is to improve students' academic performance."[33] This is a value judgment and, as such, can be challenged but not proved wrong. What does lend itself to empirical evidence is the question of how you get higher performance. Until now, I've tried to show that, paradoxically, getting everyone focused directly on this goal tends to backfire. It's better to encourage kids to focus on the task itself. Now I want to add that students attend to the task best when the task matters to them. Thus, even parents and teachers and policymakers for whom achievement is the primary objective must be concerned with interest.

Here's another way of putting it: *where interest appears, achievement usually follows.*[34] Show me a student who wants to understand what the Vietnam War was really about, and I'll show you a student who (with the right support and resources) can be helped to acquire the necessary skills to do it. Show me the kind of class where kids groan when the dismissal bell rings, and I'll show you a place where kids are doing marvelously sophisticated thinking. As one science educator observes, "There are many techniques that must be learned and practiced, of course, but the heart of science is the drive to discover, not the mastery of laboratory procedures and report formalities or the ability to recite facts from textbooks."[35] Indeed, it is interest—the drive to keep reading, to invent, to explain, to express oneself, to make meaning—that is the heart of any field of study. Some four centuries ago, Montaigne wrote that if students lack the "appetite and affection" for learning, they become little more than "asses loaded with books."[36]

There is good research to support this general point. Some of it has shown that the extent to which students are interested in the subject matter is a good way of predicting how well they'll learn it.[37] Other studies have demonstrated more specifically that, regardless of age, race, or reading skills, students are more likely to remember and really understand what they've read if they find it intriguing. Indeed, the interest level of the text has been found to be a much better predictor of what students will get out of it than how difficult it is.[38]

On one level, all of this is just common sense. Who could disagree with the proposition that what students don't care about they're unlikely to learn very effectively?[39] (As some kids I know would say, "Well, duh!") On another level, to take this observation seriously is to call into question the current direction of school reform and the way a lot of parents talk. It suggests that "the most immediate and persisting issue for students and teachers is not low achievement, but student disengagement."[40] It suggests that if we're going to hold schools "accountable," it should be for something that standardized tests do not and cannot measure: the creation of an environment that supports and enhances students' interest in learning. It suggests that people who really care about educational excellence will make this their top priority: school boards or legislatures will center their reform efforts on making schools more engaging and relevant to students.

Right now, of course, the mission of most school boards and legislatures has nothing to do with interest. Or perhaps it would be more accurate to say that their policies, including efforts to raise test scores, are not explicitly addressed to the question of interest. In reality, they do have a major effect—in *undermining* student (and teacher) motivation and therefore making excellence less likely. To skip the question of interest and proceed directly to trying to boost achievement (or "raise the bar") is to kill the goose that laid the golden egg.

•

In response to any talk about the importance of interest, some heated objections can be anticipated. "Surely," some will insist, "you're not saying that the entire curriculum has to consist of things that kids would choose to do or would regard as fun. Surely you're not proposing that we erase the distinction between school and recess." Well, no. The point isn't to turn learning into a game. There's an important difference, as Dewey emphasized, between natural interest, which grows organically "out of some question with which the student is concerned," and artificial interest, where a topic has to be made appealing by sugarcoating it.[41] Dewey's point was not only that the latter fails to work in the long run, but that the perceived need to do this indicates a problem with the original assignment.

Still, is it realistic to expect all kids to have a natural interest in everything they're doing? To answer that question, we have to distinguish between short-term interest in a particular activity and more lasting interest in a larger topic. As you may expect, researchers have found that the latter is "apt to have more consistent and positive effects on academic performance."[42] While few students are likely to be excited about every single idea or every page of every book, that may not be as important as the attitude they take toward the broader projects of which these specific activities are a part. When teachers work with students to help them see the connection between a given task and the wider interests and questions that they brought into the classroom, the whole enterprise is more likely to be experienced as engaging (and therefore is more likely to be successful).

For students to become engaged, then, they have to experience the broad contours of the lessons as relevant. But that doesn't mean the lessons have to be limited to what they already know.[43] We might say that relevance, like knowledge itself, is constructed. However, it's constructed on the basis of how natural curiosity meets up with rich and important themes. The teacher doesn't tell students to do whatever they feel like or let them just stick to what they already know. He starts with where they are and invites them to move further. He presents new ideas, surprising facts, unfamiliar voices, in such a way that their interest swells beyond where it used to be and they want to know more. That takes real skill, but, as we'll see, it's not an unrealistic goal.

Finally, we have to understand the difference between interest and fun. When people frown and declare that education isn't always fun, that it takes work, they may be guilty of a kind of black-and-white oversimplification. They have accepted a dichotomy where the only possibilities are work and play: if you agree that kids shouldn't spend their days in school playing, well, that leaves work as the only option. In fact, though, there's a third alternative: learning. Here, the primary purpose isn't playlike enjoyment, although the process can be deeply satisfying, nor is it the worklike completion of error-free products, although the process can involve intense effort and concentration.

If you'll notice, never in this book do I refer to what students do in school as "work"; I talk about their "activities" or their "projects" or their "learning" but not about how their "work" can be improved or assessed. I resist this metaphor because it suggests that what children do in classrooms to figure things out is tantamount to what adults do in offices and factories to make money. But, again, this doesn't mean that children shouldn't be challenged and shouldn't try hard. It means that work isn't the only activity that can be pursued rigorously — and play, for that matter, isn't the only activity that can be experienced as pleasurable.[44]

The goal isn't to make work playful. The goal isn't even to make school fun. The goal is to create a learning experience that arouses and sustains children's curiosity, enriching their capacities and responding to their questions in ways that are deeply engaging. Even if such a classroom doesn't manage to get every student hooked on every activity, at least we have a better shot at a high-quality education when we think in these terms — that is, when we're attentive to how excellence follows from interest. The educators and parents who understand these things are likely to work to create (or support) schools that are profoundly nontraditional — and astonishingly effective.

# ≈ 8 ≈
# EDUCATION
# AT ITS BEST

## *Overhauling the Transmission Model*

ANYONE WHO has itemized what is wrong with our schools—and knows why these things are wrong—is already looking at a blueprint for change. By inverting the characteristics described in chapter 3, we create some broad recommendations for superior schools. Thus, in place of superficial facts, we emphasize deep understanding. In place of fragmentation, we seek to integrate; we bring together skills, topics, and disciplines in a meaningful context. In place of student passivity and isolation, we value learning that is both active and interactive.

If there is a unifying theme in all these prescriptions and a common characteristic of the very best classrooms, it is that *kids are taken seriously*. The educators (and parents) who do the most for children are those who honor, and work hard to find out, what children already know. They start where the student is and work from there. They try to figure out what students need and where their interests lie. Superb teachers strive constantly to imagine how things look from the child's point of view, what lies behind his questions and mistakes. All of this represents a decisive repudiation of the Old School, where, as Dewey observed, "the center of gravity is outside the child. It is in the teacher, the textbook, anywhere and everywhere you please except in the immediate instincts and activities of the child himself."[1]

But here we have to be careful. To talk about taking kids seriously—or setting up a "learner-centered" classroom—is not necessarily to be a hopeless Romantic who believes that children are all perfect little angels. It doesn't assume that children possess a pure natural wisdom and always know what's best, and, therefore, the adult's job is to get out of the way so students can educate themselves. Exactly this sort of caricature is drawn by many traditionalists in order to discredit their challengers. This conveniently sets up a false dichotomy where you, the reader, are asked to choose between touchy-feely, loosey-goosey, fluffy, fuzzy, undemanding progressive schooling based on leftover hippie idealism, on the one hand, and, on the other, an old-fashioned defense of academic excellence based on a courageous willingness to face unpleasant realities.

Hmmm. Tough choice. But this dichotomy is a ludicrous misrepresentation of the nontraditional position(s). While some people may call themselves "progressive" and advocate a completely laissez-faire approach to teaching, I've never met any. None of the theorists, researchers, or practitioners whose work I've drawn from in this book take such a position; indeed, the vast majority of educators who embrace such labels as progressive, learner-centered, constructivist, developmental, or holistic explicitly reject a sentimental image of children and a set-'em-loose model of schooling. As Dewey put it, "Nothing is more absurd than to suppose that there is no middle term between leaving a child to his own unguided fancies and likes, or controlling his activities by a formal succession of dictated directions."[2] Piaget's followers are equally critical of the Romantic sensibility attributed to them by traditionalists.[3] Indeed, that sensibility seems to show up only in conservative polemics, where it is kept alive as a way of making the Old School look attractive by contrast.

This strategy has succeeded in causing some schools and scholars to back away from a more humanistic approach to education, and that's a shame, because such an approach not only is justified in shifting the center of gravity back to the student but is based on a solid foundation of psychological theory and research. Much of that research turns on an observation offered earlier: humans by nature are meaning makers. I've tried to avoid educational jargon and technical terms in this book, but I have felt compelled to use—and now, to return to—the word "constructivism" because it refers to a school of thought that is central to creating optimal conditions for our children's learning.[4]

Constructivists argue that it is simply inaccurate to say—indeed, dangerous to assume—that people absorb information passively. We're not blank slates or empty containers. "The pupil's mind," wrote Alfred North Whitehead, "is not a box to be ruthlessly packed with alien ideas." Indeed, he suggested, an entire educational philosophy can be summed up in four words: "The students are alive."[5] More precisely, they—and we —come into every situation already holding a set of beliefs about the way the world works. Constructivism is derived from the recognition that knowledge is constructed rather than absorbed: we form beliefs, build theories, make order. We act on the environment rather than just responding to it—and we do it naturally and continually. It's part of who we are.[6] Learning isn't a matter of acquiring new information and storing it on top of the information we already have. It's a matter of coming across something unexpected, something that can't easily be explained by those theories we've already developed. To resolve that conflict, we have to change what we previously believed. We have to reorganize our way of understanding to accommodate the new reality we've just encountered.[7]

This is what happens when astronomers suddenly notice vast areas of empty space that shouldn't be there according to widely accepted theories about how the universe began. It is also what happened when my not-quite-two-year-old daughter's own astronomical assumption ("The moon comes out at night") ran smack into contrary empirical evidence: she spotted the moon one sunny afternoon and was forced to revise her theory. Many times, that sort of challenge to one's existing beliefs comes not out of a clear blue sky, so to speak, but from seeing or hearing someone else's very different impression or belief. A student reads a play and constructs a theory about what is going on (this character is being punished for his pathetic indecisiveness) — only to be confronted by a classmate who came up with a very different reading (this character is struggling bravely to deal with forces beyond his control). Thus, the source of intellectual growth is conflict: conflict between an old belief and a new experience, conflict between two beliefs that prove to be mutually exclusive, or conflict between your belief and mine. We make sense of things and then remake sense of things, and we do it from infancy to death.

Permit me to emphasize again: this theory I've been describing is no fad. Not only educational theorists but "virtually all" cognitive researchers today "[sub]scribe to this constructive view of learning and knowledge."[8] And it is a view with powerful practical implications.[9] Because different ways of teaching will be more or less successful at taking account of how learning actually happens, some ways are more likely than others to lead to learning that is impressive and enduring. Our job is to understand and support these approaches.

## Making Trouble for Students

What can teachers do that's consistent with what is known about how students learn? Not surprisingly, they can begin by curbing the practices based on a transmission view of learning, such as simply telling students what is true or how to do things. However, as I've been at pains to point out, this doesn't mean they must sit back and wait for ideas to pop into the kids' heads. Progressive teachers are at least as active as their traditional colleagues, but they are active in different, more challenging ways. Indeed, it takes a lot more skill to help children think for themselves than it does just to give them information.

A first-grade teacher in Massachusetts[10] shoves aside all the classroom furniture and uses masking tape to outline a large boat on the floor. Its the *Mayflower,* she tells the children — the very ship we've been learning about. She hands a piece of paper to a student named Zeb and says it's a message that the king has given him to deliver to the class. Zeb reads aloud that the ship can't sail until we tell the king how big it is. "What should we do?" the teacher asks. "Who has an idea?" After some false starts and some painful silences, a boy named Tom volunteers that it can't be three feet because he knows (having just been measured by the nurse) that he is four feet and the boat looks bigger than he is. Other children now join in, one suggesting that they find out how many times Tom can fit in the boat. It turns out the boat is four Toms long. Problem solved!

But wait a minute, says the teacher. How will the king know what that means? After all, he's never met Tom. She waits for someone to remember that Tom is four feet tall. No one does. Instead, Mark suggests that the boat can be measured with hands. He does this several times (rather sloppily) and gets a different answer each time. After more discussion, the class realizes you have to start right at the end of the boat and then make sure there's no space between your hands when you put them down. Finally Mark concludes to everyone's satisfaction that the boat is thirty-six hands long. Done!

Well, just to be sure, says the teacher, let's have Sue (the smallest child in the class) measure it again. Oh, no! Now the boat is forty-four hands long! Confusion and animated discussion follow. The children realize that all hands on deck are not of equal length. By the time someone proposes using people's feet instead, time has run out. But the teacher has them return to the problem the following day. One child now remembers that the king knows Zeb and argues that the boat can therefore be measured in multiples of Zeb's foot. The class is so excited by this that they decide to use Zeb to measure everything in the room, and the teacher lets them. It isn't until the next day, returning to the topic yet again, that she begins to make the lesson explicit for them. She invites the children to think about the importance of a standard form of measurement. And only after that does she finally introduce them to the use of rulers.

Consider what the teacher does here. First, she poses a problem specifically designed to pull the kids in, making sure it won't be too hard or too easy for most of them. Then she guides their discussion without controlling it. (That alone distinguishes her from the vast majority of our children's teachers.) She doesn't correct their mistakes—and, equally important, she doesn't single out certain ideas for praise. Rather, as an expert on math instruction describes it,

> she listens and watches. And only when the children seem satisfied with a solution does she put a further question, leading them to yet another problem, their own problem, which they feel compelled to resolve. As she sees it, her task is to pose questions that will lead *through*—rather than around—puzzlement to the construction of important mathematical concepts. [Such teaching] cannot be scripted; rather, it depends on one's capacity to respond spontaneously to students' perplexities and discoveries.[11]

Some would call this teacher a "facilitator" of learning, but she doesn't facilitate "in the sense of 'making smooth or easy'"; rather, she stimulates learning "by making problems more complex, involving, and arousing."[12] She artfully complicates the situation, challenging the children to think harder and better. She sees the wisdom of " 'throwing a monkey wrench' instead of reinforcing the right answer," in Eleanor Duckworth's words. That may seem a little perverse, but it is precisely the teacher's desire "to be sure that students understand" that explains why she "remains noncommittal, resists early acceptance of a student's understanding, and searches for any soft spots that require more thinking."[13]

The lesson is hands-on—they're doing something rather than just sitting still—but it's not the typical hands-on lesson in which a teacher might, for example, have everyone measure things with rulers after she shows them how it's supposed to be done. Instead, whether or not they're aware of it, the children are grappling with the *idea* of a ruler. More: they're *inventing* the idea of a ruler. They're becoming real mathematicians without using textbooks and worksheets—indeed, one could argue, they're thinking *because* they're not using textbooks and worksheets.

Notice several other characteristics of this lesson. First, it's leisurely: the class is free to take its time with the problem, to explore it and return to it over a period of several days rather than rushing on to the next topic. Second, it's collaborative: students aren't doing solitary seatwork. Too much would be lost by depriving them of one another's ideas and disagreements. Third, it's interdisciplinary: this mathematical problem flows quite naturally from the larger social studies project on the *Mayflower* (which, in turn, probably provides extended practice in reading and writing as well).

These features are routinely used by all great teachers, regardless of the subject matter or the age of their students.[14] Such teachers see their job as providing the conditions for learning. They devise challenges and, if necessary, help illuminate for students what's interesting about those challenges. Sometimes they offer guidance and criticism, directions and suggestions—and sometimes they keep their mouths shut. They might reflect back to a student what she said, subtly reframing her idea when necessary, using different words to bring out the underlying issues. Rather than being the source of most ideas, teachers serve as "mediators," standing between the students and the idea. They offer what is needed for kids to take charge of their own learning, sometimes helping them along, offering temporary support (a strategy known as "scaffolding")[15] until the students get it. And they aren't afraid to leave some questions unanswered, some explorations unfinished, because, well, that's how life is.[16]

Again, to teach like this requires a sharp reduction in direct instruction —that is, the traditional practice of delivering information to students by giving lectures or showing them how to do a problem. An Oregon teacher in her fifties once summarized her professional growth to me in one short sentence: "The longer I teach, the less I talk." She'd come to realize that only by making sure she didn't monopolize the classroom was there a real chance for her students to talk—and therefore to learn. Given how much silence (that is, students' silence) is valued in the Old School, that last idea may be counterintuitive, but, as a British educator explained, "Talking is not merely a way of conveying existing ideas to others; it is also a way by which we explore ideas, clarify them and make them our own."[17] Every minute a teacher is doing the talking is a minute this isn't happening.

Still, that doesn't mean the teacher is completely silent. I believe there is room for some direct instruction; the amount will depend on several factors. The first variable is age: while high school or college students shouldn't have to spend whole periods listening to lectures, there should be even less lecturing to younger children—a few minutes here and there at most.

Second, the kind of knowledge is relevant. If the lesson involves logical thinking and requires students to understand ideas, then telling won't do. But on those occasions when the teacher just wants students to know some arbitrary convention, such as how to address an envelope, where to put a footnote, or the fact that September has thirty days, then it's less objectionable for the information to be given to them.[18] (Even here, though, the burden of proof should be on the teacher to show that students can't, or for some reason shouldn't, find these things out them-selves.)[19]

Finally, even when direct instruction seems appropriate, the timing is important. Usually it should occur after students have had the chance to explore, to observe at first hand, to talk and experiment and try things out. Had that first-grade teacher given the children a didactic lesson about measurement at the beginning, she would have preempted those lively exchanges and precluded much of their thinking. The teacher ties things together, makes things explicit, gives things names, checks for understanding. What she sees herself doing has implications for when she does it.

## Beyond the Right Answer

Some years ago I saw a sign posted in a classroom that said MISTAKES ARE OUR FRIENDS. I interpreted this to mean that the teacher didn't want students to feel bad about themselves when they got things wrong. Only later did I realize it was more complicated than that. This teacher understood the limits of a right-answer-oriented education. She realized not only that mistakes are an inevitable part of learning, but that learning could be described as the process of coming to make more sophisticated kinds of mistakes. Moreover, confusion drives us to understand more deeply. "You master the idea much more thoroughly if you have considered alternatives, tried to work it out in areas where it didn't work, and figured out why it was that it didn't work," says Eleanor Duckworth.[20] Teachers who want to encourage intellectual growth give students time to be confused and create a climate where it's perfectly acceptable to fall on your face.

This message can be sent in different ways. First, while students are trying to figure things out, the teacher will usually hold back rather than jumping in to correct them, mindful that "productive discussions often spring from misguided notions."[21] (Eventually the teacher will see to it that blatant errors are corrected — by the student herself, by a peer, or, if necessary, by the teacher.)[22] Second, a teacher required to give traditional grades will make sure that students have the chance to bring up those grades, if only to make it clear that "errors are part of the learning process and not indicative of failure to learn."[23] Finally, a teacher who isn't sure how to help students overcome their fear of being wrong (which they've often acquired in traditional classrooms) can simply ask them what they think would make mistakes seem less scary. As a rule, the best teachers have learned that the answer to any number of instructional challenges is to consult the students themselves.

A classroom where mistakes are "our friends" isn't a place where anything goes or accuracy doesn't count. It's a place that has transcended a behaviorist model of learning and, consequently, a place where students feel safe, take chances, and ultimately can learn more successfully. "Good schools promote displays of incompetence (strange as that may sound) in order to help students find their way to competence," in the words of Ted Sizer, who founded the Coalition of Essential Schools.[24]

But we can go even further. Mistakes typically aren't random: they reflect a particular way of (mis)understanding and thus provide a teacher with priceless information about what and how the student is thinking. To correct students promptly, or even to overvalue being right, is to lose access to that information. So we could say that great teachers don't talk very much for two reasons: to maximize student talking but also to maximize teacher listening. Like the reassuring sign on the wall about mistakes, a posture of caring and genuine interest in what students are thinking isn't just a matter of being friendly. It's a matter of being an effective educator. The teacher's explicit use of questions ("Why do you think that happened?" "What led you to say that?") is matched by a tone, a demeanor, a classroom culture, that invites students to reflect on and explain how they are making sense of things. Only when the teacher has a feel for that can he help kids make better sense of things.

Thus, if a child announces that four plus five equals ten, the teacher doesn't have to say "Wrong!" or "Ooh, you're close; try again" (a nicer way of saying "Wrong!"). Sarcastic claims by traditionalists notwithstanding, that doesn't mean the teacher is obliged to say "OK, sure, honey, if that's a valid answer for you, we'll say it's ten." Not at all. The teacher might simply ask, "How'd you get ten?" Alternatively, he could ask, "Did anyone else get a different answer? Let's talk about it." What's more, both of these responses are just as appropriate when a child announces that four plus five equals nine. It may be even more important to help students reflect on — and therefore allow the teacher to understand — how they got the *right* answer.

One day a teacher in Michigan,[25] struggling to make sense of and apply these ideas, asked her third-grade class how many legs an insect has, and a boy promptly replied that it might have "eight or ten or fifteen." The teacher's impulse was just to correct him, but she decided it might be useful to "get a feeling for what he was thinking." She asked if he could give her an example. He mentioned caterpillars, and this opened up a class discussion that suggested other students would have answered the same way. A long conversation ensued about adult insects versus larvae and about the possibility of mutations (since, in fact, all insects don't have six legs). Because the teacher asked a question rather than making a statement, this conversation was able to happen. She reflected later that this conversation also gave her alternative "ways of assessing what they know," which is one reason (among many) that great teachers don't need to give a lot of tests.

Someone once said that a student who gives a wrong answer actually may be answering another question. The teacher's job is to find out what that question is.[26] More broadly, his job is to see things from the student's point of view, to get in the habit of imagining how an idea or assignment is likely to appear to children of this particular age. How can you help students understand fractions without having a sense of how odd it is to see, for the first time, one number sitting on top of another? A terrific teacher even tries to understand how that concept will be understood differently by Sasha than by Sam, based on what she knows of how each has made sense of other math concepts.

Beyond trying to learn what students don't understand in order to help them, it's also true that teachers whose first instinct is to listen also learn how much their students already do know. I once heard an educator from Maine quote a colleague as follows: "My kids know all about my creativity in the classroom, and I just realized I know very little about theirs." A math teacher who shows students exactly what to do, then grades them on how well they imitate her, may have no idea how inventive even very young children can be in solving problems. Similarly, when one reading teacher stopped dominating discussions and transmitting facts, even some of the quiet kids began to speak up. "I was absolutely amazed by some of the responses," she reported. "The level of discussion was so high. . . . I could see thinking going on I had never seen before."[27]

To take a backseat sometimes, instead of always being the one with the answers, is to present oneself as a fellow learner—someone who is perpetually curious and, like the students, often at a loss. Such a teacher distinguishes herself from her colleagues who act like trial attorneys, never asking a question to which they don't already know the answer. Indeed, she may deliberately do things she's "no good at . . . so they can see [her] struggling."[28] That sort of deliberate vulnerability requires courage. It's as hard to be a real person in front of kids as it is to treat kids like people. That's why so many teachers, for example, wouldn't dream of letting children call them by their first names. They say it's about respect, but often it's really about their need for distance and protection. (If a teacher requires the formality of a surname to feel respected, something is very wrong.)

More generally, and more important than the name by which he's known, the kind of teacher who creates a formal environment in which he has all the power and is the source of all the knowledge is likely to be secretly ridiculed and ultimately ignored. I've come to believe that this aspect of traditional classrooms—formality—helps to explain why those classrooms are so unsuccessful. Similarly, I've noticed from visiting countless classrooms that the teachers who excel in all the other respects described in this chapter also tend to be the ones who talk with students in an open way, not all that differently from the way they talk to adults. The atmosphere in their classrooms is loose, relaxed, friendly, often jocular. "The more informal the learning environment, the greater the teacher's access to the learners' representations, understandings, and misunderstandings."[29]

It's not that such a teacher isn't—or doesn't want to be—respected; it's not that he's pretending to be one of the kids. Paradoxically, he's more likely to be respected (as opposed to merely feared), and the learning is most likely to be serious, in the kind of place where the teacher says, "Oh, wait a minute, you guys. I almost forgot. How are you doing with those chapters you're writing in the style of a famous author?" Even students with a reputation for being troublemakers in traditional classrooms often respond to this climate, no longer feeling the need to take a stand against an authority figure.

To some extent, the degree of formality reflects the personality of the teacher. For that matter, the whole package I've been describing says something about individual attitudes. But it's important to realize that attitudes and techniques can result from pressures that originate outside schools and from the structure *of* schools. For example, small classes—and large blocks of time in them—are vital so teachers can learn what students know. No wonder the best teaching is so rare at the high school level: how easy can it be for a teacher who has 120, 150, or even more students over the course of a day—and who has them for only forty-five or fifty minutes at a time—to do what I'm describing here?[30]

Bad teaching doesn't just happen. It's practically demanded by systemic factors. If students are under pressure to beat their classmates for some artificially scarce recognition, it's going to be hard for the teacher to figure out how their minds work; they'll be throwing her off by trying to impress her with how smart they are. If parents insist on the familiar sight of a teacher in front of the class presenting a conventional lesson, it's going to be hard for the teacher to grow past that model. If a very specific curriculum is imposed on teachers, with rigid requirements for what children must know at each grade level, teachers are going to be permanently set on Play rather than Record. If we allow our legislators and school boards to make schools "accountable" for producing higher standardized test scores, you can bet our children will receive an education completely out of step with the best thinking about how people learn.

## *Deep Thinking*

Consider the following fraction problem: Which is larger, $\frac{4}{11}$ or $\frac{5}{13}$? This is a question I routinely pose to parents and teachers, and very few of them (especially the math teachers) get it right because very few of them think about curriculum content from the student's point of view.

The correct answer is: Who cares?

To forget that this is the correct answer—and indeed, that it's the answer to more questions than we can count—is to leave students out of the picture, to persist in teaching bare facts that don't matter to them and therefore may not be learned by them. This, in turn, practically guarantees that schooling will continue to be experienced as an exercise in futility for all concerned. That fact is not altered just because you may happen to believe that kids ought to know which fraction is larger.

However, as I hope is clear by now, this doesn't mean we should excise fractions from the curriculum. It means we should teach them differently. In describing the role and style of effective teachers—posing problems, asking questions, welcoming mistakes, and so on—I've already offered some details of effective nontraditional instruction. What follows is a closer look at some ideas for changing the fundamentals of instruction— and thereby increasing the chances that our children will become successful learners.

•

Deborah Meier and her colleagues, who founded the highly regarded Central Park East schools in New York City, have anchored their teaching in what they call five "habits of mind." They contend that the study of virtually any topic in any discipline will benefit from raising questions about *evidence* ("How do we know what we know?"), *point of view* ("Whose perspective does this represent?"), *connections* ("How is this related to that?"), *supposition* ("How might things have been otherwise?"), and *relevance* ("Why is this important?").[31] The last of these, nominated by Meier as the one that matters most, recalls the response "Who cares?" It is both a stimulus for adults to think about what matters enough to teach[32] and an organizing principle for thinking (with students) about how to teach it.

To develop these habits of mind is to spend a fair amount of time in conversation and, inevitably, in disagreement with other people. The constructivist premise that learning is based on conflict meshes nicely with the idea that the best classrooms are those where people argue a lot. Of course, they argue in a way that's friendly rather than nasty, the point being to figure things out together rather than to win a debate. We're not talking about picking fights here but about stimulating minds.

A clash of ideas is inevitable when subjects are complex and controversial, and those are the subjects that ought to occupy our children in school most of the time. If a fact isn't controversial ($\frac{5}{13}$ is indisputably greater than $\frac{4}{11}$), it can be made controversial: How do we know that? Are some ways of finding out better than others? Students have to be given tasks that require interpretation and involve uncertainty, the kind where you can't always specify how to do something and you don't always end up with a tidy solution. Thinking is messy, and deep thinking is really messy. Traditional education, by contrast, is nothing if not orderly.

In practice, this means that the sort of activities regarded as "enrichments" (and typically reserved for the elite students) ought to constitute the bulk of the curriculum for everyone. For example, students can be invited to think about and discuss why dinosaurs became extinct, a question that will likely require them to acquire—and give them a reason to acquire—a fair amount of knowledge about how dinosaurs looked, when they lived, and what they ate. (If a unit on dinosaurs is *limited to* how they looked, when they lived, and what they ate, our children are being shortchanged.) Similarly, instead of memorizing a list of battles, students can be asked to put the Civil War in its historical context and to plumb its human costs. Perhaps each of them could take on a different role (physician, journalist, undertaker, economist, uniform manufacturer, child of a soldier) and evaluate the significance of what happened from that person's point of view. They can invent an imaginary soldier's diary, write a newspaper editorial on whether Lincoln should have just let the South secede, or prepare a speech for a conference of historians arguing for a novel parallel between the U.S. Civil War and a crisis presently taking place somewhere else in the world.

Such explorations take the place of (or swallow up) fact-based lessons, but because a fair amount of time is required, they also represent an alternative to another style of teaching mentioned in chapter 3: skimming the surface of too many things. Ted Sizer has offered a three-word slogan for a revolution in high school teaching: "Less is more."[33] (This is also the watchword for some of the best theory and practice in early childhood education.)[34] As a thought experiment, Howard Gardner likes to invite teachers to pretend they've been given only one hour with students to do something on the subject of an entire course they teach. Figure out what you would do in that single hour, he says, and then do that all year.[35] Carve off a small chunk of content and teach it thoughtfully, deliberately, deeply, presenting it from different angles. I witnessed that sensibility one morning when I visited a geometry class in Massachusetts and found to my surprise that the teacher was allowing students to spend a full class period arguing about the definition of a pyramid. As Steven Zemelman and his colleagues have remarked, "Covering less in more depth not only ensures better understanding, but increases the likelihood that students will pursue further inquiry of their own at later times."[36]

Covering less in more depth, however, is only the first step toward better education. Ultimately, we want to call into question the whole idea of a curriculum to be "covered" and to think instead about ideas to be discovered. If learning is a function of making one's own meanings and reorganizing one's own theories in response to an encounter with new ideas, then we need to maximize the impact of that encounter. As much as possible, students ought to discover things directly rather than just reading or hearing about them. They ought to explore, do, see — and reflect on what they've explored, done, and seen. This means changing what goes on in classrooms, and it means providing plenty of opportunities for students to get out of the classroom and into the community. Gardner argues that schools should incorporate the best of two models of learning: a museum, which encourages open-ended exploration, and an apprenticeship, which provides a more structured environment for practicing meaningful skills in an authentic, real-life context.[37]

The common element is giving students a chance to *do*. If you want them to learn about the conduction of heat, ask them to design a restaurant take-out container that will keep a customer's dinner hot.[38] If you want them to learn the geography of an area (and why it matters), ask them to find the major cities "on a map that contains physical features and natural resources but no place names."[39] If you want them to understand how a story is structured, invite them to dissect an episode of their favorite TV situation comedy, paying attention to the way problems are introduced and resolved — and then to write their own scripts.

In a fifth-grade social studies class in Seattle,[40] I watched as the children studied colonial Boston — by recreating colonial Boston. They built miniatures of period houses and invented period characters (specifying their ages, occupations, and Loyalist or Patriot sympathies). Then, over a number of weeks, they assumed those identities to discuss actual historical events. One day, for example, they debated whether the Boston Tea Party was morally justified, meeting with their "families" to hammer out a position, then writing a letter to a friend explaining their decision. (The teacher used these letters to get a sense of how well each student understood what was going on.)

To promote discovery, some teachers focus on the importance of careful observation, which is central to becoming a good scientist, a good thinker, or a good writer. They might tell students to light a candle and watch it vigilantly, writing down everything they see. They might have students surreptitiously record everything they notice about a friend's (or parent's) style of nonverbal communication. They might send students to a city street or a mall and ask them to notice what's impressive and what's frustrating about the way the area was designed—or to say as much as they can about the place based only on what can be heard and smelled.

Discovery learning usually entails hands-on activity, but as we saw in the distinction between using a ruler and inventing a ruler, it is also more than that. I once dropped in on a sixth-grade class in Illinois where the "hands-on" lesson consisted of gluing cotton balls on pieces of paper to represent various cloud types, whose names the students had to memorize. Completely absent were all of the ingredients that give active learning its power: the discovery of something new, a challenge to existing beliefs, interaction with other students, and sustained reflection. Similarly, it's one thing for a class to keep a garden; it's something else for the garden to prompt systematic thinking about cause and effect ("Why do you suppose these bean plants are so scrawny?") or an exploration of the plight of the American family farm.

An administrator in Florida once gave me a marvelous example of how a conventional activity can be transformed into something truly worthwhile. Visiting a middle school[41] one day, she noticed that the students were lugging around mock infants (weighted dolls) wherever they went, this being a fairly standard way of trying to convey to adolescents a sense of the responsibility entailed by parenthood. "Hey, how's your baby?" she called out cheerfully to one boy, only to be caught off guard when he replied, "Not so good. He has meningitis." Certain babies, it turned out, had been randomly designated as having a medical problem (ranging from lactose intolerance to spina bifida), and the students were obliged to research the causes and treatment, as well as to figure out how to stay within a budget for child care.

# Starting with a Question

To take children seriously is to value them for who they are right now rather than seeing them as adults-in-the-making. Thus, what we ask them to do should have "horizontal relevance," to borrow the phrase of the early childhood specialist Lilian Katz. It ought to be "meaningful to them at the time" — for example, related to something that could happen on the way home from school. Mere "vertical relevance" isn't enough: there's reason to be concerned if the only justification for learning something is that students will need to know it later — for example, as part of the following year's curriculum.[42]

On what basis, then, is (horizontal) relevance constructed and a curriculum designed? The trick is to *start not with facts to be taught or disciplines to be mastered, but with questions to be answered.* That may sound straightforward, but it's actually quite rare for learning to be organized around questions. In fact, it's even rare for classroom questions to reflect a commitment to real learning. What we find instead are those fact-based questions that Old School teachers are so fond of putting to the class: "Who can tell me . . . ?" — or the practice of "guiding children to answers by [asking] carefully chosen leading questions," which isn't much different "from just telling them the answers in the first place."[43]

No, we're talking here about questions that matter, questions that students sincerely wonder about or at least those that teachers believe students will wonder about once they're posed. These are the questions that can drive exploration and learning. Sometimes they come up naturally, and the teacher's job is to take advantage of such situations.

- In a New Jersey kindergarten,[44] recent floods in the bathroom provided the impetus for helping children think scientifically about where the water was coming from and what could be done about it.
- In a school in Illinois[45] where noisy construction was taking place right outside the window of a third-grade class, a potential headache was transformed into a learning opportunity: students watched the building to figure out what was going on at each stage, took notes in their journals, and discussed what they'd seen as well as the best words for describing it.
- In a combination first- through third-grade class in Virginia, the teacher[46] was always alert for "teachable moments" that might yield interesting questions. One day a girl brought in a small motor she had built from a kit. She attached a circular disk to the shaft and

made it spin. Before she could attach an oval disk, though, the teacher stopped her and created a little suspense, asking the class to predict what it would look like when the motor was turned back on. The question was intriguing because the answer wasn't obvious.

- Another elementary school teacher deliberately left the walls bare on the first day of school so the children could figure out together how they wanted *their* classroom to look. (It took her several summers to work up the nerve to do this.) They decided, among other things, to put up blue construction paper on one wall, which would be reserved for their own papers and projects as the year progressed. But participation can be habit-forming: having been consulted about the use of the wall, the kids wanted to do the decorating themselves. They quickly discovered that the construction paper wouldn't look nice unless it had been carefully measured. To measure it, however, they needed to know something about fractions. The teacher obliged for what may have been the most efficient fraction lesson in history.

In this last example, we have a satisfactory answer to the question "Who cares whether one fraction is bigger than another?" We care, say the children. The question is answered, not because it appears in a textbook or the teacher's lesson plan or a state standards document, but because it's directly related to something that matters to them. And even when there is no bulletin board to be decorated, the same question can arise when kids express curiosity about how fast they're growing or the fairest way to divide a pizza. Great teachers are always looking out for real-life opportunities to help students play with words, reason with numbers, and think systematically in general.

The questions that drive learning come in many varieties. Some can be answered fairly quickly; others will take a long time and, in fact, may never be completely resolved. The broader questions in particular should be open-ended enough to be challenging while still being focused.[47] The learning inheres not so much in the answers but in the process of figuring out how to ask the questions better—and how to track down the answers. As students investigate, they acquire information and come to understand important ideas more fully. The answers they devise may suggest new questions, and the learning spirals upward.

Imagine, for example, the intellectual benefits of trying to answer questions such as "Why were the Founding Fathers so afraid of democracy?" or "How could you improve the human hand?"[48] Answering questions on this scale becomes, quite literally, a real project. Back in 1918, William Kilpatrick wrote a famous article laying out what he called the "project method": a curriculum based on "wholehearted purposeful activity proceeding in a social environment . . . the essential factor [being] the presence of a dominating purpose."[49]

In progressive classrooms, that kind of learning is alive and well today, offering a model for what all our children should have the chance to do. In a fifth-grade class near Chicago, for example, one hour every morning is devoted to individual or team projects and another hour every afternoon is set aside for class exploration. The teacher describes the scene:

> Walk into our classroom during project time, and you might see children sprawled on the rug taking notes from books on the habitats of beavers or on medieval life, or two students across the room watching a videotape on Jane Goodall, or others conducting tests on the aerodynamics of paper airplanes. Go to the library down the hall (past students rehearsing a play they have written), and you might find members of the other half of the class conducting research on virtual reality or the history of Halloween. If you then go to the computer lab, you'll see, for example, one student inputting survey data while another learns to write a new computer language. In short, you never know what you might experience next, or, most important, what the students might experience next. . . . Discipline problems are minimal because students are interested in what they are doing—they see their pursuits as having *purpose*.[50]

The project approach to learning has been pursued by different educators working quite independently. Extended projects that take students out of the classroom to study the environment are among those supported by a group called the Autodesk Foundation, which sponsors conferences and publications on this approach to learning.[51] Meanwhile, Lilian Katz and Sylvia Chard have revolutionized preschool education by rejecting the two dominant models for very young children: fun and games that fail to engage the mind, on the one hand, and drill and practice to learn isolated skills such as letters, numbers, and colors, on the other. Typically they either spend their time "making individual macaroni collages" or they're put to work to satisfy "our quick-fix academic fervor."[52] The third alternative consists of creating extended studies of rich themes, such as babies or hospitals or the weather.[53] The children may spend a month learning about such a topic, visiting, drawing, discussing, thinking.

A remarkably similar approach to learning has been developed at the other end of the educational continuum. The idea of "problem-based learning," involving the extended investigation of realistic questions, began at the medical school of McMaster University in the 1960s. The idea was to teach future physicians by inviting them to seek out and apply information to solve clinical problems rather than by filling students with masses of facts that they were expected to integrate and apply some time down the line.*

This idea of using skills in a realistic context offers a refreshing alternative to the conventional high school or middle school curriculum, too. In one eighth-grade class, for example, students are designated as official "inspectors," charged with reviewing a staged drunk driving accident: they interview witnesses, visit the scene of the crash, review the medical reports, and ultimately make a recommendation to the state's attorney's office. Solving this problem requires them to distinguish between fact and opinion, to perform lab experiments to determine blood alcohol levels and reaction times, to calculate the speed of the cars, and finally to draft a report.[54]

Whether it's called "problem-" or "project-based" or "Group Investigation"[55] — or something else entirely — this approach to learning isn't a matter of gluing an occasional activity onto the regular curriculum. It replaces the regular curriculum, turns it inside out, incorporates facts and skills in the service of doing something that is as real and practical as it is intellectual and scholarly. Typically, the project leads to a real product or a presentation for a real audience.[56]

The point is that the learning has a point. By contrast, as Kilpatrick remarked long ago, the kind of instruction that consists of "an unending round of set tasks in conscious disregard of the element of dominant purpose in those who perform the tasks" tends to produce students who "at the close of a course decisively shut the book and say, 'Thank gracious, I am through with that!' How many people 'get an education' and yet hate books and hate to think?"[57] There may be no more powerful argument for project-based learning.

Notice that such projects almost inevitably involve learning across the disciplines — providing another crisp counterpoint to traditional instruction, which takes place in separate fields and rarely bothers to help students connect what they have been taught in each one. Slightly better are

---

* Ironically, traditionalists sometimes cite the example of how many facts doctors must know as a way of justifying a back-to-basics model. The reality is quite different: medical education, like other kinds, is at its best when it starts with the big picture, when it is experiential, holistic, thematic, question-driven — in a word, progressive. This has become increasingly clear to me not only as a reader of research but as the husband of a physician whose medical training I followed with some dismay.

belated efforts to combine the facts that were presented in the separate disciplines,[58] although this practice is ultimately as contrived as teaching skills in a vacuum and then injecting them back into meaningful problems.[59] If we do it right and start with the questions, students will become more competent at a range of things that can be classified as math, science, foreign languages, art, reading, and so on. "Understanding . . . does not have to be tied to the basic nature of the discipline," says Nel Noddings. "Rather, it is properly defined with respect to legitimate purposes, capacities, and interests."[60]

Figuring out what led to a car crash is one example of how the best learning is interdisciplinary. Another example began at the daily meeting of a school in southern Vermont[61] where third- through eighth-grade students get together to share news and solve problems. One morning, a ten-year-old girl from Mexico told everyone that she was very concerned about a recent earthquake in Guatemala. She held up a newspaper photo of a child caught in the rubble of his house and wanted to know what could be done to help him. The room immediately filled with questions. The children asked where Guatemala is, how many people live there, why they didn't leave before the earthquake, whether they were already being helped. Besides, they wanted to know, what causes earthquakes? Can they happen here? The teachers made a list of their questions and began organizing what turned out to be a two-month project that spanned reading and writing, English and Spanish, the natural sciences and the social sciences. In the midst of graphing earthquake intensities, the children also managed to collect money for the victims and "adopt" a Guatemalan boy.

Less spontaneous but no less engaging is a model developed for middle schools by James Beane, a pioneer in "curriculum integration," and his wife, Barbara Brodhagen. At the beginning of the year, students are asked to list all the questions they have about themselves (How long will I live? Will I be like my parents?), after which they meet in groups to share their individual lists and look for areas of overlap. Then they repeat the process for questions they have about the world (Why do people hate each other? How did religions evolve?), again listing them individually before finding areas in common. Next they're asked as teams to compare the two sets of topics to see where *they* overlap. Finally, as a whole class, the students try to reach consensus on the broad areas of concern they seem to have in common — and, with the teacher's help, design units of study to answer their questions. These investigations, on themes such as "Living in the Future" or "Conflicts and Violence," form the basis of the entire year's course of study, requiring the students to draw as necessary from (and weave together) virtually all the conventional disciplines. Experience with this method suggests that teenagers become highly motivated scholars because the curriculum is centered "on life itself rather than on the mastery of fragmented information within the boundaries of subject areas."[62]

## Decision-Making in the Classroom

When someone finally gets around to compiling a list of the ten most astonishing discoveries about education, here is one finding that won't be on it: students learn most avidly and have their best ideas when they get to choose which questions to explore. In fact, this proposition follows rather predictably from another unsurprising fact: all of us tend to be happiest and most effective when we have some say about what we are doing. If we are instead just told what to do (or, in the case of schooling, deprived of any opportunity to make decisions about what we're learning), achievement tends to drop — right along with any excitement about what we're doing.[63]

The more obvious this idea seems, the more remarkable it is that people are systematically denied the chance to make decisions about what affects them in real schools, real families, and real workplaces. Perhaps no other principle in our society is at once so commonly endorsed and so rarely applied as the value of democratic participation. Some years ago, a group of teachers from Florida traveled to what was then the USSR to exchange information and ideas with their Russian-speaking counterparts. What the Soviet teachers most wanted from their guests was guidance on setting up and running democratic schools. Their questions were based on the assumption that a country like the United States, so committed to the idea of democracy, surely must involve children in decision-making processes from their earliest years. The irony is enough to make us wince. As one survey after another has confirmed, students are rarely invited to become active participants in their own education, whether they are in kindergarten or college.[64] Indeed, the story of American schools is — and always has been — the story of doing things *to* students rather than working *with* them.

The opposite of being controlled is to be able to make decisions, to have one's voice heard. This goes well beyond conventional opportunities to choose, in which each individual selects one option from a menu: which book (from a prepared list) to write a report on, which (elective) course to take in high school or college, which activity to pursue during a narrow block of free time. Mind you, such choices are fine as far as they go; school would be a lot better if kids had more to say about what they read and what they write about or even where to sit (or stretch out) while they are doing it.

But this kind of choosing is limited, to begin with, by the quality of their options. Whenever I see children being invited to complete "any five problems" on a worksheet—or to pick a country, any country, and then go to the library and collect some facts about it—I think of Shakespeare's observation that "there's small choice in rotten apples."[65] And even when the options are more valuable, authentic decision-making consists of being able to *generate* the possibilities rather than just choosing among those provided by someone else. Nor does choice always have to be an individual matter: the benefits are multiplied if students can come together to decide. They learn to listen, to consider others' points of view, to argue carefully, to anticipate problems and work things out.

Bringing kids in on the process of designing their own education is particularly terrifying to the staunch defenders of traditional education, whose tightly regulated classroom procedures represent the polar opposite of something messy, something unpredictable—something, well, democratic. Nevertheless, it is breathtaking to be part of, or even to watch, a classroom where students have some control over what happens, where their questions and concerns help to shape the course of study, where they help to decide what they're doing, and when, and where, and how, and with whom, and why[66]—as well as how their progress will be assessed when they're done. Why, when you stop and think about it, should a teacher unilaterally determine all these things and impose them on the students? Children learn to make good decisions by making decisions, not by following directions. Besides, this model represents the ultimate in taking kids seriously, putting them at the center, helping to generate the interest that fuels excellence.

Of course, the extent to which students make these choices (individually or collectively, on their own or with the teacher) will vary depending on their age and on certain nonnegotiable requirements.[67] It's not all or nothing. One first-grade teacher in Ohio speaks in relative terms, challenging herself to be "as democratic as I can stand to be"[68]—a good motto, as long as the teacher pushes herself to be able to stand more with each passing year. Once again, the teacher continues to play a vital role in such a classroom. But the rule of thumb is that the more students' questions and decisions drive the lesson, the more likely that real learning will take place. That's why the best teachers constantly ask themselves, "Is this a decision I have to make by myself or can the students be involved?"

What does all this look like in practice? We've already seen Beane and

Brodhagen's process, a far-reaching attempt to design a curriculum around the issues that concern students. But even teachers who introduce more conventional units in the separate disciplines can involve students. Consider a sixth-grade teacher in Texas[69] who had to teach a unit on atoms and molecules. He didn't ask the students whether they wanted to learn about the whole topic, but he did introduce it by inviting them to look through books on the subject and list the questions about atoms and molecules that occurred to them. The students then came together to construct a master list, sorting the questions by category and deciding which ones they most wanted answered. The whole lesson took off from there, even though some of the questions were so tough that outside resources had to be brought in to answer them. When it was time for the teacher to evaluate the students' learning, he had them answer the questions they themselves had posed earlier.

Whether launching a study of Shakespeare or sharks or the stock market, some teachers routinely begin by checking in with students. One popular format is to ask students what they already think they know about the topic, listing their answers on a blackboard or flip chart. Then they may be asked what they want to find out, followed by how they can do so. Afterward, the teacher talks with them about what they ended up learning.[70] This framework exemplifies what I like to call a "sandwich" model of teaching, in which anything to be learned is nestled between a discussion of what we are about to do and reflection about what we just did.[71]

Even when students aren't allowed to choose what to study, they can decide how to study it and how to frame the relevant questions. Imagine a continuum of student involvement with respect to a unit about the colonial period. At the bottom, the most unimaginative and uninvolving lesson would consist of the teacher's telling students to read a textbook chapter about Adams, Franklin, Washington, Jefferson, and Henry. Slightly better would be an assignment to go dig up information about one or more of these men. Better than that, such an investigation would take place in the context of having the students decide who is worth learning about—which is to say, who were the most influential figures during that period of history? Best of all, the teacher could even involve the students in deciding on the relevant criteria for such a decision: On what basis should we choose the most influential figures?[72]

This degree of participation (and intellectual sophistication) isn't limited to older students. Once, visiting a second-grade class in Missouri,[73] I watched the teacher call everyone together to describe a party she intended to give for her son, who was about to graduate from high school.

On a flip chart, she wrote down what she needed to buy (cake, juice, ice cream) and worked with the children to estimate the number of portions she would need and the price of each item. Then she asked a question no teacher ever asked me in second grade—or in secondary school, for that matter: What's left to be figured out? After a few minutes of discussion, everyone agreed that the most important remaining question was the total cost of the party. They got into groups of three to try to find the answer to this question, which they had essentially set for themselves.

These examples only hint at all the variations on giving students more of a role in decision-making. My purpose here isn't to present an exhaustive account of how this works, a response to all possible objections, or a guide for teachers of different age levels. But if we are looking for what separates traditional from nontraditional education—or for a basic feature by which to judge the quality of our children's classrooms—we could do worse than to pay attention to how actively students are involved in making choices about their learning.

## Cooperating to Learn

Coercing students to learn is so patently counterproductive (if, indeed, it is possible at all) that we should not only stop doing it but take the affirmative step of doing the opposite—that is, helping students play an active role in their own education. In exactly the same way, making students compete against one another in the classroom is so destructive that we should not only stop doing it but take the affirmative step of helping students learn with and from one another.

Any number of theorists have argued that learning at its root is a social rather than a solitary act. Some have even suggested that the very idea of intelligence is best applied to what goes on among people rather than what happens in each person's head.[74] The exaggerated individualism of American culture has often blinded us to the role that interactions with others play in our coming to understand ideas. Success in school is a function not only of the relationship between each student and the text, or even the relationship between each student and the teacher, but also of the relationship among the students: how they show and watch, talk and listen, assert and rebut. What must be justified, therefore, are not classroom arrangements that encourage cooperation but those that separate students from one another.

Interestingly, many theorists who aren't in the habit of viewing intelligence as social, and who aren't even committed to cooperative models of classroom learning, have been convinced by the strength of the evidence. Researchers who started out "with purely individual definitions of what they were trying to teach ... arrived at the need for social interaction more through pedagogical trial and error than through theoretical analysis."[75] They may have begun with no other goal than, say, to have young children make sense of challenging mathematical ideas, but they quickly realized there has to be plenty of opportunity for "collaborative dialogue" in order for that to happen.[76] The bottom line is that students generally learn better when they learn together.

Collaboration can take place at the level of the whole class as well as in small groups. Some progressive educators are understandably suspicious of the whole class format because in most classrooms that means the teacher runs the show, spewing out information, calling on students to regurgitate it, and tightly controlling any discussion. But it is possible for a class to meet for an authentic exchange of ideas in which students address one another directly. (When I visit classrooms, one of the first things I look for is the number of exchanges between one student and another.)[77] When a student reads aloud three possible endings to the story she is writing and then calls on a few of her classmates to explain which version they prefer — or when a class brainstorms possible essay topics from which individuals can choose — their time together is truly well spent.

Meanwhile, an entire movement has grown up around the other major format for learning together, usually known as "cooperative learning."[78] At its best, the practice of having students meet regularly in pairs or small groups not only helps them develop social skills and fosters each child's concern about others, but also turns out to be powerfully effective in intellectual terms. This is true for several reasons.

1. A student struggling to make sense of an idea may understand it better when it is explained by a peer (who only recently figured it out himself) rather than by an adult.

2. The student who does the explaining can achieve a fuller understanding of the subject matter by having to make it understandable to someone else. This is why cooperative learning has been shown to benefit the one giving the explanation at least as much as the one hearing it.[79]

3. Having a group tackle a task is typically far more efficient than having one person do it alone, since students can exchange information and supplement one another's investigations.

4. Cooperative learning often leads students to become more motivated to learn; their attitude improves, and that, in turn, facilitates their achievement.[80]

5. Finally, remember that constructing meaning typically takes place through conflict, and conflict happens when students have the chance to challenge one another—in an environment that feels caring and safe. Disagreement doesn't imply an adversarial encounter; it's a "friendly excursion into disequilibrium," in the lovely phrase of David and Roger Johnson.

Not all versions of cooperative learning provide these advantages. A teacher who exclaimed, "Thank goodness for cooperative learning. Now I can get through all those boring units students hate without them complaining"[81] is unlikely to witness much intellectual growth in her classroom. Students have to be solving complex problems, pursuing meaningful projects, discussing controversial questions. A "bunch o' facts" curriculum is just as much of a dead end for groups as it is for individuals. One study found that causing students to be "fixated on finding the right answers . . . interfered with their attempt[s] to regulate each other's process of problem-solving."[82] Similarly, if the teacher exerts too much control over the process, or uses rewards (including grades) to manipulate students into cooperating,[83] the outlook is not promising.

The idea of collaboration extends beyond the use of specific strategies like cooperative learning. Ultimately, learning is most likely to be engaging and effective if it takes place in a classroom that feels like a caring community. As a rule, students need to feel safe and valued before they will take risks. They need to know they will not be laughed at or otherwise made to feel stupid before they will ask a question or propose an idea. (The same is true for adults, by the way—including teachers.)[84] Teachers who provide activities that give students a sense of belonging and connection are creating a fertile environment for the free exchange of ideas and thus for learning. They do this not by exhorting children to "work together" or reminding them to share, but by structuring opportunities for them to meet as a class, to solve problems together, to collaborate with classmates on a regular basis. Moreover, such teachers are likely to anticipate and skillfully deal with instances of exclusion, cruelty, prejudice, and competition that threaten a fragile sense of community.[85]

Yet even that is not enough. Ultimately, schoolwide changes have to be made in order for students to be able to cooperate effectively. Parents ought to be familiar with—and lend their support to—the structural factors that make it easier for collaboration to take place. One is small classes, something that teachers can't create on their own. Virtually all of the debate about class size has focused on academic achievement (often measured by standardized test scores). The best research does indeed tend to find, with certain qualifications, that kids learn better in significantly smaller classes.[86] But less attention has been paid to an indisputable proposition: students are more likely to be heard, to really know their classmates, to come to think in the plural, when there are fewer people in the room. That may be all the reason we need to keep down the numbers.

Interestingly, some prominent educators, including Deborah Meier, Thomas Sergiovanni, and the late John Holt have argued that the size of each class is less important than the size of the school.[87] Echoing Dewey, who believed no school should have more than a couple hundred students, these and other writers maintain that such a scale allows students (and teachers!) to be known, to participate directly in making decisions, and to feel part of a learning community—rather than getting lost and overwhelmed in what may feel like a factory. "There is enough evidence now of such positive effects [of small school size]—and of the devastating effects of large size on substantial numbers of youngsters—that it seems morally questionable not to act on it."[88]

Among the other changes that facilitate cooperation and community are: providing more time for each high school class, a reform usually known as "block scheduling" (see p. 270n11); letting an elementary school class, including its teacher, stay together for two or three years, which is known as "looping";[89] and teaching children of different ages in the same classroom, which is known as multiage or nongraded education.[90] These alternative arrangements have emerged from solid data about the significance of classroom relationships; when they have been tried, they've often encouraged teachers to rethink their basic assumptions about the nature of teaching and learning, thereby enhancing the quality of instruction.

## Where It All Comes Together

Now and then I see an example of classroom learning that braids together the different strands of nontraditional education, a lesson that is collaborative, interdisciplinary, project-based, dedicated to discovery, animated by student decision-making, and grounded in the construction of meaning. That was the case with Donna Migdol's third-grade class on Long Island, where the children were devoting a significant amount of class time every week over a period of more than half a year to constructing and analyzing animal habitats.

At first, they just grappled with the idea of a habitat, wandering through the halls with clipboards to collect information that would help them decide whether their school qualified as a habitat. Next, they were informed that a (fictitious) zoo curator had hired them to make wooden, desk-size models of real habitats for specific animals. The children were divided into teams to begin investigating the geography and resources of the native place of their assigned animal (Australia for the kangaroo, Florida for the dolphin, and so forth) as well as how these natural features affected the area's cultural life. While they were writing up their findings on scrolls to be placed inside the habitats, they were also learning about vertices and perpendiculars in order to construct the boxes. And they were honing their arithmetic skills by keeping a running log of the costs associated with the materials to make sure they stayed within the budget allotted by the curator.

On too many classroom walls you find commercially printed posters about the rules of grammar or reminders to listen. Here a visitor instead discovers lists of "problems we faced when designing and constructing" the habitats as well as elaborate graphs comparing the temperature in New York with those in the places they'd been studying. Here, in short, was evidence of complex thought, perseverance in overcoming problems, and classwide cooperation. No wonder Donna was able to report that parents' concerns about the project ("Where are the textbooks?" "How much longer are they going to be working on this?") tended to dissolve once they accepted her invitation to come and see for themselves what was going on.

Each habitat included some plants indigenous to their assigned region, as determined by the students' research. At the time I happen to drop by, they're describing experiments on evaporation that they had not only conducted but designed. (It was logical for them to do some of their investigations at home, so that's where they did them. This reflects a view of homework as out-of-school learning reserved for occasions when it seems appropriate rather than tasks assigned for their own sake.) One boy is talking about the fate of a drop of water on a hot pan in his kitchen the night before, and Donna gently asks him what he was trying to prove, prodding him to think more clearly and come up with the language to explain exactly what he was up to. Eventually he concludes that heat is related to the speed of evaporation.

Everyone agrees, so Donna decides to push the children further. "Steve found something that's making me ask a million questions," she announces, then asks him to explain. It turns out his experiment had consisted of leaving out two cups of water, one in the sun and the other in the shade. The difference in evaporation rate was predictable, but he also noticed "a white rough stain on the bottom of the cup" and wondered if this was some kind of leftover water. Peter pipes up: "I think it's chemicals in the water." Donna asks how they can find out for sure. Various suggestions are offered, and she reminds them to write down these ideas in their logs so they can try them out later. (The whole animal habitat project is recorded by each student in a variety of logs and journals, thereby ensuring extensive writing experience.)

Throughout the discussion that continues about evaporation, Donna emphasizes the relevance of their findings to the habitats. She responds to assertions by students with a trademark challenge: "Prove it!" A comment about "how long the plants are" is met with an invitation to "come up here and show me what you mean by 'long' " — an indication of how important it is to Donna to understand the student's point of view. She is an integral part of the conversation, guiding without telling, relaxed but requiring (and receiving) the kids' full attention to these ideas.

Earlier, the students had been encouraged to delve into the realm of what experts call "metacognition": thinking about how they are thinking. One team of three students made an entry in their habitat journal about what had been going on in this classroom. We "came up with an answer about what learning really means," they wrote. "We thought about it for a while and we thought the kids ask the questions and we go exploring to find the answer on our own instead of the teacher asking the questions and giving the answer. You are the traveler and Ms. Migdol's the north star." A drawing of a star illustrated this metaphor.

Good news: because this school uses looping, these students will navigate by the same star next year.

# ❧ 9 ❧
# GETTING
# THE 3 R'S RIGHT

## Half Truths About Whole Language

*"Kids aren't learning how to read these days because ivory-tower ideologues have eliminated the teaching of necessary basic skills in favor of feel-good, PC fads like Whole Language. We'd do a lot better if we brought back good old-fashioned phonics!"*

THESE DAYS there's no escaping pronouncements like that one. Such a position is understandably popular: it's simple and straightforward, and its urgency commands attention. Not only is it tirelessly promoted by social and political conservatives, but most of the articles that appear in mainstream newspapers and magazines about teaching children to read tend to dismiss Whole Language as a fad and claim that "studies show" children need direct instruction in phonics. Meanwhile, the supporters of Whole Language, even on those rare occasions when they manage to get their voices heard by the general public, haven't always been very effective at making their case.[1]

Frankly, if all I knew about the issue was what I read in the popular press or heard from acquaintances, I too would probably wonder why some kooky new technique had displaced the tried-and-true method of teaching children to read. But once we begin to educate ourselves, things look very different. As a matter of fact, if we go back to that italicized statement at the top of the page and review it carefully, we find that it is utterly false in every particular. It isn't true that "kids aren't learning how to read these days."[2] It isn't true that progressive reading reforms have been imposed by—or even uniformly supported by—denizens of the "ivory tower."[3] (Nor are those who favor such reforms any more "ideological" than those who oppose them.) As we saw in the first chapter, it simply isn't true that there is less teaching of necessary basic skills these days or even that traditional methods for teaching these skills are on the way out.

The key claim that needs to be evaluated, of course, is whether "we'd do a lot better if we brought back good old-fashioned phonics." Let's begin by clarifying what we're talking about here. "Phonics" refers to the relationship between symbols and sounds. A child with "phonemic awareness" is one who can "decode" a letter or pair of letters (such as *th*) and knows how to say it. To anticipate the discussion to come, we can tease apart three questions that usually get lumped together. First, do kids need to learn phonics? (Answer: yes.) Second, do kids need to be taught phonics explicitly in order to pick it up? (Answer: some do, but most probably don't.) Third, if kids *are* taught phonics explicitly, does it have to be done with the usual "drill 'n skill" techniques demanded by traditionalists? (Answer: hell, no.)

While there is no precise, universally accepted definition of Whole Language and no party line for its proponents, this much is clear: it isn't the "opposite" of phonics, and it doesn't deny the importance of phonics. Even Kenneth Goodman, a pioneer of the Whole Language movement whose views are sometimes considered extreme, agrees that "you cannot read an alphabetic language without using and learning phonics."[4] At some point, and by some means, kids have to acquire the ability to "break the code" and interpret all those phonemes.

The camp usually designated as "pro-phonics" believes in teaching sound-symbol relationships mostly, if not exclusively, through direct instruction, in a way that is intensive and explicit, by means of a very specific sequence of lessons. The point is to get children to identify one phoneme after another correctly until they can do so without thinking. In some classrooms, the reading materials are limited to contrived sentences containing only the patterns kids already know. (If your kindergartner or first-grader's school reading matter is mostly of the "Pat has lots of bats" variety, you should be worried.)[5]

Proponents of Whole Language don't challenge the significance of phonics, just the assumption that traditional *methods* of teaching phonics are the only way to help kids learn to read. It's probably true that some kids—anywhere from 5 to 20 percent—can really benefit from some direct teaching of phonics skills. But there is absolutely no justification for subjecting all students to this approach, for making it the centerpiece of classroom reading instruction for any students, or for continuing it after kids have learned to read. Nor is there any basis for insisting that such direct instruction has to take the form of repetitive drills of isolated phonemes.

A Whole Language teacher proceeds from the assumption that there are a number of ways to help beginning readers make sense of what's on the page. They may follow the words while someone reads aloud to them. They may watch a teacher write down familiar words or even pick up a pencil and try to do it themselves. Once they can recognize the first letter of the word, that, along with other clues from the context, can help them predict the rest. "Essentially," says Goodman, they "learn to read by reading."[6] As parents, we use such strategies all the time[7] — with considerable success. Most of us, after all, choose books for our young kids "as literature and not as reading instruction materials."[8] Without thinking about phonemes or decoding, without requiring them to sound out each word correctly, we explain what's going on in the story, perhaps pointing out the accompanying pictures, so that the letters they see come to be associated with the sounds they hear.

What really distinguishes Whole Language teachers, though, is not just a broader array of strategies for helping children learn to decode text, but the belief that *reading is more than decoding text*. A child filled with phonics rules may be able to pronounce a word flawlessly without having any idea what it means, much less what its relation is to the words sitting next to it. (Some critics refer to the process of getting kids to call out the words in front of them as "barking at the page.") Whole Language teachers insist that reading is first and foremost about meaning. Sure, kids have to learn a set of skills, but as a means to an end — the end being to make sense of stories and ideas. It's about communicating more than about consonants (or even words).[9] Therefore, the question to ask your child's teacher isn't "Are you going to teach phonics?" It's "*How* are you going to teach phonics? As a series of isolated skills, or as part of reading and writing real stories?"

For kids who don't seem to be picking up a phonetic concept, such as the silent *e* at the end of words like "line," some teachers will give a "mini-lesson" on that topic in the context of a story chosen (or written) by students that happens to contain that word. First comes the story, then a brief detour to explain how this particular word is pronounced (perhaps followed by a little bit of discussion about similar words), then back to the story.[10] The teacher's motto here is E. M. Forster's famous epigraph, "Only connect": symbols and sounds are taught in order to enjoy literature and in the process of enjoying literature.

In traditional classrooms, by contrast, kids face the prospect of completing worksheets filled with a bunch of unrelated silent-*e* words. They may be given contrived sentences to read, each sound of which they are expected to pronounce perfectly. (Here, the motto seems to be "Only correct.") Thus, it shouldn't have been surprising when one traditional teacher was heard admonishing a child: "Put that book away and do your reading!"[11] — because for her "reading" meant practicing skills.[12]

The worksheets that traditional teachers use are often included in giant "basal readers" that may be assigned to every young child in a school district. These typically include scripted lesson plans for the teacher so that, in effect, the entire reading curriculum comes in a package. Basals also include stories, or fragments of stories, that may have been selected more to teach a specific skill than on the basis of their literary quality. Even the better basals, attempting to capitalize on elements of the Whole Language movement by including more compelling readings, reflect a one-size-fits-all approach: here is what everyone will read, as determined by someone outside the classroom.

A Whole Language teacher would rather spend her classroom budget on the kind of children's stories that can be found in bookstores and libraries. The underlying assumption isn't just that reading material doesn't need to contain controlled vocabulary, where new phonemes or skills are introduced on a specific schedule. Rather, it's that such texts ought to be actively avoided. Better to have a child read a well-written story about an interesting subject. Better, in fact, to have children practice reading other things that matter to them: a list of their classmates, or of today's activities, or of the ingredients in their favorite cereal—or perhaps their own ideas, as transcribed by the teacher. In sharp contrast to random sentences about things like Pat's bat collection, these examples of language are used in the real world. Kids don't have to be bribed with stickers, stars, or praise to figure out what these words mean; they want to know.

Of course, the risk of a story chosen for its theme, or some other use of language chosen for its relevance, is that a child may be temporarily stumped by a tricky word. In that case, the Whole Language teacher may invite him to speculate about what the word could be. Or she may say, "Skip that word. We'll come back to it later." And if he tries and makes a mistake? Suppose a child is slowly reading aloud from a story that includes the sentence "I think my car needs new tires." He gets through the first six words and then pauses before blurting out "trees." A skills-oriented teacher would likely say, "No. Look at the letters again. What comes after the *t*?" But a Whole Language teacher is more likely to respond, "My car needs new trees? Does that makes sense to you?" Then, once he gets the word right, she'd probably call his attention to the way it's spelled.

In a Whole Language classroom, kids are helped to fall in love with the written word. They are encouraged to write even before they can spell, coming to see themselves as authors at a precocious age. They also come to see themselves as part of a community of readers and writers. Children spend a lot of time reading to, and with, one another, and the teacher helps them feel safe enough to persevere through the inevitable mistakes that occur while learning new skills. The emphasis on social interaction among beginning readers is a critical ingredient of a Whole Language classroom.

Another distinguishing feature is the chance for children to choose what books they want to read, something that teachers have learned is a surefire way of maximizing motivation. In fact, giving students a lot more control over their learning is part of what makes Whole Language so effective and exciting—and, at the same time, so disconcerting for people accustomed to having the teacher make all the decisions.[13] "Whole Language is not just about giving up the basal," says one prominent reading teacher. "Rather, it is about having teachers and students decide together what is worth knowing and how to come to know it."[14]

Here we may recall a distinction we came across earlier, between inviting kids to play an active role in constructing meaning, on the one hand, and treating them as passive receptacles to be filled up with skills, on the other. "The intensive systematic teaching of phonics that is so widely promoted reflects a transmission model of learning . . . a matter of absorbing meaning from the page," while in Whole Language classrooms, reading is seen as a "transaction between the reader and the text."[15] As parents, we ought to think about that fundamental difference and then ask which model seems to describe more accurately what reading is all about. Which model seems more respectful of children? Which is more likely to help them become enthusiastic readers—or even skillful decoders?

# The Consequences of How Kids Learn to Read

"Which model is more likely to help children become skillful decoders?" That last question is particularly provocative because it raises the possibility that Whole Language, besides being more consistent with a philosophical commitment to active learning, is also "the best phonics program there is," in the words of Jerome Harste of Indiana University.[16] Why? Because *it's easier to decode a word when you already know what it means*. By insisting that meaning should come before skills, Whole Language isn't just more enjoyable but also more effective.

A meaning-first approach is particularly sensible when the language being learned is English. Our language is very hard to learn phonetically because so many letters have more than one possible sound. If you see a *g* followed by an *e,* for example, there are five possible pronunciations: hard *g,* long *e* (gear); hard *g,* short *e* (get); soft *g,* long *e* (gene); soft *g,* short *e* (gel); soft *g,* silent *e* (George).[17] You don't know how the letters sound until you know the word of which they're a part. Of course, you can try to memorize all the rules for pronouncing different letter combinations, but their usefulness is severely limited by all the exceptions. Remember "When two vowels go walking, the first one does the talking"? This guide isn't even certain to achieve its effect for words like "guide" or "certain" or "achieve." In his infamous pro-phonics tract of the 1950s, Rudolph Flesch declared, "Teach the child what each letter stands for and he can read" — to which one educator replied that someone relying solely on that method wouldn't even be able to read the cover of Flesch's book.[18]

To the unique difficulties of English, add the unique limits of young children. It's hard for a five- or six-year-old to learn abstractly, and that's precisely what's entailed by a phonics-based approach: skills are removed from context and learned as abstract rules. To a behavioral theorist it may seem logical in principle to start with the pieces and put them together, moving from phonemes to words to sentences to stories. In the real world, though, it's far more natural and effective for the whole to come before the part. As one first-grader, struggling with a skills-based lesson, exclaimed in frustration, "You know, I could read this if I knew what it was about!"[19]

This is especially true for children who have difficulty learning or who haven't been exposed to much print before starting school. Contrary to the conventional wisdom that these kids need a steady diet of disconnected skills, they're actually the best candidates for learning in context. Or, to put it the other way around, they're the ones least likely to succeed when meaning takes a backseat to decoding. But it isn't easy to convince phonics fans: whenever their approach fails, they regard it as evidence that these children "need still more systematic instructional discipline." And when more of the same doesn't help, the children may finally be diagnosed as having some kind of learning disability. After all, they "failed to learn to read on the basis of [direct] phonics instruction." What more proof do you need?[20]

Regie Routman, a leader in the Whole Language movement, has no patience for people who invoke the "good old days" when no one questioned a skills-based approach. She remembers teaching that way,

> using scope-and-sequence charts, phonics drills and worksheets, linguistic readers with contrived stories, red pencils to correct all the work-

sheets, assigned and copied-from-the-board writing. And lots of kids were failing to learn to read successfully. In the school where I was teaching, almost 50 percent of our students needed extra support in reading by second grade. [For many of those kids] who couldn't hear sounds in words or "get" phonics . . . there was nothing wrong with their ability to learn; the problem was how we were teaching them.[21]

The story was much the same in the early twentieth century: children were failing "to read at grade level, despite drill in phonics."[22] In Appendix A, we'll look at studies that investigate more directly which approach succeeds better at helping children learn to read, but in the meantime we shouldn't forget the related question of which approach is more likely to foster a love of reading. Too heavy or too premature an emphasis on decoding leaves children with the impression that "the aim of reading is to be able to identify the words appearing in the text."[23] No wonder teachers who have shifted toward Whole Language often report that Reading goes from being the kids' most disliked subject to their favorite.[24]

Even more striking, perhaps, are the results of moving in the opposite direction. That's what happened to a little girl named Patty, who "considered herself a reader and writer" while in a Whole Language kindergarten. She wrote long, imaginative stories, one of which had this playful ending (with spelling corrected): "If you want to know more about Jane's adventures, read the next chapter in my book."

Then Patty started first grade. Her new teacher used a traditional method of teaching: the children were drilled in capitalization and had to spend their time writing letters over and over. "Instead of writing stories and poems and reading self-selected books, Patty read short, controlled-vocabulary stories in basals and worked on endless workbook pages." Within a month she had stopped writing stories, even at home. More to the point, she stopped seeing herself as someone who *could* write stories. She said she didn't know how to spell correctly and didn't know what to write about. Finally, when her parents persisted, she sat down tearfully and wrote: "The cat The cat is a pet." —and then crossed it all out.[25]

I thought of Patty not long ago when I got a call from my friend Bill, a lawyer in the Midwest. He was uncharacteristically agitated as he described his son's experience in a traditional first-grade classroom. An after-school science program emphasizing hands-on learning was working out wonderfully, Bill said, and the chapter books he was reading with his son in the evening were also a big hit. But the repetitive phonics lessons during school were taking their toll. Bill was now coming to see classroom discipline in a new way. "If I had to do this stuff, I wonder how I'd act in class," he mused. Most of all, he worried about what the intensive phonics training was doing to his son's attitude about reading. "His enthusiasm for learning is a precious resource and I'm scared he's losing it," Bill said quietly. "At the end of the year, those kids will know how to 'decode.' But so what, if they don't want to pick up a book."

•

Sometimes the response to such a discussion is that we need a "balanced" approach, a compromise that includes the best of both worlds. Most teachers like the sound of that; it's mild and diplomatic and seems an especially appealing way to deal with an especially politicized topic. Many people were relieved, for example, when a 1998 report on reading instruction, sponsored by the National Research Council and commissioned by the federal government, attempted to "neutralize the phonics vs. whole language debate" by finding common ground.[26]

The first problem with this solution is that, practically speaking, it doesn't seem to make much of a difference. Lots of people claim to support a middle-of-the-road approach but still come down clearly on one side or the other. One of the most extreme examples of rigid, phonics-based instruction in the country, a program mandated for use in all primary classrooms in Houston's public schools, has children "work[ing] their way through the alphabet . . . in the singsong tones of a military cadence." Nevertheless, it is officially described as a "Balanced Approach to Reading."[27] The moderate rhetoric may simply serve as a public relations strategy.

But here's a more basic question: Do we even want something in the middle? In my experience, most of those reassuring declarations—that the truth lies somewhere in between the two models—are based on a misunderstanding of Whole Language. Specifically, they proceed from the erroneous belief that it excludes phonics.[28] The truth is that *Whole Language itself represents a balanced approach:* it's committed to helping children acquire decoding skills, but in a context and for a purpose.

There is indeed a real choice to be made, but it's not between Whole Language and phonics. Rather, it's between using direct instruction only when appropriate and using it as the default method of teaching. The choice is whether we put meaning or skills at the center of the curriculum, whether children are active learners and choosers or passive receptacles who are expected to read what they're told. These are choices that can't be finessed by saying, "Let's have some of both."

In practice, a "balanced" approach often means that kids get to read some real literature, but separate from, and sometimes only after, the worksheet-based skills unit. People who say we should "use whatever works"[29] often evade the question "Works for what?" They don't think about the fundamental incompatibility of different goals, different methods, different views of learning and of children. It's easy to say "split the difference"; it's harder to see the difference for what it is and to take a stand.

## Sit Down for a Spell

Imagine that you're visiting some friends, chatting in the living room, when their adorable sixteen-month-old waddles up and says, "Me want 'nana." One parent glares at the toddler and says sternly, "No! You're not getting a banana or anything else until you learn to speak properly!" —then turns to you with a disgusted shake of the head, commenting, "We're raising a generation of illiterates these days! Well, that 'anything goes' philosophy doesn't fly in our house. We demand rigor and precision in communication."

I don't think I've ever met anyone who would actually react like this (and if I have, I don't want to know about it). But this response is only a slight exaggeration of how traditionalists respond when children in the primary grades are encouraged to write before they can spell correctly. "Invented spelling," closely related to Whole Language, is based, first of all, on the discovery that children go through fairly predictable stages in the way they write words. Their early attempts at spelling (like their early attempts at speaking) aren't random or sloppy but reasonable approximations that suggest a certain level of skill development. In fact, some people in the field prefer the term "developmental spelling" — if only to emphasize that children in such classrooms aren't being taught to spell incorrectly and that accurate spelling will eventually be expected.

Second, invented spelling is based on the finding that young children who write more tend to read better.[30] Not surprisingly, as we saw with Patty, kids are inclined to write more, to take risks, when they don't have to worry quite yet about spelling words perfectly[31] — which, at that age, is unrealistic in any case. The question is what we're willing to have them sacrifice for technical accuracy: Would we rather have kindergartners write about a "froshus dobrmn pensr" or about a "bad dog"?[32] (Of course, for very young children, the choice may be even more stark; either we let them use invented spelling or we don't let them write at all.)

It's "interesting that the people who rail against invented spelling are the very same people who want more phonics," notes Routman. "The irony is that invented spelling relies on phonics" and, perhaps, should even be called "phonics-based spelling" to drive home the point.[33] As we'll see in Appendix A, kids who are encouraged to listen to how a word sounds and spell it as best they can usually acquire good spelling skills eventually, in addition to being more fluent readers and writers. Teachers who allow invented spelling aren't saying that it's always going to be OK to spell words however you feel; they're saying that in the early grades, the costs of demanding perfection are too high.

•

The basic choice reflected in the difference between invented spelling and its absence, or between Whole Language and a skills-based approach, doesn't disappear once kids have learned the rudiments of reading. Phonics, to put this whole discussion in perspective, is only an issue until first or second grade.* But teachers of reading or language arts with older children continue to face the same set of questions: trade books or basal readers? choices by students or control of students? cooperation or separation? Of course, the skills are now more advanced than pronunciation: they include things like grammar and vocabulary and, yes, spelling. But the fundamental issue is exactly the same: Are these things to be learned because the teacher requires it or because they help you both communicate more effectively to readers when you write and get more out of what you read?

Pick the stuffiest, dreariest, silliest, most out-of-context and inauthentic set of practices in each domain, and that's exactly what you'll find traditionalists fighting fiercely to preserve: spelling and vocabulary quizzes based on lists of unrelated words, lessons on the separate elements of punctuation and grammar, diagrammed sentences, penmanship practice, formulaic book reports that would make anyone lose interest in even the most delightful story. Frankly, I used to do many of these things when I was teaching, offering the kind of lesson I now refer to as "Our Friend the Semicolon." My only excuse was that I didn't know any better; I suffered through it as a student, so I assumed it was what I had to do as a teacher. Then, when my students tuned out—or acted out—I simply held them responsible, announcing that they had to make "more of an effort" or

---

* More accurately, it *should* be an issue only when children are first learning to read. The sad reality is that some students are subjected to phonics instruction all the way through elementary school.

"lose the attitude." What I didn't do was examine the curriculum and my own assumptions about learning.

Take spelling. In most Old School classrooms, it's a subject unto itself, sometimes with a separate textbook. Kids get lists of words to memorize and are given regular quizzes to check their progress. (Of course, getting a word right on the test doesn't mean they'll get it right when they actually use it in their own writing, but then, the transfer of facts and skills to real applications has never really been a strong point of traditional teaching.) The alternative, as should be clear by now, is not to ignore the issue. It's to have students learn how to spell as part of writing and for the purpose of communicating more effectively.

Thus, students might be encouraged to examine words that have more than one acceptable spelling (ketchup/catsup), or whose spelling has changed over time ([a]esthetic, catalog[ue]), to get a sense of how arbitrary is the determination of which version is correct. They might be invited to write a word as many different ways as possible and then to evaluate the different spellings, finally checking which one is in the dictionary. Rather than having everyone in class working on the same list, each student might make a personal dictionary of words that she has trouble with, or that she uses regularly but isn't sure of, or simply that she's curious about. These are the words for which each student will be responsible. (Indeed, this whole approach, unlike the basic skills model, is more about having students take responsibility for their own learning.)

Instead of learning lists of words, students in a Whole Language class would probably consider the strategies that writers use for recognizing and correcting errors, thereby turning spelling into another opportunity to think rather than memorize blindly. Finally, the teacher would emphasize the difference between a rough draft, where spelling shouldn't be especially important, and a final draft, where it does matter. As Harvey Daniels puts it, "I don't care whether anybody can spell or not. I care whether they can edit. I care that they know how to find the help they need to turn their misspellings into correct spellings before they release their writing to the public."[34]

The same basic philosophy of learning is present in teaching vocabulary: it's integrated into the process of becoming more competent at reading and writing, not presented as a list of definitions to commit to memory. Students might keep their own lists of words they want to know and remember, and they might begin in each case by taking an educated guess at what a word means (based on the sentence in which it appears or a part of the word that's familiar) before looking it up.

Likewise for grammar and punctuation: our kids need to be rescued from exercises that consist of adding commas, capitalizing words, or changing adjectives to adverbs in an endless list of pointless, unrelated sentences. The teacher's job is to help kids become thoughtful observers of what they're reading—appreciating the good and criticizing the awkward—as well as skillful revisers of their own writing. They ought to edit their classmates' stories, too, perhaps after discussing as a class what students of their age can reasonably be expected to do without the teacher's help. Similarly, penmanship has better and worse purposes (writing neatly so others can understand your ideas versus conforming to someone's model of the "right way" to form a *k*) as well as better and worse methods (practicing on text that has meaning versus turning out rows of letters).

In the best classrooms, no one forgets that the point of mastering grammar and punctuation, spelling and syntax, is to be a better writer. It is the capacity to put ideas into words, to inform or move or entertain a reader, that is most important to a Whole Language teacher. Children are encouraged to write constantly. They write notes to one another (and may have mailboxes in their classroom for exchanging them) and letters to people outside the school. They write books that, at least in some schools, are actually catalogued and shelved in the library. They read their stories at Author Teas for groups of parents. They watch as their teachers show them how a writer writes—crossed-out mistakes, false starts, and all. They turn the plays they read into poems or the poems into stories. They write new endings to a favorite book, trying to imitate the author's voice.

To write well, they have to read well—and vice versa—so reading, too, is taken seriously in such classrooms. Some schools set aside time each day when everyone is supposed to Drop Everything And Read (DEAR).* Teachers read aloud to students, even those who are old enough to read to themselves. They stop periodically, asking everyone to predict what's going to happen next. And they invite students afterward to discuss what they've read, to admire and challenge it, to analyze both the style and the ideas,[35] and to get a kick out of the whole process. Routman advises teachers to ask their students the kind of questions about a book that they (the teachers) might put to a friend.[36]

All of this provides a welcome alternative to those awful book reports and comprehension questions: "What is the main idea of this story?" Reflective teachers would never dream of requiring their students to keep

---

* This could be contrasted, one supposes, with the more typical tendency to Drop Everything And Drill (DEAD).

track of how much time they spent reading or how many pages they read—the sort of assignment that can instantly transform reading into a chore. (Instead of being pulled into the narrative, students invariably think about how much longer they've got to do this.) Such teachers avoid emphasizing grades, test scores, or competition, all of which can lead students to value reading less.[37] They steer clear of reading incentives, particularly in the form of corporate programs like "Book It!," which attempts to train kids to open books by dangling pizzas in front of them. (Worse still is something called "Accelerated Reader." Not only does it get kids to think that the objective of reading is to earn points and prizes, and not only does it limit the number of books that will "count," but it makes students answer superficial, fact-based questions about each text to prove they've read it, thereby changing—for the worse—not only why they read but also how they read.) The best teachers stave off these and other dangerous remnants of behaviorist orthodoxy, which buy short-term reading behavior at the cost of producing " 'least effort' literacy styles"[38] and possibly extinguishing interest in the reading itself.[39] But mostly they work to create a long-term love of reading and critical thinking.

One last point, speaking of critical thinking: the nontraditional approach to reading and writing discussed here is notable for how much more it asks of students than the skills-based model does. In the words of a fourth-grade teacher with more than thirty years of experience, a woman who spent the first half of her career doing "traditional skills-and-drill" before moving to something closer to Whole Language, "I can honestly say I have much higher expectations for my students now. I am asking them to think, not to parrot answers I've already given them."[40]

## Why the Basics Don't Add Up

When it's time for students to put away the letters and take out the numbers, they'll likely find very little difference in the way they're taught. The still dominant Old School model begins with the assumption that kids primarily need to learn "math facts": the ability to say "42" as soon as they hear the stimulus "6 × 7" and a familiarity with step-by-step procedures (sometimes called algorithms) for all kinds of problems—carrying numbers while subtracting, subtracting while dividing, reducing fractions to the lowest common denominator, and so forth.

Once the subject is defined this way, there isn't much mystery about what technique will be used. "When the process of learning in arithmetic is conceived to be the mere acquisition of isolated, independent facts, the process of teaching becomes that of administering drill."[41] You do one problem after another until you've got it down cold. It may make you dread the whole subject (and avoid it whenever possible), but that's the way it has to be done. Moreover, doing math is pretty much the same in a high school algebra lesson as it is in a first-grade addition lesson. The teacher begins by demonstrating the right way to do a problem, then assigns umpteen examples of the same problem (with different numbers), the idea being for students to imitate the method they were shown, with the teacher correcting their efforts as necessary.

If students have trouble producing the right answer, that is "taken as evidence only of the need of further drill."[42] This, as we've seen, is exactly how the failure of direct phonics instruction is explained away: the more it doesn't work, the more you obviously need it. And, also like traditional ways of teaching children to read, most math classrooms are predicated on the transmission model: students are simply given facts and procedures by the teacher and the textbook. Math textbooks, in fact, are often regarded by student and teacher alike as the source of Truth — "a cryptic but authoritative document" — so that everyone's job is to figure out "what *it* wants you to do."[43]

One math lesson, or teacher, differs from the next only in terms of relatively trivial issues: the number of problems to be done at the blackboard versus at one's seat versus at home, the clarity of the teacher's explanations, or the difficulty of the calculations in each problem. The decisions that really matter have already been made: seeing math as a collection of truths "out there" that have to be instilled in students through repetitive drill. These elements are present even in classes that are widely judged to be of high quality, with respected teachers, attentive students, and good results on standardized tests.[44] "Mindless mimicry mathematics," as the National Research Council calls it,[45] has come to be accepted as the norm in our schools. One consequence of this process is on display every time an adult casually describes himself or herself as hating math and lacking any aptitude for it. Generations of students have written off the subject — as well as their own competence — at least partly as a result of Old School instruction.

More than seventy years ago, a math educator named William Brownell observed that "intelligence plays no part" in this style of teaching. Even now, most students are still being taught math "as a routine skill," says Lauren Resnick. "They do not develop higher order capacities for organizing and interpreting information."[46] Thus, students may memorize the fact that $0.4 = \frac{4}{10}$ or successfully follow a recipe to solve for $x$, but the traditional approach leaves them clueless about the significance of what they're doing. Without any feel for the bigger picture, they tend to plug in numbers mechanically as they follow the technique they've learned. They can't be described as "successful in quantitative thinking," because for that, as Brownell explained, "one needs a fund of meanings, not a myriad of 'automatic responses.' . . . Drill does not develop meanings. Repetition does not lead to understandings."[47]

As a result of the standard approach to math instruction, students often can't take the methods they've been taught and transfer them to problems even slightly different from those they're used to. For example, a seven-year-old may be a whiz at adding numbers when they're arranged vertically on the page but throw up her hands when the same problem is written horizontally. Or she may possess a "rich informal knowledge base derived from working with quantities in everyday situations"[48] that allows her to figure out how many cookies she would have if she started out with 16 and then received 9 more — but regard that understanding as completely separate from how you're supposed to add in school (where she may well get the wrong answer).[49]

Math educators are constantly finding examples of how kids can do calculations without really knowing what they're doing. Children given the problem $\frac{274 + 274 + 274}{3}$ set about laboriously adding and then dividing, missing the fact that they needn't have bothered — which would be clear if they really understood what multiplication and division are all about.[50] One researcher gave problems like 7 + 52 + 186 to second-, third-, and fourth-graders, and found that those who had been taught in the usual way — with a set procedure for carrying numbers from the ones place to the tens place, and then from the tens place to the hundreds place — didn't just make mistakes: they made mistakes so outlandish as to suggest a complete failure to grasp the quantities involved. The answers from these students included 29, 30, 989, and 9308.[51] (As we'll see later, students of the same age who were taught nontraditionally — without textbooks, worksheets, or any presentation by the teacher of the "right way" of adding — did far better.)

Another striking example comes from the way thirteen-year-olds dealt with a problem that appeared in the National Assessment of Educational Progress (NAEP). The question was: "An army bus holds 36 soldiers. If 1,128 soldiers are being bused to their training site, how many buses are needed?" If you divide the first number into the second, you get 31 with a remainder of 12, meaning that 32 buses would be required. Most students did the division correctly, but fewer than one out of four got the question right. The most common answer was: "31 remainder 12."[52]

This sort of robotic calculation doesn't reflect a mental defect in the students but the triumph of the back-to-basics, drill-'n-skill model of teaching math. And that's not just one person's opinion. Analysts of NAEP data for the Educational Testing Service observed that students can "recite rules" but often don't "have any idea whether their answers are reasonable." The "preposterous answers" that often result can be attributed to "a general overemphasis in contemporary curricula on computation-related skills or the tendency to teach skills and knowledge before integrating applications and problem solving into instruction."[53]

In some circumstances, it may be useful for students to practice a skill — after they've come to thoroughly understand the underlying idea. But when drill starts too early or takes up too much class time, it offers precious little benefit to the students who are already successful,[54] and does absolutely nothing for those who aren't, except to make them feel even more incompetent. Indeed, it's *most* important to avoid this scripted approach in the case of students who have trouble making sense of what's going on: the more they're given algorithms and told exactly what to do, the further behind they fall in terms of understanding.[55] By now we should hardly be surprised to find that U.S. schools get things precisely backward, subjecting these students in particular to an endless regimen of drills.

## Math Worth Doing

These problems with traditional instruction have been noticed by people who make their living thinking about how math ought to be taught. Several documents for reforming the field, including, most notably, the standards disseminated in 1989 by the National Council of Teachers of Mathematics (NCTM), have said that math classes should revolve around making meaning (just as with nontraditional approaches to reading and writing) and promote thinking rather than the memorization of rules. Students should be encouraged to write and talk about their ideas, to understand the underlying concepts and be able to put them into words. According to a group of specialists in math education at Michigan State University, they should spend their time "abstracting, applying, convincing, classifying, inferring, organizing, representing, inventing, generalizing, specializing, comparing, explaining, patterning, validating, proving, conjecturing, analyzing, counting, measuring, synthesizing, and ordering [because] these are the sorts of activities that are thought to characterize the work of mathematicians."[56]

Students in classrooms where mathematical thinking is encouraged from a very young age learn how to estimate and predict. ("How many pencils do you think there are in the whole school? Is there a way we can know for sure without counting?") They acquire basic skills in the process of solving meaningful problems—often with their peers. They may use calculators, as adults often do, so that they can tackle more challenging and engaging problems than would be possible if they had to direct their energy to computation. In contrast to a classroom whose main activities are listening to the teacher and filling out worksheets, such a learning environment is distinguished by students "sitting in groups, discussing ideas, doing experiments, making diagrams, using concrete objects to test their conjectures, following blind alleys, and now and then experiencing the satisfaction of discovering something they did not know before."[57]

Several features of such classrooms should sound quite familiar by now. For one thing, cooperation is an important part of learning. Sometimes it takes the form of children solving problems in pairs, followed by a discussion involving the whole class. Teachers make a special effort to create a caring community lest disagreeing with one another's answers turns into a competition and discourages some children from speaking out. For another thing, students are more active, more at the center of the classroom, than in the traditional model; their choices count and their voices are heard. And as with Whole Language, which takes advantage of naturally occurring uses of words and ideas, math teachers are always on the lookout for real issues and activities that can offer "opportunities for children to engage in numerical reasoning."[58] News articles from the morning paper raise questions about probability; cooking provides authentic fraction problems; even taking attendance can be put to use ("What proportion of our class is absent?").

Some of us will immediately find this vision appealing, perhaps because we see it as a refreshing contrast to the pointless tedium we had to endure in math class way back when. But others will dismiss it for exactly the same reason: it's not what they're used to. Even parents who are open to being convinced of the value of Whole Language may be skeptical about conceptual approaches to math. The idea of reading for understanding is clear enough (few adults, after all, spend their time underlining topic sentences or circling vowels), but how many of us have any experience with math instruction that emphasizes understanding?[59] We think of math as a subject in which you churn out answers that are either right or wrong, and we may fear that anything other than the conventional drill-'n-skill methods will leave our kids unable to produce the correct answers when they have to take a standardized test. Indeed, it asks a lot for people to support, or even permit, a move from something they know to something quite unfamiliar.

Nevertheless, that's precisely what most experts in the field are asking us to do—and with good reason. As with any of the issues discussed in this book, there are basically three ways to convince skeptics. First, there's theory: explaining the objectives of, and the rationale for, doing things differently. That's what I've been trying to do in this section and the preceding one. Second, there's research, which will be reviewed in Appendix A. Finally, there are examples, ideally gleaned from firsthand observation of extraordinary classrooms—or, next best, descriptions that give a flavor of what these ideas look like in practice and how they compare to the usual fare.

Consider, then, a teacher who tells her students what a "ratio" is, expecting them to remember the definition. Now imagine a teacher who has first-graders figure out how many plastic links placed on one side of a balance are equivalent to one metal washer on the other side. Then, after discovering that the same number of links must be added again to balance an additional washer, the children come to make sense of the concept of "ratio" for themselves. Which approach do you suppose will lead to a deeper understanding?

Consider a classroom where third-graders open their math textbooks to the contrived "word problems" on page 39. ("A train leaves Washington, D.C., heading west at 65 m.p.h. . . .") Now imagine a classroom where students are asked to compare the weight of two pieces of bubble gum (with and without sugar) before and after each piece has been chewed—making predictions, recording results, explaining the differences, all the while adding, subtracting, multiplying, dividing, as well as using decimals and percentages, learning to estimate and extrapolate. In which classroom are they more likely to see math as relevant, appealing, and something at which they can be successful?

Consider a ditto full of fraction problems for upper elementary-level students: "$\frac{1}{2} + \frac{1}{3} = $ _____," and so on. Now imagine that instead they are asked to explain, using words and numbers, "Why *doesn't* $\frac{1}{2} + \frac{1}{3}$ equal $\frac{2}{5}$?" Which question do you suppose will give the teacher a better sense of how each student is thinking?

Finally, consider—which is to say, remember—a conventional middle school or high school math curriculum. Now imagine a class where the students' year-long assignment, while learning various concepts, is to collaborate on writing a textbook for the students who will take their place in the same room the following year. Which is more rigorous? Which do you want for your child?[60]

## Inventing Facts

It's a pretty sharp contrast between math defined principally in terms of skills and math defined principally in terms of understanding. But if we are persuaded by a constructivist account of learning, even the latter isn't enough. When traditionalists insist that it's most important for kids to "know their math facts," we might respond not only by challenging those priorities but by asking what is meant by "know." The real question is whether understanding is passively absorbed or actively constructed. In the latter case, math actually becomes a creative activity.

In early 1998, an op-ed article in the *New York Times* mentioned the value of having students design and carry out their own experiments in mathematics. "Just think," a woman sarcastically replied in a letter to the editor, by doing that, "students might reinvent the Pythagorean theorem." She concluded: maybe this way we can "shoot for last place next year" in international comparisons.[61] Never mind that the poor showing for U.S. students in the most recent tests was likely a result of the very "facts and skills" curriculum that this letter-writer preferred. (She can be excused for ignoring this detail since it was omitted from virtually all discussions of those results in the popular press.) More interesting is her belief that it would obviously be absurd to have mathematical laws reinvented by students.

Coincidentally, Piaget offered the very same example several decades earlier to make precisely the opposite argument. "It is not by knowing the Pythagorean theorem that free exercise of personal reasoning power is assured," he wrote. "It is in having rediscovered its existence and its usage. The goal of intellectual education is not to know how to repeat or retain ready-made truths"; rather, one becomes educated by "learning to master the truth by oneself."[62] When children aren't handed rulers but in effect asked to invent them, when they construct the idea of ratios for themselves, when they recreate the marvelously consistent relation among the three sides of a right triangle (and discover its relevance to real design issues), then they are really learning.

By thinking through the possibilities, students come up with their own ways of finding solutions. They must invent their own procedures. What that means in practice is as straightforward as it is counterintuitive: *teachers generally refrain from showing their classes how to do problems.* Rather than demonstrating the "correct" procedure for adding two-digit numbers, for example, second-grade teachers might pose a problem and then let the students (individually or in pairs) find ways to solve it, encouraging them to try various techniques, giving them ample time before calling them back together so they can explain what they did, challenge one another's answers (in a friendly, supportive way), ask questions, reconsider their own approaches, and figure out what works and why.

This approach has been described in detail by Constance Kamii, a leading student of Piaget's, in a series of three books about how children in first, second, and third grade, respectively, can "reinvent arithmetic." Ultimately, of course, it matters whether students come up with the right answer, but if they're led to think that's all that matters, they're unlikely to understand what's going on. Thus, says Kamii, "if a child says that $8 + 5 = 12$, a better reaction would be to refrain from correcting him and . . . ask the child, 'How did you get 12?' Children often correct themselves as they try to explain their reasoning to someone else."[63] Because that "someone else" can be a peer, it often makes sense for children to explain their reasoning to one another. Moreover, just as correcting wrong answers isn't especially useful, neither is praising right answers. Again, what matters is the process—or, more accurately, the child's grasp of the process, which can be elicited by the question "How did you get 13?"[64]

The teacher in such a classroom has a very difficult job. He has to bite his tongue a lot and also refrain from having children put their answers down on paper too early, since that can get in the way of really thinking through the problems. He has to know when to challenge students: if they all come up with the same method and the right answer, he'd probably be inclined to ask "Is that the only way you can do it?" (The quality of math instruction at any grade level can almost be measured as a function of how often that question is asked.)

I believe this whole approach makes sense for four reasons. First, it reflects the rock-bottom reality that knowledge about numbers and how they're related *can't* be taught (that is, given) to children. It has to be constructed. As Kamii comments,

> Educators are under the illusion that they are teaching arithmetic when all they are really teaching are the most superficial aspects such as specific sums $(4 + 4 = 8, 4 + 5 = 9 . . .)$ and the conventional meaning of written signs (e.g., 4 and +). . . . If a child cannot construct a relationship, then all the explanation in the world will not enable him to understand the teacher's statements. . . . Wrong ideas have to be modified by the child. They cannot be eliminated by the teacher.[65]

Even if a teacher does nothing but demand memorization of facts and practice with procedures, students typically make up and use their own strategies anyway—in effect, constructing their own meaning—sometimes while pretending they're solving problems the way they were told to do so.[66]

Second, explicitly inviting children to make up their own procedures gives the teacher a much better sense of what they understand and where they need help. An open-ended invitation to tackle a new kind of problem lets the teacher see how they think, whether they can integrate earlier concepts, and exactly where they get stuck—as opposed to judging only whether they got the right answer. Recall that, from a constructivist point of view, one of the most important aspects of a teacher's job is to know as much as possible about each student's thinking.

The third argument for this approach is that it really works. I'll present the scientific research later, but for now, let's listen to a second-grade teacher who announced that she gave away 22 lollipops from a bag of 40. She wanted to know how many were left.

I watched the children as they struggled to solve the problem mentally. They were extremely quiet. Some of them were staring into space intently, as if they were solving the problem on an invisible chalkboard. Others sat nodding their heads as if in rhythm to the numbers. A few manipulated their fingers, and one child was biting his lip and looking quite puzzled.

After several minutes of thinking time had elapsed, most of the children had raised a hand to let me know that they had an answer to share with the group. Their proposed answers were 29, 22, 18, 28, and 12. I wrote each answer on the board without comment, and then I asked, "Are there any answers here that bother you?"

The children immediately got involved in thinking about the answers that had been proposed. . . . Allison quietly said, "I don't think the answer can be 29, but I'm not sure why." Many of the children nodded their heads in agreement.

Steve, on the other hand, was not so tentative. He simultaneously raised his hand, stood up, and began to speak. "Because 29 is too big," he insisted. "If you take 20 from 40, it's 20. So 29 is too high."

Ben barely waited for Steve to pause and take a breath. He pointed toward the board and authoritatively stated, "40 minus 20 is like 4 minus 2 equals 2. So, 40 minus 20 is 20. Take away 2 more. That's 28." . . . I was hoping that one of the children would notice the mistake and bring it to Ben's attention. I was not disappointed.

Steve commented, "I don't agree; 20 take away 2 can't be over 20, 'cause you're taking stuff away."

After more discussion, the children broke up into groups and used blocks (an example of what educators call "manipulatives") to give concrete form to the ideas they'd been discussing. Over the next few weeks they wrestled with other problems. Ultimately, the teacher reports, "they reinvented regrouping." They not only figured out on their own how to solve such problems but understood the idea behind the method.[67]

Until you see how this works, the idea of trusting children to solve unfamiliar problems—indeed, even the idea that math is a "creative" enterprise involving "invention"—can be very hard to accept. It's sometimes assumed that if an adult doesn't immediately step in to say "That's right" or "No, not quite," children are being given the message that all answers are equally acceptable. In fact, though, not only is it inaccurate to say that a constructivist math classroom is based on that relativistic premise, but exactly the opposite is true. It's precisely the fact that "40 minus 22" has only one right answer that makes this approach work. "Children *will* eventually get to the truth if they think and debate long enough because, in [math], absolutely nothing is arbitrary," says Kamii.[68] Even the kinds of errors that kids make on the way to understanding reflect certain predictable patterns, not unlike their early spelling mistakes. (For example, young children trying to figure out how many numbers separate 3 from 8 will often start counting at 3 instead of at 4, thereby coming up with an answer that's off by 1.)

Along with the charge of relativism, constructivists are sometimes accused of believing that children will just absorb mathematics automatically without the teacher's having to do anything. This, of course, is just another version of the fallacious equation of progressive education with a kind of laissez-faire Romanticism: sit back and children will learn. Because "teaching" is equated with direct instruction in the minds of many traditionalists, the absence of that particular method is taken to mean that the teacher does nothing at all. By now we understand that the teacher is vitally active, integrally involved. She sets things up so students can play with possibilities, think through problems, converse, and revise. That's infinitely harder than doing a sample problem and handing out worksheets.

But we can say more than that this approach is effective. Its final justification is that the conventional transmission approach can be positively harmful. A teacher (or parent) for whom the right answer means everything is one who will naturally want to tell the child the most efficient way of getting that right answer. This creates mindlessness. Such a student, armed with algorithms, gets in the habit of looking to the adult, or the book, instead of thinking it through herself. She feels less autonomous, more dependent. Stuck in the middle of a problem, she doesn't try to figure out what makes *sense* for her to do next; she tries to remember what she's *supposed to* do next.[69] That, in a nutshell, is the legacy of traditional education.

•

As I read the literature on nontraditional math education and watched such teaching in action, it dawned on me that an interesting paradox is at work. On the one hand, it's seen as important to wait until kids are able to understand a concept before introducing it. This caution follows from all of Piaget's findings about the qualitative changes in children's thinking. You can get toddlers to memorize the words "fifteen squared is two hundred twenty-five." Indeed, I have friends who amuse themselves and their guests by making their children recite impossibly precocious phrases. But these kids might as well be learning nonsense syllables. Parents are often amazed at how early their children can count (in the sense that they can say, "one, two, three, four . . .") but soon realize that they don't understand the relative quantities signified by each number. In this case, the developmental limitation is clear. But it's not as easy to see — though just as true — in the case of a six-year-old doing double-column addition. He can follow the steps but is almost certainly unable to understand place value — that is, how the tens column is related to the ones column.

A traditionalist like E. D. Hirsch, Jr. — a college English professor by training, incidentally — feels no compunctions about asserting that "the reported difficulty that American children under age ten have in understanding place value is very likely owing to their lack of consistent instruction and practice in arithmetic."[70] But the truth is that you can force kids to practice until the cows come home and they're still not going to understand what it means to talk about "tens" before they're ready.[71] Thus, there's no point in getting them to do by rote what doesn't make sense to them. All that does is teach them to see math as something people aren't expected to understand.

The paradox is that while constructivists are alert to what children aren't able to do, they also have an unusually generous respect for what children *are* able to do — spontaneously and at a very young age. "Children's learning begins long before they attend school," noted the famous Russian psychologist Lev Vygotsky. They "have their own preschool arithmetic, which only myopic psychologists could ignore."[72] Myopia isn't really required to miss it, though: all you have to do is make kids memorize facts and follow recipes. Teachers who spend their time telling instead of asking, instructing instead of inviting, can stand in front of children for years without having any idea of what they're capable of doing. A veteran elementary school teacher reflects:

I had never given children credit for being smart enough to invent solutions. It took a lot of extra effort as a teacher to listen to what they were trying to say, and a lot of self-control to squelch the urge to take the fast-and-easy way of imposing my adult views and methods. But there was so much that never needed to be taught, because the children invented all kinds of things that had not even occurred to me. During math, I now see excitement, enthusiasm, and concentration on the children's faces. I hear voices coming from children who are self-assured, rarely timid, and quiet only while thinking. I find myself wondering how teachers can go on depending on workbooks and drill sheets. But I also recall how skeptical and unsure I was at first of not showing the children how to solve a problem the "right" way.[73]

To say that teaching from a constructivist perspective is characterized by a paradox—don't give young children more than they can handle, but do give them a chance to show you what they can do—is to put this positively. The flip side is that the Old School manages to screw up on both counts, simultaneously failing to understand children's developmental limitations ("Just drill 'em until they get it") and failing to appreciate their minds ("Use the technique I showed you"). This double fault is what Lilian Katz may have been getting at when she talked about educators who "overestimate children academically and underestimate them intellectually."[74] Nontraditional teachers dedicate themselves to avoiding both traps.

# ∾ 10 ∾
# THE WAY
# OUT

## Explaining Educational Déjà Vu (Again)

GETTING PAST the Old School won't be easy. As we saw in the very first chapter, traditional education not only has fierce defenders but enjoys the presumption of being familiar to most of us. Now we're ready to consider an additional problem: a set of barriers to implementing alternative ways of helping children learn. Some of these barriers have to do with how this kind of change has actually been attempted, and some of them concern the nature of the change itself.

Efforts to bring about progressive school reform have sometimes foundered because well-meaning administrators or consultants (1) tried to do too much too quickly, without providing adequate training and support for teachers, (2) didn't pay enough attention to the kinds of structural changes that support better teaching, such as reducing the size of classes and the extent of departmentalization in schools, (3) tried to impose change on teachers rather than making them active partners in the process, or (4) merely provided teachers with information (about how and why to adopt new instructional techniques) rather than helping them experience a new way of teaching and thereby make sense of a radically different understanding of learning.

None of these problems is peculiar to progressive reforms; a whole literature in education addresses these and other generic stumbling blocks to change. But it is painfully ironic to try to force down teachers' throats an instructional approach that emphasizes the importance of choice. (More than once I have found myself speaking about the value of allowing students to make decisions . . . to a group of educators incarcerated in an auditorium for a mandatory district-wide "professional development" day.) It's equally ironic to find reformers using didactic methods to communicate constructivist theory, a contradiction identified by Dewey in a striking passage that could have been written this morning rather than in 1916:

Why is it, in spite of the fact that teaching by pouring in, learning by a passive absorption, are universally condemned, that they are still so intrenched in practice? That education is not an affair of "telling" and being told, but an active and constructive process, is a principle almost as generally violated in practice as conceded in theory. Is not this deplorable situation due to the fact that the doctrine is itself merely told? It is preached; it is lectured; it is written about. But its enactment into practice requires that the school environment be equipped with agencies for doing.[1]

Some years later, he added that "to train teachers in the right principles the wrong way is an improvement over teacher-training that is wrong in both respects. But it is not much of an improvement."[2]

Inconsistencies aside, progressive methods simply can't afford the mistakes of implementation that bedevil most kinds of school reform because they are at a disadvantage to begin with. New versions of old pedagogy, in which facts and skills of various kinds are transmitted to students, lend themselves to quick training sessions and easy recipes.[3] For example, compare what would be involved in training teachers (a) to use the latest version of direct phonics instruction, and (b) to help them figure out how to work with students to create a literature-rich classroom environment. Both reforms might be implemented too quickly, with little understanding on the teachers' part about what lies behind the techniques. In the latter case, however, that would be fatal. If the reform in question is *about* understanding, it has to be understood by the teacher — and that takes more time and care and support from the beginning.

Even when implemented admirably, however, nontraditional approaches to learning often don't take root; if they're adopted at all, they may be abandoned in favor of the Old School methods already in place.[4] This isn't because the new ideas don't make sense or can't work but because of how they clash with existing values — and also because of how challenging they are for teachers and students alike. Some people, of course, will immediately become defensive, viewing any meaningful departure from the status quo as an implicit criticism of their own schooling. "Am I not well educated? Of course I am. So make the kids do what I did."[5] But the particular kinds of change discussed in this book are uniquely likely to provoke resistance. Such values as "skepticism, questioning, challenging, openness, and seeking alternative possibilities have long struggled for acceptance in American society," observes Vito Perrone of Harvard University. "That they did not come to dominate the schools is not surprising."[6]

Furthermore, we are talking about a kind of education that is fundamentally about democracy—not as a vague political goal but as a commitment to giving people (including young people) more say about what happens to them every day. Nontraditional teaching also puts a premium on cooperation so that the focus is on our learning, not just mine. In a society where top-down control is the rule, where individualism and competition are venerated—and, let's not forget, where learning is often regarded as bitter medicine—a nontraditional vision of schooling will not always be popular, to say the least.

For teachers in particular, as Dewey pointed out, "progressive education is more difficult to carry on than . . . the traditional system."[7] It requires a set of skills related to teaching itself, such as asking open-ended questions and creating an environment where students can make their own sense of things. It also requires a thorough grasp of the subject matter being taught. If the goal is just to transmit a body of knowledge, it may be sufficient to stay one chapter ahead of the students. But that won't do if the goal is for students to really understand ideas. Any kind of teaching that's more rigorous and demanding of students is likely to be so for teachers, too. In math, for instance, the skillful facilitation of children's understanding requires a strong grasp of quantitative principles. "One reason drill and memorization have dominated mathematics teaching may be that teachers' knowledge of the subject [is] too weak for anything deeper"—perhaps because of their own traditional training.[8]

Indeed, nontraditional teaching is distinguished not only by being humanistic or progressive, not only by taking kids seriously and treating them as active learners, but also by its sheer rigor. There is a common misconception, deliberately perpetuated by some traditionalists, that high standards are kept alive primarily by Old School methods. Yet the way progressive educators have rethought education from preschool to high school (as reflected, for example, in the work of Lilian Katz and Ted Sizer, respectively) amounts to a detailed criticism of traditional schooling precisely on the grounds that it is insufficiently challenging. When you watch students slogging through textbooks, memorizing lists, being lectured at, working on isolated skills, and preparing for standardized tests, you begin to realize that nothing bears a greater responsibility for undermining excellence in American education than the success of the back-to-basics movement and the continued dominance of traditional instruction.

By contrast, where a constructivist model of learning informs the teaching, kids are "expected to explain and give reasons for their thinking, as well as to understand and question the reasoning of others."[9]

More is asked of students: the assignments are "more complex and demanding when students try to make sense of biology or literature than when they simply memorize the frog's anatomy or the sentence's structure."[10] Students in such classrooms are thinking and arguing about controversial issues from the very beginning, playing an active role in making sense of ideas. In short, they're "always operating at the very edge of their competence"[11]—and that puts an extraordinary burden on their teachers. We might say that what is so impressive about this kind of teaching is precisely what explains why we don't have more of it.

Even those educators who have the cognitive skills to function this way may find it difficult to give up some control, to live with uncertainty — not only to move beyond the comforting, predictable search for the "right answer" but to let students play an active role in the quest for meaning that replaces it. That takes guts as well as talent.[12] It flies in the face of the way most teachers are still being trained—namely, to stay in control of the classroom at all times. Ultimately, says one high school educator, "teachers have to let students take ownership." That isn't just a matter of adjusting one's instructional technique. "Teachers' attitudes about students have to change,"[13] too—with the help of parents.

Furthermore, a classroom experience that is at once less orderly and more rigorous is hard to create in light of explicit pressures to teach in a less ambitious way (for example, as reflected in the imperative to increase standardized test scores)—and, more subtly, in light of the image of schooling that teachers, like all of us, have absorbed from all their years as students. Even teachers who attended relatively progressive schools of education will usually "teach as they were taught in fact, not as they were taught *about* teaching," as Dewey put it.[14]

One has to make a concerted, courageous effort to dispense with the textbooks and grade books, the teacher-directed lessons and the assumption that math must be separated from social studies. These forces conspire to create a kind of undertow that threatens to pull the classroom back to the traditional model, back to the familiar practices. It takes constant effort *not* to say, "All right, boys and girls, just sit quietly and read chapter 17; the quiz is tomorrow." At best, it's tempting to make only a little bit of change, to tinker with the methods or improve the delivery while leaving the old assumptions about learning securely in place.[15]

Finally, anyone searching for explanations of the stubborn persistence of traditional education will have to consider the students themselves. While children in progressive classrooms often seem convinced that the greater demands of such an education are worth the effort, that's not true of all children, particularly when they're first asked to give up the security of workbooks, the comfort of predictable lessons, the relative ease of memorizing and regurgitating facts. The introduction of a nontraditional science program led one tenth-grader to exclaim "We see what all this is about now. You are trying to get us to think and learn for ourselves." Exactly, replied the teacher, relieved and grateful that the message was getting through. "Well," said the student, "we don't want to do that."[16]

Philosophers and novelists have reminded us that it's often easier to decide not to decide, to take refuge in being told what to do[17] — an inclination that may be just as human as, if less admirable than, the desire for self-determination. A number of educators, meanwhile, have described the games that are played in the traditional classroom, the way students and teachers seem to wink at each other as if to say "We both know how this works: you don't have to do much of anything if I don't. So let's not rock the boat."[18] In a way, it's reminiscent of how children sometimes respond to traditional discipline. However unpleasant punishment (including physical punishment) may be, it's also relatively undemanding: one need only grit one's teeth until it's over — as opposed to taking responsibility for one's actions, reflecting on how they have affected other people and what else one might have done.

In the case of traditional academics, it is the students who are most successful under the old system and their parents who are most likely to resist efforts to improve the quality of the learning. Jerome Bruner tells the story of a boy who, thanks to his father, had acquired exceptional math skills. On the first day of school, he felt obliged to "demonstrate his prowess by multiplying two large and ugly numbers on the board, announcing the while, 'I know a lot of math.' He was probably our best student, but he made no progress until he got over the idea that what was needed was hard computation."[19] Students who are accustomed not only to impressing their teachers and peers but to racking up good grades and high test scores as a result of their facility at getting right answers are likely to be thrown for a loop when real understanding is valued instead. This may help to explain why not only new methods of teaching but new (and more authentic) ways of assessing learning come under attack: those who are used to being successful tend to oppose changes that would put their status at risk.[20]

In one classroom, a girl grew increasingly uneasy with an open-ended scientific exploration and finally demanded to be told "the answer." The teacher responded by asking whether she wanted some words to explain the phenomenon they had been investigating or whether she wanted to understand it herself. The girl thought about this for a while and finally chose the latter. Any teacher facing a roomful of traditionally instructed students "must be prepared for an initial reluctance and moments of obvious frustration." But we can be hopeful that when students are encouraged "to become participants in constructing their own knowledge," they may develop a taste for real understanding[21] — and so, too, may the teacher.

## Moving Beyond Grades

One obstacle to developing a taste for real understanding is the practice of giving grades. Notwithstanding all the arguments and evidence to that effect presented in chapter 2, however, some parents may still fear that their children will be unsuccessful in life if they haven't been strongly encouraged to bring up (and keep up) their grade-point averages in school. After all, most people — notably admissions officers and employers — still care about grades regardless of how useless or destructive they may be. There is some validity to this concern, but perhaps less than is normally assumed. In fact, the argument rests on a chain of assumptions that is only as legitimate as its weakest link.

1. Does encouraging one's children to get good grades make them share that concern? It depends. Heavy-handed techniques, such as rewards for good grades and punishments for poor ones, may lead kids to feel resentful and to try to reclaim a sense of autonomy by staging a quiet rebellion. The harder you press, the more they resist. (Also, recall the Vermont and California studies cited on page 33, which showed that parents who push their children to get good grades cause them to be less interested in what they're learning, which, in turn, appears to have negative effects on later school achievement.)

2. Assume a child comes to share the parents' concern about getting good grades. Does that actually *produce* good grades? Often, but not always. Some stressed-out grade-grubbers end up undercutting their own effectiveness, while some students who are able to take pleasure in learning wind up with good grades that they weren't directly chasing.

3. Assume a student does get good grades. Does that translate into acceptance by a good college? Before high school, grades are essentially irrelevant to college admission.[22] But while colleges obviously look at high school grades, that is not the only thing they care about, nor does it guarantee admission to the most selective institutions. More than two thirds of the high school valedictorians who apply to Princeton University, for example, are rejected.[23] That's worth thinking about in advance: if acceptance to such a college is the sole reason for sacrificing everything else

in high school in order to get straight A's, what happens if it doesn't work? Of course, we're talking here about the most elite colleges, but that fact cuts both ways: about three quarters of American colleges accept just about everyone who applies, so again one wonders about the wisdom of devoting one's early years to a costly, nonstop effort to get better grades.[24]

4. Does getting into a good college mean economic success? While there is undoubtedly a correlation between the two, it doesn't mean that the first causes the second. It may be that certain factors associated with one (such as family income) also happen to be associated with the other. If that's true, then admission to the school of one's choice (or one's parent's choice) may be neither necessary nor sufficient for financial well-being. People without the usual credentials but with determination and a genuine love for what they're doing often manage quite well in material terms, while people with superlative credentials may be summarily sacked. (The prevalence of mass firings, euphemistically referred to as "downsizing," makes many nervous parents push their kids even harder to get good grades — and, in effect, to see education as little more than a credentialing ritual.[25] But if the conventional approach offers no guarantees, perhaps we should respond instead by questioning our basic assumptions about the purpose of school and the role of grades.)

5. Finally, we shouldn't forget to ask whether economic success is the same as, or even positively related to, fulfillment or psychological well-being. The degree to which one spends one's life in pursuit of material gain is a matter of basic values. However, researchers have found that the more people are driven by a desire to be wealthy, the poorer their mental health tends to be on a range of measures.[26]

The more we're apt to take for granted that it's good to emphasize grades so our kids will be successful, the more important it is to probe each step in the argument. If there is reason to doubt any of these connections, the ostensible advantage of focusing children's attention on getting A's may be outweighed by the demonstrated harms of doing so.

Then there's the separate question of whether a school should give grades as a matter of policy. The evidence suggests that, all things being equal, students in a school that uses no letters or numbers to rate them will be more likely to think deeply, love learning, and tackle more challenging tasks. But here again some will immediately ask whether those gains will come at the expense of college admission. It would seem not. Again, because colleges pay no attention to students' records before high school, there is absolutely no justification for using traditional grades in elementary or middle school. But there are also some high schools that avoid grading students[27]—and many more that at least avoid ranking them[28]—without jeopardizing their chances for getting into college.

If your child's high school decided to do likewise, imagine a letter that might be included with each student's college application:

> We at _____ High School believe our graduates are uniquely qualified to take advantage of what your institution of higher learning has to offer. Why? Because they are interested in what they will be able to learn rather than in what grade they will be able to get. By the time they leave us, our students have grown into scholars, and that's largely because we don't use traditional ratings. Students in other schools spend much of their time and mental effort keeping track of their grade-point averages, figuring out what is required for an A and then doing only that and no more. At _____, time and energy are devoted to encountering great ideas and great literature, using the scientific method, thinking like a historian or a mathematician, and learning to speak and write with precision. Our students not only think clearly—they take joy in doing so . . . precisely because their efforts have not been reduced to letters or numbers.
>
> The enclosed transcript includes a wealth of other information about the applicant—a descriptive list of the courses s/he has completed and the special projects and extracurricular activities s/he has undertaken, as well as what selected members of our staff have to say about the student as a thinker and as a person. We believe that these data, together with the personal essay you may request and the interview we hope you will conduct, will give you a rich and complete portrait of this applicant; a list of grades would add little in any case.

•

The recommendation to move away from grading is based not on a romantic vision but on a large quantity of scientific data and the experience of real students in real classrooms. It may be naïve to believe that, given the current social and educational climate, grades will be abolished anytime soon, but it's not naïve to believe that we can and should work toward that goal. What's really naïve is to believe that children's minds and dispositions to learn will emerge unscathed from more than a dozen years of looking at school assignments as little more than something standing between them and a good grade.

Of course, legitimate questions and concerns do arise in response to a proposal to eliminate grades, but everything depends on how they are posed. There's a big difference between asking, "Yes, but will this prevent my child from getting into college?," a question that begins a conversation; and flatly asserting, "Grades are necessary for getting into college," a statement that ends the conversation. It also matters whether one's point of departure, so to speak, is the difficulty of implementing such a change, in which case one is unlikely to persevere, or the recognition of how much harm grades can do, in which case one is likely to see the practical difficulties as problems to be solved.

## What Replaces Grades

What we put in place of grades depends entirely on our goal. How we evaluate students' learning can be addressed only after we've figured out why we want to do so. In 1995, a coalition of educational organizations called the National Forum on Assessment proposed some basic guidelines on the subject, the first one of which was this principle: "The primary purpose of assessment is to improve student learning."[29] That may sound obvious, but it implies that other purposes, such as using assessment to sort students or "motivate" them, may be inherently problematic. And the trouble isn't limited to letter grades: other techniques, too, will be objectionable if adopted for purposes other than helping kids to learn.[30]

Jerome Bruner once said that we should try to create an environment where students can "experience success and failure not as reward and punishment, but as information."[31] A more profound or practical sentence on the subject is hard to imagine. Its first implication is that traditional grades have got to go because they are unavoidably experienced as reward and punishment. But Bruner's formulation also serves as a cornerstone on which to build substitutes for grades. He is challenging us to make sure that whatever assessment systems we devise as alternatives are experienced as information — rather than degenerating (or perhaps we should say "degrading") into a new set of carrots and sticks.

Before considering alternatives to grades, which are used to *communicate* information about student performance, we should take a hard look at how teachers *collect* that information. There's good reason to think that the best teachers do not rely much on pencil-and-paper tests[32] because they rarely need them to know how their students are doing. Teachers who base their practice on a constructivist theory of learning are always watching and listening. Everything from the kinds of tasks assigned to the way the classroom is organized has been designed to help the teacher know as much as possible about how the students are making sense of things. This kind of informal assessment is continuous, making things like quizzes very nearly superfluous. We might even say that the more a teacher needs formal tests to gauge student achievement, the more something is wrong.[33] (With direct instruction, of course, the teacher is talking more than listening, so traditional exams would be seen as necessary.) As parents, we shouldn't be worried about teachers who rarely give tests; we should be worried about those who need to give frequent tests because they may have no feel for how their students' minds work.

Consider this testimony from a classroom teacher:

> In the real world of learning, tests and reports and worksheets aren't the most meaningful way to understand a person's growth, they're just *convenient* ways in a system of schooling that's based on mass production. . . . I assess my students by looking at their work, by talking with them, by making informal observations along the way. I don't need any means of appraisal outside of my own observations and the student's work, which is demonstration enough of thinking, their growth, their knowledge, and their attitudes over time.[34]

It isn't an accident that this statement appears midway through a description of this teacher's rich, project-oriented approach to learning. A meaningful curriculum is virtually a prerequisite of meaningful assessment. Indeed, the two go together not only logically but chronologically: tasks that are especially useful for evaluating students' progress are woven through their projects and activities. Assessment can be done while the student is learning, not just afterward. Remember the fifth-grade social studies class in Seattle studying colonial Boston (pp. 143–44)? Students, taking on the identities of period characters, wrote letters to imaginary friends to defend their positions on the Boston Tea Party. This activity was designed both to help them learn and to give the teacher a chance to check their progress.

Even if such an assignment is used purely for the purpose of assessment, note that it's a way of having students show what they've learned that's more authentic than a test. It's an example of what educators have come to call *performance assessments:* opportunities for students to demonstrate their proficiency by actually *doing* something: designing and conducting (and explaining the results of) an experiment,* or speaking in a foreign language, or writing a play. Ideally, the students themselves help to decide the best medium for showing what they can do.

One especially intriguing version of a performance assessment is called

---

* Most of us are familiar with this kind of performance assessment through science fair projects. Unfortunately, many schools ruin what could be a productive assessment and an opportunity to share ideas by turning the event into a contest.

a "portfolio," modeled on what adults in some fields compile to document their professional accomplishments. Here, students collect what they've done over a period of time, not just because it's helpful to have all that material in one place, but because the process of choosing what to include—and deciding how to evaluate it—is an opportunity for them to reflect on their past learning as well as to set new goals. The portfolio's contents may be selected to demonstrate improvement over time or to reflect how many different kinds of projects have been attempted. Students may share their portfolios with the rest of the class or consult with their peers on what should go into them. In short, portfolios can be used to help students play an active role in their own assessment,[35] just as, we hope, they've had the chance to play an active role in their own learning. Like other forms of performance assessment, they provide data far more meaningful than what could be learned from a conventional test.

The information about students' performance has three potential audiences: teachers, students, and parents. The teacher who is always observing carefully is doing so partly to learn what instructional practices are working and which are not. (Even in conventional classrooms, a batch of test scores say a lot about the effectiveness of what the teacher has been doing, a fact that isn't always acknowledged.) Through informal monitoring and occasional performance assessments, the teacher receives useful feedback.

But what can take the place of grades for helping the students themselves get a sense of how they're doing? The answer is that, in the best classrooms, feedback is readily available to students, just as information is provided *by* them while they're learning. With some tasks it's immediately clear to a student whether she has been successful: either the experiment worked or it didn't. In such a case, there may be no need for a teacher's evaluation. Even when it may be useful to get someone else's opinion—for instance, to judge what aspects of a story flowed smoothly and where the narrative became confusing—that role can sometimes be filled by a fellow student. When the teacher does weigh in, he can do so with a written comment or, better yet, in the course of a conversation with the student. The latter is preferable because the feedback can be part of a two-way discussion rather than a one-way communication. In addition to informal conversations of this kind, time can also be set aside for more formal occasions to assess progress and make plans.

Finally, what about communicating to parents? We would hope that the purpose is to offer information that can assist them in helping their children rather than simply rating past performance. Either way, grades aren't terribly informative (to say nothing of the way they interfere with learning). Some schools have moved to replace A-B-C-D-F with what amounts to a different nomenclature for a very similar set of ratings. This isn't much of an improvement; what's more, parents will often try to translate the new system into the familiar one ("Is an Outstanding the same as an A?")—not because grades are inevitable but because the school hasn't made a clean break with a system that's broken.

Other schools, meanwhile, have replaced grades with a more elaborate series of checklists and "rubrics"[36] so that students are rated on a range of subskills. By using a detailed scoring guide, for example, a student's performance in English class can be judged on the basis of many different criteria. At its best, this can help teachers and students think more precisely about what constitutes successful learning and how a given student is doing. Clearly, such a report would be a lot more informative than a single summary letter. Yet we have to wonder whether pigeonholing children on a greater variety of fixed rating scales really represents an improvement. It's too easy to forget, given the apparent specificity of a rubric, that these ratings are still based on a series of subjective judgments. Moreover, some schools have been tempted to use rubrics to compare children to one another, in effect grading them on a curve.

Finally, the troubling consequences of an excessive focus on performance, in which students are led to be preoccupied with how well they're doing, may well be exacerbated when their performance is explicitly evaluated on a long list of criteria. To someone primarily concerned with techniques of assessment, rubrics may represent a wonderful advance because they provide more information about achievement. But to someone primarily concerned with the way students come to look at learning, rubrics may actually be seen as worse than traditional grades.

The answer to the question "How can information about student progress be conveyed to parents?" lies not in a new rating system but in straightforward conversation: as they do with students, teachers write to parents and talk with them. The latter can take place at any time, but a period may be set aside for just this purpose at a parent-teacher conference. Some schools have taken this concept a step further by inviting the student to be part of the event. Better still, the student can plan and facilitate it, deciding how to share information about his accomplishments.[37] Remarkable conversations can occur at such an occasion as the student, for example, walks his parents through his portfolio, responding to questions about its contents (Why did you decide to include this? How did you manage to do that? What's the difference between these two items?).

The value of portfolios can easily be undercut if the point of all that effort and care is to yield a letter or number. It's important to emphasize that the real value of this approach depends on its replacing grades rather than being just another technique for deriving them. Likewise, we can imagine a hierarchy of parent-teacher conferences: at the first stage, the student is invited; at the second stage, the student runs the show; at the final stage, this method of keeping parents informed is used in lieu of a report card. To continue to give grades while doing something as constructive as a student-led conference is to take away with one hand what we've just given with the other.

Of course, the best way for parents to know what's going on at school is to talk with their children directly. Far more of these casual conversations should concern what kids are doing rather than how well they're doing. Children who aren't afraid of their parents' reaction, who are free of the pressures created by rewards (including praise) and punishments, feel safe to describe what excites them, bores them, angers them, and scares them about school. (Make a big deal about your kid's report card, one way or the other, and you'll probably be treated to less daily information about what your child is doing at school and how she feels about it.) Parents who show genuine, uncritical interest in what their children have figured out how to do are likely to be entrusted with the child's perspective on where she's succeeding and where she's struggling. But we have to trust and value that information rather than assuming we won't know what's really going on until we hear it from the teacher.

We may as well admit it: not all parents will immediately accept the abolition of traditional grades no matter how much better the alternatives prove to be at providing information and helping students remain excited about what they're learning. Even relatively minor changes, such as shifting to a new rating scale, sometimes meet with howls of protest. This may be due to how such a policy is implemented as much as to the nature of the change itself. If a school or district announces the abolition of grades as a fait accompli, something decided behind closed doors and imposed on the community, then opposition is virtually inevitable (and deserved).

Likewise, a change this significant can be implemented too quickly. In most communities, it makes more sense to take one step at a time. This can be done by first eliminating the most pernicious versions, such as grading on a curve, or the most offensive practices related to grading, such as ranking high school students or posting honor rolls that make grades even more salient (and destructive) than would otherwise be the case. Alternatively, grades can be phased out one year at a time, starting with the youngest children and gradually moving up to high school. Even where opposition to getting rid of grades at the secondary level is too strong, we need to move as far as possible: every year that children don't have to worry about report cards is another year in which the climate favors intellectual excellence. At a minimum, we should take the advice of early childhood experts and commit ourselves to using no numbers or letters for rating children below the fourth grade.[38] Meanwhile, teachers can be encouraged to make grades as invisible as possible for as long as possible — for example, by not putting any letters or numbers on individual assignments.[39]

To be sure, some people will object not merely to the way such changes are implemented but to the changes themselves, even when done incrementally. This too happens for different reasons. If parents are simply suspicious of abandoning things like grades, which they know and understand, it may be possible to convince them that this change will give them even more information about how their kids are doing, that it won't spoil the chances of college admission or gainful employment down the line, that it isn't part of some diabolical experiment with their children. Other parents, however, seem less receptive to evidence. We can prove to them that alternative assessments are better at promoting learning, but they may be more interested in having grades serve other functions, such as making students work harder or demonstrating how much better their children are than everyone else's. In that case, A's will always be necessary — and it will always be necessary for some people's kids not to get them. We will have to engage such parents in an ongoing conversation about issues of fairness as well as to help them understand all the ways that grades and other traditional practices adversely affect even their own children over the long haul.[40]

Most members of the public aren't wedded to grades, though, according to two educators at Indiana University. They simply haven't been "provided with convincing alternative[s]."[41] I've heard anecdotal reports of schools that give parents a choice on back-to-school night: either they get a letter grade and go home, or they receive a detailed briefing from their child, a student-led discussion of her portfolio, but with no grade attached. Even some of the most traditional parents choose the second option — after seeing it in practice.

One last point needs to be emphasized. Because of the perils of placing too much emphasis on how well students are performing, it's vital that any assessment procedure not be overdone. Whether a school relies on a superficial fill-in-the-blank quiz or an impressively rigorous performance assessment, a preoccupation with results can derail students' engagement with the learning itself. Most of the time they are in school — particularly younger students but arguably older ones, too — they should be able to think and write and explore without worrying about how good they are. Only now and then does it make sense for the teacher to help them attend to how successful they've been and how they can improve. On those occasions, the assessment should proceed along the lines of what educators have found to be most useful, as described here. The rest of the time, students should just be immersed in figuring things out.

## What Replaces Standardized Tests

Standardized tests are used for two reasons: to collect information about the performance of individual students and to monitor the performance of entire schools or districts. It's important to distinguish between these purposes as we think about alternatives, because what works for one may not work for the other. It's equally important to distinguish between testing as a means of collecting information (so that schooling can be improved) and as a means of holding people accountable. It's hard to get an accurate sense of how children (or schools) are doing by using a test that is also going to be the basis for public judgment. The latter typically leads to a desperate effort to raise scores, thereby providing a skewed picture of what kids can do and where teachers need help.

For all the reasons discussed in chapter 4, standardized tests are not very useful measures of children's learning. It is therefore profoundly depressing to see how seriously they are regarded by many teachers and parents, even when there are no "high stakes" involved. A friend of mine remembers visiting his daughter's sixth-grade teacher to ask about some problems she was having in school. The teacher immediately walked over to the closet and fished out the girl's last set of test scores. This impulse illustrates what some writers call the "de-skilling" or "disempowering" of teachers: they have been led to distrust their own impressions of students, formed and reformed through months of close observation and interaction. Instead, they defer to the results of a one-shot, high-pressure, machine-scored exam, attributing almost magical properties to the official numbers. Even a teacher who has her priorities straight may have to defend the validity of her judgment to parents who have been mesmerized by the aura of standardized scores. A computer printout is regarded as authoritative not in spite of the fact that it's removed from personal experience but precisely because of that feature.

To the extent that some people will continue to demand wide-scale testing regardless of its limits, we should at least minimize the intrusiveness and harm of any such system. We can do that, to begin with, by restricting the student population involved. Children below the age of seven or eight simply should not be subjected to any kind of standardized testing. It's difficult, if not impossible, to devise such an assessment in which very young children can communicate the depth of their understanding. Moreover, skills develop very rapidly and at very different rates during that period, so tests that expect all first-graders to have acquired the same set of capacities create unrealistic expectations and lead to one-size-fits-all teaching.[42]

In fact, that same lack of attention to developmental variations—that same expectation that everyone must learn at the same pace—is reflected by testing students every single year. Even well-designed assessments can have an adverse impact on teaching and learning if they're given too often. Checking in, as the NAEP exams do, once in elementary school, once in middle school, and once in high school should be enough. "Testing must become an *occasional adjunct,* used for obtaining certain basic but limited information"[43]—which is to say, as only one part of a much broader picture of student achievement.

Then there's the matter of test design. For reasons already explained, assessments should compare the performance of students to a set of expectations, never to the performance of other students. Rather than providing useful information, norm-referenced tests lead people to think that the goal is just to triumph over others. Parents must then be helped to understand that the scores on criterion-based tests refer to the level of their child's achievement rather than to how she compares to her peers.

This, in turn, raises the question of what kind of achievement is being tested. Parents and teachers who feel the need for an assessment that is somehow authoritative—including a determination of whether a high school student is ready to be graduated[44]—don't have to resort to the usual standardized tests. Better assessments tap students' understanding of ideas rather than their ability to memorize facts and definitions. In place of a multiple-choice or short-answer format, such tests closely resemble the performance assessments being used in some classrooms: students respond at length to open-ended questions and explain their answers.

Traditionalists often object to the mass use of performance assessments,[45] not only because they're expensive,[46] but because of the difficulty of scoring the responses in a consistent, and therefore statistically reliable way.* A multiple-choice exam yields a straightforward score be-

---

* Anyone who is seriously bothered by this problem would be in the forefront of opposition to classroom grades, which are about as unreliable as an evaluation can be. Curiously, critics of performance assessments tend to be silent on this point.

cause each question has one right answer. Any two raters will therefore have little trouble agreeing on how well each student did. But this agreement (known by statisticians as "interrater reliability") is bought at a steep price, given the inherent limits of what such a test can tell us about a student's level of understanding.[47] An essay test, which asks students to offer and justify their opinions, is far richer, far better able to tell us something meaningful and valid about the student, even though it may be harder to get every reader of an essay to agree on how good it is. At some point we may have to decide which feature is more important, authenticity or reliability.

On the other hand, these two features may not be mutually exclusive. It may be possible to get raters to agree more often than you'd think while scoring performance assessments. Lauren Resnick and her colleagues insist that "open-ended responses can be scored with sufficient reliability" by training professional readers of these exams to apply a fixed set of criteria. After the readers discuss some sample essays, there eventually emerges a "remarkable convergence of judgments."[48] Resnick has been involved with the New Standards Project, and it, like a unique, portfolio-based state testing program in Vermont,[49] has been quietly challenging the assumption that if we want to test large numbers of students, we have to make them fill in bubbles with number two pencils.

For all the progress they represent, however, these newer, more ambitious assessments are still external to the classroom. Like traditional standardized tests, questions are designed and answers are scored at a central location, and to that extent something is lost. Less well known but more promising is an approach that has teachers evaluate their own students' projects in a way that is standardized across schools. One such venture, called the Learning Record, uses a defined format to help teachers document each student's learning by sampling different things she has done, including her own interpretations of what she's learned, thereby allowing the teacher to analyze "a pattern of performance observed and documented over time in natural settings."[50] Another system, known as Work Sampling, is also based on a bottom-up rather than top-down approach, but again within a structure that gives the teacher's perceptions more weight.[51]

Even with structured formats and standardized criteria, though, there's no denying that performance assessments are messier than multiple-choice exams. One response, as we've seen, is to say that it's worth it, given how much more of value we can learn from the former. A second response is that the messiness can be minimized by increasing the reliability of performance assessments. But there's another way to look at the fact that the people who are scoring tests won't always see eye to eye about what the students have done, and that's to remind ourselves that disagreement is a fact of life and not necessarily a bad thing. You and I will inevitably differ in our judgments about politics and ethics, about the quality of the movies we see and the meals we eat. It is odd and troubling that in educating our children, "we expect a different standard of assessment than is normal in the rest of our lives."[52] Too much standardization suggests an effort to pretend that evaluations aren't ultimately judgments, that subjectivity can be transcended. This is a dangerous illusion.[53]

It's completely understandable that parents, like patients, often seek out a second opinion. We want to be reassured that a teacher's assessment of our child is credible; we want some kind of confirmation from an outside source about how well our kids are doing. Tragically, this desire has led us to standardized tests, which fail to offer meaningful information and do a great deal of damage in the process. What makes far more sense is some kind of system that begins with the teacher's judgments, like the Learning Record or Work Sampling, and then makes sure that those judgments are periodically checked by an evaluator outside the classroom. The best of all possible worlds would seem to be an arrangement that (a) bases assessment on an analysis of students' learning over a period of time by a teacher who knows them well, but (b) uses other educators to authenticate that analysis as a way of increasing our confidence in it.[54]

•

To this point, we've been concerned with the improvement of, and alternatives to, standardized tests to find out how our kids are doing. That still leaves the question of how we can judge the adequacy of a whole school or district if not by these tests. Criticisms of standardized exams, no matter how devastating, are sometimes met with a shrug: "Well, we need *some* way to evaluate schools."[55]

As parents, we already have a way: if our kids come home chattering excitedly about something they figured out in class, if they not only can read but do read (on their own), if they persist in playing with ideas and come to think carefully and deeply about things, then the chances are they attend an excellent school. It's not that these behaviors correlate with evidence of school success: these behaviors *are* the evidence of school success. Is it hard to quantify such things? Yes. That suggests a limit, not of these indicators, but of quantification itself. Sometimes people who say we need some way of evaluating schools really mean we need some way of reducing schools to numbers, which is not the same thing.

To reject the most meaningful criteria because they are qualitative is to put "the quest for accurate measurement—and control—above the quest for educationally and morally defensible policies."[56]

If we continue to probe this need to evaluate schools, it turns out that the demand for standardized testing not only reflects a preference for a judgment that is quantified but for a judgment that is relative. We don't need test scores if our goal is to get a sense of what is going on at a school and whether it's benefiting our children. But we do need test scores if our goal is to rank schools. Once we understand how silly and irrelevant such comparisons are, how they reflect a sensibility that has little to do with excellence and everything to do with competition, we may come to question the demand for standardized tests.

There are two further reasons to question the assumption that such testing is essential for holding our schools "accountable." First, how is it that parents considering a private education for their children feel less need for test scores to reassure them about the quality of a given school? Testing isn't altogether absent in the realm of nonpublic schooling, but it is far less frequent and prominent. We may not approve of all the other bases on which such parents decide where to enroll their kids, but the fact that they can get a sense of the value of a school without consulting a table of ITBS or Stanford scores contains a lesson for the rest of us.

Second, even though student achievement tests have existed for the better part of a century, they have traditionally been used *in* schools for student placement or remediation. Only in the last generation have scores been published in the newspaper and used to determine policy—to the point that they are now the primary way of evaluating public schools.[57] It's hard to argue that we can't get along without them since we did just that for decades. Of course, it may be objected that more attention is paid to test scores today because the quality of schools has declined so dramatically. But it's also possible that this belief that the quality of schools has declined is mistaken and, moreover, whatever the state of our schools, the pressure to jack up the test scores has only made things worse. In any event, information that is local and even somewhat impressionistic is not necessarily less accurate or useful.[58]

The best way to judge schools is by visiting them and looking for evidence of learning and interest in learning. I've offered one set of indicators in Appendix B, but I recognize that not every parent or public official who spends time wandering through schools will be looking for exactly the same thing. We won't all agree on good signs and bad signs, but then, that lack of unanimity will at least be out in the open if we judge schools by spending time in them—as opposed to camouflaging our disagreements by making standardized test results the main criterion. Thoughtful observation is still the best way to gauge the quality of a school.

For those who insist on something more formal or tangible, we have to go back to the kinds of assessment of individual students discussed earlier. Learning takes place in classrooms, not in districts or states. To get a sense of how our schools are doing, we have to start where the learning is and move out from there. That can be done by using the same kind of classroom performance assessments described above and relying on outside readers or validated rating scales to increase our confidence in the teachers' evaluation of students' learning. To look at the projects of a number of students (and the evaluations of those projects) is to get a sense of the quality of the school as a whole.[59]

However, whether we're using these kinds of assessment or more conventional standardized tests, it's worth offering two cautions. The first is that if our goal is to monitor a school or district, it's not necessary to test every single student — any more than monitoring public opinion requires pollsters to question every voter in the country. It makes sense to sample a student body — that is, to test a cross section of students. One version of this technique consists of giving each batch of students a different part of a larger test. When the results are combined, a picture emerges of how well the whole population did. But even if all the students are given the entire test (which is, of course, more expensive), their individual scores shouldn't be released. That way we can distinguish between monitoring students and monitoring schools — without all the problems that occur when one test is used to achieve both objectives.

The second caution is that, just as students should never be compared to one another, so norm-referenced testing (or a norm-referenced version of performance assessment) doesn't make sense for schools, districts, or states. What matters is how each one is doing with reference to a standard, not whether it's doing better than others. Moreover, the results should always be evaluated in light of the special challenges faced by a given school or district: a large number of students with special needs, or a low-income community, provides a context in which to understand a set of results.

The question we ought to keep in mind in weighing any sort of assessment system is how it will ultimately affect the kids, whether giving tests — along with the nature of those tests and how the results are used — is going to do more good than harm. This is a very different point of reference than talking about holding schools accountable for maximizing productivity. Even some supporters of performance assessments who are critical of current standardized testing still talk about Tougher Standards, still describe education as an investment, and still couch the need for school reform in terms of what will benefit business. These critics may have us measure learning differently, but their fundamental model of schooling remains the same.

When the traditional approach to education remains unquestioned, it's likely that the newer assessments will be presented as part of a "high-stakes" proposal — that is, the tests will be used as levers to make teachers change what they do in order to be rewarded or avoid being punished. The assessment is thereby used to manipulate classroom practice rather than to provide information, an idea defended on the grounds that forcing teachers to prepare their students for a more authentic assessment will necessarily improve their teaching.

This should make us nervous. First, it's another example of doing something *to* people rather than working *with* them to bring about improvement. No matter how laudable the new standards for teaching, they simply cannot be shoved down teachers' throats. Rather, teachers have to want to change what they're doing. "We don't need or want teachers to simply accept the new gospel . . . just because some authority figures say it is a good idea or because we're going to scare them with an external test," argues Ken Jones, an educator in Kentucky.[60] What's more, educators require help to be able to teach in a way that promotes creative and critical thinking; pressure in the form of better tests isn't sufficient even if it were desirable.[61]

And here's a related problem that should be familiar by now: focusing disproportionate attention on results tends to distract students from attending to what they're learning. Similarly, it's not good practice to get *teachers* to keep asking, "Is this going to be on the test?" In the words of two leading educational psychologists, Martin Maehr and Carol Midgley, "An overemphasis on assessment" — on measuring how well students are achieving — "can actually undermine the pursuit of excellence."[62] That's true regardless of the quality of the assessment.

Attempts to hold teachers accountable for improving scores on more ambitious tests will likely lead them to second-guess these new measures and drill students on *their* specific formats and contents. As the education writer Robert Rothman points out, "Teachers can narrow instruction to the type of performance demanded by a performance-based assessment just as they can teach to a multiple-choice test."[63] To help teachers improve the curriculum, we have to do better than issuing a new version of the same old threat: "If you don't teach the way we demand, your kids will flunk this test."

We ought to keep in mind not only the inherent limits of a coercive model of school reform but also the limits of assessment itself. Some people who specialize in this field seem to forget that even the newest, jazziest, most informative and authentic measure of learning isn't enough. It's perfectly legitimate for us to want to check up on our children, and we may as well have the means for doing so that tells us (more effectively than grades and multiple-choice tests) whether they have succeeded in learning what they've been given. But the more important question remains: Have they been given something worth learning?[64]

## Pulling the Plug

Whether our children will continue to be subjected to standardized testing is ultimately a political question. No amount of evidence about its effects (or about the feasibility of other approaches to assessment) counts for anything unless we use that evidence to demand that school superintendents and state legislators steer a different course. When seven-year-olds are prevented from reading wonderful stories because their teachers feel obliged to spend class time drilling them on basic-skills test questions, the matter is already political. The only question is whether opponents of the status quo will make their voices heard, too.

What can be done? The first, and least controversial, step for any community is to conduct a survey to discover the actual impact of standardized testing. A group of psychologists at the University of Michigan have found it useful to ask these questions:

> Do the tests improve students' motivation? Do parents understand the results? Do teachers think that the tests measure the curriculum fairly? Do administrators use the results wisely? How much money is spent on assessment and related services? How much time do teachers spend preparing students for various tests? Do the media report the data accurately and thoroughly? Our surveys suggest that many districts will be shocked to discover the degree of dissatisfaction among stakeholders.[65]

The process of reflecting as a community on the actual impact of standardized tests (rather than just repeating clichés about "accountability" and "higher standards") will take time. During this period, teachers cannot just ignore the fact that they and their students are going to be judged on the basis of these scores. In the short term, therefore, they may have to strike a balance between doing the kind of teaching that is best for kids and the kind that prepares them for tests. Teachers may grit their teeth, do as much test preparation as they feel is necessary, and then get back to the real learning—making sure that this distinction is also clear to students and their parents.[66]

Fortunately, a relatively short period of introducing students to the content and format of the tests may be sufficient to produce scores equivalent to those obtained by students who have spent the entire year in a test-prep curriculum.[67] But whatever time is devoted to such preparation need not take the form of traditional drilling: several educators have figured out how to turn these tests into a kind of puzzle that children can play an active role in solving. The idea is to help students become adept at the particular skill called test-taking so they will be able to show what they already know.[68] Fortunately, test scores in some subject areas will be sensitive to good teaching that isn't specifically geared to those tests at all.[69]

We need to keep in mind, however, that figuring out how to make sure children are not trampled by the testing juggernaut is only an interim solution. Our challenge over the long haul is not to accommodate ourselves to what doesn't make sense but to work together to replace it with something more productive. For every workshop on how to help kids do well on standardized tests, there should be three on how to fight for the abolition of these tests. If many people in our communities are surprised to hear about alternatives, this suggests that the apparently high level of support for, and interest in, such tests may reflect simple ignorance about better ways of evaluating students and schools.

One example: a survey of parents of third-graders in an ethnically diverse, working-class district near Denver found higher levels of support for performance assessments than for standardized tests *once the former option was presented and explained.* When parents were shown examples of standardized test questions ("How much change will you get if you have $6.55 and spend $4.32? [a] $2.23 [b] $2.43 [c] $3.23 [d] $10.87") and performance assessment questions ("Suppose you couldn't remember what $8 \times 7$ is. How could you figure it out?"), many remarked that the latter were more challenging and "likely to give teachers better insights about what children are understanding and where they are struggling."[70]

This is why it's so important for us to educate ourselves about the effects of standardized tests and the existence of alternatives—and then to educate our friends and acquaintances, raising questions in the supermarket and the hairdresser's, at dinner parties and playgrounds. (If the information in chapter 4 is useful for this purpose, you have my permission to copy and distribute it.) We can create alliances with teachers, many of whom are already disgusted with these tests. We can make our voices heard in our school system: if an administrator or politician brags about how high the local test scores are, or how much they improved since last year, we can respond (and suggest that others respond) by saying, "Frankly, if this is what matters to you, then I'm worried about the quality of education my child is getting."

We can lobby the school board. We can write to our state legislators and submit a letter to the editor (or opinion piece) to the local newspaper. Better yet, we can organize a delegation of teachers and parents to meet with the newspaper's education reporter(s) and top editors, telling them, "Every time you treat standardized test scores as a legitimate measure of learning—or, worse, publish a chart ranking local schools by their scores—you inadvertently make our schools a little bit worse. Here's why . . ." (If we get a sympathetic response, we can even offer to draft a statement for the newspaper to publish that explains why it has decided to eliminate such charts.)

We can talk to real estate brokers, urging them to stop using test scores as indicators of the quality of schools in a given neighborhood. Suggest they wax enthusiastic instead about how small the schools are, how students feel as though they're part of a caring community, how even kindergartners get the chance to write stories, how the teachers here feel secure enough to create democratic classrooms so kids learn how to make good decisions, how the students can't stop talking about the projects they do. In short, we can suggest more descriptive and less destructive ways of explaining how good the schools are.

Any of the people we approach—school board members and administrators, journalists and legislators and real estate agents—may respond by saying that their focus on test scores is just "giving people what they want." There is obviously some truth to this, but the truth is partial and self-serving, just as it is when producers of graphically violent movies use the identical argument. We can reply, first, that higher test scores aren't what many of us are concerned about, and second, when people do seem to want this, it is often an uninformed preference, one that may change when they're helped to understand the broader picture. (Then we can set about helping our neighbors to do just that, calling into question an uncritical acceptance of this kind of testing.) Finally, we can argue that anyone who claims to be responding to a public fixation on test scores is also feeding it, actively contributing to a phenomenon that is then used to justify that very behavior.

No one has a greater opportunity to make an impact with these arguments than the teachers and parents associated with schools that are known for having high test scores. It's easy for traditionalists to dismiss critics by using a "sour grapes" argument: Well, you're just against standardized testing because it makes you look bad. That's why it's so important for people from high-scoring areas to say, in effect, "Actually, our students happen to do well on these stupid tests, but that doesn't blind us to the fact that they're stupid. High test scores are nothing to be proud of. We value great teaching and learning, which suffer when people become preoccupied with test scores. Please join us in phasing them out."

If letters to the editor and pointed questions at school board meetings fail to make any headway, we may want to consider more direct measures, such as boycotting these tests. To date, there have been scattered examples of students taking collective action by agreeing to deliberately flunk a given standardized test in order to "send a message to administrators who they believe place too much emphasis on the exam."[71] In parts of Colorado, some parents have kept their children home on test day to protest all "the classroom hours their children were spending on testing."[72] In Michigan, "parents statewide exempted 22.5 percent of students" from the high school proficiency portion of the Michigan Educational Assessment Program (MEAP) in 1998–99, and "some districts had up to 90 percent of their students waived from the test," suggesting a "grassroots revolt by parents and students."[73] Some educators in that state are working to create a more organized opposition, setting up conferences and using the Internet to spread the word about the destructive impact of the MEAP on teaching and learning and to urge more parents and students to consider boycotting it.[74] A parents' group in Ohio is taking similar actions against that state's proficiency tests,[75] and some students in Massachusetts are acting on their own, refusing to participate in a new statewide exam.[76]

In some areas, parents can simply follow a routine procedure to request that their children be exempted from a test. An organized group of parents who pledge to do this repeatedly, who offer a cogent and pointed explanation of why they're doing so, and who attract press attention as a result, can create a ripple effect, encouraging parents in other communities to do likewise.

It takes more organizing, and perhaps more courage, for teachers to refuse to participate in standardized testing. But teachers have two considerable advantages: many already understand quite clearly how much harm is done by such tests, and many are already members of a union that can theoretically provide a framework for organizing around this issue. Few Americans know of the striking, inspirational examples from other countries. Recall that Japanese teachers have successfully stopped their country from testing elementary school children ever since the 1960s "through their collective refusal to administer" such tests.[77] In 1993, teachers in England and Wales basically stopped the new national testing program in its tracks, at least for a while, by a similar act of civil disobedience. What began there "as an unfocused mishmash of voices became a united boycott involving all teacher unions, a large number of governing bodies, and mass parental support." The English teachers made it clear—as their U.S. counterparts must too, should they undertake a similar action—that their opposition was not a complaint about extra work or a fear of being held accountable, but an act in behalf of students, based on their understanding that "to teach well for the tests was in effect to teach badly."[78]

From quiet letters to the editor and small gatherings in living rooms can grow organizations, perhaps with names like Standardized Testing Offends Parents (STOP), perhaps by using an existing organization such as FairTest.[79] But let's remember that standardized testing is just the most visible manifestation of the whole Tougher Standards model of school reform. That model should be opposed in all its particulars—its faulty assumptions about achievement and motivation, about challenge and improvement, about models of change and models of teaching. Efforts are already under way to create a loose confederation of local groups that share these concerns. (For information about becoming involved in your state, visit www.alfiekohn.org and then click on "Standards and Testing.")

Teachers *and* parents need to be part of any such activity, to share information and complement each other's perspectives. After all, to paraphrase Arlo Guthrie, if just one person in a town comes forward to denounce the current approach to education, he or she will probably be ignored. If two or three people speak out, they'll be considered extremists. But if fifty people in a community take a stand, the powers-that-be may think it's a movement. And that's just what it is: a movement to demand the schools our children deserve.

*Appendix A:*

# THE HARD
# EVIDENCE

Some readers have been impatient for the stories to give way to studies, for descriptions to be supplemented by data. These results, as they see it, will be decisive in weighing the merits of the different models of education discussed throughout the book. Others, however — and this is true regardless of ideological persuasion — will be more likely to respond, with a wave of the hand, "Ah, you can prove anything with research." Such cynicism may come from years of listening to people *claim* that research proves their particular point. Given enough declarations that turn out to be groundless, you may eventually come to distrust any reference to research.

One example may be enough to make the point. *The Schools We Need,* written by E. D. Hirsch, Jr., in 1996, purports to provide solid evidence in support of Old School practices and against progressive education. However, anyone who actually takes the trouble to track down the studies cited will find that many simply don't show what Hirsch claims they do.[1] Consider the following statement: "It has been shown convincingly that tests and grades strongly contribute to effective teaching" — and again, on the following page: "Research has clearly shown that students learn more when grades are given."[2] In light of a considerable body of evidence showing precisely the opposite (see pp. 41–42), I was immediately curious to know what research Hirsch had uncovered.

His footnote contained five references, but it turned out that all of them dealt only with the use of pass-fail grading options at the college level rather than with elementary and secondary education (the focus of the book and the context of his claim about grades). Furthermore, four of the five sources were more than twenty-five years old, and two were unpublished reports and therefore impossible to verify. Of the three published references, one was just a commentary and another, a survey of opinions of the instructors at one college. Only one of Hirsch's sources contained any real data: it found that undergraduates who took all their courses on a pass-fail basis would have gotten lower grades than those who didn't. But the researchers went on to conclude that "pass-fail grading might prove more beneficial if instituted earlier in the student's career, before grade motivation becomes an obstacle."[3] In other words, the only published study that Hirsch cites to support his sweeping statement about how the value of grades is "clearly shown" by research actually raises questions about the use of grades during the very school years addressed by his book.

This is far from the only example in Hirsch's book where the research fails to substantiate its claim[4] — and this book is far from the only example of this phenomenon. Thus, it's not hard to understand how some readers have learned to discount claims about what "studies show." But even where research is cited accurately, its value depends on how it was conducted. We might say that the strength of a study is a function of three factors, all of which readers would do well to keep in mind: how the relevant terms are defined, how the experiment was set up, and what the researchers were looking for.

Readers may become impatient with claims and counterclaims, wondering why scientists don't just look at the available studies to tell us once and for all whether traditional or nontraditional teaching works better. Part of the problem rests with the many possible meanings of "traditional" and "nontraditional." Fifty researchers may have fifty different things in mind when they use these terms, so two studies allegedly on the same topic may produce findings that aren't really comparable.

One experiment, to take a real example, found better results for a "discovery method" of learning than for an "expository method." This would seem to capture a relevant aspect of progressive education except that other relevant aspects of progressive education were ignored in the study, and one feature — cooperation among students — was for some reason explicitly excluded from the discovery condition.[5] Another example: even assuming we can arrive at a sufficiently precise definition of what must be present in reading instruction to qualify as Whole Language, can we take studies of those classrooms and combine them with studies of "literature-based" instruction? What about weighing a curriculum that uses a combination of basals and literature with one that uses basals alone? Can a study showing that children learn to read faster with direct phonics instruction than without it be counted as evidence against Whole Language, even without looking at any Whole Language classrooms?

You get the idea. One of the reasons that almost any position can be supported by a study — and one of the reasons that no one can ever find a study so definitive that it finally ends the debate on a question

—is that there is so much variation in how the relevant terms are defined. Another complicating factor is the way a given study is set up. Should we follow a group of students over time to see how much they learn under a particular teaching method? (And, by the way, how much time is enough?) Or do we also need a control group—that is, do we need to compare them to a bunch of students who were taught the usual way? How can we be sure that the "usual way" in the study represents what happens in real classrooms?

More: How did the experimenters decide which children would be placed in each kind of classroom? (Probably the largest comparative study of teaching methods,[6] cited by behaviorists as proof that their approach works, failed to assign students randomly to the various conditions. Could some difference between the students in each kind of classroom have accounted for the different outcomes?) We also need to know how many students are being studied. If there aren't enough, we have a weak basis for drawing conclusions, yet huge samples can produce statistically significant differences even when the practical effect of those differences is slight.

Some of these issues—and many more besides—have no clear-cut answers, and specialists continue to argue about the best experimental designs as well as the appropriate statistical techniques for interpreting the data. Still, some studies are clearly designed better than others. Whenever anyone says, "Here's some research that proves $x$ style of schooling is better than $y$," we should immediately ask how that research was conducted.

Finally, before citing or evaluating research, we have to know what the "dependent variables" were—that is, what the researchers were looking for. How did they measure the benefit or harm of a particular educational approach? The vast majority of studies in the field look at how this or that intervention affects academic achievement. Furthermore, academic achievement usually ends up being measured by (indeed, defined as) standardized test scores. If you have doubts about the validity of these tests, claims about the value of whatever kicked up the scores must be regarded skeptically also.

Apart from the specific tests used, one of the key questions we need to keep in mind is the extent to which researchers are mostly just interested in increasing *temporary compliance or temporary retention of facts and low-level skills.* Let's call this Goal 1. Someone for whom this is a primary objective has a good chance of showing a positive effect by doing any of the following: offering people in the experiment a reward (including grades, money, and other incentives) or threatening a punishment, setting up a competition (in effect, turning a reward into an artificially scarce *a*ward), or using a concentrated form of traditional education (including direct instruction and drills that focus on the "basics" and relegate students to a passive role).

As I've described in two previous books, research suggests that the use of carrots, sticks, and competition can indeed "work" to reach Goal 1.[7] Now I want to add that the same is true of the teaching methods described here in chapter 3: studies can be cited to prove that the Old School is successful. But here's the catch: success can be claimed only by those who don't care about three other goals: (a) *long-term retention* of these facts or skills, (b) *a real understanding of ideas,* along with critical thinking, creativity, the capacity to apply skills to different kinds of tasks, and other more sophisticated intellectual outcomes, or (c) *students' interest in what they're doing,* and the likelihood that they'll come away with a continuing motivation to learn.

The rough rule-of-thumb, to anticipate what will follow here, is that the more we are concerned about any of these outcomes, the more that research supports not traditional education but its opposite: the various overlapping versions of the progressive model of education described in chapters 8 and 9. Thus, it's not really accurate to conclude from conflicting claims that "anything can be proved with research" and therefore we may as well ignore it. Rather, we need to evaluate any study in terms of the outcomes being investigated. We need to consider assertions concerning "what studies show about effective education" in terms of what is meant by "effective," and specifically whether the effect could be characterized as short term or long term, low level or high level, and relevant or irrelevant to motivation.

Because I'm willing to concede that traditional schooling can be effective (under certain circumstances) at meeting Goal 1, I won't be citing many of those studies here. Instead, I want to demonstrate that nontraditional schooling is backed by research that is even more impressive, particularly if your values lead you to be more concerned about those other goals. Without attempting the impossible feat of a comprehensive review of every study relevant to all the issues raised in this book, my aim is to give you enough of a feel for the research to show just how ridiculous are the claims that only traditional education is backed by science.

# Teaching Young Children

Some of the most ambitious and expensive educational evaluations in this country have looked at programs growing out of Head Start, begun in the 1960s to help disadvantaged young children. One of those efforts, known as Follow Through, was originally intended to provide support for children after they left preschool. Threatened by the Nixon administration with a loss of funding, Follow Through was hastily reinvented as an experiment involving more than a dozen different models of instruction at more than a hundred sites around the country. Among the results was the finding that some programs emphasizing basic skills—in particular, a model known as Direct Instruction, in which teachers read from a prepared script in the classroom, drilling young children on basic skills in a highly controlled, even militaristic fashion, and offering reinforcement when children produce the correct responses—appeared to produce the best results. Proponents of this kind of teaching have trumpeted this finding ever since as a vindication of their model.

Of course, even if these results could be taken at face value, we don't have any basis for assuming that the model would work for anyone other than disadvantaged children of primary school age. But it turns out that the results can't be taken at face value because the whole study was, to put it bluntly, a mess. It's worth elaborating on that assertion at least briefly because of the role these findings have played in giving the appearance of empirical support for a drill-'n-skill approach to teaching— and also because it will help us understand why other studies have supported exactly the opposite conclusion.

To begin with, the primary research analysts wrote that the "clearest finding" of Follow Through was not the superiority of any one style of teaching but the fact that "each model's performance varies widely from site to site."[8] In fact, the variation in results from one *location* to the next of a given model of instruction was greater than the variation between one *model* and the next. That means the site that kids happened to attend was a better predictor of how well they learned than was the style of teaching (skills-based, child-centered, or whatever).

Second, the primary measure of success used in the study was a standardized multiple-choice test of basic skills called the Metropolitan Achievement Test. While the children were also given other cognitive and psychological assessments, these measures were so poorly chosen as to be virtually worthless.[9] Some of the nontraditional educators involved in the study weren't informed that their programs were going to end up being judged on this basis.[10] The Direct Instruction teachers methodically prepared their students to succeed on a skills test, and, to some extent at least, it worked. As the study's authors put it, Follow Through proved that "models that emphasize the kinds of skills tested by certain subtests of the Metropolitan Achievement Test have tended—very irregularly—to produce groups that score better on those subtests than do groups served by models that emphasize those skills to a lesser degree. This is hardly an astonishing finding; to have discovered the contrary would have been much more surprising."[11]

Finally, outside evaluators of the project—as well as an official review by the U.S. General Accounting Office—determined that there were still other problems in its design and analysis that undermined the basic findings.[12] Their overall conclusion, published in the *Harvard Educational Review,* was that "because of misclassification of the models, inadequate measurement of results, and flawed statistical analysis," the study simply "does not demonstrate that models emphasizing basic skills are superior to other models."[13] Furthermore, even if Direct Instruction really was better than other models at the time of the study, to cite that result today as proof of its superiority is to assume that educators have learned nothing in the intervening three decades about effective ways of teaching young children. The value of newer approaches—including Whole Language, as we'll see—means that comparative data from the 1960s now have a sharply limited relevance.

That suspicion is strengthened by recent anecdotal evidence about Direct Instruction and similar programs in which children are trained, not unlike pets, to master a prescribed set of low-level skills. Reporters for the *New York Times* and *Education Week* visited Direct Instruction (DI) classrooms—in North Carolina and Texas, respectively—and coincidentally published their accounts in the same month, June 1998. The *Education Week* reporter found that sixth-grade students, successfully trained to do well on the main standardized test used in Texas, couldn't explain what was going on in the book they were reading or even what the title meant. Apparently, she concluded, "mastering reading skills does not guarantee comprehension." The *Times* reporter had been told by the for-profit company running a DI school that all of their kindergartners had been trained to read. "All you have to remember" as a teacher, he was told, "is that you can't go off the script." But when the reporter showed the children "something basic they'd never seen," they couldn't make heads or tails of it. A regimented drill-'n-skill approach had trained them to "read" only what had been on the teachers' script.[14]

Even apart from journalistic investigation, it's common knowledge among many inner-city educators that children often make little if any meaningful progress with skills-based instruction.[15] But this failure is typically attributed to the teachers, to the limited abilities of the children, or to virtually anything except the model itself. In contrast, whenever problems persist in nontraditional classrooms, they are immediately cited as proof of the need to go "back to basics."

Not only does this attitude represent an indefensible double standard, but a lot more research dating back to the same era as the Follow Through project supports a very different conclusion. Several independent studies of early childhood education have compared tightly controlled, skills-oriented classrooms (such as DI) to an assortment of "developmentally appropriate" (DA) approaches, including those referred to as child-centered or constructivist and those using the Montessori or High/Scope models.[16]

For example, an Illinois study of poor children from the mid-1960s found immediate gains in reading and arithmetic for the DI group, a result that might have given the traditionalists something to boast about if the investigators hadn't continued to track the students after preschool. With each year that went by, the advantage of two years of regimented reading skills instruction melted away and soon proved equivalent to "an intensive 1-hour reading readiness support program" given to another group. One difference did show up much later, though: almost three quarters of the DA kids ended up graduating from high school compared to less than half of the DI kids. (The latter rate was equivalent to that of students who hadn't attended preschool at all).[17]

Research that follows people over a considerable period of time is expensive and therefore relatively rare, but its findings are far more powerful than those from short-term studies. Frankly, given how much happens to us over the years, it would be remarkable to find that *any* single variable from our early childhood had a long-term effect. That's why the results from another such study are nothing short of amazing. Back in the 1960s, a group of mostly African-American poor children from Michigan were randomly assigned to DI, free-play, or High/Scope constructivist preschools. They were followed from that point, when they were three or four years old, all the way into adulthood. As in the Illinois sample, the academic performance of the DI children was initially higher but soon became (and remained) indistinguishable from that of the others. By the time they were fifteen years old, other differences began showing up. The DI group had engaged in twice as many "delinquent acts," were less than half as likely to read books, and generally showed more social and psychological signs of trouble than those who had attended either a free-play or a constructivist preschool.[18]

When the researchers checked in again eight years later, the situation had gotten even worse for the young adults who had attended a pre-school with a heavy dose of skills instruction and positive reinforcement. They didn't differ from their peers in the other programs in their literacy skills, total amount of schooling, income, or employment status. But they were far more likely to have been arrested for a felony at some point and also to have been identified as "emotionally impaired or disturbed." (Six percent of the High/Scope and free-play preschool group had been so identified at some point compared to a whopping 47 percent of the DI group.) The researchers also noted who was now married and living with his or her spouse. The results: 18 percent of the free-play preschool group, 31 percent of the High/Scope group, and not a single person from the DI group.[19]

It might be tempting to say that these disturbing findings have to be weighed against the academic benefits of a back-to-basics preschool model—except that both studies showed that any such benefits are washed away very quickly. Moreover, a third experiment, with kindergartners in Louisiana, failed to find even a short-term boost in test scores. There were no significant differences between the two groups at the end of the year or at the end of first or second grade. What did distinguish the different models in this study was that the children who had been taught with the skills-based approach were "more hostile and aggressive, anxious and fearful, and hyperactive and distractible" than those who had attended more developmentally appropriate kindergarten classrooms—and they remained so a full year later. (Other research has confirmed the presence of much higher levels of "stress-related behaviors" as a result of direct instruction techniques.)[20] Furthermore, when the researchers broke the results down by race, economic background, and gender, they found that low-income black males were "most likely to be hurt by . . . teach-to-the-test instruction." This was true, first, because they experienced an unusual amount of stress, and second, because for this group there was a difference in academic achievement: those in the skills-oriented class-rooms didn't do as well even on skills-oriented tests.[21]

Three other studies conducted in the 1980s and '90s seem to clinch the case:

- When DI was compared to a constructivist model not unlike High/Scope in six Alaskan kindergarten classrooms (whose students were mostly white and from economically diverse backgrounds), the latter students did as well or better on standardized tests of reading and math.[22]
- When a didactic, basic skills focus was compared to a child-centered

focus in thirty-two preschool and kindergarten classes in California, children in the former group did better on reading tests (consistent with the short-term advantage found in some of the other studies), neither better nor worse on math tests, and terribly on a range of nonacademic measures. The skills kids had lower expectations of themselves, worried more about school, were more dependent on adults, and preferred easier tasks.[23]

- A study of more than 250 children in Washington, D.C., that began in 1987 compared those from "child-initiated," "middle-of-the-road," and "academically directed" preschool and kindergarten classrooms. Those from the child-initiated preschools "actually mastered more basic skills by initiating their own learning experiences" and continued to do well as the years went by. The middle-of-the-roaders fell behind their peers. As for those from the academically directed group, their "social development declined along with mastery of first-grade reading and math objectives. . . . By fourth and fifth grades, children from academic pre-K programs were developmentally behind their peers and displayed notably higher levels of maladaptive behavior" — particularly in the case of boys.[24]

In keeping with my earlier cautions about deriving a single conclusion from a range of very different studies, I should emphasize that the research with young children includes many variables that can affect the results: social and economic class, age (what's true of preschoolers may not be true of second-graders), the specific nature of the child-centered alternative(s), and a focus on short-term versus long-term effects as well as on academic versus nonacademic issues. Still, with the single exception of the Follow Through study (where a skills-oriented model produced gains on a skills-oriented test, and even then, only at some sites), the results are striking for their consistent message that a tightly structured, traditionally academic model for young children provides virtually no lasting benefits and proves to be potentially harmful in many respects.

# Whole Language: Rethinking the Case Against

There aren't many topics in education where you will find so wide a chasm between what the evidence actually says and what the public assumes it says. It is widely believed that Whole Language (WL) has nothing to support it except good intentions, and that scientific evidence shows that systematic phonics instruction (and, more generally, a skills-based approach) is strongly preferable, if not absolutely necessary, for teaching children to read. This belief has been stated as fact so often by proponents of that kind of instruction that by now journalists, politicians, and many parents feel no need to defend it. It has become part of our folk wisdom.

The truth, as three Illinois educators explained, is that "the main body of educational research, amassed over six decades, strongly and consistently validates [those] progressive approaches to teaching reading now grouped under the name 'Whole Language.' "[25] We'll get to some of that proof shortly, but first let's take a closer look at the claims made to the contrary. To begin with, the studies brandished by WL opponents usually fail to support the claims for which they are being cited. There's a gap, in other words, between the arguments and the data. Exhibit A is the tendency to cite research showing that phonics is important. The proper response to this claim is, "Yeah. So?" The relevant question, remember, is not whether phonics matters but how it will be taught. You can't take a study showing that kids have to recognize and know how to pronounce all the phonemes and then pretend you've justified a particular method of teaching that skill (such as the use of drills) or a particular schedule for this instruction (such as teaching phonics before letting kids read literature). As a matter of fact, "hardly any researcher advocates [teaching] phonics first—not even most phonics advocates."[26]

A second problem is that the overwhelming majority of the research used to support the direct instruction of phonics skills (and to oppose WL) consists of tallying up children's scores on standardized reading tests. The problem is that most of those tests measure decoding and word identification, not comprehension.[27] Skills tests are a perfect match for skills instruction, and it's not surprising that the latter often produces good results on the former. Sometimes those tests are literally nonsense: they require kids to sound out collections of letters that don't make any sense. They tell us nothing about what kids can do with their skills. Because they don't measure literacy at all, they fail to capture what WL can achieve.

Conversely, explicit training in phonemic awareness is most likely to produce an effect on this kind of test and least likely to produce an effect on those involving comprehension.[28] This is clearest in the case of extreme methods like DI, where, as we've seen, kids can be trained to call out letters or words on command but without any understanding. If their test scores go up, that says more about what's included in (and excluded from) these tests than it does about the value of this style of instruction.[29]

Third, studies do show that "phonemic awareness" is associated with being a good reader. The problem is that causality is assumed where only correlation has been shown. In other words, the fact that these two things tend to occur together shouldn't be (but often is) used to justify the claim that phonemic awareness causes, and is necessary for, kids to read well. It's entirely possible — and consistent with this line of research — that the relationship also works the other way around or that some third factor, such as spending a lot of time with books, leads kids to be better readers *and* better decoders. This is not nit-picking: it may not make sense to focus on isolated phonics skills if it turns out that this isn't the cause (or at least the only cause) of higher reading achievement.[30]

What's interesting about all the claims that research proves the superiority of intensive phonics instruction to WL is that a lot of the studies described in research reviews were conducted before WL, as such, even existed. What they were really comparing with a systematic focus on phonics was a "whole word" approach to decoding, which is completely different.[31] The latter didn't work very well, but that doesn't count as an argument against Whole Language any more than it counts as an argument against something else with the word "whole" in it (such as "whole class" instruction). Even some newer studies that claim to evaluate WL are actually looking at something a little different, such as a "language experience" model of instruction, which may exclude such elements of WL as having children do their own writing.

In any case, the timing of the research is relevant since more recent studies have been especially supportive of WL. Also relevant is the population of children being studied. Some experiments, notably those sponsored by the National Institute of Child Health and Development (NICHD), have been limited to students "identified as experiencing some severe reading difficulties" — and yet are casually cited as though they justified using a certain method for teaching all children to read.[32]

In an effort to discredit WL, some opponents have lately made a different kind of argument. Look at California, they say: when the state switched from phonics instruction to WL, reading test scores, notably on the 1994 NAEP exam, dropped. This claim, too, has been repeated endlessly and uncritically in the popular press, reflecting at best an ignorance of what was really going on and, at worst, a calculated attempt to discredit WL by twisting the facts. First of all, while a change in California's framework for language arts instruction in the late 1980s did call for more literature in teaching reading, it wasn't a legal mandate and it never endorsed WL per se. More important, there is no evidence that it was widely implemented. It's likely that more teachers began to use literature-based basal readers, but not necessarily in a manner consistent with WL (at which few had been trained). Many teachers simply assigned the same story to the whole class; when that didn't work very well, the fault was said to lie with WL.[33]

Of course, we're taking for granted that there actually was a surge in reading difficulties during the period in question, a claim that is open to debate.[34] But even if this did occur, any reasonable observer would have to conclude that there are other, far more plausible explanations. Serious budget cutbacks resulted in large numbers of students in each class and one of the most inadequate school library systems in the country. In the early 1990s, California ranked dead last among the fifty states in librarians per pupil and next to last in books per pupil.[35] Then there is the explosive growth in the number of students from other cultures: in 1988, 652,000 California students were identified as having limited English proficiency; a decade later, the number had more than doubled, to 1.4 million.[36] One would have to be pretty desperate to claim with a straight face that WL explains why children are having trouble reading in California.

## Whole Language: Reviewing the Case in Favor

Complementing the deficiencies of arguments against WL are quite a lot of data to support it. As someone who doesn't subscribe to professional journals on reading research, I was frankly unprepared for the sheer number of studies demonstrating its effectiveness. Some of them evaluated relatively few students, and not all of them mean the same thing by "Whole Language" or by the traditional alternative to which it is being compared. Still, the cumulative effect of this research literature is truly impressive, particularly in demonstrating that WL kids hold their own even on standardized reading tests. It seems that spending time reading and talking about real books, writing and rewriting, and generally being steeped in language-rich activities not only gives children an enormous advantage in terms of real literacy but also provides sufficient preparation for the low-level measures of skills that many people seem to care more about.

The 1980s saw a sprinkling of such studies, not all of which were published. At a girls' parochial school in the Northeast, a WL kindergarten produced better results across the board, including on formal measures of phonetic knowledge, than a kindergarten with a highly structured phonics program.[37] At a public school in the South, low-income minority kindergartners were followed and tested for three years. The result was similar: those in the WL group not only became better readers but, even though they were "not drilled on words or word parts in isolation, they scored significantly higher" on two standardized measures of basic word skills than those who had been taught the traditional way.[38] A huge study in Utah, featuring 1,149 children in fifty classrooms, confirmed that "the use of children's literature to teach children to read had a positive effect upon students' achievement and attitudes toward reading — much greater than the traditional methods."[39]

In 1989, an article in *The Reading Teacher* caught the attention of people in the field by describing a number of studies that favored a literature-based approach to teaching reading.[40] It had no sooner been published than more such studies started appearing. Two showed up in the same issue of the *Journal of Educational Research*: one found that after a year of WL instruction, first-graders did better on reading tests than their counterparts who had spent the year with skill lessons and worksheets.[41] The other found that WL helped second-graders to write better, when judged on content, than those who had been in a traditional classroom; there were no differences between the two in terms of their mastery of mechanics.[42]

Meanwhile, Lesley Mandel Morrow and her colleagues at Rutgers University were evaluating "at-risk kindergarten classes in an urban school district in New Jersey," comparing a group that did mostly story reading with a group that spent the year with a commercially produced reading-readiness program (Living with the Alphabet). The former group ended up being better readers in terms of comprehension while scoring about the same on a skills test.[43] Two years later, Morrow moved up to second grade, trying out a curriculum that spent less time on the district's standard basal reader and more time with independent reading and writing. Again, those children did better on a variety of measures of comprehension and just about as well on standardized tests.[44]

Even with the odds stacked against WL — teachers just learning how to teach this way and tests favoring traditional skills instruction — still other researchers have found it to be every bit as effective for helping first-graders learn the mechanics of reading[45] and for helping kindergartners (both high and low achievers) to become competent writers.[46] The researcher who directed the latter study also discovered another sort of difference between the children who came from literature- as opposed to skills-based classrooms: when presented with incomprehensible text (for example, "To bus was it Mrs. the go the"), many of the skills kids said they couldn't read it because it was too hard, whereas most of the literature kids just laughed.[47]

Additional studies seem to roll in every year. One reviewer concluded in 1998, "The notion that an emphasis primarily on skills and phonics instruction produces superior results to programs centered on providing children with a lot of interesting and comprehensible texts is not supported by the available evidence."[48] And from another: "The evidence seems fairly strong that whole language teaching produces about the same results on standardized tests . . . as does traditional skills-oriented instruction, including teaching that has emphasized phonics [while producing] substantially greater advances in a variety of literacy-related skills, strategies, behaviors, and attitudes."[49]

Naturally, all of this flies in the face of the conventional wisdom, which is that an intensive skills-based approach makes up in effectiveness what it lacks in appeal. Nor does the research support the fall-back position of WL opponents — that progressive classrooms may work for high-achieving, affluent white kids, but everyone else needs a heavy dose of basic skills. Until I combed through the journals, I didn't understand how thoroughly this claim misrepresents what researchers have actually found.

Consider the children who seem to have a tougher time in school. In the overwhelming majority of American classrooms, these kids will receive a heavy diet of isolated skills and a lot less literature than their more proficient peers. "Good readers are more likely to be presented lessons that emphasize meaning, while poor readers' lessons more often emphasize words, sounds, and letters," reports the reading researcher Richard Allington.[50] This continues to be the case despite research showing that poor readers need to spend time reading real books (as opposed to practicing skills) as much as good readers do — and maybe more.[51] Specifically, researchers have discovered that "low progressing" first-graders (in one study) and "low scoring" kindergartners (in another) made more progress in WL classrooms than in traditional classrooms. More proficient children did as well or better with WL, too.[52]

Minority children from low-income families typically get the same kind of drill-'n-skill instruction that low achievers do, sometimes because individual teachers arrange things that way and sometimes because it's imposed on teachers in the form of heavily scripted programs like Success for All[53] or Direct Instruction. (One group of researchers, looking to compare minority students who were in such classrooms to those in WL classrooms, had trouble finding enough examples of the latter to conduct their study.)[54] To the extent that this represents a deliberate strategy — as opposed to another example of how the least thoughtful, lowest quality teaching is once again most common in the poorest neighborhoods — the rationale goes like this: privileged white children have often learned phonics from their parents before they get to school. Their peers who haven't had this luxury need to learn phonics in order to catch up.[55]

One problem with this argument is the tendency, once again, to confuse learning phonics with a particular (intensive, systematic, drill-based) method of teaching phonics. Remember: WL includes phonics, but in the context of meaningful stories and other authentic uses of language. The children who show up at kindergarten already reading are typically coming from homes that are more like WL than drill-'n-skill environments. That's why WL proponents point out that "overemphasizing phonics may be especially damaging for children who have had few experiences with books prior to school."[56]

This argument is supported by some of the studies already mentioned here, notably Morrow's evaluation of at-risk children in New Jersey and the comparison of minority kindergartners in the South. Now we can add three separate studies of kindergartens and/or first grades, all published in the 1990s and all focusing on children of low socioeconomic status. All found that some variation of WL instruction (in one case with a scant fifteen minutes a day of skills instruction tacked on) was superior to traditional reading instruction for these students.[57]

Beyond the studies comparing individual classrooms, there is one other kind of evidence worth mentioning. The NAEP—the source of the allegedly lower scores of California students used to argue against WL—includes a questionnaire that provides some information about students and teachers that can be correlated with the scores. Data from fourth-grade teachers throughout the 1990s turned up some intriguing findings. First, the more frequently students could read books of their own choosing in class, the higher their scores. (Those who could do so every day had the best scores, those who were never permitted to do so had the worst, and those who could do so occasionally were in the middle.) Second, those students who never used workbooks or worksheets had the highest scores, those who used them every day had the lowest, and those who used them occasionally again fell in between. Finally, those who never took quizzes or tests had the highest scores, those who took them every day had the lowest, and those who took them occasionally were in the middle.[58]

Although this evidence is indirect, it's hard to deny that a class with more tests, more worksheets, and less choice does bear a striking resemblance to the Old School model of teaching, whereas the reverse has an awful lot in common with WL. More direct evidence comes from simply asking teachers whether they have a "whole language," "literature-based," or "phonics" approach to reading instruction. There are, to be sure, several reasons for exercising caution in drawing conclusions from the answers: WL and phonics are not opposites; what teachers say in a questionnaire isn't necessarily what they do; and these are fourth-grade rather than primary-grade teachers. Still, the students of those teachers who picked "phonics" had a lower average score (208) than those who picked WL (220) or literature (221). Moreover, when you look at the state-by-state results, the more fourth-grade teachers who said they used phonics, the lower that state's average NAEP score.[59] If we assume there is some correlation between the way a school's fourth-grade teachers and its first-grade teachers approach reading instruction, these results are suggestive indeed. Oddly, they weren't reported in any newspapers or popular magazines.

•

Some academics who are partial to traditional instruction have claimed that standardized tests reveal no clear advantage for WL. (Notice the "spin" here: proponents of WL might describe the same result by saying that their approach manages to do just as well as skills-centered instruction even though it doesn't concentrate on teaching skills explicitly.) Based on my own reading of the research, I would challenge this summary: as we've seen, WL often pulls ahead of explicit phonics instruction on decoding measures and almost always proves superior when children are tested on comprehension.

But assume for the moment that the critics are right: WL is neither better nor worse than traditional instruction on achievement measures. Even if this is true, wouldn't it still make sense to use WL in light of its other advantages? Giving students more choice about their learning has its own set of benefits and may even be regarded as intrinsically preferable. WL creates a sense of community, which is also valuable in its own right. And, perhaps most important, WL is much more likely to foster a love of reading. It's only common sense that stories are more appealing than worksheets, and this view is supported not only by anecdotal accounts (see chapter 9) but by research. Regardless of race or class, kids in WL classrooms typically report having more positive attitudes about reading —and, in one study, actually did more reading on their own—than those in traditional classrooms.[60] For some of us, the ultimate objective is not just for children to know how to read but *for them to read*. If WL is more likely to lead to that result, it would seem to be the obvious choice, all else being even close to equal.

•

Finally, two areas related to reading—spelling and grammar—have attracted a modest amount of research, with surprising results. Consider first the practice of "invented spelling," in which young children are encouraged to write before they can spell correctly. Because they end up writing so much more than kids in traditional classrooms, they do indeed make a lot more mistakes. But they also spend more time rereading what they've written, and they tend to pay attention to the relation between letters and sounds rather than just memorizing correct spellings. The result is that they "gradually adopt appropriate symbols for sounds and . . . progress to traditional spelling."[61] Typically, they wind up scoring "as well or better on standardized tests of spelling *by the end of first grade* than children who are allowed to use only correct spellings in first drafts."[62] One study found that first-graders in invented spelling classrooms continued to make more errors in their writing through the year, but on a spelling test given in March, they actually got a higher score than those in traditional classrooms. Low achievers benefited the most from invented spelling.[63] As for older students, a study of nearly 3,000 children in 22 states found that explicit spelling instruction seemed to produce no advantage at all after fourth grade. Students who had not been taught spelling as a separate subject did just as well on a test as those who had used any of three leading commercial programs.[64]

Grammar instruction provides a spectacular lesson on how old-fashioned dogma continues to drive beliefs and practices in direct contradiction to scientific findings. In the mid-1970s, a group of New Zealand researchers reviewed the available literature and wrote that "sixty years of empirical studies on the practical value of teaching grammar have failed to demonstrate any consistent measurable effects on students' writing skills." Nevertheless, they set out to design a test of their own, dividing 164 secondary school students into three carefully matched groups and exposing them to traditional grammar instruction, to a new "transformational grammar" curriculum, or to a course that just used the grammar time for more reading and creative writing. Three teachers rotated through each approach, so each group of students was exposed to all three teachers doing the same kind of instruction. At the end of three years, there were virtually no differences among the groups, which is to say there were no measurable benefits of formal grammar instruction.[65]

Returning to the question in 1991, two U.S. scholars contributed a definitive chapter to a research handbook published by the International Reading Association and the National Council of Teachers of English. They found absolutely nothing to challenge the New Zealanders' conclusion. Indeed, a meta-analysis performed by one of the authors a few years earlier had discovered that students studying grammar actually did worse than their peers on some measures, raising the possibility that almost "any focus of instruction is more effective in improving the quality of writing than grammar and mechanics." The major question suggested by all the data was why grammar retains its appeal "when research over the past 90 years reveals not only that students do not learn it and are hostile toward it, but that the study of grammar has no impact on writing quality." The best answer they could come up with is that grammar is easy to teach, easy to grade, and "provides security in having 'right' answers." The grammar sections of a textbook should be used as a reference tool, they concluded, and not as a course of study.[66]

# Math Results

Whether U.S. students are doing "well enough" in math is, of course, a judgment call. But to whatever extent we are dissatisfied with their proficiency, there is good reason to believe that the traditional model of instruction bears a large part of the responsibility.

In the mid to late 1990s, a comprehensive international comparison of math and science teaching, known by the acronym TIMSS, was conducted and then released piecemeal. Part of the study involved a series of conventional tests given to students all over the world in the equivalent of fourth, eighth, and twelfth grades. U.S. students did rather well in fourth grade, rather poorly in eighth grade, and miserably in twelfth grade — although questions have been raised about the data underlying these conclusions (see p. 246*n*62).

TIMSS wasn't limited to standardized test results, however; it also included an analysis of curriculum materials and classroom practices. For one segment of the study, James Stigler and his colleagues videotaped more than two hundred eighth-grade math teachers to review their methods and distributed questionnaires to get a sense of their objectives. Three out of five U.S. teachers said they were chiefly concerned with "skill building." Only one out of four Japanese teachers responded that way: the overwhelming majority said they wanted their students to understand a particular math concept. That goal led those teachers to include deductive reasoning in their instruction, which played a role in 62 percent of Japanese lessons and 0 percent of U.S. lessons. Japanese teachers also explored the intricacies of specific mathematical concepts with their students rather than just naming those concepts, American style. In Japanese classrooms, fewer math problems were considered in more depth, and students participated actively in suggesting different ways of solving those problems. Also, interestingly, homework was rarely assigned.[67]

The overall conclusion reached by the TIMSS researchers—which somehow didn't make it into the headlines, or even into the news stories—was that *traditional forms of teaching, and an emphasis on the basics, contributed significantly to the low standing of older American students.* Even before the last phase of the study was reported (looking at the final year of high school and finding the worst results for U.S. students), the TIMSS authors wrote: "Instruction in this country still seems—compared to instruction in some other countries—more centered on students as passive absorbers of knowledge rather than as active participants who construct, transform, and integrate knowledge."

They went on to predict that "a widespread choice to focus on 'basics'" in American schools would probably lead to "corresponding differences in student achievement, and the differences should be cumulative, with U.S. students falling further behind as they move through the grades"—which is exactly what happened. These findings can't be explained in terms of "natural differences" among students—that is, innate ability—or even in terms of how much effort students put in, since "curricular differences . . . affect how much students can achieve even by working hard." Looking at data from around the world, the researchers found that students lucky enough to live in countries that avoided the "back to basics" approach to instruction "performed comparatively far better" on tests of real understanding.[68]

Recall that these conclusions precisely mirror those of the NAEP, the major U.S. assessment of student achievement, in terms of math instruction. They're also corroborated by a study of math instruction in the upper elementary grades, which found that "heavy emphasis on skill development and slight attention to concepts and applications may help to explain the United States' relatively poor standing among other nations on mathematics problem-solving ability of students."[69]

Another kind of support came in 1998, when a researcher compared students' use of computers to their NAEP math scores. The overall finding, surprisingly enough, was that the more time students spent on computers during school, the worse they did on the exam. But, on closer inspection, it turned out that nontraditional uses of computers, such as for simulations and learning games, were beneficial. The negative achievement effect was confined to those students who used computers primarily for practicing basic skills.[70] Apparently even the use of new technology is not enough to mitigate the destructive effects of the old pedagogy.

So much for recent evidence on traditional approaches to math instruction. What can we say about efforts to introduce more conceptual and constructivist alternatives? The research on such programs has been concentrated in the primary grades, and it points to a result that can be summarized in six words: *better reasoning without sacrificing computational skills*—an interesting echo of what we've just seen about a nontraditional approach to teaching reading (namely, better comprehension without sacrificing decoding skills).

In one study, forty first-grade teachers in Wisconsin were given special training in how to make problem solving the organizing focus of teaching arithmetic. When achievement tests taken by their students were later compared to those of traditionally taught children, the results showed a modest, though consistent, edge for the former group. "A focus on problem solving does not necessarily result in a decline in performance in computational skills," the authors wrote.[71]

A few years later, some researchers in Delaware attempted something similar with a smaller group of second-grade teachers. Children in nontraditional classrooms solved a lot fewer problems over the course of the year but presumably with more thought and understanding, because they ended up doing better on tests—particularly when they had to solve problems they hadn't seen before.[72] A third study confirmed that a more conceptual approach to math instruction at both the elementary and secondary levels didn't entail a sacrifice in standardized test scores, even during the transition from traditional instruction.[73] And a fourth project, in Maryland, found that such math instruction boosted achievement for low-income, mostly minority students—although it took a couple of years for the benefits to reach statistical significance.[74]

Still another group of researchers, at Purdue University in Indiana, developed a very specific framework for teaching the local school district's math objectives to second-graders. Problems were presented for children to work on in pairs, after which the whole class came together to talk about their results. There were no grades, no praise for right answers, no textbooks or worksheets, no requirements for getting through a certain number of problems, and no demonstration by the teacher of the "correct" way to solve them. Teachers took care to encourage productive collaboration and to create a supportive environment where kids could safely challenge one another's ideas.[75]

After a pilot classroom had been set up and analyzed, the researchers were ready to compare the effects of their model to those of traditional classes in three schools. There was virtually no difference in how well the children did basic computation, but those in the alternative classrooms demonstrated significantly higher levels of mathematical reasoning.[76] All the students then spent the next year in conventional classrooms and were tested again. Those whose second-grade experience had been nontraditional were still more advanced at conceptually challenging tasks.[77]

Meanwhile, the researchers were extending their project to more second-grade classrooms as well as to some third-grade classrooms, thus allowing them to gauge the effects of spending two consecutive years in a place where "patterns, relationships, and meanings are constituted by students" and where math class is reconfigured as "a community in which mutual exchange and in-depth interaction occurs." The additional year in such a setting did indeed make a difference. Many different kinds of math competence were tested, and while not all measures showed a statistically significant effect, none indicated better performance for traditionally instructed students than for those who had had the two years of alternative math. The latter students were far more proficient at understanding problems presented in nontextbook formats, and they also did better at basic computation—even after they had gone on to spend a year in a conventional classroom. Those who had had only one year of constructivist math were more likely to be dragged back down to the level of drill-'n-skill students—not only in their achievement but in their attitudes: they came to accept that math is about "solving problems using a single method" rather than believing, as they once had, that it's about "trying to understand and figure out for oneself."[78]

On a smaller and more informal scale, the constructivist theorist Constance Kamii has tested a few elementary classrooms in which children worked all the problems on their own without being given any algorithms. Consistent with the other studies, she discovered that two constructivist second-grade classes did about as well as two conventional classes on a standardized achievement test but performed better on measures of thinking.[79] A subsequent comparison of third-graders also found that the "Constructivist Group used a variety of procedures, got more correct answers, and made more reasonable errors when they got incorrect answers. The Comparison Group by and large had only one way of approaching each problem—the conventional algorithm—and tended to get incorrect answers that revealed poor number sense."[80]

Finally, a small British study published in 1998 suggests that the same pattern holds true for older students. A researcher compared math instruction at two very different schools and followed students for three years, starting when they were thirteen years old. The first school was very traditional, with a sequential, skill-based math program; the other one used an open-ended, project-based approach. In the end, students at the second school not only were more adept at solving problems that involved applying math principles to "realistic situations," but also did better on conventional tests of content knowledge.[81]

•

One last point, which is not so incidental: a teacher working with Kamii commented that after she adopted the constructivist approach to instruction, her classes "displayed a love of math that I had not seen during my first decade of teaching."[82] While there are no hard data to confirm this impression (as there are with Whole Language), it certainly matches what the Purdue researchers witnessed in their experimental classrooms. They reported that visitors "invariably remarked about the excitement for mathematics displayed by the children as they solved the activities. Children frequently jumped up and down, hugged each other, and rushed off to tell the teacher when they solved a particularly challenging problem." Moreover, they persisted at difficult problems to an unusual degree and took pleasure in one another's successes.[83] Of course, this is probably related to the absence of stickers, grades, praise, and other reinforcers that tend to interfere with children's delight in the learning itself. But the tasks must be sufficiently engaging and open-ended so that success is potentially delightful—something far less likely to happen when children are just expected to go through the approved steps to get the correct answers on a worksheet.[84]

# Open Classrooms, Progressive High Schools, and Other Experiments

The benefits of progressive education are not peculiar to early childhood education, nor are they limited to reading and math. Studies published from the 1960s through the mid-1980s have confirmed the same basic pattern. A middle school geography program based on group discussions and active learning was far more effective than traditional instruction even at helping students retain basic factual knowledge.[85] A review of some fifty-seven studies of "activity-based" and "process oriented" elementary school science programs (in which no textbooks were used, by the way) found that students emerged as much better thinkers than their counterparts in traditional classrooms—and they didn't sacrifice any learning of basic content. The benefit of the nontraditional instruction in these studies was especially significant for disadvantaged students. The "one caution" offered by the authors was that the advantages of such teaching "may be lost for elementary students when they are later enrolled in classrooms where more traditional methods prevail."[86]

Many other studies were conducted in the 1960s and '70s to evaluate so-called open classrooms, a term that has been variously defined but loosely coincides with some of the progressive ideas set out in chapter 8. Although some classrooms classified this way have been, shall we say, less than rigorous in their implementation of a nontraditional philosophy, the consensus on the part of reviewers of the relevant research has been that "students' academic achievement did not suffer in open classrooms, and in several areas—creativity, self-concept, attitudes toward school—students in open classrooms did better than students in traditional classrooms." Some studies find no statistically significant difference between the two models, but when such a difference does turn up, it almost always favors open rather than traditional classrooms.[87]

The research already reviewed on Whole Language as well as preschool programs suggests that the Old School particularly fails children of color, children of poverty, and children who have difficulty keeping up. This conclusion is powerfully confirmed by a three-year, in-depth study of 140 first- through sixth-grade classrooms with high concentrations of poor children. Here, the comparison was between conventional, basic-skills instruction and that which "emphasized meaning and understanding." Not surprisingly, perhaps, the latter group exhibited a greater grasp of advanced skills. But they were also more successful overall at acquiring *basic* skills than were the children subjected to the kind of teaching designed to produce exactly that result. The researchers noted that, as a rule, "schooling for the children of poverty . . . emphasizes basic skills, sequential curricula, and tight control of instruction by the teacher." Their findings, however, suggest that this makes no sense when we consider that "alternative practices work at least as well for low-performing as [for] high-performing students in all three subject areas"—reading, writing, and mathematics.[88]

It would be nice to be able to say with assurance that a curriculum emphasizing meaning and understanding, or a classroom based on student decision-making and collaboration, has been proven more successful at the secondary school level as well. Neither that proposition nor the reverse can be stated with confidence, however, because it's not easy to find high school classes that aren't teacher-centered, didactic, fueled by grades and tests, and otherwise thoroughly traditional. Partly for that reason, it's difficult to find empirical tests of progressive teaching at this level. In fact, the best example I know of dates back to the 1930s! That experiment, known as the Eight-Year Study, ought to have made far more of an impact than it did—and ought to be a lot better known than it is. It has quite rightly been called the best-kept educational secret of the twentieth century.

Here's what happened: thirty high schools around the country set about turning traditional practice on its head, particularly for students planning to go on to college. In place of grade-driven, teacher-controlled, competitive instruction, the learning was interdisciplinary, conceptual, experiential, collaborative, often ungraded, and fashioned jointly by teachers and students. Specifically for the study, hundreds of colleges agreed to set aside their usual admissions requirements so that students from these progressive programs wouldn't be penalized.

More than fifteen hundred students over four years were compared to an equal number of carefully matched students at conventional schools. The result: when they got to college, the experimental students did just as well as, and often better than, their traditionally educated counterparts on all counts: grades, extracurricular participation, and drop-out rate, as well as on measures of such things as intellectual curiosity and resourcefulness. And here's the kicker: "The further a school departed from the traditional college preparatory program, the better was the record of its graduates."[89]

Like Whole Language and child-centered preschools, the Eight-Year Study gave students more say about what they were doing. A separate line of research has convincingly demonstrated that students of all ages and in all subjects tend to learn more effectively whenever this is true.[90] To wit: Young children did more creative collages when they could choose which materials to use. Second-graders were more efficient in completing their tasks when they were given more control over their schedules. High school chemistry students learned better if they could design their own experiments instead of following set procedures. Low-income minority children fared better in terms of academic achievement if their teachers had been trained to bolster their sense of control over what was happening to them. Sixth-graders who had the chance to make decisions about their learning got higher standardized test scores.[91]

Indeed, performance was positively affected even when students were given the opportunity to make relatively trivial choices about relatively unengaging curricula: the specific method of instruction for an elementary school vocabulary lesson, which questions to answer on a middle school math quiz, or how to set the criteria for grading in a tenth-grade typing class.[92] Attempts to correlate NAEP scores with reports of student choice have produced mixed results,[93] but, with the exception of one study of undergraduates,[94] the research comparing classrooms with and without choice have all demonstrated a bottom-line benefit for the former.

Once again, if we allow ourselves to look beyond achievement, the case for giving students more opportunity to make decisions becomes even more compelling. When elementary school teachers (in a South African study) or high school teachers (in a Canadian study) were less controlling, students became more interested in learning. When undergraduates had some choice about which puzzle to work on and how long to work on it, they ended up finding the task more appealing than the students who spent the same amount of time on the same puzzle but had no say in the matter. Beyond interest, it appears that the chance to make decisions about what one is learning also encourages people to try more difficult tasks and to gain confidence about their abilities.[95]

Other specific features of progressive education arrive trailing equally impressive research backing. The idea of learning by cooperating with others (as opposed to individually or competitively) has become virtually a field unto itself, with literally hundreds of studies to support it.[96] More recently, researchers have begun to demonstrate the value of transforming classrooms and whole schools into "caring communities"; this, too, can profoundly affect students' experience of school, of learning, and of themselves.[97] Specific school reforms such as multiage education, block scheduling, and "looping" have also demonstrated encouraging results, as reported elsewhere in this book.

However, even the most promising examples of school restructuring — having students learn in groups, in smaller classes, or in classes that stay together longer — will have limited effectiveness if we fail to change the fundamental approach to teaching. The root of the problem is a school experience that is essentially passive, fragmented, and based on skills. And the basis for saying that lies with yet another strand of research: that conducted by experimental constructivists as well as by cognitive scientists whose investigations into how people learn provide a reason in itself to question traditional classroom practice.[98]

•

It would seem that traditional education sometimes provides students with basic skills but rarely with a penetrating understanding of what lies behind those skills, how they're connected, or how they can be thoughtfully applied. By contrast, a nontraditional education, at least as defined and measured in the studies reviewed here, nearly always enhances understanding and often helps with basic skills to boot. Realizing that students in the latter classrooms may not have to sacrifice anything on standardized tests[99] should be enough for us given how little those tests really tell us and how much these students gain when judged by more meaningful criteria.

Some readers, of course, were already enthusiastic about progressive education before they opened this book. They will feel validated, and they may duplicate and distribute the evidence reviewed here because it supports what they already believed. Other readers, meanwhile, are so invested in the Old School, or so contemptuous of what presumes to supplant it, that it doesn't matter how good or plentiful the data are; they will find some reason to dismiss them and continue believing what *they* already believed. This appendix is primarily intended for those in the middle: those who haven't yet formed an opinion or whose opinions are susceptible of being changed by what the research actually says. I believe any open-minded readers cannot help but be impressed, if not surprised, by all the studies that demonstrate the superiority of nontraditional schools.

# Appendix B:
# WHAT TO LOOK FOR
# IN A CLASSROOM

In evaluating the schools that our children attend (or may attend), there are four overlapping questions we can ask. First, to what extent does a given school meet the basic psychological needs shared by all students—for example, the need to have some say about what one is doing, the need to feel connected to other people, and the need to feel competent at doing things that are seen as meaningful?[1] Second, to what extent does it meet my child's unique needs (or, for that matter, any child's unique needs)? Third, to what extent is it likely to promote the long-term goals I have for my child (pp. 120–21)? Will it help him or her to grow into a caring and responsible person, an independent lifelong learner, and so on? Finally, to what extent does it reflect my general sense of the purposes of education (pp. 115–20)? Is this school more concerned with promoting democratic skills or with preparing students to take their place as workers, more interested in teaching everyone or in deciding who's better than whom?

This chart is meant to bring such questions down to a concrete level, to point to specific, observable features of a classroom or school that exemplify the ideas offered in this book. Here we leave the abstractions behind and try to make sense of what may actually be seen or heard during a visit.

If the school or individual classroom you're observing matches a number of features in the right-hand column, you'll have to decide whether it is sensible (or possible) to enroll your child elsewhere or whether to stay and press for change. If you opt for the latter, you will likely have to pick your battles as well as thinking about whether it makes sense to approach administrators or individual teachers, when it can help to organize other parents, and how you can preserve good relationships with educators while respectfully expressing concerns.

This chart can, in any case, put certain classroom practices (as well as their consequences) in a context. If your child seems bored or unhappy in school, this may reflect problems with the school rather than with your child. Conversely, this chart may be useful in reassuring you about certain things your child's teacher is doing; if they show up in the left-hand column, that may help to turn a reaction of puzzlement and suspicion into one of gratitude and even delight.

•

NOTE: An earlier version of this chart was published in *Educational Leadership* (Kohn, 1996b), then reprinted as the title chapter in Kohn, 1998b, reflecting some helpful suggestions from Jim Beane, Harvey Daniels, Rheta DeVries, and the late Sylvia Kendzior. I subsequently embellished it a bit, incorporating ideas from three other, remarkably similar lists: Routman, 1991, pp. 475–76; Wood, 1992, pp. xiii–xv (from whom I borrow the phrase "sense of purposeful clutter"); and Zemelman et al., 1998, pp. 213–15.

*Table 2: A Visitor's Guide*

| | GOOD SIGNS | POSSIBLE REASONS TO WORRY |
|---|---|---|
| FURNITURE | • Chairs around tables to facilitate interaction<br>• Comfortable areas for learning, including multiple "activity centers"<br>• Open space for gathering | • Chairs all facing forward or (even worse) desks in rows |
| ON THE WALLS | • Covered with students' projects<br>• Evidence of student collaboration<br>• Signs, exhibits, or lists obviously created by students rather than by the teacher<br>• Information about, and personal mementos of, the people who spend time together in this classroom | • Nothing<br>• Commercial posters<br>• Students' assignments displayed, but they are (a) suspiciously flawless, (b) only from "the best" students, or (c) virtually all alike<br>• List of rules created by an adult and/or list of punitive consequences for misbehavior<br>• Sticker (or star) chart — or other evidence that students are rewarded or ranked |
| FACES | • Eager, engaged | • Blank, bored |
| SOUNDS | • Frequent hum of activity and ideas being exchanged | • The teacher's voice is the loudest or most often heard<br>• Frequent periods of silence |
| LOCATION OF TEACHER | • Typically working with students so it takes a few seconds to find her | • Typically front and center |
| TEACHER'S VOICE | • Respectful, genuine, warm | • Controlling and imperious<br>• Condescending and saccharine-sweet |

| | | |
|---|---|---|
| STUDENTS' REACTION TO VISITOR | • Welcoming; eager to explain or demonstrate what they're doing or to use visitor as a resource | • Either unresponsive or hoping to be distracted from what they're doing |
| CLASS DISCUSSION | • Students often address one another directly<br>• Emphasis on thoughtful exploration of complicated issues<br>• Students ask questions at least as often as the teacher does | • All exchanges involve (or directed by) the teacher; students wait to be called on<br>• Emphasis on facts and right answers<br>• Students race to be first to answer teacher's "Who can tell me . . . ?" queries |
| STUFF | • Room overflowing with good books, art supplies, animals and plants, science apparatus; "sense of purposeful clutter" | • Textbooks, worksheets, and other packaged instructional materials predominate; sense of enforced orderliness |
| TASKS | • Different activities often take place simultaneously<br>• Activities frequently completed by pairs or groups of students | • All students usually doing the same thing<br>• When students aren't listening to the teacher, they're working alone |
| AROUND THE SCHOOL | • Appealing atmosphere: a place where people would want to spend time<br>• Students' projects fill the hallways<br>• Library well stocked and comfortable<br>• Bathrooms in good condition<br>• Faculty lounge warm and inviting<br>• Office staff welcoming toward visitors and students<br>• Students helping in lunchroom, library, and with other school functions | • Stark, institutional feel<br>• Awards, trophies, and prizes displayed, suggesting an emphasis on triumph rather than community |

# NOTES

## 1. FORWARD...INTO THE PAST

1. Kamii et al., 1994, p. 675.
2. Everything quoted in this paragraph appears in Pines, 1982, pp. 112–15, 119. For another, very similar definition, see Brodinsky, 1977.
3. Kantrowitz and Wingert, 1989, p. 52.
4. Zemelman et al., 1998, p. 287.
5. This is from the behaviorist Alyce Dickinson (1989, p. 12), who puts the phrase *intrinsic motivation* between quotation marks in the title of her article, as though to call the very existence of the phenomenon into question. (This is a telltale sign of Skinnerian orthodoxy.) Nevertheless, Skinner and his acolytes insist that their theory sees the learner as active because he or she (or it) overtly responds to environmental stimuli, emitting certain behaviors that are reinforced. But, as a group of scholars hasten to explain, this is quite different from what cognitive theorists mean by *active*. "Rather than passively receiving and recording incoming information, the learner actively interprets and imposes meaning through the lenses of his or her existing knowledge structures, working to make sense of the world" (Putnam, 1990, p. 87).
6. These terms are a trifle misleading because the kind of schooling defended in this book requires both students and teachers to be actively involved, making decisions and pursuing ideas. By contrast, in this era of imposed standards and mandated curricula, teachers and students have both been relegated to the periphery (a point made by Goodman, 1992, p. 127). Our children are more likely to receive a legislature-centered education.
7. E. D. Hirsch, Jr. (1996, p. 49), refers with a straight face to "decades of progressivist intellectual dominance." William Damon (1995, pp. 102, 104), one of the many conservative education professors whose collective existence belies conspiratorial claims about how radicals have taken over the field, sounds a similar theme: "child-centered doctrines are fast dominating schooling" and "the constructivist perspective has come to dominate the educational scene." The same claims are made by right-wing talk show hosts, newspaper and magazine columnists, and others too numerous to list. I don't believe I've ever seen any of them offer empirical evidence to document these assertions, although the same few anecdotes of nontraditional classrooms get passed around and repeated endlessly.
8. "To most people—even most educators—there isn't a dominant paradigm of

schooling because there is only one kind of schooling, the kind we have" (Wolk, 1998, p. 5).

9. Many of them look the same because they are the same. But even recently constructed schools typically have the same walkway to a central entrance, the same flagpole, the same brick construction. Inside, meanwhile, Linda Darling-Hammond (1997, p. 149) describes how it's still the case that "the office is the first thing one sees, the quietest and best-outfitted part of the school, a forbidding place with its long high counter separating the office staff from others who enter. The next sight is a glass-enclosed trophy case and a bulletin board of announcements about meetings, sports events, and rules to be followed. Long clear corridors of egg-crate classrooms are broken by banks of lockers and an occasional tidy bulletin board. Classrooms look alike, teachers' desks at the front of each room commanding the rows of smaller desks for students." A high school in particular is likely to set aside most of its public display areas for documenting how its students have defeated those from other schools and which of its students are better than others.

10. For a challenge to this view from a group of optimistic progressives, see Zemelman et al., pp. 276–77: "The cyclic vacillations between authoritarian and progressive education in this culture are not random pendulum swings, but advances and retreats along a battlefront—the playing out, over a huge span of time, of a war for the soul of schooling in this society. In the end, the student-centered, developmental approach will win out over the authoritarian model because it parallels the direction in which civilization itself progresses.... Each time the progressive set of ideas comes back, it gains strength and coherence from the new research and practice that connects with it, and each time it appears it exerts more influence on the schools before it is once again suppressed." I don't know if this assessment is accurate, but I'd certainly like to think so.

11. The first quotation is from Cuban, 1988, p. 341; the second, from Cuban, 1984, p. 238.

12. Newmann, 1992a, pp. 186, 203. "We have seen numerous examples of teachers and students engaged in the 'new' pedagogy: interesting, hands-on science projects; students working cooperatively to solve applied mathematics problems; intense debates where students analyze historical episodes to clarify their reasoning on persisting public issues; creative writing that uses literature to illuminate a personal experience. These provide glimpses of an alternative curriculum model. But the isolated examples have not yet been synthesized into total school programs. Only a few teachers, students, and parents have experienced them" (p. 186).

13. Cohen and Barnes, 1993, p. 241.

14. Dewey, 1952, pp. 129–30.

15. Ellen Lagemann is quoted in Gardner, 1991, p. 196. (Exactly the same contrast between Dewey and Thorndike—and the same conclusion—is offered by Farnham-Diggory, 1990, p. 28.) Even in the mid-1970s, supposedly a high mark for progressive teaching, David Hawkins (1974, p. 162) observed that Dewey actually had an "almost negligible influence in our educational theory and practice." At least one scholar, Lawrence Cremin, would dispute that view. Perhaps the most persuasive conclusion is that "Dewey's educational philosophy is widely cited as theory" but has almost always been "widely ignored in practice" (Sharan, 1990a, p. 33).

16. Goodlad, 1984, esp. p. 229.

17. Mitchell, 1992, p. 183.
18. Goodlad, 1999, p. 573. He also wrote, "I have no doubt that a study today would reveal equally traditional procedures. . . . Almost everywhere I go, individuals endeavoring to bring about change report that teachers are paying less and less attention to the needs of individual children and more and more to the 'standards' being imposed on them" (personal communication, 1998).
19. The first quotation is from Meier, 1996b, p. 271; the second, from Stipek et al., 1995, p. 209.
20. Cathy Drees, a kindergarten teacher in South Carolina, is quoted in Manzo, 1998d, p. 27. The reporter introduces this comment by saying, with apparent satisfaction, that "even the littlest of South Carolinians are learning what it means to meet higher standards."
21. Kantrowitz and Wingert, p. 52. Also see Darling-Hammond (p. 121): "Hands-on learning in the early grades has been replaced in many schools by deskbound learning conducted with basal readers and workbooks, and curriculum packages that emulate standardized tests. Play corners, blocks, picture books, easels, and sand tables have disappeared from many classrooms as teachers have been directed to teach for the tests. Young children are asked to learn in ways that are inappropriate for them and ineffective for nearly anyone."
22. Meier, 1995, pp. 32–33. Meier herself and Ted Sizer have made heroic efforts to rethink the nature of high school and to implement a more progressive and rigorous vision of learning; they have offered impressive models for anyone who cares to be guided by them. The trouble is that so few seem able or willing to take that journey.
23. Battista, 1999, p. 426.
24. The study was conducted by the Center for the Study of Testing, Evaluation, and Educational Policy. See Madaus et al., 1992, p. 14. Emphasis added.
25. Results of the National Survey of Science and Mathematical Education, which gathered data in 1993 from 6,000 teachers at all grade levels, were summarized in Willis, 1995, p. 2.
26. Baumann et al., 1998.
27. Most teachers described themselves as having a "balanced approach" to teaching reading, but other details suggest that traditional beliefs and practices are still prevalent. Two out of three teachers surveyed said they used systematic direct phonics instruction, giving explicit skill lessons before letting kids try to make sense of words. Fewer than one out of five taught phonics "on an as-needed basis," while only one of six teachers taught with trade books exclusively—that is, the kind of stories you might find in a library or bookstore—presumably meaning that the great majority were still using those textbooks known as basal readers. When asked directly, roughly one out of three respondents said he or she could be described as a Whole Language teacher, but the other answers suggest that many identify themselves that way when their practice indicates otherwise.
28. Daniels, 1993, p. 4. While not attempting to offer any quantification, a leading academic opponent of Whole Language agreed that "very few teachers identify themselves as purely 'Whole Language' " (Stahl, 1994, p. 139).
29. Manzo, 1998b.
30. Paterson, 1998. Moreover, she found that such bills are disproportionately introduced by Republican lawmakers in states where the Christian Right "has substantial or dominant influence in the state's Republican party."
31. See the first paragraph of note 34, below.

32. Bond, 1997, p. 28. An updated report the following year noted that "the number of states that use alternative forms of assessment exclusively has decreased over the last five years" (Bond, 1998, p. 13).

33. Bradley, 1998.

34. Reading: A 1987 framework for language arts instruction in California called for a literature-based approach to teaching reading, with skills taught in the context of understanding real stories. In 1995 this policy was essentially reversed, and isolated skills were again the order of the day. According to two leading professional associations, the California Reading Association and the California Association of Teachers of English, the newer standards document is "overly prescriptive, overemphasizes decodable text in the early grades, and treats the reading process as a simple sequence of skills" (Manzo, 1998e). What's more, the state legislature now mandates that professional development for reading teachers must be limited to traditional phonics methods; instructors must sign a form stating that they will not teach other approaches (Manzo, 1997). Those who work with teachers are prohibited from using "any program that promotes or uses reading instruction methodologies that emphasize contextual clues in lieu of fluent decoding, or systematically uses or encourages inventive [sic] spelling techniques in the teaching of writing."

    Mathematics: A set of guidelines offered in 1992, echoing the recommendation of national experts, suggested that math classes should emphasize problem-solving and help students understand the ideas behind the formulas. Five years later, California's Board of Education moved to reverse that policy and return to computational skills and drill-and-practice techniques. The new policy "emphasizes a direct instructional model that focuses on memorizing the steps necessary to solving math problems, but fails to build an understanding of math concepts," according to the president of the California Mathematics Council, which represents math teachers (Manzo, 1998e. See also Lawton, 1998, and Jackson, 1997.)

    Testing: The California Learning Assessment System (CLAS) was introduced in the early 1990s to tap "a broader range of student abilities than traditional tests" did, and to provide "information on what students know and are able to do, not just how they compare with one another." The emphasis shifted a bit toward real understanding and away from memorizing right answers. But not for long. Within a couple of years CLAS was history and multiple-choice testing was back. (See Rothman, 1995, pp. 90–103, and Kirst and Mazzeo, 1996.)

35. Cuban is quoted in Bronner, 1998a, p. 32.

36. The first quotation is from Brodinsky, p. 523; the second, from Feinberg, 1997, p. 32. On the use of standardized tests, see p. 92.

37. Berliner and Biddle, 1995, p. 306.

38. Lemann, 1998, pp. 96, 104. The program is called Success for All.

39. Winerip, 1998, p. 47. The mayor, Bret Schundler, a white Republican Harvard alumnus, enrolled his own daughter in private school. In the same vein, Jonathan Kozol (1992, p. 78) dryly describes the conservative educational theorist Chester Finn's opposition to allocating money for the purpose of reducing class size. That "is 'not a very prudent investment strategy,' said Mr. Finn, who sent his daughter to Exeter, where class size is 13."

40. Strickland is quoted in Routman, 1996, p. 43. Furthermore, this kind of teaching is likely to "bore the students (turning them off to education even more)" (Singham, 1998, p. 13).

41. Singham, p. 15.
42. Rothman, 1995, p. 6.
43. Lemann, 1997, p. 130. For more information, see Goodman, 1998. Note that some right-wing groups use names that sound neutral, such as Citizens for Excellence in Education, Concerned Citizens for Educational Reform, and the National Right to Read Foundation.
44. "Are Teachers of Teachers Out of Touch?" was the way the *New York Times* headlined its report of a "survey by a nonpartisan research group" that found many professors of education are more interested in helping students to become lifelong learners than in making them memorize the rules of grammar or training them to be punctual (Sengupta, 1997). As with other newspapers' coverage of that survey (which, as it turns out, was actually underwritten by the conservative Thomas B. Fordham Foundation, headed by Chester Finn), the reporter simply assumed that the professors were wrong. One wonders whether a survey finding that physicians have different priorities than their patients — promoting long-term health rather than just reducing discomfort, for example — would have been presented so as to exclude the possibility that we might have something to learn from the doctors.
45. Zemelman et al., p. viii. Of course, the fields of medicine and education are not altogether analogous, but it makes little sense in either case to ignore the progress that has been made in theory and practice.
46. As a rule, two Stanford University researchers argue, "higher education institutions place a premium on students' mastery of facts and reproduction of transmitted knowledge as the definition and measure of learning." Even when this is not the case, the admissions committees of these institutions certainly place a premium on that, with the result that even parents who might value critical thinking and problem solving — and therefore might endorse a nontraditional approach to instruction — end up "press[ing] teachers of college-oriented high school students to embrace a transmission-oriented pedagogy" (Talbert and McLaughlin, 1993, pp. 182–83). For different reasons, non-college-bound high school students are at least as likely to be subjected to the same kind of teaching, albeit at a lower level (see Oakes, 1985).
47. The party and even the name of the president don't seem to matter. Virtually all of Bill Clinton's lengthy remarks on education in his 1997 State of the Union message could have been delivered by George Bush or even Ronald Reagan — and indeed, the speech reportedly pleased Republican governors. Clinton went out of his way to assure social conservatives that he supported "not Federal Government standards but national standards." He framed the task at hand not as enhancing the quality of student learning but as making sure the USA was number one in educational performance. He called for competition among public schools and for rewards and punishments to "motivate" teachers. Most of all, he said the solution to our educational problems was more testing (Clinton, 1997). The groan from teachers across the country was almost audible.
48. Interestingly, the Christian Right has opposed not only national standards and testing but also some dreadful state tests, such as the Texas Assessment of Academic Skills (TAAS), which was fought by the most conservative Republicans on that state's Board of Education. One national leader of the Christian Right regards standardized tests as evidence of government mind control. Those of us who arrive at our opposition from a very different point of departure may be tempted to make common cause with this constituency. Such an alliance

will not last long, however, given that these same people are vociferous supporters of a back-to-basics agenda for classroom instruction. ("To those whose world is bounded and defined by religious faith," writes one conservative, "it would be sacrilegious to oblige their children to become critical thinkers and independent questioners of authority" [Manno, 1995, p. 723].) Moreover, the alternative to federal (or even state) mandates is a kind of control at the local level that often continues to exclude the active participation of teachers and students.

49. To cite a few examples: the Committee for Economic Development, consisting of executives from about 250 large corporations, demands that school curricula be linked more closely to employers' skill requirements; it also calls for "performance-driven education," incentives, and a traditional "core disciplinary knowledge" version of instruction (Archer, 1996; Manegold, 1994). Ditto for the Business Roundtable, which describes schooling as "competing in the education Olympics": besides endorsing narrow and very specific academic standards, punishments for schools that fall behind, and more testing, it approvingly cites the example of teaching high school students how to write personnel evaluations (Business Roundtable, 1996). The National Association of Manufacturers, meanwhile, insists on more testing as well as "a national system of skills standards designed by industry" (Zehr, 1998). And the Business Task Force on Student Standards says that "workplace performance requirements of industry and commerce must be integrated into subject-matter standards and learning environments" (Business Task Force, 1995, p. 2). These reports typically receive generous attention from the press. More to the point, such recommendations are increasingly being adopted.

50. Some people in the business world have insisted that their current goals are really aligned with those of educators: corporations today want employees who are critical thinkers and problem solvers, who are skilled at teamwork, and so forth. But if this were true, we would see cutting-edge companies taking the lead in demanding a constructivist approach to instruction, where students' interests drive the curriculum—as well as a Whole Language model for teaching literacy. They would be demanding that we throw out the worksheets and the textbooks, the decontextualized skills and rote memorization. They would demand a greater emphasis on cooperative learning and complain loudly about the practices that undermine collaboration (and ultimately quality)—practices like awards assemblies and spelling bees and honor rolls. They would insist that heterogeneous, inclusive classrooms replace programs that segregate and stratify and stigmatize. They would stop talking about "school choice" (meaning programs that treat education as a commodity for sale) and start talking about the importance of giving students more choice about what happens in their classrooms. They would publish reports on the importance of turning schools into caring communities where mutual problem-solving replaces traditional obedience-based discipline.

The sad truth, of course, is that when business leaders do address these issues, they take precisely the opposite approach: they write off innovative, progressive educational reforms as mere fads that distract us from raising test scores. While there may be more talk in boardrooms these days about teamwork, it is usually in the context of competitiveness—that is, working together so we can defeat another group of people working together. While "social skills" are often listed as desirable attributes, business publications never seem to mention such qualities as generosity or compassion. While it is common to talk about the need for employees who can think critically, there is reason to doubt that corporate executives want people with the critical skills to ask why they (the executives) just received multimillion-dollar stock option packages even as several thousand employees were thrown out of work. Corporations may, as we have seen, encourage high school English teachers to ask students to write a sample personnel evaluation, but they seem less keen on inviting students to analyze critically whether such evaluations make sense or who gets to evaluate whom. What business wants from its workers — and, by extension, from our schools — in the twenty-first century may not be so different after all from what it wanted in the nineteenth and twentieth centuries.

51. I'm not suggesting that corporations should be silenced. Ideally, we would thank business leaders for their advice and say that we'd be happy to consider it . . . right alongside the opinions of labor unions, college admissions officers, philosophers, social scientists, journalists, elected officials, and other interest groups. We'd make it clear that when their prescriptions seem out of step with what others are saying and ultimately of benefit only to themselves, those suggestions will be viewed with the appropriate skepticism. Finally, we would acknowledge that the leaders of giant corporations represent financial resources far beyond those of other groups but add that, as we're sure they realize, to give their recommendations any greater weight would violate core democratic principles.

52. As one critic puts it, after summarizing a number of government reports, "The purpose of these reforms, the motivation behind the narrowing of the curriculum, is simply to prepare children for work (and, in *A Nation at Risk,* for the military)" (Wood, 1988, p. 173).

53. Hunt, 1984.

54. See American Federation of Teachers, 1998; and *Education Week*'s report *Quality Counts.*

55. A 1998 editorial in the *Boston Globe* may as well have appeared in the *Wall Street Journal* or the *National Review*: it called for "rigorous academic standards and high-stakes assessments," setting children against one another in contests to "motivate" them, making more students repeat a grade, and bringing instruction in line with whatever appears on standardized tests. An educator who wondered if a state exam "is a test that I believe in" is ridiculed for his "confusion" ("A Moment of Truth"). *The New Republic* likewise endorsed "competitive pressure throughout school systems" and more emphasis on standards, testing, and incentives ("School Haze"). For its part, the influential *New York Times* seems to have a coordinated policy of advancing a similar agenda in its reporting of education news, its choice of op-ed essays (where balance consists of publishing pieces by commentators ranging from the conservative Lynn Cheney all the way to the conservative Diane Ravitch), its articles in the Sunday *Magazine,* and the selection of books featured in the *Book Review* (and who reviews them). Much the same could be said about most other major newspapers and newsweeklies. The only topic on which liberal politicians and publications diverge from conservative has to do with support for proposals that would shift funds from public to private education, such as voucher plans.

56. Daniels, 1993, p. 4. The version of school reform "geared toward accountability and testing . . . actually doesn't have any reform in it at all," he adds. "It doesn't say you should teach this differently, you should add this content. It doesn't say anything about the substance or the process of schooling. It of-

fers no resources. It doesn't offer any professional development for teachers. Instead, it issues threats."

57. The late Al Shanker, the influential former president of the AFT, was nearly indistinguishable from right-wing union bashers on pedagogical issues. He demanded more punitive discipline, more testing, more tracking of students, more use of incentives, and a more structured curriculum emphasizing " 'error-free' student work" (Sontag, 1992; Shanker, 1995). Conservatives loved him: Chester Finn said he "agree[d] with Al Shanker four days out of every five" (in Mosle, 1996, p. 56); Linda Chavez said she "went from [working for] Al Shanker to Ronald Reagan, and it wasn't such a long leap" (in Hill, 1996). Through its Web site and its magazine (*American Educator*), the AFT continues to promote remarkably conservative theories and practices and to endorse some of the most prescriptive, behaviorally oriented teaching programs, including Direct Instruction and Success for All.

58. The most visible and energetic challengers of the "scores are falling, schools are failing" position are David Berliner and Bruce Biddle, particularly in chapter 2 of their book *The Manufactured Crisis;* Richard Rothstein, in a 1998 report entitled *The Way We Were?;* and Gerald Bracey, who writes a monthly column for the education journal *Phi Delta Kappan.* Bracey also puts together a lengthy annual report for that journal each October and has published a book on the topic, *Setting the Record Straight.*

59. This comment comes from *Student Literacy: Myths and Realities* by Michael Kibby, and is quoted in Calkins et al., 1998, p. 37. Overall, only about half of American high school students take the test; moreover, that percentage varies considerably from state to state. Only 4 or 5 percent of high school graduates —an elite, self-selected sample—take the test in the states that have the highest average scores, while 70 percent or more take the test in some of the states that wind up with the lowest average scores (Rotberg, 1998b, p. 27). Overall, the negative correlation between a state's average score and the proportion of eligible students taking the test is very high: $r = -.86$, according to McQuillan 1998, p. 96n3. Thus, "if Americans want to raise the nation's SAT scores, they do not need to improve schools. They can do so simply by discouraging any but the top students in every high school from taking the test" (Rothstein, 1998, p. 54). The test is also useless for looking at trends over time because of variations in how many students take the test from one year to the next.

60. I've left out tests of writing because that subject wasn't included until 1984. When scores from that first year are compared with those in 1996, the performance of 8th- and 11th-grade students dropped a little while students in 4th grade did a little better. The 1996 results are from the *NAEP 1996 Trends in Academic Progress,* prepared by the National Center for Education Statistics in August 1997; the 1998 reading results, which reported small additional gains over 1996 for all three age groups, were released in February 1999 (see Pear, 1999). A mountain of data is available on the Web at http://nces01. ed.gov/naep.

Beginning a few years ago, certain NAEP scores were characterized as "basic," "proficient," or "advanced"—allowing critics of the schools to cite the results as evidence of inadequacy even though the scores haven't changed much over time. Many researchers, however, have called these designations into question because they are arbitrary, because the conclusions based on them "are not consistent with other data on student achievement," and because they "seem to have been established primarily for the purpose of con-

firming preconceptions about the poor performance of American schools" (Rothstein, pp. 70–74).
61. See Elley, 1992. Incidentally, the U.S. score was judged quite high even after the social and economic circumstances of each country were factored into the equation. Fourteen-year-olds were also tested; here, the U.S. score was not quite as high but still respectable: 535, where the range was from 330 to 560.
62. Critics have argued that only a handful of the countries taking part in the study met the stated testing guidelines, with the result that some were testing unrepresentative groups of students in terms of age, income, or number of years studying science or math. "Countries had such different patterns of participation and exclusion rates, school and student characteristics, and societal contexts that test score rankings are meaningless as an indicator of the quality of education" (Rotberg, 1998a, p. 1031; also see Bracey, 1998b).
63. A front-page *New York Times* article (Bronner, 1998b, p. A1) began as follows: "A major new international study shows that American high school graduation rates, for generations the highest in the world, have slipped below those of most industrialized countries." The reporter than struggled to explain what has happened to our schools, quoting an academic who believes "we should be quite alarmed by this." (The same week, a front-page article in *Education Week* [Hoff, 1998a] carried the ominous headline "U.S. Graduation Rates Starting to Fall Behind.") It turns out, though, that the study in question actually reported no slippage in absolute terms; on most measures, the U.S. is actually doing better than ever. In 1990, an American five-year-old was expected to attend school for 16.3 years; six years later, that had increased to 16.8 years. Furthermore, 77 percent of Americans between the ages of 55 and 64 had completed "at least an upper-secondary education" in 1996, while 87 percent of a younger cohort (those between 25 and 34) had done so. The drop in rank just reflects the improvement of other countries, which would be regarded as bad news only by someone who is more rivalrous than rational.
64. For decade-by-decade examples of such claims, see Rothstein, pp. 9–20.
65. For one thing, the availability of meaningful work is far more likely to influence the study habits of students than the other way around. For another thing, labor force skills don't contribute meaningfully to the productivity level of a specific industry, given all the other factors that matter a lot more. (See Paris, 1997; Ray and Mickelson, 1997; Berliner, 1996; and the sources cited in Gelberg, 1997, p. 212).
66. Labaree, 1997b, p. 51.
67. Rothstein, p. 25.
68. Bracey, 1996a.
69. Along with a number of conservative politicians and pundits, an economist named Eric Hanushek has challenged the relationship between funding levels and quality of schools. This dispute, like most, is not as simple as it is sometimes made out to be. No one argues, on the one hand, that money makes no difference or, on the other hand, that money is the only thing that matters. Rather, the issues include: Is there a funding level beyond which more money buys less return? Is there a difference between simply correlating achievements to spending across schools (or states) at a given point in time as opposed to investigating what money can do over a period of years? Does money interact with other variables such that it makes more of a difference in certain kinds of schools? And what happens when we look beyond standardized tests to other measures of quality? From a common-sense point of view, it is hard to accept

the argument that more money won't help poor schools, if only because affluent school districts seem quite firmly convinced that there are substantial benefits from all the amenities that money has bought them. (No one in the suburbs says, "Money isn't correlated with achievement, so here, you may as well take some of this extra cash off our hands.") From a scientific point of view, a reanalysis of Hanushek's position has suggested that money actually matters quite a lot: Hedges, 1994; also see Wainer, 1993; and Berliner and Biddle, pp. 70–78.

70. Berliner and Biddle, pp. 12, 144.
71. The Dewey story appears in Paul et al., 1989, p. 41.
72. When "Horace Mann's committee of examiners administered the nation's first standardized test in 1845 to five hundred Boston fourteen-year-olds," they found that "when children did answer a question correctly, they frequently did not understand the answer they had given because, as the examining committee put it, the children had been taught 'the name of the thing rather than the nature of the thing'" (Rothstein, pp. 33–34). For modern echoes of this same phenomenon, see the discussion of recent math results on pp. 173–74.
73. See especially Gardner, 1991, pp. 152–66. David Perkins (1992, chap. 2) makes a similar point.
74. Dickinson is quoted in Covington, 1992, p. 181.
75. Rothstein, p. 31.
76. I should point out that some educational researchers and theorists are explicitly critical of standardized tests—indeed, have built careers on making such criticisms and developing alternative ways of assessing the quality of students' learning—and yet seem to accept other aspects of the Tougher Standards approach to school reform I discuss here, including the economic rationale for pursuing school reform in the first place.
77. Holt, 1982, p. 155.


## 2. GETTING MOTIVATION WRONG

1. Nicholls, 1992, p. 282. The specialist in educational testing, meanwhile, may not "think of children except as they distribute themselves across deciles" (Paul Hogan, former director of the National Council of Teachers of English, quoted in Freedman, 1993, p. 28).
2. Fred Gross, an educator in Sudbury, Mass., is quoted in Willis, 1994, p. 6. He was speaking in particular about teachers who spend a lot of time lecturing to students.
3. Miserandino, 1996, p. 205.
4. Researchers have contrasted a "learning" or "mastery" or "task" orientation with a "performance" or "ego"' orientation. See especially the work of Carol Dweck, Carole Ames, and the late John Nicholls, cited below.
5. Maehr and Midgley, 1991, p. 420.
6. Carol Midgley has documented that "middle school classrooms emphasize performance goals more, and task goals less, than do elementary classrooms," and she has also shown that students' orientations come to match those of the school environment. See Midgley, 1993, and Anderman and Midgley, 1997. (A performance orientation may be stronger in some subjects, such as English and social studies, than others. See Maehr and Midgley, 1996, p. 80.) It is in-

teresting to juxtapose these studies showing an increase in performance goals as students move up through the grades with another line of research showing that their interest in learning tends to decline over approximately the same period of time. See p. 125.

7. John Nicholls, who distinguished between a task and an ego orientation, believed that these are separate constructs rather than two ends of a single continuum. It is possible, as he saw it, to be high on both or low on both. Still, classroom structures often encourage one or the other, leading students, for example, to be a lot more concerned with how they are doing relative to their peers than with whether they have understood something. Nicholls (1989, p. 107) noted that "a person who is task-involved will choose any task that she believes offers an opportunity to exercise or extend her competence. But a person who is ego-involved may have to face the prospect that a gain in competence . . . will still leave her feeling incompetent" because success has been defined in comparative terms.

8. Dweck, 1986, p. 1042.

9. Anderman et al., 1996. A study of college students found this sort of interest-dampening effect on the part of those students who did well: the negative effects of being performance oriented (wanting to get good grades or do better than others) didn't hold for students who thought they weren't as successful. This study also found that interest was positively related to being mastery oriented (wanting to learn and understand); see Harackiewicz et al., 1997. Yet another study discovered that the difficulty of the task may be relevant. In this experiment, where fifth-graders were asked to search for words hidden in a page full of letters, those kids who had just been told to do their best were much more likely to return to a difficult version of this task on their own time than were those who had been told that their scores would be reported to their teacher (Hughes et al., 1985).

10. See especially Diener and Dweck, 1980. The quotation is from Heyman and Dweck, 1992, p. 238.

11. See, for example, Anderman and Midgley; Miserandino, 1996; Mueller and Dweck, 1998.

12. On this point, see Dweck, p. 1045, and Henderson and Dweck, p. 325. Positive feedback can be decidedly damaging if it refers to how smart the student is (Mueller and Dweck).

13. Dweck, p. 1041.

14. Harter, 1992, pp. 89–90, cites three studies to this effect. Also see Elliott and Dweck, 1988; Maehr and Stallings, 1972; and Pearlman, 1984. It's possible to conclude that people's "natural" inclination is to choose something that requires them to stretch beyond what they're capable of doing easily. The fact that so many children (and adults) play it safe would thus reflect a fact not about human nature but about the exaggerated emphasis on performance in the environments in which they find themselves.

15. A 1985 study to this effect by Bandura and Dweck is cited in Heyman and Dweck, p. 237.

16. Anderman et al., 1998.

17. Ames and Archer, 1987.

18. Researchers have found that when "an extrinsic motivational set develops, children avoid the pursuit of challenge even when they are no longer being rewarded or evaluated" (Flink et al., 1992, p. 193).

19. Milton et al., 1986. A subsequent study confirmed that a "learning orientation" and a "grade orientation" are inversely related (Beck et al., 1991).

20. Carol Dweck (personal communication, 1993) suggests that parents can encourage their children to associate challenge with enjoyment by saying similar things: "That was no fun—let's do something harder!"
21. Ames and Archer, 1988; Meece et al., 1988.
22. Some evidence, though not all, suggests that college students who are performance-focused may get higher grades than those who are learning-focused (see Elliot and Church, 1997, and Harackiewicz et al., 1997). Also, Conti et al., 1995, found that undergraduates led to think about their scores on a forthcoming test succeeded in recalling more facts in the short run—though not in the long run—than those who were encouraged to think more about the task itself. On the other hand, Beck et al., 1991, found a negative correlation between students' grade-point averages and the extent to which they were "grade oriented"—possibly because students who were less proficient worried more about their grades. More relevant to our concerns here, however, there is contradictory evidence as to whether the grades of younger students are more closely associated with task or performance goals (see Middleton and Midgley, 1997).
23. The study, by Farrell and Dweck, is cited in Dweck, p. 1043.
24. Utman, 1997. One study published too late to be included in that review (Newman and Schwager, 1995) found that low-achieving students solved significantly fewer math problems if they were induced to think about their performance than if they were led to think of them as "puzzles" that would help them "learn new things."
25. First study: Ginsburg and Bronstein, 1993; quotation appears on p. 1470. Second study: Gottfried et al., 1994.
26. For a different, but somewhat overlapping, list of "five separate cognitive and affective factors that would impair performance for performance-oriented individuals," see Dweck and Leggett, 1988, p. 262.
27. Ryan and Pintrich, 1997.
28. Newman and Schwager.
29. Stipek and Weisz, 1981, p. 130.
30. Dweck et al., 1978, p. 268. There is an important caveat here, however: students may think that effort makes the difference and as a result continue to try hard—but only because they feel they're supposed to, not because they take any real satisfaction in it. This is why some researchers argue that the distinction between different *goals* that students may have for their actions isn't as useful as the different *motives* or reasons for what they do or for having a particular goal. (See Deci et al., 1996; Covington [1992, p. 71] also contends that "attributions are no substitute for the concept of motivation." Also see pp. 39–40.)
31. Heyman and Dweck, p. 235. Elsewhere, Dweck (p. 1042) observed, "Research shows that children with performance goals are more likely to interpret negative outcomes in terms of their ability."
32. Ames and Archer, 1988.
33. Arguably, it's even worse than attributing success or failure to luck. Luck, like effort, can change. It is widely believed that ability cannot. See Weiner, 1979, p. 9.
34. Anderman, 1992.
35. Butkowsky and Willows, 1980.
36. Mueller and Dweck. Apart from its effect on achievement, having been told that they are smart (as opposed to that they "must have worked hard") also led children to prefer easier tasks, to enjoy them less, to give up sooner, and to

compare their performance to others'. These effects held regardless of actual ability level or ethnic background. "Thus, praise for intelligence does not appear to teach children that they are smart; rather, such praise appears to teach them to make inferences about their ability versus their effort from how well they perform" (p. 39)—with potentially devastating consequences when their performance drops.

37. These two ideas are theoretically distinct but closely related, particularly in Carol Dweck's research. She finds it useful to distinguish between people who believe that intelligence is set for life—some people are born smart and some aren't, and there's nothing to be done about it—from those who think that intelligence can be improved through learning. The former view may be faulted as unduly pessimistic or dangerously close to the assumption that whole groups of people are less successful because they're born deficient. But Dweck and her colleagues have also found a very specific, very practical consequence: just by virtue of believing it, students may be in real trouble. And it isn't just harmful to believe this about failure. Kids who do very well in school but believe that people's intelligence is fixed—and who presumably see their own high intelligence as responsible for their success—are also at a disadvantage.

   In one study, a group of students were followed from the end of elementary school into junior high school to see how they fared. It turned out that even very confident students didn't do nearly as well in seventh grade as might have been expected from their earlier achievement test scores *if* they believed that nothing can be done about a person's intelligence. This belief was associated not only with lower grades (even when earlier achievement was taken into account) but with more anxiety about school and a tendency to attribute failure to ability rather than effort. Students were better off if they had a more flexible view of intelligence. Indeed, even those who weren't terribly confident about themselves did better than expected when they got to junior high school if they looked at intelligence this way. (See Henderson and Dweck, 1990; also, MacGyvers and Dweck, 1994).

38. The three explanations that follow, along with evidence to support them, are listed in Heyman and Dweck, p. 235.

39. "Attributing past failure to lack of ability was associated with low expectations of future success" for young children in one study (see Stipek and Hoffman, 1980, p. 864).

40. Licht and Dweck, p. 628.

41. This phenomenon, vividly described years ago by John Holt (1982), is generally known by social and educational psychologists as "self-handicapping" (see Covington, and Riggs, 1992). It can also explain why some students, instead of picking easy tasks where success is all but guaranteed, pick tasks that are much too hard so they can blame their failure on that fact and thereby continue to believe they're very smart. This is more likely to happen in classrooms where students' performance is emphasized and compared (see Urdan et al., 1998).

42. Dweck and Leggett, p. 260.

43. On the Japanese vs. American contrast, see Holloway, 1988. (American children are also more likely than their Japanese peers to point to "some external 'carrot or stick' " when explaining why they do what they do in school: see Hamilton et al., 1989.) For general references on both gender and cultural factors, see Stipek, 1993, p. 131. A study by Ellen Leggett found that "bright girls were twice as likely as bright boys" to view intelligence as something that one

possesses in a fixed amount (see Henderson and Dweck, p. 323). On the other hand, there is a fair amount of evidence suggesting that boys are more performance-oriented than girls overall (Middleton and Midgley, 1997).

44. One of the first psychologists to attend to this human need, and the consequences of failing to meet it, was Richard de Charms. Edward Deci and Richard Ryan (e.g., 1985) have refined our understanding of the subject and conducted numerous studies on the role of autonomy in various aspects of human life. Also, there is a huge psychological literature on the related issue of perceived control.

45. Skinner et al., 1990, p. 22. (No, not *that* Skinner.)

46. Duckworth, 1987, p. 63. The results of that California parent study (p. 33) lend support to that recommendation.

47. See Kohn, 1992a.

48. Nicholls, 1989, p. 117. This book is an extraordinarily cogent discussion of competition, achievement, and learning. Also on this topic, see Covington.

49. Nolen, 1988.

50. Ames, 1978. Interestingly, this effect was found to be most pronounced in children who have high levels of self-esteem; these children were also more self-critical after losing than after failing.

51. One study (Fry and Coe, 1980) looked at sixty classrooms in twenty junior and senior high schools and found a similarly negative effect when students perceived their teachers as controlling. A second study (Anderman and Young, 1994) looked specifically at students' attitudes toward science and found that they were more negative when teachers encouraged competition, even when students' achievement levels were taken into account. These researchers concluded, in fact, that improving the nature and content of science education may be futile if teachers and schools have created a competitive atmosphere for students. Carole Ames (1992a, p. 266) made a similar point: all the good stuff we offer with one hand, by "designing tasks with challenge or offering choices" to students about their learning, we end up taking away with the other hand if we compare students to, or set them against, each other.

52. See the encyclopedic review of research in Johnson and Johnson, 1989, as well as Kohn.

53. We can readily concede that students are not equally good at what they do, and, moreover, that they will pick up on who among them is a particularly effortless reader or imaginative painter. But this does not justify exaggerating those differences, calling attention to them (for example, by announcing or posting rankings), or making students try to defeat one another. If anything, it's a reminder that we ought to work to reduce the salience and significance of kids' relative standing, to do everything possible to prevent an observation ("I'm better than Stephen in math") from becoming a motive ("I want to be better than Stephen in math").

Here are other things we can do in the face of differences in ability. First, we can expand the number of capacities that we value by having teachers offer students different kinds of tasks to do and encourage different ways of doing them. For the most part, being "smart" or "good in school" is overwhelmingly associated with a narrow band of verbal and analytical abilities. This is problematic for many reasons, one of which is that a large number of students whose strengths lie elsewhere almost immediately come to think of themselves as inferior. (Howard Gardner's work [1983] on multiple intelligences has helped a number of educators to rethink what it means to be capable; others,

252 · Notes to Page 39

following his lead, have thought about the practical implications of this theory for schools.)

Second, we ought to encourage students to see ability as something that isn't set for life (see p. 250, note 37). At the least, we can help them understand that higher ability often just means that something comes more easily to one person than to another. I may well have a poorer sense of direction than you do, but that's another way of saying that I have to work harder than you to find my way around. This way of reframing the concept of ability differences can be remarkably liberating.

Finally, teachers can give students a different way of understanding that Allison picks up certain concepts faster than Allen does: it's not that Allison wins and Allen loses, but that Allison is able to help Allen. (This idea is offered in Nicholls and Hazzard, 1993, p. 30.) If some students are always the helpers and others are always the helped, however, this can create a status hierarchy in the classroom that isn't particularly healthy. The answer may be to combine the opportunity to help with the earlier suggestion to provide tasks that require a broad range of skills to complete. The student who was receiving explanations from a peer about the mechanics of long division may switch to *giving* explanations if the assignment requires students not only to do calculations but to put them to use in designing and constructing a building. For more on the use of varied tasks in cooperative learning for this very purpose, see the work of Elizabeth Cohen.

People who resist such suggestions for minimizing the impact of differences in ability often do so because they think that competition will "motivate" students to improve. Apart from the empirical evidence indicating that this usually doesn't happen (see Kohn, esp. chap. 3), such a belief may suggest a failure to distinguish between different *kinds* of motivation, a distinction to which I'll return in chapter 5. Or it may suggest a tendency to attribute to "human nature" or "life" what is actually a function of specific practices and institutions. One researcher confirmed that "young people in achievement situations do not always exhibit a clear preference for normative comparisons." Only some students in her study were concerned about how well they did compared to everyone else — namely, the ones who had been encouraged beforehand to focus on how well they could do a task. Others, who had been encouraged to be imaginative (and were therefore focused on the task itself) were later curious to see *what* their classmates had done rather than to look at everyone's scores. (See Butler, 1992; for a summary of this study, see Kohn, 1993a, pp. 157–58. Another situational factor found to influence whether students look for information about how well they did compared to their peers — versus what their peers did — is whether they were led to explain performance in terms of ability or effort; see Mueller and Dweck, experiments 3 and 4.)

In short, the fact that people have different abilities doesn't justify the significance we attach to ability (as opposed to, say, effort), and it doesn't justify the practices that highlight those comparisons and turn them into a competition. We can "find learning and the exercise of our skills inherently satisfying and gain a sense of competence and accomplishment in the absence of explicit concerns about our ability — without reflecting on how we stand relative to our peers" (Nicholls, p. 95).

54. Elliot and Harackiewicz, 1996; Skaalvik, 1997. These psychologists are less persuasive, I think, when they try to claim that *only* this version of a performance orientation is harmful, which is to say that chasing success is not a

problem. First of all, the best that can be said about the success-oriented performance condition is that it may not reduce intrinsic motivation; there is no evidence that it *enhances* such motivation, which is often true of the nonperformance (mastery or learning) condition. Second, both ways of emphasizing performance—demonstrating competence and demonstrating the absence of incompetence—have the effect of generating high levels of anxiety (Skaalvik) and discouraging students from asking for help (Ryan and Pintrich). Finally, one pair of researchers clearly failed to replicate the main finding. They discovered that students who were actively seeking success looked pretty similar to those actively trying to avoid failure, and concluded that it's the "distinction between task and performance that is influential," not distinctions between different versions of the performance orientation (Middleton and Midgley, p. 716).

55. Powers, 1993.
56. Wood, 1996, p. 86.
57. Deci and Ryan, p. 124.
58. For a review of research on self-esteem that debunks its purported connection to academic achievement—but challenges the conservative critics of self-esteem—see Kohn, 1994. (Some of the discussion about failure is taken from that article.)
59. Of course, all things are rarely equal. Different aspects of the situation and different characteristics of the individual help to determine how a given failure will be perceived—and, as we keep seeing in other contexts, the way it is perceived then helps to determine its effects. It matters whether a student was deliberately given too difficult a task in the hope that she would somehow be a better person for failing at it. It matters whether failure was defined on the basis of someone else's judgment as opposed to something intrinsic to the task itself. It matters whether the failure took the form of losing to someone else in a public competition. It matters whether the failure took place in the context of intense pressure to succeed as opposed to a relaxed climate of exploration. It matters whether the student fears ridicule or punishment (such as an F) for having failed or is part of a supportive community where setbacks are no big deal. It turns out that the conditions *least* likely to make failure a "terrific motivator" (or even to prevent subsequent performance problems) are things like tough standards, grades, competition, rewards and punishments—in short, the practices associated with traditional instruction promoted by many of the same people who extol the motivational benefits of failure.
60. For example, see Parsons and Ruble, 1977.
61. One study (Allen and Wuensch, 1993) found that failure undermined subsequent performance for younger children. Another study (Boggiano et al., 1993) found that it happened for older children, too. Also see Hiroto and Seligman, 1975, and the references in Covington, p. 65.
62. Wigfield, 1988.
63. See Deci and Ryan, p. 612; and four studies cited in Deppe and Harackiewicz, 1996, p. 869.
64. See Wigfield; and four studies cited in Stipek, 1993, pp. 130–31.
65. For an empirical demonstration of the difference between mere perseverance at a task and genuine intrinsic motivation, see Ryan et al., 1991.
66. De Zouche, 1945, pp. 339, 341.
67. This quotation accompanies eight citations in Crooks, 1993.
68. For example, see some of the early research reviewed in Kirschenbaum et al., 1971.

69. One of many examples of the success of that masquerade: the National Honor Society has been criticized for inducting students on the basis of their character, leadership, and community service as well as grade-point average. "Three of the four are pretty much subjective," commented the superintendent of an Illinois school district that has begun honoring students instead purely on the basis of their grades, a criterion evidently regarded as nonsubjective (Hoff, 1998b, p. 1).

70. Cullen et al., 1975.

71. Clark, 1969. Also see Gold et al., 1971.

72. Moeller and Reschke, 1993.

73. Yarborough and Johnson, 1980.

74. Grolnick and Ryan, 1987.

75. Butler and Nisan, 1986; Butler, 1987; Butler, 1988.

76. Benware and Deci, 1984.

77. Anderman and Johnston, 1998.

78. Additional studies: Salili et al., 1976; Hughes et al., 1985 (which found a reduction in interest for challenging tasks but not for easy ones); Kage, 1991; and Harter and Guzman, 1986 (described in Harter, 1992, pp. 89–90). Harter (1978) also found that children seemed to take less pleasure from their success at a task when they knew it was for a grade.

79. See Milton et al., 1986; Beck et al., 1991.

80. Bruner, 1977, p. 51.

81. Many of the studies already mentioned have found this effect as well: Harter, 1978; Harter and Guzman, 1986 (described in Harter, 1992, pp. 89–90); Kage, 1991; and Milton et al., 1986. See also the evidence finding the same effect from inducing a performance orientation—pp. 29–31.

82. Jerome Bruner (p. 66) makes this point. The relationship is reciprocal, however, since an unengaging curriculum virtually requires the use of grades: without bribes (A's) and threats (F's), students would have no reason to do the assignments. "Let's face it," one group of writers remarked. "Most of our courses are so boring that if you [students] didn't get graded, you'd do only enough work to get by" (Kirschenbaum et al., p. 37). The fact that students are likely to dive in, and do well at, lessons that really are worth doing (see note 72, above) belies the claim that grades are always necessary to keep students "on task." The problem, we might say, is with the pedagogy, not with the species.

83. Krumboltz and Yeh, 1996, p. 325.

84. "No teaching and learning takes place when pop quizzes are given, nor can they be justified as 'motivational.' Pop quizzes are simply punitive measures that teachers employ when they suspect that their students have not learned the material. Rather than spend class time determining what the students have not learned and why, many teachers assume that students have not studied and decide to 'get even.' . . . [In the case of one such teacher,] confidential discussions with her students revealed that those who cared about grades were learning as much about how to cheat on the quizzes as about the material. Other students decided that they could not win at [her] game and simply gave up. Her colleagues regarded [her] as a tough teacher who maintained high standards. No one asked the students" (Canady and Hotchkiss, 1989, p. 70).

85. Kirschenbaum et al., p. 115.

86. Covington, p. 263.

87. Nicholls and Hazzard, p. 77.

88. Two facts stand out about the research on this question. First, most of it was conducted in the 1970s with undergraduates, and those findings may not apply to younger students. Second, student performance was almost always defined as the number of facts retained temporarily as measured by multiple-choice exams. In any case, the research has produced mixed results, with three investigations finding that harder grading produces limited gains in test scores (Powell, 1977; Johnston and O'Neill, 1973; Semb, 1974), and four finding no difference (Abrahami et al., 1980; Vasta and Sarmiento, 1979; Goldberg, 1965; Driscoll et al. 1983 [cited in Driscoll, 1986]). Again, recall that with meaningful material taught in an interesting way, even the complete absence of grades didn't reduce the quality of students' learning.

89. Goldin, 1995.

90. It is sometimes forgotten that grades are not inherently competitive. If everyone in a class can theoretically wind up with an A, there is no competition involved—although the grade orientation is still harmful for all the reasons already discussed. But if students are graded on a curve, with the number of top grades artificially limited, then any form of cooperation among students has been discouraged because each student now stands to benefit from the failure of others. Moreover, it seems egregiously unfair on its face to decide in advance that no matter how high the level of student achievement, only a few will receive A's. Any instructor who does this is sending a message, not only that her classroom isn't really about learning, but that it isn't even about performance: it's about winning. Sadly, many teachers who do not formally grade on a curve end up making sure the grades wind up distributed in pretty much the same way, perhaps because they believe that this is the way final grades are "supposed to" look: a few very high grades, a few very low grades, and everyone else somewhere in the middle. In fact, this result is "not a symbol of rigor" but "a symbol of failure—failure to teach well, failure to test well, and failure to have any influence at all on the intellectual lives of students" (Milton et al., p. 225).

91. In decrying the alleged proliferation of good grades, one writer offers these analogies: "What good would Siskel and Ebert be if they gave every film 'two thumbs up'? Why would anyone subscribe to *Consumer's Digest* if every blender were rated a 'best buy'?" (Cizek, 1996, p. 22). Indeed, such ratings would not be useful for their intended purpose—which is to sort movies and appliances for the convenience of people purchasing them. The relevant question, however, is whether this marketplace analogy makes sense for education. If students were commodities to be rated, then one would naturally become indignant that too many were rated highly. But if the purpose of assessment is to provide information that will help students learn more skillfully and enthusiastically—and if an emphasis on sorting actually compromises an emphasis on learning—then our critique will look very different.

92. That finding isn't based on only one study but on a synthesis of thirty-five studies completed in the 1950s, '60s, and '70s (Samson et al., 1984).

93. Davidson and Lewis, 1997.

94. Glasser, 1969, p. 69.

95. Milton et al., pp. 147–48.

## 3. GETTING TEACHING AND LEARNING WRONG

1. Darling-Hammond (1997, p. 228) quotes from 1993 draft standards for history at the fourth-grade level.
2. Ibid., p. 60. The question is taken from the study guide for the 1995 New York State Regents test.
3. Howe, 1995, p. 376. He added that standards are misconceived not only when they are too specific but also when they are developed "narrowly within particular disciplines" (p. 377). Most of what we'd like students to be able to do consists of ideas and capabilities, each of which embraces many different fields. To that extent, distinguishing science standards from social studies standards from language arts standards is not just artificial but counterproductive.
4. House et al., 1978, p. 137.
5. Campione et al., 1988, p. 95.
6. Ibid. Similarly, the "basics" approach to teaching younger children has resulted in their achieving some mastery of "the rules of reading and writing, even as they are learning their addition and multiplication tables," writes Howard Gardner. "What [they are] missing are not the decoding skills, but two other facets: the capacity to read for understanding and the desire to read at all" (1991, p. 186).
7. Whitehead, 1929/1967, p. 1.
8. This teacher is quoted in Prawat, 1989, p. 317. The same position is defended by E. D. Hirsch, Jr. (1996, p. 150): "Higher-level skills critically depend upon the automatic mastery of repeated lower-level activities."
9. Yager, 1991, p. 54. Emphasis added.
10. Labinowicz, 1987, p. 2.
11. This is analogous to claims one sometimes hears in favor of the Old School model of discipline or classroom management: at the beginning of the school year, the teacher has to get "control of the classroom" and impose his or her expectations, rules, and punishments on students because an orderly environment today is a prerequisite for helping kids to take responsibility and become empowered tomorrow. In reality, though, teachers who start that way rarely give up control and create a democratic environment later on (see Kohn, 1996a). This may be related to the argument that children can't participate in making decisions about how to act and learn and solve problems because they're not old enough to be given responsibility. Until they've developed sufficient maturity, they just have to do what they're told. Unfortunately, the kind of treatment that follows from that assumption means they may never get to that point.
12. The National Science Teachers Association has been pushing for a reform effort, known as Scope, Sequence and Coordination of Secondary School Science, in which all these different branches of science would be integrated into the curriculum taught every year from seventh to twelfth grade.
13. Whitehead, p. 16. He added: "The uncritical application of the principle of the antecedence of some subjects to others has, in the hands of dull people with a turn for organisation, produced in education the dryness of the Sahara" (pp. 16–17).
14. Resnick, 1987, p. 8.
15. Wolf et al., 1991, p. 51. Piaget, whose work provides a powerful empirical refutation of behaviorist theories of learning, helped us to understand that there are several distinct stages in children's mental development. The way they think after each of those cognitive reorganizations is different in kind, not

merely in degree, from the way they thought before. Jerome Bruner (1966, p. 27), who was greatly influenced by Piaget's findings, explained that "mental growth is not a gradual accretion" but "more like a staircase with rather sharp risers, more a matter of spurts and rests."

16. This example is adapted from one offered by Phil Daro, as quoted in Mitchell, 1992, p. 178.
17. This is true regardless of age and regardless of whether we are quick or slow to understand things. On the latter point, Perkins (1992, p. 14) declared that "thoughtful learning is just as important for slow learners as anyone else."
18. Joy Donlin is quoted in Willis and Checkley, 1996, p. 6. From another source: "It is contrary to what we know about the way children think to begin with contentless computation and only afterwards move on to applications of that know-how in the real world" (Kamii, 1985b, p. 120).
19. Gluck, 1995, p. 40.
20. Other aspects of the Old School (discussed elsewhere in this book) are similarly hard to square with the "real world": spending the day with people of one's own age; being evaluated largely on the basis of performance at timed, multiple-choice exams; and the typical high school schedule. On the last point, one writer wonders "how many adults would do well at dealing with different job requirements and a different boss every 47 minutes" (Ohanian, 1996b, p. 281).
21. Glasser, 1969, p. 72. In response to this point, E. D. Hirsch, Jr. (p. 156), says that maybe we *could* look up the facts rather than memorize them, "but few of us will" actually do so. Perhaps this is true; I don't know how many people actually own almanacs, visit libraries, or use the Internet to do research. But what interests me is *why* it may be true, why some people lack the proficiency or the propensity to go and find out what they need to know. My hunch is that it is precisely the traditional style of fact-based education that often leaves them either unable or unwilling to acquire information after they've graduated. If I'm right, it takes a lot of nerve to turn around and use this outcome to argue for that very style of education.
22. Langer, 1997, p. 69.
23. Novak, 1993, p. 52.
24. For example, when students in the equivalent of an honors class were asked by a researcher how long they usually remember the content of most of their lessons, one replied, "Ten minutes," and another said, "I've forgotten it straight after the lesson." So you wouldn't be able to recall most of what you're being taught six months later? the researcher asked. "None at all." "Oh no, oh my God no" (Boaler, 1997, p. 175).
25. Perkins, p. 8.
26. Dewey, 1916, p. 137.
27. Darling-Hammond, p. 272. And no wonder: "It is easier to organize drill and practice in decontextualized skills to mastery, or to manage 164 behavioral objectives, than it is to create and sustain environments that foster thought, thought about powerful ideas" (Brown, 1994, p. 11).
28. Shepard, 1989, p. 6.
29. See, for example, Campione et al., 1988, p. 96.
30. Kamii, p. 60.
31. After "intensive drilling on all the kinds of problems they will have to do on the test . . . the children are conditioned, like Pavlov's dog; when they see a certain arrangement of numerals and symbols before them, lights begin to flash,

wheels begin to turn, and like robots they go through the answer-getting process, or enough of them [do] to get a halfway decent score. . . . But is this a sensible way to carry out the education of our children?" (Holt, 1982, p. 260).

32. Langer makes a particularly strong argument along these lines, drawing from research to show that "when we drill ourselves in a certain skill so that it becomes second nature," we may come to perform that skill "mindlessly." "Learning the basics in a rote, unthinking manner almost ensures mediocrity" (pp. 13–14).

33. Dewey, 1916, p. 175.

34. Even "Close!" rankles the really reactionary, who firmly insist that close just isn't good enough, that the answer is either right or wrong. This is just the hard-assed version of the more general phenomenon I'm describing here; my point is that the kinder, gentler version is similarly misguided. Whether we welcome approximations of the right answer or accept nothing short of the real thing, we're still guided by the same problematic pedagogy that stifles thinking.

35. Duckworth, 1987, pp. 64, 131, 6.

36. Bruner, p. 72.

37. Brooks and Brooks, 1993, p. 86.

38. Apart from Piaget himself, other people whose work I have cited here, notably Bruner, Kamii, and Duckworth, might be considered his protégés. Thus it is intriguing to consider the possibility that even Piaget didn't go far enough in challenging the preoccupation with right answers. While children make different kinds of errors, Piaget's main point was that their thinking was erroneous, argued John Nicholls. Young children can't see, for example, that a taller, thinner container doesn't necessarily hold more liquid than a shorter, fatter one. "Applied to the classroom, this approach is easily assimilated into the ethic that students must discover the correct answers that are known to their teachers." While conceding that "this is not a necessary consequence of Piaget's perspective," Nicholls went on to say that the model "has no obvious place for dialogue about what question should be asked or what paradigm, in the Kuhnian sense of world view, one should try out. Piaget's is a psychology of puzzle-solving rather than of paradigm-choosing. The later Piaget, if not the early one, always knew what question he wanted to put to children and framed his questions to ensure that they answered his questions rather than others they might have been more disposed to ask. Here lies the key to the power of his work as well as to its limitations" (Nicholls and Hazzard, 1993, pp. 130, 202). James Beane (1997, p. 63) is similarly critical of the versions of constructivist teaching "that simply involve young people in finding their own way to predefined answers within one or another subject area."

39. For example, see Stigler and Stevenson, 1991; Lewis, 1995.

40. The analogy isn't perfect because over the course of a week or two these tourists will at least have tasted the food, met a few people, heard snatches of the language. To be more like traditional education, they would simply stay home and memorize the chief exports of each country.

41. Darling-Hammond, p. 228.

42. This reminds me of a story told by David Hawkins (1990, p. 138) about another elementary school science teacher who was told she must use some fill-in-the-blank workbooks. " 'So,' she said, 'We used them. We weighed them singly and by twos and by threes. We weighed them dry and we weighed them wet.' "

43. Theoretically one could hold such a view while being selective about the facts to be

covered, but the reality is that once learning is seen in that way, the sheer number of facts out there creates pressure to cover as many of them as possible.

44. Gardner et al. are quoted in Darling-Hammond, p. 113. Likewise, Lauren Resnick (p. 48) has remarked that "thinking skills tend to be driven out of the curriculum by ever-growing demands for teaching larger and larger bodies of knowledge."

45. Newmann, 1992, p. 84.

46. This is even more true if, as one study suggests, the tendency to cover things rapidly, so that students are merely "exposed" to them, is most in evidence with "topics having to do with conceptual understanding and application," whereas more time is spent with skill-building exercises (Porter, 1989, p. 12). Of course, it's possible to imagine a style of teaching that errs in the direction of too much depth—graduate education in many fields comes to mind, where students are expected to know everything there is to know about one tiny area and nothing about anything else—but elementary and secondary education now lean so far over in the direction of breadth that we have a long way to go before this becomes a real worry.

47. Newmann, p. 84. Beyond the question of how long these facts are remembered, we could ask an even more telling question: "How much of all that content is an important part of who [we] are today" (Wolk, 1998, p. 35).

48. "Teaching for exposure also may communicate to students that knowing a very little about a lot of different things is more valuable than a deep understanding of a few key concepts" (Porter, p. 12).

49. McNeil, 1986, p. 174. Also, "most teachers felt they could cover more material more efficiently if controversial topics were omitted."

50. Dewey, 1916, p. 158.

51. Freire, 1970, p. 53.

52. Wisconsin's governor Tommy Thompson is quoted in Harp, 1996.

53. The beauty of the *Reader's Digest* is that you can't really tell whether any given item appeared last month or in 1935. This one was published in October 1969 and was quoted in Silberman, 1970, p. 148.

54. Ayers, 1991, p. 128.

55. Resnick and Klopfer, 1989, p. 5.

56. No matter how many times it proves fruitless simply to tell, Deborah Meier points out (1995, pp. 138, 144), "we keep feeling sure that if we could but 'tell it right . . .' " Moreover, "we worry whenever we're not doing the talking. . . . Teachers who were good at the old style . . . miss being star performers."

57. Brooks and Brooks, pp. 39–40.

58. Perhaps it is because the overwhelmingly conservative constituency that supports traditional education can sense that there are political implications to vesting all knowledge and authority in the leader (of the classroom) as opposed to inviting students to play a more vital role in their own education. "The more students work at storing the deposits entrusted to them, the less they develop the critical consciousness which would result from their intervention in the world as transformers of that world. The more completely they accept the passive role imposed on them, the more they tend simply to adapt to the world as it is and to the fragmented view of reality deposited in them" (Freire, p. 54).

59. There's no contradiction for E. D. Hirsch, Jr. (p. 22), however, who sympathizes with such a sentiment and holds that if only students had been given more facts beforehand, they would have learned what the teacher had just taught them. Needless to say, this view is a lot more convenient for teachers,

which may help to explain why the transmission approach to teaching remains so widespread.

60. The quotation is from Darling-Hammond, p. 114. For a good discussion of this dilemma, see Searfoss and Enz, 1996.

61. Gardner, p. 243. He adds that schooling is often "done to" the teachers, too, by which he presumably means that a curriculum (and, by extension, a style of teaching) is often mandated by administrators, school boards, state legislatures, and others who presume to control education in the name of "accountability."

62. Dewey, 1899/1990, p. 80.

63. This metaphor comes from Patrick Shannon. Another group of writers, citing the work of Larry Cuban, notes that this kind of teaching grew out of a search for "new ways to convey the requisite skills to large numbers of average students seen by educators as headed for semiskilled labor. The models they drew on included application forms, shipping invoices, and business letters rather than experiments, essays, or journals. Out of these choices have come the media of most public education: fill-in-the-blank exercises, multiple-choice items, sets of preestablished chapter-end questions, five-paragraph essays, book reports, and science labs that entail no more than verification of someone else's hypotheses and procedures in a highly specified order. The verbs that dominate directions for seat work, class instruction, or tests are *complete, choose,* and *match,* not *ask, analyze, investigate,* or *revise*" (Wolf et al., p. 40).

64. I discuss this issue at length in Kohn, 1996.

65. Hirsch, p. 218. We'll overlook for the moment his equation of "naturalistic" and "integrated" learning.

66. Piaget, 1948/1973, p. 93.

67. Meier, p. 4. John Goodlad (1984, p. 244) saw this, too: "We have not fully considered the implications of the grand phrases. How many creative thinkers do businesses need? What kind of nation is one awash with autonomous individuals?" For a classic essay on how schools are designed to prepare people for a life of essential passivity because that is what our economic system requires, see Bowles and Gintis, 1976.

68. Traditionalists who speak of rigor and challenge and excellence usually take for granted that these qualities describe academic subjects such as history and physics. Other skills and tasks are denigrated and even used as a shorthand for lack of challenge: the prototypical easy course is "basket-weaving." As Nel Noddings (1992, p. 147) asks, however, "How many of us can actually weave a serviceable basket?" If challenge were really our criterion, then a rigorous education for people like me would be geared to teaching auto mechanics rather than verbal skills, since public speaking comes pretty easily to me but I have no idea why my car's engine has been hesitating lately. One comes to understand why Dewey (1916, p. 239) flatly stated that "we cannot establish a hierarchy of values among studies. It is futile to attempt to arrange them in an order." Moreover, even if we prefer to confine the discussion to the intellectual realm, Deborah Meier (p. 171) reminds us that "traditional academics [is] but one example of important intellectual activity."

69. For example, a publication by the Council for Basic Education asserts that "standards' significance depends on their relationship to the traditional core academic disciplines" (Pritchard, 1996, p. 5). Not every proponent of standards for instruction in this or that field is an apologist for the current separation of disciplines, but that may well be the effect of their actions.

70. The research, by the Mid-continent Regional Educational Laboratory, found

that "even the brightest students would need nine additional years of schooling to master the nearly 4,000 benchmarks experts have set in 14 subject areas" (Marzano et al., 1999, p. 68).

71. Whitehead, p. 6. This, he added, "kills the vitality of our modern curriculum. There is only one subject-matter for education, and that is Life in all its manifestations."

72. Putnam et al., 1990, p. 127. This violates a newer understanding "of learning and knowledge as structured and connected," these researchers add (p. 128).

73. Few schools today rigidly adopt the "mastery learning" model developed by Benjamin Bloom and his colleagues, but "much of the prevalent traditional practice still in place stems from this behaviorist psychology. Behaviorist theory often explains behavioral change well, but it offers little in the way of explaining conceptual change" (Fosnot, 1996, p. 9).

74. Traditional teaching has a way "of taking vitally important material—exciting material—and reducing it to mush" (Noddings, p. 85).

75. Brown et al., 1989, pp. 32–33.

76. It's worth remembering that reading, writing, and math were invented in a context, and for a purpose—namely, to keep track of trade. "Instruction was embedded in practical enterprises that had important consequences" (Farnham-Diggory, 1990, pp. 117–18).

77. One result of—some would even say a reason for—keeping students with same-age peers is that competition among them is more likely to take place. It's certainly easier to sort them by achievement if all the eight-year-olds are together, doing the same thing (see Labaree, 1997b, p. 62). One of the many advantages of "multiage" or "nongraded" schooling is that it fosters a culture of collaboration instead of competition.

78. The best single source on ability grouping continues to be Oakes, 1985. Notice how neatly this practice fits with the dominant model of learning: once it has been decided that knowledge is something transmitted to students, the transmission may be thought to occur more efficiently if the students are sorted by putative ability.

79. Goodman, 1992, pp. 22–23. Carole Ames (1992a, p. 266) similarly remarks that "the prevalence of children 'working on their own' in many U.S. classrooms cannot be viewed as supporting autonomous achievement activity. Students may be doing their own work, but their activity often lacks meaningful direction or is in fact teacher defined and structured."

80. Darling-Hammond, p. 114. She continues: "Their acquisition of these sounds would be tested and graded periodically, but they would receive little practice in real-world contexts or feedback on their efforts. After four or more years of study, they would probably speak about as fluently as most foreign language students do when they graduate from school—that is, far less easily and knowledgeably than today's entering kindergartner does" (pp. 114–15).

81. David Zahren, an instructional specialist in Maryland, is quoted in Welsh, 1990, B1.

82. Dewey, 1938/1963, p. 46.

83. McNeil, p. 79.

84. This veteran high school math teacher is described as maintaining "standards with a vengeance, regularly ejecting students from his classes and awarding a preponderance of Ds and Fs. This teacher's talk, like that of other teachers who shared his view of students as the problem, was filled with military

metaphors—combat pay, front-line, kick butt, line of fire—which reflect his general view of the classroom as a battlefield" (McLaughlin, 1993, p. 91).

85. Dewey, 1938/1963, p. 49.

## 4. GETTING EVALUATION WRONG

1. Here are four facts about the SAT that everyone should know:

1. We've come to think of it as a necessary part of going to college, but in its current (multiple-choice) form it has been used only since the 1940s. Realizing that something hasn't always been done helps to remind us that it doesn't have to be done. So does realizing that something isn't done everywhere. Canadian universities, for example, don't use the SAT or anything like it for college admission. Moreover, at least 280 U.S. colleges and universities have stopped requiring that applicants take the SAT—or its equally pernicious Midwest counterpart, the ACT. (See "ACT/SAT Optional," 1997.) The organization that released that information, FairTest, subsequently surveyed some of those colleges and found that most were pleased with the results; applicants, for example, were no less capable when test scores were not required. (See " 'Test Score Optional' Admissions," 1998. For a list of colleges that no longer require SATs or ACTs, send a self-addressed stamped envelope to FairTest, 342 Broadway, Cambridge, MA, 02139, or download it from www.fairtest.org.)

2. The SAT doesn't tell us how smart students are. Several years ago the Educational Testing Service, which designs and administers the test, gave up the pretense that it measures students' "aptitude," which used to be what the *A* in SAT stood for. (For a while it stood for "assessment," but now ETS says the initials don't stand for anything.) The verbal section is basically just a vocabulary test, but even that description is too generous. One study classified students' approaches to studying as "surface" (doing as little as possible and sticking to rote memorization), "deep" (understanding ideas and connecting new material to existing knowledge), or "achieving" (trying to get good grades and beat everyone else without interest in what was being learned). It turned out that those who adopted either a surface or achieving style did the best on the SAT. Scores were *negatively* correlated with a deep approach to learning (Hall et al., 1995).

3. The only remotely defensible rationale for the test, given how little it tells us about the test-taker's aptitude, is that it helps colleges predict who will succeed if admitted. But studies indicate that it isn't even very useful for that: SAT scores predict only about 16 percent of the variation in students' grades even in the freshman year, and they're worthless for predicting anything beyond that, such as eventual occupational success (Sacks, 1997, pp. 26–27).

4. Far from being a measure of merit (sometimes pointedly contrasted with affirmative action criteria), what the test mostly tells us about is money. There is a direct relationship between SAT scores and family income. The average score for students whose families made less than $10,000 was 873; for $10,000–$20,000, 918; for $20,000–$30,000, 972; for $30,000–$40,000, 993; for $40,000–$50,000, 1015; for $50,000–$60,000, 1033; for $60,000–$70,000, 1048; for $70,000–$80,000, 1062; for $80,000–$100,000, 1084; for $100,000 and above, 1130 ("College Admissions Test Scores by Family Income," 1998; the information is also available at www.collegeboard.org). Even without a graph, you can see that in every single case, the richer the family, the higher the score. One reason for this (though by no means the only one) is that more affluent

families can afford those expensive test prep sessions. The fact that such tutoring really does seem to bring up scores should be cause for outrage, not relief.

2. Sacks, 1997, p. 25.

3. "Few countries today give these formal examinations to students before the age of sixteen or so" (Resnick and Nolan, 1995, p. 102). Moreover, "it is interesting to note that European countries, whose education systems are often touted as superior to ours, have not historically relied on standardized tests at all" (Wagner, 1998, p. 516).

4. "By the time they were ready to graduate to sixth grade last June, New York City fifth graders had taken eight standardized tests over the previous 14 months; this year's fourth-grade reading test . . . will take three days to administer. In Chicago, pupils took 12 standardized tests from the winter of third grade through the spring of fourth grade" (Steinberg, 1999).

5. A survey of 250 representative school districts across the U.S. in 1995 found that more than 93 percent reported giving standardized reading tests to children before they had reached the third grade (Dougherty, 1998).

6. Compared to other forms of assessment, standardized tests are a bargain. But given the sheer scope of testing these days, they cost hundreds of millions of dollars that could instead be spent to help children learn.

7. Frederiksen, 1984, p. 201.

8. See Morgan, 1970, chap. 6.

9. McNeil, 1986, p. xviii. W. Edwards Deming was one of the few people in his field to understand that this is also true in the business world. He frequently commented that the most important management issues simply cannot be reduced to numbers.

10. Mitchell, 1992, p. 134. We may not know who "they" are, but "their" fallibility is brought home to us every so often, particularly when a student taking one of these tests can make a case that, say, "b" is the best answer, or at least that there is sufficient ambiguity in the question to permit several legitimate answers, but at the same time knows full well that "they" are looking for "c" and will count only that response as correct. Anyone who has ever had this experience should understand on yet another level how wide the gap is between higher achievement and higher test scores.

11. Ayers, 1993, p. 118. At the very least, reports of a school's (or district's) average test score should always be accompanied by information about the income levels of the community in question.

12. Rotberg, 1998b, p. 28. A chart in this article provides striking evidence of a correlation between the child poverty rate in each state and its ranking on the NAEP math test for eighth-graders in 1992. The average poverty rate for the five states with the highest test scores was 15 percent; for the bottom five states, it was almost exactly twice that.

13. Glaser, 1963, p. 520.

14. Norm-referenced tests were used by thirty-one states in 1997, two more than the year before, and they are "not going away" (Bond et al., 1998, pp. 7, 9). Worse, individual school districts often use more of these tests than the states require.

15. Popham, 1999, p. 10.

16. For example, far and away the most common method for determining whether students are "reading on grade level" is to look at whether they score above a certain percentile (such as the 50th) on a norm-referenced test. At least two out of every five districts in the country do this, compared with only one out of six that use a criterion-referenced test and fewer still that use other definitions. See Dougherty.

17. The reverse situation actually happened in late 1998 on an international scale. See p. 246n63.

18. Thus, "the better the job that teachers do in teaching important knowledge and/or skills, the less likely it is that there will be items on a standardized achievement test measuring such knowledge and/or skills" (Popham, p. 12; also see 1993, pp. 106–11). Furthermore, because these tests are designed to maximize "response variance" (that is, to spread out the students' scores), they also tend to include the sort of questions that "tap innate intellectual skills that are not readily modifiable in school" and information "learned outside of school." Yet the results of these tests are then used to rate the effectiveness of schools. Popham (1999, p. 14) also points out that the relevance of knowledge acquired outside school, which of course is not acquired equally by all children, helps to explain the high correlation between test scores and socioeconomic status.

19. A survey of parents' understanding of a test in Michigan revealed that "an overwhelming majority . . . interpreted the criterion-referenced score as a normative percentile" (Paris et al., 1991, p. 14).

20. Popham, 1998, p. 383.

21. Resnick, 1987, p. 34.

22. Resnick and Resnick, 1990, pp. 71–72. Their overall conclusion: "The tests most widely used to assess achievement are unfriendly to the goals of the thinking curriculum" (p. 73).

23. Madaus et al., 1992, p. 2.

24. Constance Kamii (1989, p. 157) has pointed out that standardized tests may look as though they're tapping logical-mathematical knowledge but to a significant extent are really just tapping arbitrary conventional knowledge. Two math educators give a good example from a Massachusetts test for high school students. The question reads as follows:

$$n \; 1 \; 2 \; 3 \; 4 \; 5 \; 6$$
$$t_n \; 3 \; 5$$

The first two terms of a sequence, $t_1$ and $t_2$, are shown above as 3 and 5. Using the rule: $t_n = t_{n-1} + t_{n-2}$, where n is greater than or equal to 3, complete the table.

This is actually just asking the test-taker to add 3 and 5 to get 8, then add 5 and 8 to get 13, then add 8 and 13 to get 21, and so on. "The problem simply requires the ability to follow a rule; there is no mathematics in it at all. And many 10th-grade students will get it wrong, not because they lack the mathematical thinking necessary to fill in the table, but simply because they haven't had experience with the notation. Next year, however, teachers will prep students on how to use formulas like $t_n = t_{n-1} + t_{n-2}$, more students will get it right, and state education officials will tell us that we are increasing mathematical literacy" (Cuoco and Ruopp, 1998).

25. Wood and Sellers, 1997, p. 181.

26. Bruce Alberts's comments, delivered at the academy's annual meeting in May 1998, were reported in "Science Leader Criticizes Tests," 1998.

27. One study classified fifth- and sixth-graders as "actively" engaged in learning if they went back over things they didn't understand, asked questions of themselves as they read, and tried to connect what they were doing to what they had already learned; and as "superficially" engaged if they just copied down answers, guessed a lot, and skipped the hard parts. It turned out that the superficial style was positively correlated ($r = .28$, significant at $p < .001$) with

composite scores on the CTBS and Metropolitan standardized tests (Meece et al., 1988). A study of middle school students, meanwhile, found that those "who value literacy activities and who are task-focused toward literacy activities" got lower scores on the CTBS reading test (Anderman, 1992). And, as already mentioned, the same pattern shows up with the SAT (see p. 262*n*1, par. 2).

28. Piaget, 1948/1973, p. 74.
29. Kamii, 1985a, p. 7.
30. Delisle, 1997, p. 44. He continues: "With many of the multiple-choice questions having several 'correct' options in the eyes of creative thinkers, scores get depressed for children who see possibilities that are only visible to those with open minds." And from another source: "Good readers, for example, take lots of risks in the process of reading most materials. These risks lead to errors. Depending upon their impact on meaning, these errors may or may not be corrected by the reader. But reading tests, which involve fairly short passages followed by trick questions and answers, require being constantly alert to precisely the kind of insignificant errors that good readers let fall by the wayside" (Calkins et al., 1998, p. 47).
31. The teacher, Marcia Burchby, is quoted in Wood, 1992, p. 32.
32. Goodman, 1986, p. 358.
33. Peck et al., 1989.
34. Ayers, 1993, p. 116.
35. Robert J. Mislevy is quoted in Mitchell, 1992, p. 179. Actually, it's more like twenty-first-century statistics at this point, and the psychology in question didn't come into its own until the early part of the twentieth century, but you get the idea. Dennie Wolf and her associates (1991, p. 47) contend that "the technology of scoring has become one of the most powerful realizations of behaviorist views of learning and performance."
36. See Frederiksen, p. 199, for a discussion of Herbert Simon's distinction between well-structured and ill-structured problems, the latter being more realistic and important, the former showing up on standardized tests.
37. Bond et al., p. 10; Neill, 1997.
38. "Short-answer questions and computational exercises presented in formats that can be scored quickly and 'objectively'" represent a "typically American style of testing [that] is quite different from traditions in other countries, where more complex problem solving is the norm on both classroom and external examinations" (Schoen et al., 1999, p. 446).
39. Farr is quoted in Checkley, 1997a, p. 5.
40. Frederiksen, p. 199. And from another source: "No multiple-choice question can be used to discover how well students can express their own ideas in their own words, how well they can marshal evidence to support their arguments, or how well they can adjust to the need to communicate for a particular purpose and to a particular audience. Nor can multiple-choice questions ever indicate whether what the student writes will be interesting to read" (Gertrude Conlan is quoted in Freedman, 1993, pp. 29–30).
41. This is roughly analogous to how norm-referenced testing is inherently objectionable but not all criterion-referenced testing is worth celebrating either. In fact, putting the two observations together, it's not hard to find criterion-referenced essay exams that require students to analyze a contrived chunk of text or cough up facts about the Victorian era. The results may not be valid, and the exercise may not be worth it. Moreover, the way these exams are scored raises even more concerns. For example, the essays written by students from two

dozen states are not evaluated by educators; they are shipped off to North Carolina, where low-paid temp workers spend no more than two or three minutes reading each one. " 'There were times I'd be reading a paper every 10 seconds,' " one former scorer told a reporter. Sometimes he "would only briefly scan papers before issuing a grade, searching for clues such as a descriptive passage within a narrative to determine what grade to give. 'You could skim them very quickly ... I know this sounds very bizarre, but you could put a number on these things without actually reading the paper,' " said this scorer, who, like his coworkers, was offered a "$200 bonus that kicked in after 8,000 papers" (Glovin, 1998).

42. Wolf et al., p. 46.
43. Wiggins, 1993, p. 72. "Thoughtful and deep understanding is simply not assessable in secure testing," he continues, "and we will continue to send the message to teachers that simplistic recall or application, based on 'coverage,' is all that matters—until we change the policy of secrecy" (p. 92).
44. If we need an analogy that evokes the heartland, this one seems more apt: "Measuring the richness of learning by giving a standardized test is like judging chili by counting the beans" (Ferri, 1998, p. 20).
45. Mitchell, 1992, p. 15, and Resnick and Resnick, p. 73, respectively. Lauren Resnick (1987, p. 47) adds that multiple choice tests "can measure the accumulation of knowledge and can be used to examine specific components of reasoning or thinking. However, they are ill suited to assessing the kinds of integrated thinking that we call 'higher order.' "
46. Delisle, p. 41.
47. Shepard, 1989, p. 5.
48. For example, see Goldstein, 1990a.
49. Antonucci is quoted in Daley and Hart, 1998.
50. Bushweller, 1997.
51. Freedman, 1995, p. 29. I am reminded of how the management theorist Douglas McGregor once explained why corporate executives are so fond of incentive plans. He said, in effect, that they like to dangle money in front of their employees because they *can*—that is, because while they cannot control how people will feel about their work, they can unilaterally determine how much people are paid.
52. Jones and Whitford, p. 280. Also see Frederiksen on this point.
53. Departmentalization, in turn, tends to support other problematic practices, such as giving letter grades and segregating students by alleged ability.
54. Gloria Hoffman, principal of Randolph Elementary School in Arlington, Va., was quoted in Mathews and Benning, 1999.
55. Herman and Golan, 1993, p. 22. It was also common to find staff meetings, as well as conversations between principals and individual teachers, devoted to reviewing test scores and strategies for raising them.
56. Madaus et al., p. 16. This survey included more than two thousand teachers of grades four through twelve in six diverse districts. Also see Herman and Golan.
57. I borrow here from the analyses of Linda McNeil and Lorrie Shepard.
58. The Arizona anecdote comes from a study reported in Smith, 1991, p. 10. The Texas examples are from Kunen, 1997, and Johnston, 1998. (In response to this situation, incidentally, the director of the Texas Business and Education Coalition reportedly commented that "what the state needs is even more testing" [Johnston, p. 21].) The Illinois example comes from Smith et al., 1998; the New Jersey quotation from Glovin, 1998; the North Carolina quotation

from Simmons, 1997; the Maryland example from Goldstein, 1990a; and the New York example from Hartocollis, 1999.

59. Calkins et al., pp. 2, 73.
60. For example, see Mathews, 1998a.
61. Campbell, 1997, p. 641.
62. This finding by Susan Stodolsky is cited in Noble and Smith, 1994.
63. Zemelman et al., 1998, p. 218.
64. Cenziper, 1998, p. 1C. "About half [of the teachers surveyed] said they spent more than 40 percent of their time having students practice for end-of-grade tests. Almost 70 percent thought the [tests] would not improve education at their schools" and "almost half the teachers surveyed in the UNC study said preparation for the tests has decreased students' love of learning." A press release about the study revealed that two thirds of teachers have changed their teaching strategies to prepare students for the tests, with many relying more on worksheets, lectures, and tests in class than they otherwise would.
65. Paris et al., p. 15.
66. Darling-Hammond's analogy, which originally appeared in a 1989 article in *Rethinking Schools,* is paraphrased in Calkins et al., p. 44.
67. Noble and Smith, p. 6.
68. Principals, politicians, and journalists routinely cite just such a predictable jump in scores as evidence that the desperate efforts to prepare students for those very tests has been successful. For example, a reporter for the *Los Angeles Times* asserted that a high-stakes testing program in Texas—perhaps the most educationally destructive program in the nation—"has shown signs of dramatic success," meaning that scores on the test itself have risen (Kolker, 1999).
69. The story appears in Calkins et al., p. 47.
70. Kathy Greeley of Graham and Parks School. Personal communication, 1998.
71. National Association for the Education of Young Children, 1987, p. 1. Piaget (p. 74) anticipated this problem decades ago: "The school examination becomes an end in itself because it dominates the teacher's concerns, instead of fostering his natural role as one who stimulates consciences and minds, and he directs all the work of the students toward the artificial result which is success on final tests."
72. Personal communication, 1998.
73. The work of FairTest (see note 1) is relevant here. Recall also that the questions on a norm-referenced test are more likely to be included not only when just some students get them right but when they are answered correctly by those who answer the other questions correctly, too. Thus, "a test item on which African-Americans do particularly well but whites do not is likely to be discarded because of the interaction of two factors: African-Americans are a minority, and African-Americans tend to score low" (Neill and Medina, 1989, p. 692).
74. Virtually no one, including defenders of standardized tests, will deny this fact; it is evident to anyone who visits schools around the country. Those looking for empirical confirmation can find it in Madaus et al., pp. 2, 15–16; and in Herman and Golan, who discovered a particularly striking discrepancy in how much time was spent taking practice tests in poor versus rich schools. In the most extreme cases, such as Baltimore elementary schools serving low-income African-American students, "teachers are now spending the entire school year teaching for the standardized tests." Sadder still, some teachers don't seem to mind: "Their scores went up this last time, so it's worth it," one third-grade teacher remarked (Winerip, 1999, p. 40).

75. Dorn, 1998, p. 16.
76. Jones is quoted in Cenziper, p. 7C.

## 5. GETTING SCHOOL REFORM WRONG

1. This distinction grew out of a conversation I had in 1993 with Eric Schaps, who directs the Developmental Studies Center in Oakland, Calif.
2. The original meaning of "standard" is noted in Jervis and McDonald, 1996, p. 568.
3. Eisner, 1995, p. 763. "Uniform standards may be appropriate for business—a manufacturer wants all its microwave ovens to meet specified standards of quality. That's good. But to what extent do we want all students to be alike?" (Reigeluth, 1997, p. 204).
4. "The TIMSS data provide examples of countries with centralized curriculum and educational control that achieve both higher and less high than the US" (Schmidt, in press).
5. Those who *do* know something about the field may be dismissed rather than consulted. My favorite example of this comes from a state legislator in Montana whose pet proposal was blocked by some of his colleagues who happened to be former teachers and administrators. He remarked, "We screwed up. We just put too many educators on the education committee" (Lindsay, 1995, p. 14).
6. Dewey, 1916, p. 170.
7. Jones and Whitford, 1997, p. 279.
8. Flink et al., 1990.
9. Note the irony here: policy makers not only dictate what and how to teach, but then insist that teachers be held accountable for what they were compelled to do! As one teacher put it, "I have no problem being held accountable for the content and direction of my classroom, but I would ask that this accountability extend only to factors within my control" (Smith, 1999).
10. "Stating precise and definite curricular objectives in advance of any educational activity . . . is, of course, an argument by analogy from the world of manufacture where, at least, according to Taylor, precise specifications and standards had to be established in advance in order to achieve the desired product with maximum efficiency" (Herbert M. Kliebard, quoted in Wolk, 1998, p. 33). Ironically, Taylor's assembly line paradigm continues to drive the corporate view of educational standards even though many corporations no longer see it as useful in the business world.
11. We ought to rethink the idea that accountability means "to an external authority." At the least, we ought to demand broader, more meaningful measures of success. Purely "statistical accountability, with the abstraction of student performance into numbers without context, removes classroom practices from the discussion of educational reform" and fails to "encourage deeper discussion of educational problems" (Dorn, 1998, pp. 23, 22). In smaller schools that are more democratic, Deborah Meier argues, "the accountability we owe to parents and the public is a matter of access, not of complex governing bodies or monitoring arrangements. In small schools we know quickly which teachers are absent, and don't need to depend on time clocks." In large schools, by contrast, "administrators can be held accountable only for indirect indicators of performance because that's all they know — 'standardized' stuff,

easily manipulated and inauthentic" (Meier, 1995b, pp. 112–13). Beyond the specific point Meier is making here, her style of criticism is worth noticing: rather than just calling for more or less accountability, she questions the usual definition and invites us to see how our positions are effectively constrained by the features of schooling (in this case, the sheer size of schools) that we take for granted. This sort of analysis contrasts sharply with talking about how high, how much, how fast, how hard.

12. Deci et al., 1982. This phenomenon has been noticed by a number of educators, including Seymour Sarason and Linda McNeil. Once again, though, Dewey (1916, p. 109) anticipated long ago what researchers would later discover. Often, he remarked, "the intelligence of the teacher is not free; it is confined to receiving the aims laid down from above. . . . This distrust of the teacher's experience is then reflected in lack of confidence in the responses of pupils."

13. See Kanter, 1977, pp. 189–90.

14. The mother of an honor roll student in Alabama who was denied a high school diploma because he failed that state's graduation test says that she "might as well have told him to skip school, fail his classes, and get into trouble because nothing matters except the almighty exit exam." (From an unpublished letter sent to an administrator in Baldwin County; her name has been withheld on request.)

15. See Olson, 1998, for an example of this way of framing the debate.

16. For more than you could ever want to read on the issues raised in the next few paragraphs, see Kohn, 1993a.

17. Harackiewicz et al., 1984, p. 293.

18. Shepard, p. 8. Those gains from teaching to the test may not last very long.

19. There is evidence that retention "increases dramatically in historically low-achieving schools following the implementation of a statewide high-stakes assessment," a practice that two researchers describe as "egregiously unethical" — to say nothing of the fact that it tends to "contaminate accountability data" (McGill-Franzen and Allington, 1993, pp. 20–21).

20. Berliner and Biddle, pp. 192–92.

21. Steve Frommeyer is quoted in Keller, 1998, p. 16.

22. Kellaghan et al., 1996, p. 23.

23. "Contrary to the popular view, dropouts are not always the worst students. According to one estimate, nearly 30 percent of all dropouts in America would test out as gifted" (Covington, 1992, p. 59).

24. Darling-Hammond, 1997, p. 238.

25. A review of scores by FairTest found that "students were *less likely* to reach a level of "proficient" or higher on the NAEP math or reading tests in states which had mandatory high school graduation tests" ("High-Stakes Tests," 1997–98, p. 1). Bracey (1998a) then looked for changes in students' status on these tests from 1990 to 1996 and drew the conclusion quoted here.

26. See Kellaghan et al., 1996. For additional evidence about the British experience with high-stakes exams, see Freedman, 1995.

27. The superintendent, John A. Murphy, is quoted in Goldstein, 1990b. He went on to say, "If it can be taught, it can be measured."

28. Rothman, 1995, p. 44.

## 6. GETTING IMPROVEMENT WRONG

1. This is confirmed by the AFT's "Making Standards Matter" report, which deserves credit at least for recommending that low-achieving students be provided with extra help.
2. Covington, 1996, p. 24.
3. Labaree, 1997b, pp. 72, 51. Another group of writers made much the same point: "The result of strictly meritocratic reforms will not be a better future for the majority, but new convenience in designating the victims of both educational and economic deprivation. Today's get-tough policies work, in practice, as new ways to justify the enlargement of an underclass and the lowering of expectations for most others. . . . In too many cases, excellence has become a code word for retrenchment in public education, signaling a retreat from egalitarian commitments and from public responsibility in schooling" (Bastian et al., 1986, pp. 55–6, 4).
4. This quotation, from page iii of *Hard Work and High Expectations: Motivating Students to Learn,* released by the U.S. Office of Educational Research and Improvement (OERI), is cited in Kellaghan et al., 1996, p. 1.
5. Shanker, 1994.
6. Wood, 1992, p. xxii. This conclusion is consistent with the research conducted by the educational historian Larry Cuban (1988, pp. 342–43), who found that recent reforms "seek to make the existing system more productive, not to disturb basic classroom roles or the governance structure of schools." More serious proposals to change the traditional nature of education "have seldom found a permanent home in the classrooms and schools of the nation"—as we saw in chapter 1.
7. Wood, p. 10. Also see Sizer, 1992, p. 11: "'Tougher' courses often simply meant 'more' to cover, maintaining the 'exposure' metaphor and further trivializing a grotesquely overloaded curriculum. 'More homework' usually meant more mindless busy work. A longer school year or school day translated into more of the existing regimen."
8. "Evidence indicating that, when districts or states that represent the full panoply of American students and schools set high standards, they also generate greater levels of achievement . . . has not yet appeared, nor is it likely that we will ever see it" (Biddle, 1997, p. 10).
9. Karweit, 1984, pp. 33, 34.
10. For math in particular, researchers have found "a significant positive linear relationship between observed 'engaged time' of the learner in low-level mathematics activities and tasks (knowledge, facts, and skill) and students' subsequent low-level mathematics achievement." But that clear relationship isn't apparent "for higher level mathematics activities, including mathematical applications and problem solving" (Putnam et al., 1990, p. 129).
11. Moving to fewer classes that last longer is usually referred to as "block scheduling." It has been enthusiastically supported by a number of educators (e.g., Queen and Gaskey, 1997) but hasn't always led to better results when teaching methods haven't changed along with the schedule (see Sommerfeld, 1996). The power of this reform, though, is that with proper support and coaching, high school teachers often find that a much longer period of time with a class is an invitation to rethink the traditional, lecture-based way of teaching. The added time thus acts as a catalyst for improvement rather than itself being the source of achievement gains.
12. "We are intent on improving academic performance," said the superintendent

of schools in Atlanta, and "you don't do that by having kids hanging on the monkey bars" (quoted in Johnson, 1998, p. A1).

13. Levin, 1984, p. 3.
14. Schmidt et al., in press. Surveys that report U.S. students don't spend as many days in school as some of their counterparts in other countries generally fail to measure actual hours of instruction. For example, Japanese, Korean, and Canadian students spend more days in school than those in the U.S. but have fewer actual hours of instruction. (See National Center for Education Statistics, 1994.)
15. Martin Burne, the principal of Deerfield Elementary School in Milburn, N.J., is quoted in Winerip, 1999, p. 28. The writer of this article goes on to observe that "there are many ways to measure a successful school—the creativity of the students, their happiness, their hunger to learn new things, their love of reading. But at this point in American history, the most important measure . . . is performance on standardized tests. And as long as that is true, those backpacks are likely to be full each night starting in grade 1 and maybe earlier" (p. 40).
16. Cooper, 1989.
17. Sadler and Tai, 1997.
18. Cooper et al., 1998. The quotation appears on p. 81.
19. Black, 1996. Fortunately, some teachers assign homework only when there is something important to do that can't be done in school, such as conducting a scientific investigation at home. Some teachers figure that homework is far more likely to be useful if students have been brought in on the process of deciding what ought to be done, by what date, in what manner, and for what purpose. In Japan, meanwhile, homework for older students doesn't consist of the dreaded (and often pointless) teacher-directed assignment, such as "read chapter 12 and do the even-numbered questions"; rather, there is the expectation that students will spend time "reviewing the day's lessons and anticipating the lessons for the following day" (Stevenson, 1998, p. 529). In Japanese eighth-grade math classes, homework is rarely assigned at all (Stigler and Hiebert, 1997, p. 18).
20. For another thoughtful critique, see Corno, 1996. Others who have challenged conventional ways of thinking about the subject include Etta Kralovec, who teaches at the College of the Atlantic in Bar Harbor, Me., and Patricia Hinchey, who teaches at the Pennsylvania State University. Cooper's research was featured in a *Newsweek* article that also quoted Corno's conclusion: "Homework is more a part of the problem than a part of the solution" (see Begley, 1998; the quotation appears on p. 51).
21. Retention can also be a deliberate strategy to boost a school's overall test scores (see p. 99). Thus, one part of the Tougher Standards agenda (preventing low-achieving students from advancing to the next grade) is encouraged by the adoption of another part (high-stakes testing).
22. See Labaree, chap. 2. The irony here is that it is traditionalists who are fond of accusing progressives of being driven by ideology and political considerations.
23. Natriello, 1998, p. 15.
24. House, 1989, pp. 204–5, 215; Shepard and Smith, 1989, p. 10. Investigations by other researchers, including a study of young children in Washington, D.C. (see Marcon, 1994), has confirmed these conclusions. Also see Reynolds et al., 1997; Darling-Hammond and Falk, 1997; Owings and Magliaro, 1998; Allington and McGill-Franzen, chap. 2; and, most recently, a report by the National Research Council described in Hauser, 1999.
25. For more on multiage education and looping, see p. 156.

272 · Notes to Pages 107–109

26. Stevenson, p. 526; Lewis, 1995, p. 15. "Asian children are not divided into high- or low-ability groups [so] Asian teachers must therefore present each lesson in a variety of ways for children with different skills" (Chira, 1992).
27. Lewis, p. 15, citing the U.S. Department of Education's report *Japanese Education Today*.
28. Lewis, pp. 201, 16. The national curriculum standards in Japan are much shorter and less detailed than the model to which many Americans seem to aspire.
29. Lewis, passim; and Baris-Sanders, 1997.
30. Stigler and Stevenson, 1991; Lewis, passim. All of this seems to be turned on its head, with a reversion to teacher-directed, fact-based instruction, when students get to high school (see Paul George's observations, cited in Bracey, 1996b, p. 642; Lewis, p. 198).
31. Lewis and Tsuchida, 1998. Nor can this success be put down to Japan's more homogeneous population. "It is diversity in children's educational backgrounds, not in their social and cultural backgrounds, that poses the greatest problems in teaching. Although the United States is culturally more diverse than Japan or China, we have found no more diversity at the classroom level" in Asia. "Teachers everywhere must deal with students who vary in their knowledge and motivation" and "the variability in levels of academic achievement differs little between the United States and Japan, Taiwan, or China" (Stigler and Stevenson, p. 19).
32. Dewey, 1913, p. 2. Also see his discussion in chapter 3 of *Democracy and Education*. Psychological research has borne out Dewey's concern: "Simply increasing the pressure on students to try harder in the face of failure is to invite disaster" (Covington, 1992, p. 78).
33. Marianne Moody Jennings, quoted in Bryant, 1998.
34. Marshall, 1994, p. 43. Emphasis added.
35. Flink et al., 1992, p. 208. In fact, rewards are more likely to undermine interest, but they can increase the probability that someone will do the work, like it or not, at least temporarily.
36. Some high school and college instructors deliberately make their courses very difficult, particularly at the beginning of the year. They may do this because, by some macho calculus, they think a tougher course is a better course. Even more disturbingly, they may be deliberately trying to force out students who can't handle the challenge or the pressure or who don't want to devote most of their time to this particular course. This is especially pervasive among science teachers, but the fundamentally antidemocratic sensibility it suggests isn't all that different from that of a teacher in the arts whose professional pride is invested in the occasional student who becomes famous. In both cases, the point is not to help most students cultivate a love of, and competence in, the field; the point is to sift through most students, even weed them out, in search of the very few who can triumph.
37. Bruner, 1977, p. 40.
38. See Danner and Lonky, 1981. For evidence that the chance to choose increases people's willingness to risk failure, see Kuhl and Blankenship, 1979. That a performance-oriented environment (and especially one that involves competition) can reduce this natural desire to challenge oneself was discussed in chapter 2; also see Nicholls, 1989, chap. 7. Danner and Lonky's study makes it clear that offering rewards, including praise, for success similarly induces children to pick tasks they can do easily (so that they'll receive the reward) instead

of tasks that provide an optimal level of challenge. Of course, if students spend most of their time in environments featuring rewards, competition, and the pressure to perform well, their logical preference for easier tasks may be misinterpreted as laziness, or as a reflection of "human nature." These conclusions may then convince a teacher or parent to reduce children's chance to choose or to increase the use of rewards—which is precisely what caused the problem in the first place.

39. Dewey, 1913, p. 58.
40. Meier, 1995a, p. 373. See also Meier, 1995b, p. 183; Meier and Kohn, 1998.
41. "Many Fail New Nevada Tests," 1998; Barnett, 1997; Walsh, 1997.
42. Personal communication with Deborah Meier, 1997. A similar point was made by Allington and McGill-Franzen, 1995, p. 50.
43. A new test for teachers in Massachusetts asks them to define the word "preposition." As a writer and former English teacher, I don't know that I could produce an abstract definition of the term, but I do know that neither role requires me to be able to do so. True to form, low scores on the test led politicians, businesspeople, and newspaper editorial writers to denounce the ignorance of teachers—but not to inquire whether the content of the test made any sense.

## 7. STARTING FROM SCRATCH

1. Noddings, 1992, pp. 12, 174. She adds that "moral purposes have, until recently, been more important than academic ones" in U.S. schools (pp. 64–65), although the traditional "moral" purposes were often quite different than those she endorses. Even today, "71 percent of Americans believe it is more important to teach values than academics," according to a survey by the Public Agenda Foundation (cited in Wagner, 1998, p. 514).
2. Sarason, 1995, p. 85.
3. Reynolds and Martin, 1996, p. 19.
4. The first quotation is from Gardner, 1991, p. 128; the second, from Resnick, 1987, p. 5.
5. Nicholls and Hazzard, 1993, p. 91.
6. Katz and Chard, 1989, p. 21. "As children grow older," Katz (1998, p. 34) added, "it is the responsibility of schools to help them make better, fuller, and deeper sense of other people's experiences and environments" rather than of just their own.
7. Daniel Resnick is paraphrased in Gursky, 1991, p. 28.
8. Durkheim, 1938, p. 6.
9. Piaget is quoted in Sherry, 1976.
10. Wilson is quoted in Lapham, 1991, p. 10.
11. Sizer, 1992, p. 143.
12. Brooks and Brooks (1993, p. 9) contrast this remark of Dewey's with one by Franklin Bobbitt (an early proponent of applying factory-style scientific management to schools): "Education is primarily for adult life, not for child life." The latter view still seems to be implicit in contemporary business prescriptions for school reform, which see schooling as an "investment" and students as future workers (see Kohn, 1997a).
13. Kilpatrick, 1918, p. 323.
14. This model was articulated most famously by one Elwood Cubberly in 1916: "Our schools are, in a sense, factories, in which the raw products (children)

are to be shaped and fashioned into products to meet the various demands of life. The specifications for manufacturing come from the demands of twentieth-century civilization, and it is the business of the school to build its pupils to the specifications laid down" (quoted in Gelberg, 1997, p. 27). On this factory model, and on the training of students to take their place as workers, also see Darling-Hammond, 1997, pp. 39–47; Bowles and Gintis, 1976. Ted Sizer (1984, p. 88) suggests that compulsory school attendance may have had another economic motive: a simple desire to protect adults' jobs.

15. Gelberg, pp. 210, 215.
16. Bronner, 1998a, p. 32.
17. Fromm, 1960, p. xvi.
18. The quotations are from Labaree 1997a, p. 38; and 1997b, pp. 258 and 32, respectively. Labaree goes on to argue that one consequence of viewing education this way is that the quality of learning itself is likely to decline. "We have credentialism to thank for the aversion to learning that, to a great extent, lies at the heart of our educational system," he observes. The point is not to get an education but to get ahead — and therefore, from the student-consumer's point of view, "to gain the highest grade with the minimum amount of learning" (1997b, p. 259). This perspective was borne out by a college instructor who offered familiar complaints about his students' ignorance of history and current events but then, rather than attributing it to low standards, insufficient homework, laziness, television, or other commonly cited causes, noted that the students "said they wouldn't need the information in their future jobs.... 'When is any of this stuff going to matter in my career?' " asked one student (Craig, 1997). This attitude may be nothing more than the logical result of all the talk by businesspeople and politicians about education's primary role as preparing students for the workplace.
19. It's also possible that the private and public goals are held by different people. Educators and policymakers may think in terms of what we need schools to do for our economic (or political) system, whereas a parent may be more concerned about what school can do (materially or otherwise) for his or her own child. If this is true, then it isn't altogether accurate to describe what's going on as a situation where "we" have to choose between this or that educational objective so much as a situation where the more accurate question is: Who gets to choose? (Of course, even if everyone in the country agreed that education should be viewed primarily as a means for maximizing the competitive advantage of one's own child, that goal in itself guarantees conflict because each child has to triumph over all the others.)
20. See pp. 41–43.
21. Tony Wagner, now at the Harvard Graduate School of Education.
22. See Daniels, 1996; Daniels, 1993, p. 7; and Zemelman et al., 1998, pp. 263–65.
23. "Teachers often described factors within the student or within the home that might be contributing to these problematic behaviors.... Rarely was the classroom environment mentioned as a possible contributor to the use of these troubling strategies" (Urdan et al., 1998, p. 115).
24. "Given particular outer conditions and approaches to education, an inner world will eventually emerge which conforms to and matches it," as one group of researchers (Ryan et al., 1992, p. 168) put it. For substantiation of how school culture significantly shapes students' motivational orientation, see Maehr and Midgley, 1996, esp. chap. 4.

25. In a recent book concerned with "teaching for understanding," for example, the emphasis is on using meaningful assessments in place of standardized tests, giving students a more active role in that process, and facilitating the construction of meaning rather than trying to transmit facts and skills. All of this is to the good. Somewhat troubling, however, is the implicit assumption that there is no such thing as too much assessment or too much attention to performance: we're told that "assessments occur frequently, from the beginning of a curriculum sequence until the end. Specific assessment activities are conducted in conjunction with every significant performance of understanding." Indeed, "one is continually comparing one's present performance with where one was earlier and where one wants to be" (Wiske, 1998, pp. 80, 77). The general sensibility of this project may be progressive and the specific form of the assessments irreproachable, but one senses a hidden similarity with a traditional, Tougher Standards approach to school reform in that both fail to distinguish between a performance orientation and a learning orientation, thereby overlooking the potential harms of the former.

26. Meier is quoted in Scherer, 1994, p. 7.

27. For evidence of the decline, see Harter, 1992; Harter and Jackson, 1992 (for a replication); Anderman and Young, 1994 (for evidence that it happens in science); and Lepper et al., 1997 (for still further confirmation).

28. For more on this topic, see Kohn, 1993a.

29. Covington, 1992, p. 17.

30. One researcher did just this at a traditional school and found that "most students would tell me the textbook chapter title, and, if I inquired further, the exercise number. It was generally very difficult to obtain any further information." At a progressive school, by contrast, "students would describe the problem they were trying to solve, what they had discovered so far, and what they were going to try next" (Boaler, 1998, p. 50).

31. Ames, 1990.

32. Similarly, "inadequate achievement is merely a symptom" of motivational problems (Covington, p. 158).

33. Beyond the implicit repudiation of other possible reasons (such as fostering a continuing motivation to learn, helping children to grow into good people, or creating a more democratic society, to name three), the single-minded pursuit of "academic performance" seems in context to refer not to intellectual sophistication but simply to higher standardized test scores ("Text of Policy Statement," 1996). Even apart from political documents like that one, it has been observed that "the study of human motivation has not played a major role in either the study of school reform, or the development of school reform programs and policies" (Anderman, 1997, p. 329). And when people do talk about motivation, it is "too often equated with quantitative changes in behavior (e.g., higher achievement, more time on task) rather than qualitative changes in the ways students view themselves in relation to the task, engage in the process of learning, and then respond to the learning activities and situation" (Ames, 1992a, p. 268).

34. This is not to deny that interest can also follow from competence: under some circumstances, "we get interested in what we get good at" (Bruner, 1966, p. 118). The relationship may well be reciprocal, with one leading to the other, which then enhances the first. But I believe the phenomenon deserving of more attention, and typically receiving much less, is how interest drives competence.

35. Farnham-Diggory, 1990, pp. 93–94.

36. Montaigne, 1958, p. 131.
37. For example, see Pintrich and De Groot, 1990.
38. Of course, this supports the last chapter's argument that we put far too much emphasis on whether the assignments given to students are hard enough and too little emphasis on whether students regard these assignments as worth doing. Among the many studies on the relevance of interest level to reading recall and comprehension: Anderson et al., 1987; Asher, 1979; Ryan et al., 1990; and Schiefele, 1996.
39. The same is true for teachers. If the curriculum "cannot change, move, perturb, inform teachers, it will have no effect on those whom they teach," remarked Jerome Bruner (1977, p. xv).
40. Newmann, 1992c, p. 2. He continues: "Until we learn more about the fundamental problem of how to engage students in schoolwork, there is no reason to expect improvements in achievement" (pp. 3–4).
41. Dewey, 1916, pp. 186, 213.
42. Alexander et al., 1994, p. 218.
43. As William Kilpatrick (1918, pp. 328–29) put it, "We contemplate no scheme of subordination of teacher or school to childish whim. . . . It is the special duty and opportunity of the teacher to guide the pupil through his present interests and achievement into the wider interests and achievement demanded by the wider social life of the older world." Likewise Bruner (1966, p. 161): "To personalize knowledge one does not simply link it to the familiar. Rather one makes the familiar an instance of a more general case and thereby produces awareness of it."
44. I've made the argument against the nomenclature of "work" in Kohn, 1997b, and in so doing have drawn from the thinking of Hermine H. Marshall (e.g., 1990/1997, 1994).

## 8. EDUCATION AT ITS BEST

1. Dewey, 1899/1990, p. 34.
2. Dewey, 1900/1990, p. 130. Similar comments are woven through virtually all of Dewey's books.
3. For example, see Kohlberg and Mayer, 1972, which explicitly distinguishes the Romantic views of Jean-Jacques Rousseau from the progressive approach of Dewey and Piaget. (It's become almost de rigueur for conservatives to invoke Rousseau's name and pin it on those who disagree with them.)
4. Constructivism is primarily a philosophical position (see note 7); its relevance to education is derived mostly from the explorations of child development by Jean Piaget, who only began to use the word "constructivism" toward the end of his life. His work was systematically applied to the classroom beginning in the 1970s by Rheta DeVries and Constance Kamii, among others. Today there are numerous books on the subject for educators, including Brooks and Brooks, 1993; Fosnot, 1996; and Marlowe and Page, 1998.
5. Whitehead, 1929/1967, pp. 30, v.
6. This contradicts the behaviorists' assumption that students must be prodded with artificial inducements, such as "positive reinforcement" for learning. When such devices do appear to be necessary, it is not a statement about children or human psychology but about what is being taught and how.
7. Constructivism calls into question not only traditional ideas of knowing and

learning but our understanding of knowledge itself—specifically, the idea that the world to be known is "out there," independent of people, waiting to be taken in. Constructivists argue that reality, including scientific phenomena, are construed and ultimately constituted by us as much as observed. Galileo may have "collected measurements of falling objects"; however, the idea of acceleration "did not emerge in a nonproblematic way from observations but was imposed upon them." Science, like history, literature, and other fields, is not the story of the world impinging on us but of "constructs that have been invented and imposed on phenomena in attempts to interpret and explain them, often as results of considerable intellectual struggles" (Driver et al., 1994, p. 6). A milder form of this argument is more epistemological than ontological: it doesn't deny the independent existence of reality but holds that "the only thing we can know is our own understanding of [that reality]—our own construction of it" (Zahorik, 1997, p. 30). Such arguments are obviously complicated and controversial, and it's impossible to do justice to them here. For a good overview of constructivism, and its implications for philosophy, psychiatry, mathematics, sociology, and other disciplines, see Watzlawick, 1984.

8. Putnam et al., 1990, p. 89. Resnick and Klopfer (1989, pp. 3–4) make the same observation; also see Battista, 1999, p. 432. The only real exceptions are orthodox behaviorists, whose numbers are dwindling.

9. Not everyone agrees with this. Writers like E.D. Hirsch, Jr. (1996, p. 134), forced to concede that traditional *descriptions* of how people learn are seriously misconceived, fall back on the claim that no *prescriptions* for schools are entailed by the new theory. Because everybody always constructs knowledge, "there is no necessary relation between the mode of instruction offered by the teacher and the amount of active meaning construction engaged in by the student." It's a clever argument, but I believe it's wrong, for the reasons indicated in the text. If knowledge is actively constructed *by* the learner rather than simply transmitted *to* the learner, then "one cannot assume that what is presented through curriculum or instruction is what students will learn. Instruction can no longer be viewed as a matter of simply laying out, however carefully, the knowledge and skill to be acquired" (Putnam et al., p. 92). A lot will therefore turn on the kind of teaching that takes place.

When asked, Lauren Resnick (personal communication, 1998) explicitly says she disagrees with Hirsch's contention that constructivism doesn't yield prescriptions for instruction, and further argues that the prescriptions it does yield "aren't his." Another group of researchers, meanwhile, acknowledge that constructivism is technically a "descriptive theory of learning" but add that this doesn't deny that there are "several principles for practice that would seem to facilitate the learning process" that constructivism describes. The four principles they list are incorporated in what follows in the text: the teacher should attend to students' prior knowledge, "emphasize opportunities for higher-order thinking and in-depth understanding," offer multiple opportunities to process information, and act as a "coach, facilitator, guide, or mentor in a 'cognitive apprenticeship'" (Newmann et al., 1996, p. 285).

10. The teacher is Anne Hendry, and her account, originally published elsewhere, was excerpted in Schifter, 1996, pp. 73–76.

11. Ibid., pp. 79, 81.

12. Edwards, 1993, p. 157. The essay in which this comment appears is a wonderful discussion of the role of the constructivist teacher.

13. Duckworth, 1987, p. 133.

14. For a description of a college-level physics course where the instructor plays a role very similar to that of the first-grade teacher, see Dykstra, 1996.
15. The term "scaffolding" was first used in this context by Jerome Bruner, and it derives from the work of the Russian psychologist Lev Vygotsky (e.g., 1978), who wrote during the first third of the twentieth century. His emphasis on the social nature of learning usefully supplements the work of Piaget. Some constructivists have challenged the metaphor of scaffolding, however: see Fosnot, 1996, p. 21; Fyfe, 1997, pp. 5–6.
16. The importance of resisting the desire for closure is a point made by Eleanor Duckworth and also by Deborah Meier. Meier has other thoughts on what defines good teachers: they are reflective about how they themselves learn (and don't learn); enjoy working collaboratively; want to share their interests with others; are committed to getting things right; and have "a sympathy toward others, an appreciation of differences, [and] an ability to imagine [their] own 'otherness' " (Meier, 1995b, p. 142). That last characteristic suggests the capacity to see oneself as one is seen by others, which is one more facet of taking the student's point of view.
17. Michael Marland is quoted in Green and Myers, 1990, p. 330.
18. That the teaching style is related to the type of knowledge involved is a point made by DeVries, 1997, p. 15; and DeVries and Zan, 1994, pp. 193–97, drawing from Piaget's distinction between conventional, physical, and logico-mathematical knowledge.
19. One additional feature of the task might also be relevant. There is some evidence that reading and thinking skills, as opposed to that which is being read and thought about, can be taught directly. Teachers might help students learn and apply very specific techniques such as silently summarizing what they've just read, anticipating what's coming next in the book, or making up relevant questions and figuring out what information they'd need to answer them. Ann Brown and her colleagues have done some interesting work with such instructional techniques and have argued that "the more complex the strategy in question, the more explicit the instruction needed" (Campione et al., 1988, p. 99; for a review of related research, see Fielding and Pearson, 1994). These methods can be "transmitted," but ideally they will then be used by students who spend most of the day constructing rather than absorbing. Moreover, the disposition to *use* the skills in question may count for at least as much as the skills themselves.
20. Duckworth, pp. 71–72.
21. Strachota, 1996, p. 52.
22. The balance between students' understandings and "experts' constructions" is discussed in Zahorik, 1997.
23. Ames, 1992b, p. 341.
24. Sizer, 1984, p. 174.
25. Carol Miller's account appears in Wilson, 1993, pp. 97–98.
26. This idea is attributed by Bruner (1966, p. 4) to someone named David Page.
27. The teacher, Peg Gerhart, is quoted in Routman, 1991, p. 131.
28. Holt, 1982, pp. 282–83.
29. Katz and Chard, 1989, p. 44.
30. Dewey (1952, p. 130) had the same concern: "In the secondary schools and colleges . . . the conditions still too largely prevailing in the school—the size of the classes, the load of work, and so on—make it difficult to carry on the educative process in any genuinely cooperative democratic way."

31. Meier, 1995b, pp. 41, 49–50.
32. Recalling a friend who "gave up teaching high school mathematics because she could not answer, to her own satisfaction, the students who asked, 'Why do we gotta do this stuff?' " John Nicholls reflects that "much of what we teach is hard to justify, and we might expose ourselves to the challenge of justifying it to our students and changing it when reason demands this. . . . If adults spent more energy provoking children to think about what knowledge is worthwhile and less energy trying to hold their noses to the grindstones assigned by test and textbook selection committees, everyone might have more energy" (Nicholls and Hazzard, 1993, pp. 183–84).
33. See Sizer, 1992, pp. 76–77. In an earlier book, Sizer quoted Whitehead (1929/1967, p. 2), who maintained that the prescription for guarding against "mental dryrot" is to observe "two educational commandments. 'Do not teach too many subjects,' and again, 'What you teach, teach thoroughly.' "
34. This is true, for example, in the world-famous Italian model of early childhood education known as the Reggio Emilia approach, where "young children are not marched or hurried sequentially from one different activity to the next, but instead encouraged to repeat key experiences, observe and reobserve, consider and reconsider, represent and rerepresent" (Edwards et al., 1993, p. 7).
35. Gardner made these comments during an address at the annual convention of the Wisconsin Education Association Council, Milwaukee, October 1997. He has written that we should "involve students as deeply as possible in the central problems of a discipline, so that they can acquire a fully rounded view of the data and the evidence. A month or even an entire term devoted to a particular topic proves effective" (1991, p. 237).
36. Zemelman et al., p. 140.
37. Gardner, 1991.
38. The example is from Gerhard Salinger, a program director at the National Science Foundation, quoted in Willis, 1995a, p. 8.
39. Bruner (1960, pp. 21–22) describes how a sixth-grade class given this assignment "rapidly produced a variety of plausible theories concerning the requirements of a city—a water transportation theory that placed Chicago at the junction of the three lakes, a mineral resources theory that placed it near the Mesabi range, a food-supply theory that put a great city on the rich soil of Iowa, and so on. The level of interest as well as the level of conceptual sophistication was far above that of [traditionally taught] classes. Most striking, however, was the attitude of children to whom, for the first time, the location of a city appeared as a problem, and one to which an answer could be discovered by taking thought."
40. Betsy Rupp Fulwiler, a teacher at the John Rogers School, borrowed this activity from an approach to teaching social studies called Storypath, developed by Margit McGuire at Seattle University. See McGuire, 1997.
41. The Brown-Barge Middle School in Pensacola.
42. Katz, 1998, p. 35; also see Katz and Chard, p. 4. The *reductio ad absurdum* of vertical relevance is to make decisions about school curriculum and children's lives primarily on the basis of what will maximize their chances of getting into the best college. "We must be guided by the present lives of children, not by the shadow of the college admissions officer lurking in the corner," says Susan Ohanian (1996b, p. 279).
43. The answer can be put in question form, but the learning is still in jeopardy. The comment in the text was offered by John Holt (p. 199), who continued:

"The only answer that really sticks in a child's mind is the answer to a question that he asked or might ask of himself."

44. John Furey, at the Rand School in Montclair, N.J.
45. The Francis Parker School.
46. Anne Davis at the Drew Model School in Arlington, Va.
47. For discussions of the criteria for good questions, see Perkins, 1992, pp. 92–95; Perrone, 1994; and especially Traver, 1998.
48. The Founding Fathers question, posed by the historian Bernard Bailyn, is cited in Gardner, 1991, p. 238; the hand question comes from Bruner, 1966, p. 98.
49. Kilpatrick, 1918, pp. 320–21.
50. Wolk, 1994, pp. 43–44. At the time, he was teaching at the Baker Demonstration School in Evanston, Ill. For a more comprehensive account of project-based learning, see chapter 6 in his subsequent book: Wolk, 1998. (Among other things, he describes how he, the teacher, chooses and carries out a project and then makes a presentation just as the students do [pp. 122–23].) In a discussion of project-based learning from the perspective of researchers concerned about student motivation, Blumenfeld et al. (1991) warn that even willing and competent students may not pursue the project "in a manner that promotes understanding" if the teacher "emphasize[s] grades and comparative performance, discourage[s] risk-taking, use[s] evaluation criteria that stress right answers, enforce[s] accountability for work by imposing externally controlling events such as rewards and punishments, or assign[s] primarily low-level tasks" (p. 380).
51. The Autodesk Foundation is located at 111 McInnis Parkway, San Rafael, CA 94903, and at www.autodesk.com/foundation.
52. Katz, 1988, p. 16.
53. See Katz and Chard, 1989.
54. This example of problem-based learning appears in Checkley, 1997b, p. 4. For a more comprehensive treatment of the idea that contains many more examples, see Delisle, 1997.
55. There are various models of cooperative learning, which is to say, various ways of structuring a classroom so that students can meet in pairs or small groups to learn together. The version most consistent with constructivism is Group Investigation, developed by a group of Israeli educators: Shlomo Sharan, Yael Sharan, and Rachel Hertz-Lazarowitz. Here, students break a subject into specific questions, sort themselves into groups to explore those questions, plan and conduct an investigation, and figure out how to share what they have learned with the rest of the class. (See Sharan and Sharan, 1992.)
56. Making sure that there is an audience (beyond the teacher) for students' projects is a core principle of the kind of teaching supported by the Foxfire Network, which grew out of Eliot Wigginton's work in rural Georgia. (See, for example, Smith, 1994 — or contact the Foxfire Fund, P.O. Box 541, Mountain City, GA 30562.)
57. Kilpatrick, pp, 328, 327.
58. I scarcely need to mention the inadequacy of contrived and superficial connections between separated disciplines, such as inserting Chinese names into otherwise unrelated math word problems when students are being taught about China during social studies.
59. "The reason school needs to integrate curriculum is because *it falsely separated it from the start*. But with projects, we start *with the whole*. Therefore, there's nothing to integrate. When doing projects, the integration of multiple

disciplines occurs naturally, just like it does in real life. There are no 'subjects' in life" (Wolk, 1998, p. 102).

60. Noddings, 1992, p. 172. See especially the work of James Beane (e.g., 1997) on the topic of "curriculum integration."

61. The Westminster West Community School in Westminster, Vt. The account that follows is adapted from Watts, 1994, p. 146.

62. This approach to curriculum design is described in Beane, 1997, esp. pp. 50–62; the quotation appears on p. 18. It has been used at the Marquette Middle School in Madison, Wisc., among other places.

63. See pp. 232–33, 251*n*44.

64. For example, see Silberman, 1970; Goodlad, 1984; McNeil, 1986; and the data cited in chapter 1 concerning the continued pervasiveness of traditional schooling. As students grow older and feel even more acutely the need to participate in making decisions, they have less opportunity to do so. Whatever openness may have existed in the early grades gives way to an increasingly controlled environment. By the time they get to college, students find themselves in a state of enforced passivity in the classroom; they're handed a preset syllabus and spend class time listening to lectures. A report released in 1998 by the Carnegie Foundation for the Advancement of Teaching, entitled "Reinventing Undergraduate Education," recommended, among other things, that "the freshman program should be carefully constructed as an integrated, interdisciplinary, inquiry-based experience." Shirley Strum, chair of the commission that produced the report, remarked, "What we need to do is to create a culture of inquirers, rather than a culture of receivers" (quoted in Arenson, 1998; the report itself is available on the Web at www.sunysb.edu/boyerreport).

65. *The Taming of the Shrew,* Act I, Scene 1.

66. The last of these—inviting students to think about why they are learning—was emphasized by Dewey (1938, p. 67). He talked about "the importance of the participation of the learner in the formation of the purposes which direct his activities in the learning process."

67. I have discussed some specific ways of involving students in curricular decisions, as well as some limits on and barriers to this process, in Kohn, 1993b.

68. Joette Weber is quoted in Wood, 1992, p. 5.

69. Matias Jasin at the Hockaday School in Dallas.

70. A version of this technique, called K-W-L, was first described in Ogle, 1986. It's useful to give students time to reflect on each of these questions, perhaps inviting them to take an evening to consider what they'd like to know about a given topic or having them discuss some possibilities with a peer or read a little bit about the topic first. After all, we want their questions to be genuine rather than perfunctory.

71. Lessons are far more effective when they are introduced properly, when the reason for learning them is clear, and when students can participate in making decisions about process and content. Subsequent reflection about what questions were answered, what questions remain, what new questions were generated—as well as how the next unit can be even better—is also critical for learning. "We don't learn from our mistakes; we learn from thinking about our mistakes," said Ralph Tyler—a comment Catherine Lewis (1995, p. 212) quotes in the context of describing the depth of reflection in Japanese classrooms. Alas, these critical steps that precede and follow each unit are most likely to be sacrificed when there is pressure to cover a large quantity of material.

72. The last, most sophisticated question appears in Wiske, 1994, p. 20.
73. Terry Anderson's second grade in Robinson Elementary School in Kirkwood, Mo.
74. For example, see the work by Roy Pea and others on the idea of "distributed intelligence."
75. Resnick and Klopfer, 1989, p. 8.
76. For example, see Yackel et al., 1991.
77. This is somewhat less true with young children and, in any case, is unlikely to happen at the beginning of the year. It takes talent and skill and time for a teacher to empower students in this way.
78. I've summarized some of the theory and research on cooperative learning, providing a number of references to relevant sources, in Kohn, 1992a, chap. 10. Also see Cohen, 1994, for a more scholarly treatment of small group learning. Any survey of the literature must include the work of David and Roger Johnson (e.g., 1994), brothers who teach at the University of Minnesota and cooperate in the study of cooperation. I also recommend Sharan and Sharan, 1992.
79. The research of Noreen Webb (e.g., 1985) has been especially important in demonstrating the cognitive benefits of explaining ideas to others. For evidence that high-ability or high-achieving students tend to benefit from cooperative learning—thus refuting the canard that they gain nothing while teaching their slower peers—see Kohn, 1992a, pp. 51–52; and, more recently, Carter and Jones, 1994.
80. This point has been demonstrated empirically: see Sharan, 1990b, pp. 290–91.
81. This teacher is quoted in Sapon-Shevin and Schniedewind, 1992, p. 15. Elsewhere, Sapon-Shevin has referred to this as the Hamburger Helper model of cooperative learning.
82. This account of research by Paul Vedder appears in Cohen, 1994, p. 6.
83. See Kohn, 1991; 1992a, pp. 225–26; 1993a, pp. 340–41*n*44.
84. A number of researchers have found that teachers who do exemplary work in helping students engage deeply with what they are learning are invariably part of collegial communities of educators (see, for example, McLaughlin, 1993; and Newmann, 1992a). Conversely, any number of valuable educational reforms have failed to take root because of a sense of isolation on the part of teachers (see Fullan, 1982).
85. I've dealt with the importance of caring classroom communities in Kohn, 1996a, chap. 7, but the best source of theory and research on the topic, as well as practical resources for creating and sustaining a sense of community, is the Developmental Studies Center in Oakland, Calif. Among the organization's studies: Battistich et al., 1995 and 1997, which found that the extent to which a school is experienced by students as a caring community is significantly associated with their liking for school and their motivation to learn. The positive effects of community are especially pronounced in schools in low-income areas. Among the group's books and videos: *At Home in Our Schools: A Guide to Schoolwide Activities that Build Community; Ways We Want Our Class to Be: Class Meetings that Build Commitment to Kindness and Learning;* and *Among Friends: Classrooms Where Caring and Learning Prevail.* A complete catalogue of materials is available by writing to the DSC, 2000 Embarcadero, Suite 301, Oakland, CA 94606, or calling 800-666-7270.
86. Reviews of recent studies, the most conclusive of which is the so-called STAR project in Tennessee, can be found in Viadero, 1995; Bracey, 1995; Achilles et al., 1997/1998; and, for a description of an update showing that the benefits of

small classes continue right through high school graduation, Viadero, 1999. The size of the effect is naturally affected by the difference in the sizes of the classes being compared (40 vs. 15 has more of an impact, as you might predict, than 35 vs. 25), and it also appears that class size makes more of a difference in the younger grades. Two significant caveats to the basic finding: first, you wouldn't expect to see much benefit if teachers were basically hired off the street in a rush to lower the teacher-student ratio; and second, the style of teaching must change to take advantage of the smaller size. If a teacher continues to rely on the transmission model of instruction (and to minimize opportunities for student collaboration), even a tiny class might not produce any advantage. Conversely, some Asian schools manage to promote cooperation and active learning even in very large classes. Smaller classes may be helpful but not absolutely necessary to do much of what is described in this book.

87. See Meier, 1995b and 1996a; Sergiovanni, 1996, chap. 6; and Holt, p. 87. The best, and to my mind, most persuasive case for smaller schools is Meier's book *The Power of Their Ideas* (1995b), which reflects her firsthand experience in founding and leading such schools.

88. The quotation is from Raywid, 1997/1998, p. 35, who reviews some of that evidence. Also see Berliner and Biddle, 1995, pp. 295–98. One study, by the American Legislative Exchange Council, found that rural schools are unusually successful on conventional academic measures not because of what is delicately referred to as "racial homogeneity" but rather because rural schools are more likely to be small. Schools with fewer than three hundred students fared the best of all (Johnson, 1994).

88. On looping, see Burke, 1996; Jacobson, 1997; and Rasmussen, 1998.

90. On multiage education, see, for example, Katz et al., 1990; Pavan, 1992; Viadero, 1996; and McClellan and Kinsey, 1997. The last of these describes a study finding that children whose classmates were of different ages tended to be more helpful and less aggressive than children in conventional, same-age classrooms.

## 9. GETTING THE THREE R'S RIGHT

1. The movement is not without persuasive defenders, some of whom are quoted in this chapter, but one can't help noticing that claims about how research supports direct phonics instruction are frequently left unanswered. To be more precise, some teachers have responded by saying, in effect, "Well, I know what works in my classroom" or "I don't trust research anyway." Some theorists, meanwhile, have responded by asserting that Whole Language isn't a technique that can be tested but a worldview — and then launching into a discourse about patriarchal hegemony and liberatory praxis. Some of the leading figures in Whole Language, when questioned about research findings, reply that right-wing activists are behind all opposition to the approach, and let it go at that. Now, I believe there is some validity to each of these responses, but I also view with consternation the failure to give direct and potent answers to reasonable challenges about the empirical base of Whole Language. The impression is sometimes given that there isn't any research to support the practices associated with Whole Language, and this, as we'll see, couldn't be further from the truth.

2. The argument that children's reading scores are miserable because schools

have stopped teaching phonics is rather difficult to defend from the outset because, in fact, children's reading scores *aren't* miserable. See p. 17 for some of
the evidence. Also see McQuillan, 1998, chap. 1.

3. Academics can be found taking all possible positions on the question of how
children should learn to read. (That conservatives are quick to cite any study
that seems to support their cause is ironic, given their penchant for dismissing
researchers in education and their work, referring to them derisively as "edu-
cationists" or part of what E. D. Hirsch, Jr., calls Thoughtworld.) More to the
point, teachers who have adopted a Whole Language approach have done so
not because it was rammed down their throats by crusading educational theorists but because the idea seemed appealing and the results have been persuasive. Indeed, Whole Language is notable for being a "bottom-up," grassroots
reform, driven by classroom teachers.

4. Goodman is quoted in Steinberg, 1997. It may be possible to find a teacher
who doesn't agree with this, who provides inadequate instruction, or who, in
any number of other ways, implements a good theory badly. But it would be a
mistake to attribute any of these things to Whole Language itself.

5. If your child's school is using a packaged program like Success for All—for a
description, see p. 300*n*53—you should be outraged. Programs like this are
typically reserved for low-income, mostly African-American schools, a fact
that should outrage all of us.

6. Goodman, 1986, p. 361.

7. Even traditional phonics teachers may go home and "create much richer literary environments for their own children" than they do with ours (Gallimore
and Goldenberg, 1992, p. 204).

8. Sulzby et al., 1993, p. 186. This is true regardless of race or income, the authors point out.

9. Whole Language is sometimes confused with the "whole-word" (or "look-
say") approach to reading instruction, which lies behind those deadly "See
Dick run. Run, Dick, run" primers lurking in our repressed early memories.
From a Whole Language perspective, the difference between phonics and
whole-word techniques is insignificant compared to the difference between either of these and an approach based on meaning. One teacher, thinking about
various skills-based models, was reminded of Calvin Trillin's comment about
fruitcakes: "The worst one isn't that much different from the best one" (Ohanian, 1994, p. 10).

10. Dorothy Strickland (1998) calls this approach "whole-part-whole."

11. From a journal entry by Rita Roth, quoted in Wirth, 1983, p. 142.

12. The approach to reading is also reflected in the children's own comments.
When first-graders in a skills-based classroom were asked by a researcher
what they could do, they said they could read "words, sentences, and the
basal reader." When children in a Whole Language classroom were asked the
same question, they replied that they could read books (Manning et al., 1989,
p. 10).

13. Some have speculated that this aspect of Whole Language may also help explain the virulent opposition by ultraconservatives.

14. Routman, 1991, p. 26. Thus, it's possible for a teacher to use trade books instead of basal readers but to see the stories as separate from, and coming after,
the skills work. "It is not unusual to see classrooms with no basals but where
books of literature are read whole class, round-robin style. Seatwork consists
of packets of vocabulary words to look up and lots of questions to answer in

written form for each chapter. Even though literature is being used, children have few actual choices during reading time" (p. 25). Conversely, even where teachers do end up using basal readers—perhaps because they're required to do so—they can "skip the worksheets and meaningless activities and involve students in authentic responses to literature, including literature discussion groups and author study in connection with basal selections and/or supplemental trade books" (Routman, 1996, p. 126).

15. Weaver et al., 1996, pp. 107, 31.
16. Harste is quoted in Willis, 1995b, p. 2.
17. Thanks to Smokey Daniels for pointing out the fifth variant.
18. Plenty of similar examples, along with the remark about Flesch (attributed to Beverly Regelman), can be found in Weaver et al. At one point, these authors cite a study showing that even using three hundred such rules, fewer than half of a list of 17,000 words would have been spelled correctly (p. 105).
19. The first-grader is quoted in Johnson, 1992.
20. Smith, 1992, p. 439.
21. Routman, 1996, pp. 77–78.
22. Rothstein, 1998, p. 92.
23. Campione et al., 1988, p. 98. An analogously skewed and sad impression is created by a skills-based focus in teaching math, they add. Of course, we could dismiss this concern by saying that children will be taught later on that reading is about meaning. But an initial skills emphasis has taught children to define reading "as a process of linking sounds to symbols," so when they subsequently encounter unfamiliar words, "they may revert to sounding it out. Unable to integrate the new concept of reading for meaning in a context, they fall back on their old perceptions and phonetic strategies and are no closer to understanding the word" (Noble and Smith, 1994, p. 9).
24. Likewise for writing. "When I started to love writing," one first-grader commented, "is when we stopped copying letters and I got to write everything I know about dolphins" (quoted in an unpublished manuscript by Catherine Lewis, Eric Schaps, and Marilyn Watson, 1994).
25. Patty's experience is related in Watson, 1989, pp. 138–41.
26. Manzo, 1998a.
27. Manzo, 1998c, pp. 32, 34.
28. For an example, see Matson, 1996.
29. One administrator comments, "When I interview prospective teachers, I always ask them how they teach reading. If a teacher says, 'I use what works, use whatever works,' I quickly show them to the door." After all, workbooks and "trivial questions at the end of chapters" could be said to "work"—at keeping kids "at their seats, silent, and busy. [But] not everything that works is good. Children who become hooked on phonics get a deceptive picture of what reading is. Children who read watered-down texts get used to them. Poor quality texts become the given. Children who must answer endless, inane questions after reading get a dangerous view of response to reading. If 'eclectic' means using phonics kits, flash cards, and laminated fill-in-the-blank passages, alongside a shelf of library books, I'm not interested" (Harwayne, 1994, p. 120).
30. For research on this point, see Dickinson and DiGisi, 1998, p. 24.
31. "I am reminded of a kindergartner who would not show me the sentence he had just written on the computer because not all the words were spelled correctly. I was delighted that he had phonemic awareness and could work independently at the computer. However, even though he was obviously very ad-

vanced, instead of being pleased with his accomplishment, he was anxious about his lack of perfection and felt inadequate. He felt far less satisfaction with his efforts than another child who busily and thoughtfully wrote sentence after sentence in his journal using a less advanced level of invented spelling. All other characteristics of these two 5-year-olds being equal, who is more likely to develop the disposition to be a writer?" (Wakefield, 1997, p. 236).

32. This contrast comes from an unpublished, undated manuscript by Susan Sowers.
33. Routman, 1996, p. 8.
34. Daniels, 1993, p. 6.
35. That includes paying attention to the writer's craft even while reading textbooks or other nonfiction. The quality of writing isn't relevant only to stories and poetry.
36. Routman, 1991, p. 48.
37. Anderman et al., 1996.
38. Sweet and Guthrie, 1996, p. 661.
39. See Kohn, 1993a; McQuillan, 1997.
40. Joan Servis is quoted in Routman, 1996, p. 44.
41. Brownell, 1928, p. 197.
42. Ibid., p. 200.
43. Lampert, 1986, p. 340.
44. "A year-long intensive study of the teaching and learning that took place in a 10th-grade geometry class . . . in a highly regarded suburban school district in upstate New York" produced just such results. While "a classroom observer unfamiliar with mathematics would necessarily give the class high marks," students basically spent the year copying proofs and then doing exercises "designed to indicate mastery of relatively small chunks of subject matter." ("Over the period of a full school year, none of the students in any of the dozen classes we observed worked mathematical tasks that could seriously be called problems.") Indeed, this exemplary teacher, mindful of the standardized test the students would eventually have to take, commented at one point, "You'll have to know all your constructions cold so you don't spend a lot of time thinking about them" (Schoenfeld, 1988, pp. 145–46, 152, 159).
45. The National Research Council is quoted in Battista, 1999, p. 427.
46. Resnick, 1987, p. 14.
47. Brownell, 1932, p. 10. He added: if arithmetic somehow does become "meaningful, it becomes so in spite of drill" (p. 12).
48. Putnam et al., 1990, p. 85.
49. This real example comes from Paul Cobb by way of Gardner, 1991, p. 164.
50. This example, from Max Wertheimer's *Productive Thinking*, is cited in Schoenfeld, p. 148.
51. Kamii, 1994, pp. 36–40.
52. Cited in Schoenfeld, p. 150, among other places. Another example: a startling number of young children taught in traditional classrooms give the answer "36" to the question "There are 26 sheep and 10 goats on a ship. How old is the captain?" (Kamii, 1989, p. 160).
53. Dossey et al., 1988, pp. 67, 54.
54. "Because really bright students generally learn symbolic algorithms quickly, they appear to be doing fine when their performance is measured by standard mathematics tests. But a closer look reveals that they too are being dramatically affected by the mathematics miseducation of traditional curricula [ending up with learning that is] only superficial" (Battista, p. 426).

55. Kamii (e.g., 1994, pp. 43, 46) is especially persuasive on this point.
56. Putnam et al., 1990, p. 96.
57. Jackson, 1997, p. I: 1.
58. Kamii, 1985b, p. 3. For examples of fortuitous events that can provide the opportunity for children in first, second, and third grade to think about numerical concepts, see Kamii, 1985b, pp. 123–35; 1989, pp. 91–97; and 1994, pp. 92–98. Like some other constructivists, Kamii also swears by the use of certain games—such as those involving dice or play money—for teaching purposes. All the games in question, however, are competitive, suggesting both a lack of familiarity with cooperative games (where the same numerical skills are often required) and a lack of sensitivity to the social and psychological disadvantages of setting children against one another (see Kohn, 1992a).
59. Joseph Kahne at the University of Illinois, Chicago, makes this point. As a rule, he argues, parents "aren't nervous about Whole Language because they know their kids will be reading; their literacy skills aren't threatened" (personal communication, 1997). However, this may understate the extent to which Whole Language diverges from most people's school experience. One writer notes: "Sadly, many parents don't recall being given the opportunity to read 'real books' in their early elementary classrooms unless (as in my case) it was after all their 'work' was done. Thus, attacks on whole language that focus on literature grow partly from parents' discomfort that their children's school experience isn't like their own" (Brinkley, 1998, p. 59). And this from another writer: "When you take away the two school rituals that parents understand —math facts and spelling quizzes—you scare them to death" (Ohanian, 1996a, p. 9).
60. The washer lesson is described in Brooks and Brooks, 1993, pp. 73–75. The bubblegum lesson was used by Pam Hyde and appears in Zemelman et al., 1998, p. 85. The fraction problem comes from Joy Donlin and is reported in Willis and Checkley, 1996, p. 7. The idea of having students write a textbook is attributed to Bill Elasky by Wood, 1992, p. 140.
61. Kahramanidis, 1988.
62. Piaget, 1948/1973, p. 106.
63. Kamii, 1985b, p. 46.
64. Another, more practical reason for asking this same question about a correct answer is that otherwise children will just assume "How did you get that?" is teacher code for "Nope—try again."
65. Kamii, 1985b, pp. 25, 36. Her constructivist premises have led Kamii to offer only a partial endorsement of the NCTM standards. She argues that, despite their emphasis on a deeper understanding of mathematical truths, the standards still reflect an empirical view that those truths have a reality entirely independent of the knower. Further, while collaboration among students is recommended, Kamii believes the standards fail to reflect a constructivist appreciation for the necessity of understanding through resolving conflict among disparate ideas (see Kamii, 1989, pp. 59–62).
66. This point was made by Brownell, 1928, pp. 199, 208–9, and also by Jean Lave, cited in Brown et al., 1989, p. 36. Unfortunately, students in this situation aren't being appropriately challenged (by the teacher or other students) to rethink and improve their initial ideas, so they probably won't learn as effectively as they would in a nontraditional classroom.
67. Lester, 1996, pp. 146–52. For another teacher's description of how—and how well—this approach works, see Strachota, 1996, chap. 3.
68. Kamii, 1994, p. 67.

69. Not every math educator agrees that primary-grade children shouldn't be given algorithms at all, but Kamii makes a strong case for this position. Rob Madell (1985, p. 20) similarly recommends that no algorithms be taught until the end of third grade and that no conventional procedures for working with fractions be introduced until sixth grade (even though students will have studied fractions intensively for at least two years before that).
70. Hirsch, 1996, p. 83.
71. "Research has shown, however, that most children think that the 1 in 16 means one, until third or fourth grade" (Kamii, 1989, p. 15). "Even in fourth and fifth grades, only half the students interviewed demonstrated good understanding of the individual digits in two-digit numerals" (Ross, 1989, p. 50).
72. Vygotsky, 1978, p. 84.
73. Linda Joseph's account appears in Kamii, 1989, p. 156. A nearly identical piece of testimony from another teacher—"I have been teaching all this time [fifteen years] and I never knew second-graders knew so much about math"—is quoted in another discussion of what it means to become a constructivist math teacher (Wood et al., 1991, p. 601).
74. Katz, 1993, p. 31. Also see Katz and Chard, 1989, pp. 4–5.

## 10. THE WAY OUT

1. Dewey, 1916, p. 38. For an example of how school reform must itself by informed by constructivist principles, see Wagner, 1998; Noble and Smith, 1994.
2. Dewey, 1952, pp. 132–33. Progressive principles "have been converted into a fixed subject matter of ready-made rules, to be taught and memorized according to certain standardized procedures and, when occasion arises, to be applied to educational problems externally, the way mustard plasters, for example, are applied" (p. 132).
3. "In the back to basics crusade, reformers urged a set of changes in classrooms that fit relatively well with established practice, which itself was didactic, teacher-centered, and oriented to skills and facts. They presented the reform ideas in practical, easy-to-adopt formats, and blanketed American education relatively effectively. The pedagogy of the reform fit quite nicely with the pedagogy that reformers urged on teachers. [By contrast, nontraditional] curriculum reforms urged a very different sort of instruction that would have required immense changes in teaching. But while these reforms were pedagogically very ambitious, they were much less effective in reaching teachers. Reformers only weakly understood practice and the problems their ideas posed for practitioners" (Cohen and Barnes, 1993a, p. 227).
4. I've discussed some of these issues with special reference to cooperative learning in Kohn, 1992b.
5. Sizer, 1992, p. 10.
6. Perrone, 1998, p. 23
7. Dewey, 1938/1963, p. 40.
8. Jackson, p. II: 6. See also Cohen, 1990. "The major impediment to improving students' mathematics learning is adults' lack of knowledge—both of mathematics and of research on how students learn mathematics" (Battista, 1999, p. 431). Note that it is a lack of knowledge on the part of parents and policy makers, not only teachers, that helps to explain why students continue to be subjected to ineffective, traditional methods.

9. Wood, 1996, p. 90. Progressive educators and their students already know that "engaging" and "rigorous" can go hand in hand, just as they know that traditional education manages to be simultaneously less rigorous and more disagreeable. A lot of other people, however, may need to be reminded. "Someday," Harvey Daniels sighs, "progressives are going to get smart and start talking about the *rigor* of whole language, the *challenge* of critical thinking, the *demands* of collaborative learning, the *requirements* of student-directed inquiry, the *scrutiny* of authentic assessment, and the *elevated standards* of integrated curriculum." Contrary to the carefully cultivated conventional wisdom, it is the nontraditional educators "who really challenge children" (1995, p. 5; emphasis added).

10. Cohen and Barnes, 1993, p. 245.

11. Smith, 1994, p. 43.

12. There is a relationship between knowledge and openness to student participation: the more unfamiliar teachers are with a given topic, the more likely they are to keep a tight grip on what happens in the classroom, presumably because of their insecurity (see Prawat, 1989, p. 322).

13. Ginny Hanley is quoted in Willis and Checkley, p. 4.

14. Dewey, 1952, p. 133.

15. Sometimes teachers catch themselves at this, however belatedly. One high school English teacher confesses that her "authoritarian practices went unquestioned" for years. She wanted her students "to think for themselves, but only so long as their thinking didn't slow down my predetermined lesson plan or get in the way of my teacher-led activity or argue against my classroom policies" (Coe, 1997, p. 7). Other teachers pride themselves on transforming their instructional practices even when they have actually not come as far as they might like to think. David Cohen (1990), an educational researcher, has brilliantly described one such math teacher. While she had introduced cooperative learning and was teaching "math for understanding," the class was still "conducted in a highly structured and classically teacher-centered fashion." While she was teaching better than before, she still "did not see mathematics as a source of puzzles, as a terrain for argument," but as a series of "fixed truths" that she had to impart to them. (Those of us who try to help teachers change their practice know that one of the most challenging obstacles to reform is the tendency of such teachers to respond to descriptions of constructivist classrooms by saying, rather airily, "Oh, I'm already doing all of that.") For another example, see Campbell, 1996, pp. 466–67; for a case study describing a more successful change in teacher practice (also in mathematics), see Wood et al., 1991.

16. This exchange was reported in White, 1992, p. 55.

17. This idea plays an important role in the work of Jean-Paul Sartre and Erich Fromm and is the core of Dostoyevsky's classic "Grand Inquisitor" chapter in *The Brothers Karamazov*.

18. John Holt and Ted Sizer are only two of the more prominent educators who have identified this phenomenon.

19. Bruner, 1966, p. 69. On this point, also see Gardner, 1991, pp. 208–9.

20. This may help to explain the rapid demise of the California Learning Assessment System (CLAS), a major improvement over the conventional standardized tests that preceded and succeeded it (Kirst and Mazzeo, 1996). On the more general point, see Kohn, 1998a.

21. Julyan and Duckworth, 1996, p. 68.

22. Of course, one could ague that getting students to work for A's at age seven may create a habit that will last right through age seventeen—and more's the pity if that's true.

23. Mitchell, 1998. Princeton also turned down more than three quarters of applicants with perfect or near-perfect SAT scores (750–800). Presumably the same is true for other elite colleges.

24. Lilian Katz's distinction between horizontal and vertical relevance is pertinent here. See p. 145.

25. On this point, see Labaree, 1997b.

26. Kasser and Ryan, 1993, 1996. This research was described in Kohn, 1999.

27. These include the Carolina Friends School in Durham, N.C.; the Poughkeepsie Day School in Poughkeepsie, N.Y.; the School Without Walls in Rochester, N.Y.; the Waring School in Beverly, Mass.; Saint Ann's School in Brooklyn, N.Y.; and the Metropolitan Learning Center in Portland, Ore. (I would be glad to hear about other high schools that don't use grades; please write to me in care of Houghton Mifflin.) While hundreds of colleges no longer require that applicants take the SAT or ACT (p. 262n1, par. 1), the reality is that grades will probably count more for a student who doesn't submit a test score, and test scores will probably count more for a student whose high school courses weren't graded. At least we should recognize that it's not always necessary to subject students to both. Another reality is that large state universities are more resistant to unconventional applications than are small private colleges simply because of economics: it takes more time, and therefore more money, for admissions officers to read meaningful application materials than it does for them to glance at a GPA or an SAT score and plug it into a formula. But I have heard of high schools approaching the admissions directors of nearby universities and saying, in effect, "We'd like to improve our school by getting rid of grades. Here's why. Will you work with us to make sure our seniors aren't penalized?" This strategy, reminiscent of what was done on a wide scale in the 1930s as part of the Eight-Year Study (see pp. 231–32), may well be successful for the simple reason that not many high schools are requesting this at present and the added inconvenience for admissions offices is likely to be negligible. Of course, if more and more high schools abandon traditional grades, the universities will have no choice but to adapt. This is a change that high schools will have to initiate rather than waiting for colleges to signal their readiness.

28. A survey of college admissions officers revealed that most enjoy the convenience of having applicants ranked against one another but that relatively few actually insist on this practice. Asked what would happen if a high school stopped computing class rank, only 0.5 percent said that that school's applicants would not be considered for admission, 4.5 percent said it would be a "great handicap," and 14.4 percent said it would be a "handicap." In other words, it appears that the absence of class ranks would not interfere at all with students' prospects for admission to four out of five colleges. High schools are slow to change, however. In the same study, about 7.5 percent of high schools reported that they didn't rank students—although the validity of the survey is unclear, given that fewer than one third of the high schools receiving questionnaires responded (Levy and Riordan, 1994). In any case, the number of high schools that do not calculate class rank "will increase, observers suggest, as schools replace traditional student-assessment tools with other types of evaluations" (Diegmueller, 1994, p. 13).

29. National Forum on Assessment, 1995, p. 6.
30. Similarly, getting rid of grades may be necessary but not sufficient for helping students focus on the learning itself. In another of those early monographs on the subject, a California principal wrote that we have to take a look at "the classroom practices from which our grades have inherited most of their weaknesses. . . . Abolishing grades would not in and of itself alter the attitude of the youth who had grown up under the belief that he is working for the teacher, whose inner pressure for accomplishment goes up and down in response to the teacher's judgment, and who regards assignments as distasteful tasks to be courageously faced until the teacher's demand for the tangible fruits of effort has been appeased" (Linder, 1940, pp. 25–26).
31. Bruner, 1961, p. 28. This is not bad advice for people in offices either. Taken seriously, it would mean an end to performance appraisals, which, in their usual form, do not really provide feedback but "feeddown" — that is, an evaluation (from one's superior) in place of descriptive data. For more on this, see Scholtes, 1998, chap. 9.
32. Interviews with fifty teachers identified as being exceptional at their craft revealed a consistent lack of emphasis on testing, if not a deliberate decision to minimize the practice. See Jackson, 1968/1990. Also, fewer classroom tests were associated with higher scores on the NAEP fourth-grade reading exam (see p. 223).
33. Of course, something may be wrong not with the teacher but with features of the school structure, such as classes that are too large or periods that are too short. This isn't an argument for continuing to grade under those circumstances but for calling those circumstances into question.
34. Wolk, 1998, pp. 111–12.
35. Involving students in assessing their own learning isn't limited to portfolios. Before beginning any unit, teachers can invite the class to think about the criteria by which their assignments (essays, poems, paintings, math solutions, translations, or whatever) ought to be judged — perhaps on the basis of reviewing other examples of the genre and figuring out together what makes the good ones good and the bad ones bad. Later, students can apply the criteria that they helped to formulate to their own efforts, thereby playing an active role at both stages in the process.
36. The word "rubric" originally described the letters "used in Christian prayer books to give directions on the proper conduct of the religious service" (Mitchell, 1992, p. 34).
37. On this topic, see Le Countryman and Schroeder, 1996, and Stiggins, 1994, pp. 418–21. (The latter book is a useful reference on the whole question of assessment.) There's no reason students can't also be involved in *written* evaluations of their own learning rather than leaving that up to the teacher (see Routman, 1996, pp. 159-63).
38. For example, see Katz, 1997.
39. This and other interim suggestions for reducing the salience of grades are discussed in Kohn, 1993a, pp. 208–9.
40. See Kohn, 1998a.
41. Farr and Greene, 1993, p. 21.
42. "Development in young children occurs rapidly; early childhood educators recognize the existence of general stages and sequences of development but also recognize that enormous individual variation occurs in patterns and timing of growth and development that is quite normal and not indicative of

pathology." Therefore, "the younger the child, the more difficult it is to obtain reliable and valid results from standardized tests"—although "the ritual use even of 'good tests' (those that are judged to be valid and reliable measures) is to be discouraged in the absence of documented research showing that children benefit from their use" (National Association for the Education of Young Children, 1987, pp. 3, 2).

43. Neill and Medina, 1989, p. 695.

44. High school graduation is usually contingent on passing a certain number of courses, which seems unsatisfactory to a number of critics. Traditionalists, however, merely demand that students should have to pass an exit exam to receive a diploma—an exam that often reflects the worst of standardized tests and is also much more difficult. Marching as usual under the banner of "higher standards," these reformers would make graduation harder rather than making school better (or an assessment of students' learning more meaningful). Ted Sizer (1992) and others affiliated with the Coalition of Essential Schools have instead proposed a series of "exhibitions": elaborate projects that provide evidence of sustained serious thought and proficiency across the disciplines.

45. For example, see Hirsch, 1996, chap. 6.

46. For a summary of relative cost estimates of performance assessments and multiple-choice tests, see Rothman, 1995, p. 168.

47. Here's another interesting example of how a concern with statistical reliability on the part of test manufacturers can eclipse issues of validity: suggestions that the College Board's SAT II biology test ought to be reconfigured to include fewer and better questions have been dismissed by those who design the test on the grounds that such a dramatic change would make it impossible to "say that a 600 score meant the same thing year after year. But why care if a 600 score always means the same thing if it does not measure anything important, [the National Academy of Sciences president Bruce] Alberts asked" ("Science Leader Criticizes Tests," 1998).

48. These quotations are from Resnick and Resnick, 1990, p. 74, and Resnick and Nolan, 1995, p. 115, respectively.

49. For details, see Rothman, pp. 77–89, 158–60, and Darling-Hammond, 1997, pp. 243–44. Kentucky has also developed some innovative performance assessments but unfortunately implemented them within a larger program that uses carrots and sticks to impose and enforce changes (Jones and Whitford, 1997).

50. This is taken from the first page of an unpublished document by Mary A. Barr, "The Learning Record Assessment System." It, along with other documents, is available from the Center for Language in Learning, 10610 Quail Canyon Road, El Cajon, CA 92021—or on the Web at www.learningrecord. org/lrorg. Also see Barr et al., 1999. The Learning Record was adapted from the Primary Language Record, developed in England.

51. For example, see Meisels, 1993. More information on Work Sampling is available from Rebus, Inc., P.O. Box 4479, Ann Arbor, MI 48106, or by calling 1-800-435-3085.

52. Mitchell, 1992, p. 115.

53. In fact, Deborah Meier argues that impressively high interrater reliability in evaluations of students' writing or other projects implies that the scorers are obediently setting aside their own judgment in order to apply a rigid set of criteria.

54. For a useful discussion of these and other issues pertaining to alternative assessments, see Neill et al., 1995.
55. Indeed, someone who is attentive to systemic causes of problems may agree with Alfred North Whitehead (1929/1967, p. 13) that "primarily it is the schools and not the scholars which should be inspected." This, it is important to add, is not an argument for the *kind* of "inspection" entailed by standardized tests.
56. Howe, 1994, p. 31.
57. See Dorn, 1998.
58. Many of the ideas in the preceding half-dozen paragraphs have grown out of conversations I've had with Deborah Meier. I owe a great deal to her incisive analysis of these issues.
59. One example: the Central Park East Secondary School in New York City brings in external reviewers — experts who don't teach at the school — to look at, talk about, and rate a sample of what students have done through the year "in order to provide all concerned parties with a 'second' look at our criteria and standards. This is for the purpose solely of assessing the school's standards, not the individual's right to a diploma" (Central Park East, 1993, p. 24).
60. Jones, 1998. Two other authors point out that "measurement-driven instruction" is "merely an extension of behaviorist psychology," so when policy makers continue to depend on "coercion to create uniformity" — except now as a way to get higher-quality instruction — they just create a fatal inconsistency between what is done to teachers and what teachers are expected to do with students (Noble and Smith).
61. On this point, see Airasian, 1988.
62. Maehr and Midgley, 1996, p. 7. This point is frequently overlooked by educators who promote more "authentic" assessments without attending to the psychological significance of evaluation itself.
63. Rothman, p. 153. Also see Farr and Greene, p. 26.
64. One concrete illustration: "Using portfolios makes little sense if instruction is dominated by worksheets so that every portfolio looks the same" (Neill et al., p. 4).
65. Paris et al., 1991, p. 17.
66. Along the same lines, one first-grade teacher in Kentucky worked with her students to develop "their own reading program, which moves them faster and more effectively through (and beyond) the district's reading program objectives than the basal. Even so, she is required by her school's administration to put her class through a basal reader program on a prescribed weekly schedule. The solution, quickly evolved by the class: they do each week's work in the basal on Monday, with little effort, then work on the meaningful curriculum — theirs — Tuesday through Friday" (Smith, 1994, p. 29).
67. "You don't need to study only the test and distort your entire curriculum eight hours a day, 180 days a year, for 12 years," says Harvey Daniels (1993, p. 5), a leading teacher educator at National-Louis University. "We've got very interesting studies where teachers do 35 or 38 weeks of what they think is best for kids, and then they'll give them three weeks of test cramming just before the test. And the kids do just as well as kids who have 40 weeks of test-driven curriculum." This is corroborated by a study that found a one-hour intensive reading readiness tutorial for young children produced test results equivalent to two years of skills-oriented direct instruction (Karnes et al., 1983). Of course, this will vary depending on the nature of the test.

68. Two excellent guides for teachers along these lines: Taylor and Walton 1998; and Calkins et al. 1998. Several articles in the December 1996/January 1997 issue of *Educational Leadership* are also relevant. One teacher suggests using tests as part of the curriculum so students can critically analyze their content (Christensen, 1999).
69. On this general point, see Appendix A. On the relevance of the discipline being tested, see p. 302*n*99.
70. Shepard and Bliem, 1993. The quotation appears on p. 29.
71. Stolberg, 1989. See also Rossi, 1999.
72. See "Testing Boycott in Denver," 1992.
73. The first two quotations are from Van Moorlehem and Audi, 1998; the third is from Van Moorlehem, 1998. National attention was briefly focused on the fact that two thirds of the 500 juniors in a very wealthy suburb of Detroit had requested waivers from the test the previous year (see Johnston, 1997). Overall, "those opting out of the test tend to be average or above-average students," some of whom wore T-shirts that urged their peers to JUST SAY NO to the test (Van Moorlehem).
74. For example, see the following Web site: www.pipeline.com/~rgibson/meap. html.
75. Contact Mary O'Brien at sobrien@columbus.rr.com or 614-487-0477.
76. Vigue and Daley, 1999.
77. Lewis, 1995, p. 16.
78. Coles, 1994. Quotations are taken from pp. 16, 23.
79. FairTest: 342 Broadway, Cambridge, MA 02138; 617-864-4810; www. fairtest.org.

## APPENDIX A: THE HARD EVIDENCE

1. This is especially ironic in light of Hirsch's pointed assertions that the position he supports has "strong scientific foundations" in the sort of "consensus mainstream science" that is "published in the most rigorous scientific journals," while the other side "invokes research very selectively" (Hirsch, 1998, pp. 38, 39; 1996, p. 127).
2. Hirsch, 1996, pp. 181, 182. And yet again: "Effort and learning have declined wherever grades and tests have been abolished. Human nature has proved to be robust. Evolutionary psychologists have argued that all humans retain a residue of competitiveness" (p. 245). Note the conflation of grades, tests, and competition, which are, of course, three distinct phenomena: grades aren't competitive if everyone in the class can theoretically receive an A; not all tests are graded and not all grades are based on tests. (Elsewhere he seems to equate "extrinsic motivation" with "discipline, toil, or sweat," implying that those who criticize the first are enemies of the second [p. 214].)
3. Gold et al., 1971. The quotation appears on p. 20.
4. In a previous book, Hirsch referred to a "recent consensus among reading researchers that adequate literacy depends upon the specific information called 'cultural literacy.'" But this claim is "simply not accurate," rejoined Stephen Tchudi (1987/1988, p. 72), director of the Center for Literacy and Learning at Michigan State University. "To the extent that a consensus exists among reading researchers, it does *not* include a mandate to 'impart traditional literature culture to children at the earliest possible age.' A considerable amount of read-

ing research *does* emphasize the informational background of the reader, but 'background' includes not only factual information, but also the experiences, attitudes, and values the reader brings to a text."

Similar examples from his more recent book (1996):

1. *Hirsch's claim: "Cultural Literacy's* general argument is confirmed" (p. 12). *The reality:* The first study cited to support the idea that children should memorize a compendium of facts in order to become "culturally literate" discovered nothing more than a correlation between fifth-graders' scores on a cultural literacy test and their scores on a standardized test and an IQ test — hardly surprising in light of the kind of knowledge with which one must be familiar to do well on the latter tests. Moreover, the researchers list several possible "plausible interpretations" of the correlation, concluding that "because the study was not able to establish definite causality between cultural literacy and academic achievement, it should not be considered unequivocal or strongly prescriptive" (Kosmoski et al., 1990, p. 271; Hirsch omits this key disclaimer). The next study Hirsch cites (Pentony, 1992) reported nothing more than a moderate correlation between verbal SAT scores and freshman English grades, which hardly qualifies as substantiation for Hirsch's theories.

2. *Hirsch's claim:* In the course of arguing against the kind of curriculum intended to promote critical thinking skills, he writes, "People who have just finished a one-semester course in logic are only marginally more logical than people who have never taken logic. Other experiments show that training in abstract 'higher-order skills' does not much improve thinking" (p. 137). *The reality:* The first sentence assumes that efforts to promote critical thinking skills are equivalent to a course in logic, a pretty good example of illogic in itself. As for the second sentence, even apart from Hirsch's omission of a large body of research supporting the usefulness of training in critical thinking skills, the single source cited in his footnote (Klaczynski and Laipple, 1993) doesn't support anything close to a generalized recommendation to avoid such training. Rather, it examines the narrow, highly specialized hypothesis that "when incorrect strategies for solving domain-specific problems were contradicted, a domain-general rule would be induced and would subsequently facilitate transfer to problems outside of the original domain" (p. 653).

3. *Hirsch's claim:* "In a highly significant but rarely discussed study, [W. James] Popham showed that because of the failure to instruct prospective teachers about the best research into effective pedagogical methods (the findings of which happen to contravene the naturalistic approaches that continue to be advocated), uncertified persons, plopped into the classroom without having taken education courses, got results that were as good as those obtained by certified and experienced teachers" (p. 230). *The reality:* (a) The key to Hirsch's argument is not that uncertified teachers were successful but the statement that certified teachers did no better because they weren't properly instructed. Contrary to the impression he gives, however, this attribution was not a finding of the study at all but merely a speculation offered by Popham (1971) in his discussion section. (b) The claim that "the best research into effective pedagogical methods" challenges "naturalistic approaches" (which Hirsch equates with virtually any educational model that isn't his) wasn't even addressed by Popham's paper. (c) Finally, the "results" were based on highly specific indicators of performance, suggesting the possibility that these measures and the kind of instruction they favored may have accounted for the relative success of untrained teachers.

Sometimes Hirsch makes assertions that are debatable, to put it charitably, claiming that research backs him up but offering none. To wit: "an appropriate emphasis on transmitting knowledge results in students who actually possess . . . skills such as critical thinking and learning to learn" (p. 219); "the research also shows that external incentives combined with intrinsic ones work better than intrinsic incentives alone" (p. 230); "research into teaching methods has consistently shown that discovery learning is the least effective method of instruction" (p. 250); "hands-on, project-style teaching has been shown to be highly ineffective" (p. 269); and "anti-rote-learning reforms being advocated are already firmly in place" since they are "essentially the project-oriented, child-centered methods that have long dominated American educational thought and have prevailed for decades in our schools" (pp. 49, 132). (The kindest interpretation of this last unsubstantiated and demonstrably false assertion is that Hirsch "mistakes the talk of some professors of education, often misconstrued and taken out of context, as the reality of the American public school" [Feinberg, 1997, p. 29]). Not every assertion in a book needs to be backed by a study, of course, but it seems slightly suspicious when specific empirical claims, particularly those dressed up with phrases such as "research . . . has consistently shown," are bereft of citations. This is all the more true when a good deal of evidence contradicts such claims.

On other occasions, Hirsch does cite research, and does so accurately, but he presents the findings in such a way as to imply falsely that his recommendations for traditional education (or his criticisms of progressive education) are bolstered by these findings:

• "Lack of stimulation has depressed [some children's] IQs" (p. 20). This reasonable proposition is used to imply that "stimulation"—or, in a later passage, making sure children are "ready to learn" (p. 228)—signifies the practice of having children focus on lists of facts that every *n*th grader should know.

• "There is a great deal of evidence, indeed a consensus in cognitive psychology, that people who are able to think independently about unfamiliar problems and who are broad-gauged problems solvers, critical thinkers, and lifelong learners are, without exception, well-informed people" (p. 144). No sources are offered here, but let's stipulate that it's true. Because people who think effectively are also well informed, Hirsch invites us to infer that the former is *caused by* the latter—which is to say, that making children acquire more information will turn them into problem solvers and lifelong learners. Not only is there no reason to accept this, but precisely the reverse may be true: this kind of teaching may undermine an interest in learning and reduce the time available for learning how to solve problems.

• "Every decent job available in a modern economy is dependent upon communication and learning—two activities that take place primarily through the medium of words" (p. 110). Few would dispute this, but many would dispute his larger point, that becoming familiar with "the medium of words" entails his specific model for teaching language arts.

• "Psychological research has shown that the ability to learn something new depends on an ability to accommodate the new thing to the already known" (p. 23). There is no citation here, so we can only guess that he is talking about the work of Piaget and other constructivists. Unfortunately, the "already known" refers to the *theories* that people have developed about the world; this research in no way supports (and, in some respects, actually challenges) the idea that acquiring more *facts* is a condition for later learning.

Later, Hirsch faults this same tradition of "developmentalism" for believing that "there is a natural age (usually after age eight) for introducing bookish content" (p. 84). The actual caution concerns the introduction of concepts beyond children's cognitive capacity. The invocation of "bookish content" suggests an attempt to saddle the developmental tradition with a naïve Romanticism that makes an easier target.

Apart from his questionable use of research, Hirsch frequently tries to get away with a kind of intellectual sleight of hand, arguing for one thing and then proceeding as if he's demonstrated something else entirely. One minute he is talking about people who want to educate the "whole child"; the next, he is criticizing the "faith in the unerring goodness of whatever comes forth from the child" (p. 78) as if these two were equivalent. He collapses interdisciplinary learning into the Summerhill model (p. 96) and equates a rejection of his cultural literacy model with "anti-intellectualism" (pp. 106, 245). After making fun of academic standards that lack specific content, he proceeds as if he's proved there's something wrong with a lack of specific content in the teaching itself (p. 32). He is keen to attack something he calls "natural pedagogy"—the straw man of Romanticism again—and then goes a step further, attributing to it the belief that "innate ability is the royal road to all learning." (Not surprisingly, no proof is offered that *anyone* actually believes this.) He, by contrast, proudly defends an emphasis on "effort," which we are encouraged to believe is tantamount to the use of "drill and practice" (p. 87).

A number of conservatives have welcomed Hirsch's book as the best case that can be made for traditional education. They may be right.

5. Worthen, 1968.
6. See the discussion of Follow Through, below.
7. Kohn, 1992a, 1993a.
8. Stebbins et al., 1977, p. 166.
9. There is strong reason to doubt whether tests billed as measuring complex "cognitive, conceptual skills" really did so. Even the primary analysts conceded that "the measures on the cognitive and affective domains are much less appropriate" than is the main skills test (Stebbins et al., p. 35). A group of experts on experimental design commissioned to review the study went even further, stating that the project "amounts essentially to a comparative study of the effects of Follow Through models on the mechanics of reading, writing, and arithmetic" (House et al., 1978, p. 145). (This raises the interesting question of whether it is even possible to measure the conceptual understanding or cognitive sophistication of young children with a standardized test.)
10. House et al., p. 158.
11. Anderson et al, 1978, p. 164.
12. The outside evaluators concluded that the original data analysts had defined an "effect" in such a way as to confound "the effectiveness of a program with its number of pupils" so that "larger programs could appear to be more effective" (House et al., p. 146). They also argued that the level of analysis—individual children rather than schools or sites—had the effect of biasing the results in favor of the Direct Instruction model (pp. 151–52). Meanwhile, the General Accounting Office's official review of the Follow Through research found that problems "in both the initial design and implementation of the experiment will limit OE's [the Office of Education's] ability to reach statistically reliable overall conclusions on the success or lack of success of the approaches for teaching young disadvantaged children. The problems cannot practicably

be overcome, and, when combined with the OE contractor's reservations about design and measurement problems, raise questions about the experiment's dependability to judge the approaches" (Office of Education, 1975, p. 25).

13. House et al., pp. 130, 156.

14. Manzo, 1998c, p. 37; Winerip, 1998, pp. 88–89.

15. Linda Darling-Hammond (1997, p. 50) gives the example of the failure of the "heavily prescriptive, rigidly enforced competency-based curriculum (CBC) [which] was introduced [into Washington, D.C., schools] in the 1980s and has continued in effect throughout the years the district's performance has plummeted."

16. The High/Scope curriculum, based on Piaget's ideas, sees "the child as a self-initiating active learner" and places "a primary emphasis on problem solving and independent thinking. . . . Teachers do not simply stand out of the way and permit free play, but rather guide children's choices toward developmentally appropriate experiences" (Schweinhart and Hohmann, 1992, pp. 16–18). "Developmentally appropriate" practice emphasizes meeting the "individual needs" of the "whole child," providing "activities that are relevant and meaningful," with plenty of opportunity for "active exploration and concrete, hands-on experiences" in order to tap "children's natural curiosity and desire to make sense of their world." Developmentally *inappropriate* classrooms, by contrast, segment the preschool or kindergarten curriculum into the traditional content areas, rely heavily on rewards and punitive consequences, give children little choice about what they're doing, ignore individual differences, and use standardized tests (Hart et al., 1997, pp. 4–5).

17. Karnes et al., 1983.

18. Schweinhart et al., 1986. The difference in book reading didn't reach conventional levels of significance ($p=.09$). Advocates of Direct Instruction conducted a longitudinal study of their own, comparing some of the original DI Follow Through students in four communities to those from matched comparison schools when they were in high school. They reported finding either better standardized test results or higher graduation rates (but not necessarily both) for DI students (Gersten and Keating, 1987). However, unlike the Ypsilanti study and the others described here, there was no attempt to compare the results for DI and distinctly different types of programs. It's unclear what model of instruction, if any, characterized the primary school experience of the comparison students. If they received a less systematic version of the same kind of basic skills training that the DI students got—which is entirely possible in light of how pervasive this kind of teaching was and is in the United States—then these results hardly lend support to the basic philosophy common to both conditions.

19. Schweinhart and Weikart, 1997.

20. Hart et al., p. 7

21. Charlesworth et al., 1993, pp. 18–22.

22. Rawl and O'Tuel, 1982.

23. Stipek et al., 1995. A little over half of these children were Latino or African-American, and 42 percent were from low-income households.

24. Marcon, 1994, pp. 11–12.

25. Daniels et al., in press.

26. Weaver and Brinkley, 1998, p. 137.

27. Much has been written on this subject by proponents of Whole Language, but one of the best articles is still a relatively early essay by Deborah Meier (1981) entitled "Why Reading Tests Don't Test Reading."

28. See Krashen, 1998.

29. When claims are made for the effectiveness of Direct Instruction and other skills-based techniques, it's worth asking not only what kind of effect has been shown (simple decoding vs. comprehension) but how the study was designed. This would seem to be a clear case where a comparison group using a different approach to reading instruction would be necessary. To show that DI produced gains doesn't say much in itself: the children may have grown more proficient even without the intervention, or they may have benefited from the extra resources and attention that came from the introduction of DI rather than from some characteristic of the program itself.

30. For a review of research on this question, see Weaver et al., 1996, esp. pp. 283–85. Also see McQuillan, 1998, chap. 5.

31. On this point, see p. 284*n*9 and Weaver et al., p. 104.

32. Allington and Woodside-Jiron, 1998, p. 149.

33. Freeman and Freeman, 1998, p. 77.

34. NAEP scores weren't broken down by state before 1992, so California's scores that year can't be used to prove a decline from previous years. Nor do other kinds of tests permit the conclusion that reading achievement dropped during the period in question. See McQuillan, pp. 12–14.

35. McQuillan, pp. 82–83.

36. Freeman and Freeman, p. 78.

37. Ribowsky, 1985.

38. Manning et al., 1989.

39. Eldredge and Butterfield, 1986.

40. Tunnell and Jacobs, 1989.

41. Reutzel and Cooter, 1990.

42. Varble, 1990. The same study compared two sixth-grade classrooms as well and found no significant differences on mechanics or content between the two conditions.

43. Morrow et al., 1990.

44. Morrow, 1992.

45. Klesius et al., 1991.

46. Freppon et al., 1995.

47. Freppon, 1991.

48. McQuillan, p. 66.

49. Weaver et al., p. 286. The authors acknowledge that the direct instruction of phonics, "particularly with children labeled at risk or reading disabled, when they are tutored one-on-one or in very small groups," can produce "higher initial scores on phonemic awareness and word attack skills and sometimes on comprehension tests," but "this advantage appears not to last very long, particularly for comprehension tests."

50. Allington, 1983, p. 554. A subsequent study of second- and fourth-graders in five varied school districts confirmed that "low achievement instructional groups frequently focused on oral reading accuracy and concentrated instruction at the word level. When larger units of text were the focus—stories, for instance—accuracy remained the critical feature of instruction, with oral reading tasks that evidenced little, if any, emphasis on comprehension" (Allington and McGill-Franzen, 1989, p. 83).

51. See the discussion of this point and the accompanying citations in Fielding and Pearson, 1994.

52. The first-grade study: Milligan and Berg, 1992. The kindergarten study: Sacks and Mergendoller, 1997.

53. Success for All, designed by Robert Slavin and his colleagues at Johns Hopkins University, "tells schools precisely what to teach and how to teach it—to the point of scripting, nearly minute by minute, every teacher's activity in every classroom every day of the year. . . . Teachers must use a series of catch phrases and hand signals developed by Success for All. In kindergarten and first grade every piece of classroom material (readers, posters, tapes, videos, lesson plans, books—everything) is provided by the program. . . . Success for All . . . teaches reading primarily through phonics. . . . Students are tested, put into groups based on their skills levels, drilled in reading skills, regrouped, and drilled some more. . . . [A first-grade] teacher stands at the blackboard and says, 'Okay, let's get ready for our shared story. Ready, read!' The students read the first page of the story loudly, in unison. . . . 'Okay, do your first word,' she says. The students call out together, 'Only! O[clap] N[clap] L[clap] Y[clap]. Only!' . . . 'If you work right, you'll earn points for your work team! You clear?' Twenty voices call out, 'Yes!' " (Lemann, 1998, pp. 98–99). Keep in mind that this account is offered by a journalist who supports the program, at least for poor schools.
54. Purcell-Gates et al., 1995, p. 678.
55. Lisa Delpit, with whom this argument is often associated, has added that "literacy instruction should be in the context of real reading and real writing, and reading and writing for real purposes. This means using literature that children like and that connects with them in their homes and lives. It means writing for purposes the children find useful" (Delpit, 1992).
56. Weaver et al., p. 104.
57. Eldredge, 1991; Otto, 1993; and Purcell-Gates et al., 1995.
58. The NAEP questionnaire results appear on pp. 451, 471, and 501 of the National Reading Assessments, Data Almanac, available on the Internet at www.nces.ed.gov/naep/y25alm/n04r1c.pdf. Data for 1998, released just as this book was going to press, confirmed that there was a significant correlation between fourth-graders' test scores and how often they were permitted to read books of their own choosing. This was not true in eighth or twelfth grade, however, suggesting that letting students read whatever they wanted may have had a different meaning, and different implications for the quality of instruction, in the context of a 45-minute English class.
59. These NAEP results were cited in McQuillan, pp. 14, 90.
60. Mixed results (a difference favoring WL in one study, no differences in two others) were obtained by one group of researchers who have generally been critical of WL (McKenna et al., 1995), but every other study I could find that measured attitudes, motivation, or reading outside of school demonstrated a clear advantage for WL or a literature-based program: Eldredge, 1991; Eldredge and Butterfield, 1986; Morrow, 1992; and Kasten and Clarke, 1989, a study that looked at disadvantaged minority children. (Also see the review of research on this topic in McQuillan, pp. 63–64.) Interestingly, even a recent study spearheaded by long-time advocates of direct instruction that claimed to show an advantage for that approach—a study widely cited by people of similar persuasion and harshly criticized for its methodology by WL advocates—found significantly more positive attitudes toward reading among the children receiving something that was supposed to resemble WL than among those getting a skills-based approach (Foorman et al., 1998, p. 50).
61. Five studies are cited in support of this conclusion by Clarke, 1988, p. 281.
62. Weaver et al., p. 270.
63. Clarke, esp. pp. 295, 304.

64. Hammill et al., 1977.
65. Elley et al., 1976. The quotation appears on p. 5.
66. Hillocks and Smith, 1991. Quotations appear on pp. 597 and 600. A more recent review of the research arrives at the same conclusion. "There simply is not a high correlation between knowledge of grammatical terminology and the ability to use the language. [We should] stop teaching traditional schoolroom 'grammar' entirely" (Schuster, 1999. Quotations appear on pp. 523, 524).
67. See Stigler and Hiebert, 1997; and Lawton, 1997. Other differences between U.S. and Japanese instruction may also contribute to differences in results. Japanese teachers meet regularly in small groups so they can evaluate their teaching and improve their craft (Stigler and Hiebert, p. 20). Also, Japan, like many other countries, does not "track" students by putative ability (Schmidt et al., in press).
68. Schmidt et al., pp. 10, 15, 18, 25–26.
69. Porter, 1989, p. 11.
70. Mathews, 1998b. The report, prepared by Harold Wenglinsky of the Educational Testing Service, also found that African-American children were especially likely to use computers for drill-'n-skill purposes. Once again, a back-to-basics approach to instruction is disproportionately used for children of color —to their detriment.
71. Carpenter et al., 1989. Quotations appear on pp. 525, 527.
72. Hiebert and Wearne, 1993.
73. Simon and Schifter, 1993.
74. Campbell, 1996.
75. Yackel et al., 1991.
76. Cobb et al., 1991.
77. Cobb et al., 1992.
78. Wood and Sellers, 1996, 1997.
79. Kamii, 1989, pp. 158–78.
80. Kamii, 1994, p. 205.
81. Boaler, 1998.
82. Linda Joseph, quoted in Kamii, 1989, p. 155.
83. Cobb et al., 1989, pp. 137, 139, 144.
84. For example, the students in traditional classrooms who "worked hard and stayed on task" in one study nevertheless "found mathematics lessons . . . extremely boring and tedious" (Boaler, p. 45).
85. Mackenzie and White, 1982.
86. Bredderman, 1983. Quotation appears on p. 513.
87. Rothenberg, 1989, p. 70. Also see Horwitz, 1979; and Walberg, 1984. "Several widely reported studies that found students in open classrooms had significantly lower academic achievement . . . were later shown to be erroneous. . . . One particularly flawed study . . . 'trumpeted the failure' of open classrooms . . . and helped turn the tide against them (Rothenberg, p. 77).
88. Knapp et al., 1992. Quotations appear on pp. i, 27.
89. This is from the introduction to Volume 5 of the report *Adventure in American Education,* quoted in Adams, 1988, p. 161. All five volumes were published in the early 1940s, each with a different author. Of special interest are Volume 1: *The Story of the Eight Year Study,* by Wilford M. Aiken, and Volume 4: *Did They Succeed in College?* by Dean Chamberlin et al. Apart from the Adams article just cited, also see descriptions of the study in Ritchie, 1971; and Irwin, 1991.
90. This, in turn, is but one slice of a much broader and deeper line of psycho-

logical research demonstrating the positive effects of having a sense of control and the negative effects of feeling powerless, something that seems to be true at all ages.

91. Collages: Amabile and Gitomer, 1984. Second-graders' schedules: Wang and Stiles, 1976. High school chemistry: Rainey, 1965. Low-income minority children: de Charms, 1972. Sixth-grade standardized achievement scores: Boggiano et al., 1992.

92. Elementary school vocabulary: Berk, 1976. Middle school math: Keinan and Zeidner, 1987. Tenth-grade typing: Alschuler, 1969.

93. One review of NAEP data from the 1970s found that the extent to which teachers were perceived as having control of the science classroom was positively related to science achievement scores but negatively related to students' continuing motivation to learn about science (Pascarella et al., 1981). However, recall that in the 1990s, NAEP reading results for fourth-graders were positively related to how often students could read books of their own choosing (p. 223).

94. Undergraduates required to participate in an experiment did not perform better on tests just because they were allowed to choose which of two or three essays to read. They did, however, report more interest in the text than those told which ones to read (Schraw et al., 1998). Another experiment that offered undergraduates what might be viewed as a more substantive opportunity for decision-making—namely, which strategy to use in solving difficult conceptual problems—did find better test performance for this group than for students told how they should solve the problems, even though the strategies themselves were identical in the two conditions (Boggiano, Flink, Shields, Seelbach, and Barrett, 1992, reported in Boggiano et al., 1992, p. 280).

95. South African elementary school: Green and Foster, 1986. Canadian high school: Fry and Cole, 1980. Undergraduate puzzles: Zuckerman et al., 1978. Try more difficult tasks: Kuhl and Blankenship, 1979. Gain confidence: Ryan and Grolnick, 1986.

96. See the sources cited in chapter 8.

97. For example, see Battistich et al., 1995, 1997.

98. For example, Lauren Resnick, Howard Gardner, Ann Brown, and others.

99. Monty Neill, a thoughtful critic of standardized tests, has pointed out (personal communication, 1998) that this may be more true in some subject areas than in others. While some talented students will test poorly, even silly, superficial tests in reading and math will often reflect something of what children have gained from the rich, conceptual learning that goes on in progressive classrooms. But the truly horrendous standardized tests that many of our children must take in science and social studies are often no more than lists of specialized vocabulary words. To that extent, in-depth, interdisciplinary projects may not be good preparation for such exams. It will take courage to persevere with such teaching in the face of this gap.

APPENDIX B: WHAT TO LOOK FOR IN A CLASSROOM

1. Deci and Ryan (e.g., 1985) have labeled these three needs *autonomy, relatedness,* and *competence.*

# REFERENCES

Abrami, Philip C., Wenda J. Dickens, Raymond P. Perry, and Les Leventhal. "Do Teacher Standards for Assigning Grades Affect Student Evaluations of Instruction?" *Journal of Educational Psychology* 72 (1980): 107–18.

Achilles, Charles M., Jeremy D. Finn, and Helen P. Bain. "Using Class Size to Reduce the Equity Gap." *Educational Leadership,* December 1997/January 1998: 40–43.

"ACT/SAT Optional Colleges List Soars to 280." *FairTest Examiner,* Summer 1997: 5.

Airasian, Peter W. "Measurement Driven Instruction: A Closer Look." *Educational Measurement: Issues and Practice* 7, 4 (1988): 6–11.

Alexander, Patricia A., Jonna M. Kulikowich, and Tamara L. Jetton. "The Role of Subject-Matter Knowledge and Interest in the Processing of Linear and Nonlinear Texts." *Review of Educational Research* 64 (1994): 201–52.

Allen, Scott, and Karl L. Wuensch. "Effects of an Academic Failure Experience on Subsequent Performance on Anagram and Paired-Associate Tasks." *Journal of Genetic Psychology* 154 (1993): 53–60.

Allington, Richard L. "The Reading Instruction Provided Readers of Differing Reading Abilities." *Elementary School Journal* 83 (1983): 548–59.

Allington, Richard L., and Anne McGill-Franzen. "Different Programs, Indifferent Instruction." In *Beyond Separate Education: Quality Education for All,* edited by Dorothy Kerzner Lipsky and Alan Gartner. Baltimore: Paul H. Brookes, 1989.

———. "Flunking: Throwing Good Money After Bad." In *No Quick Fix: Rethinking Literacy Programs in America's Elementary Schools,* edited by Richard L. Allington and Sean A. Walmsley. New York: Teachers College Press, 1995.

Allington, Richard [L.], and Haley Woodside-Jiron. "Thirty Years of Research in Reading: When Is a Research Summary Not a Research Summary?" In *In Defense of Good Teaching: What Teachers Need to Know About the "Reading Wars,"* edited by Kenneth S. Goodman. York, Me.: Stenhouse, 1998.

Alschuler, Alfred S. "The Effects of Classroom Structure on Achievement Motivation and Academic Performance." *Educational Technology,* August 1969: 19–24.

Amabile, Teresa M., and Judith Gitomer. "Children's Artistic Creativity: Effects of Choice in Task Materials." *Personality and Social Psychology Bulletin* 10 (1984): 209–15.

American Federation of Teachers. *Making Standards Matter.* Washington, D.C.: AFT, 1998.

Ames, Carole. "Children's Achievement Attributions and Self-Reinforcement: Effects of Self-Concept and Competitive Reward Structure." *Journal of Educational Psychology* 70 (1978): 345–55.

————. "Achievement Goals and Classroom Structure: Developing a Learning Orientation in Students." Paper presented at the annual meeting of the American Educational Research Association, Boston, April 1990.

————. "Classrooms: Goals, Structures, and Student Motivation." *Journal of Educational Psychology* 84 (1992a): 261–71.

————. "Achievement Goals and the Classroom Motivational Climate." In *Student Perceptions in the Classroom*, edited by Dale H. Schunk and Judith L. Meece. Hillsdale, N.J.: Erlbaum, 1992b.

Ames, Carole, and Jennifer Archer. "Mothers' Beliefs About the Role of Ability and Effort in School Learning." *Journal of Educational Psychology* 79 (1987): 409–14.

————. "Achievement Goals in the Classroom: Students' Learning Strategies and Motivation Processes." *Journal of Educational Psychology* 80 (1988): 260–67.

Anderman, Eric M. "Motivation and Cognitive Strategy Use in Reading and Writing." Paper presented at the National Reading Conference, San Antonio, Tex., December 1992.

————. "Motivation and School Reform." In *Advances in Motivation and Achievement*, vol. 10. Greenwich, Conn.: JAI Press, 1997.

Anderman, Eric M., Jacquelynne Eccles, Robert Roeser, Kwang Suk Yoon, Phyllis Blumenfeld, and Allan Wigfield. "Classroom Influences on the Value of Reading." Paper presented at the annual meeting of the American Educational Research Association, New York, April 1996.

Anderman, Eric M., Tripp Griesinger, and Gloria Westerfield. "Motivation and Cheating During Early Adolescence." *Journal of Educational Psychology* 90 (1998): 84–93.

Anderman, Eric M., and Jerome Johnston. "Television News in the Classroom: What Are Adolescents Learning?" *Journal of Adolescent Research* 13 (1998): 73–100.

Anderman, Eric M., and Carol Midgley. "Changes in Achievement Goals Orientations, Perceived Academic Competence, and Grades Across the Transition to Middle Level Schools." *Contemporary Educational Psychology* 22 (1997): 269–98.

Anderman, Eric M., and Allison J. Young. "Motivation and Strategy Use in Science: Individual Differences and Classroom Effects." *Journal of Research in Science Teaching* 31 (1994): 811–31.

Anderson, Richard B., Robert G. St. Pierre, Elizabeth C. Proper, and Linda B. Stebbins. "Pardon Us, But What Was the Question Again?: A Response to the Critique of the Follow Through Evaluation." *Harvard Educational Review* 48 (1978): 161–70.

Anderson, Richard C., Larry L. Shirey, Paul T. Wilson, and Linda G. Fielding. "Interestingness of Children's Reading Material." In *Aptitude, Learning, and Instruction*, vol. 3: *Conative and Affective Process Analyses*, edited by Richard E. Snow and Marshall J. Farr. Hillsdale, N.J.: Erlbaum, 1987.

Archer, Jeff. "New School Role Seen Critical to Respond to Modern Economy." *Education Week*, 8 May 1996: 1, 8.

Arenson, Karen W. "Undergraduate Education Is Lacking, Report Finds." *New York Times*, 20 April 1998: A12.

Asher, Steven R. "Influence of Topic Interest on Black Children's and White Children's Reading Comprehension." *Child Development* 50 (1979): 686–90.

Ayers, William. "Grounded Insight." In *Progressive Education for the 1990s: Transforming Practice*, edited by Kathe Jervis and Carol Montag. New York: Teachers College Press, 1991.

————. *To Teach: The Journey of a Teacher.* New York: Teachers College Press, 1993.

Baris-Sanders, Marcia. "Cooperative Education: Lessons from Japan." *Phi Delta Kappan,* April 1997: 619–23.

Barnett, Earl. "If You Can't Jump Eight, Then Try Eleven." [Jasper, Ala.] *Daily Mountain Eagle,* 15 June 1997.

Barr, Mary A., Dana A. Craig, Dolores Fisette, and Margaret A. Syverson. *Assessing Literacy with the Learning Record.* Portsmouth, N.H.: Heinemann, 1999.

Bastian, Amy, Norm Fruchter, Marilyn Gittell, Colin Greer, and Kenneth Haskins. *Choosing Equality: The Case for Democratic Schooling.* Philadelphia: Temple University Press, 1986.

Battista, Michael T. "The Mathematical Miseducation of America's Youth: Ignoring Research and Scientific Study in Education." *Phi Delta Kappan,* February 1999: 425–33.

Battistich, Victor, Daniel Solomon, Dong-il Kim, Marilyn Watson, and Eric Schaps. "Schools as Communities, Poverty Levels of Student Populations, and Students' Attitudes, Motives, and Performance: A Multilevel Analysis." *American Educational Research Journal* 32 (1995): 627–58.

Battistich, Victor, Daniel Solomon, Marilyn Watson, and Eric Schaps. "Caring School Communities." *Educational Psychologist* 32 (1997): 137–51.

Baumann, James F., James V. Hoffman, Jennifer Moon, and Ann M. Duffy-Hester. "Where Are Teachers' Voices in the Phonics / Whole Language Debate? Results from a Survey of U.S. Elementary Classroom Teachers." *Reading Teacher* 51 (1998): 636–50.

Beane, James A. *Curriculum Integration: Designing the Core of Democratic Education.* New York: Teachers College Press, 1997.

Beck, Hall P., Sherry Rorrer-Woody, and Linda G. Pierce. "The Relations of Learning and Grade Orientations to Academic Performance." *Teaching of Psychology* 18 (1991): 35–37.

Begley, Sharon. "Homework Doesn't Help." *Newsweek,* 30 March 1998: 50–51.

Benware, Carl A., and Edward L. Deci. "Quality of Learning with an Active Versus Passive Motivational Set." *American Educational Research Journal* 21 (1984): 755–65.

Berk, Ronald A. "Effects of Choice of Instructional Methods on Verbal Learning Tasks." *Psychological Reports* 38 (1976): 867–70.

Berliner, David C. "Uninvited Comments from an Uninvited Guest." *Educational Researcher,* November 1996: 47–50.

Berliner, David C., and Bruce J. Biddle. *The Manufactured Crisis: Myths, Fraud, and the Attack on America's Public Schools.* Reading, Mass.: Addison-Wesley, 1995.

Biddle, Bruce J. "Foolishness, Dangerous Nonsense, and Real Correlates of State Differences in Achievement." *Phi Delta Kappan,* September 1997: 9–13.

Black, Susan. "The Truth About Homework." *American School Board Journal,* October 1996: 48–51.

Blumenfeld, Phyllis C., Elliot Soloway, Ronald W. Marx, Joseph S. Krajcik, Mark Guzdial, and Annemarie Palincsar. "Motivating Project-Based Learning: Sustaining the Doing, Supporting the Learning." *Educational Psychologist* 26 (1991): 369–98.

Boaler, Jo. "When Even the Winners Are Losers: Evaluating the Experiences of 'Top Set' Students." *Journal of Curriculum Studies* 29 (1997): 165–82.

————. "Open and Closed Mathematics: Student Experiences and Understandings." *Journal for Research in Mathematics Education* 29 (1998): 41–62.

306 · *References*

Boggiano, Ann K., Marty Barrett, and Teddy Kellam. "Competing Theoretical Analyses of Helplessness: A Social-Developmental Analysis." *Journal of Experimental Child Psychology* 55 (1993): 194–207.

Boggiano, Ann K., Ann Shields, Marty Barrett, Teddy Kellam, Erik Thompson, Jeffrey Simons, and Phyllis Katz. "Helplessness Deficits in Students: The Role of Motivational Orientation." *Motivation and Emotion* 16 (1992): 271–96.

Bond, Linda, Edward Roeber, and David Braskamp. *Trends in State Student Assessment Programs: Fall 1996.* Washington, D.C.: Council of Chief State School Officers, 1997.

Bond, Linda, Edward Roeber, and Selena Connealy. *Trends in State Student Assessment Programs: Fall 1997.* Washington, D.C.: Council of Chief State School Officers, 1998.

Bowles, Samuel, and Herbert Gintis. *Schooling in Capitalist America: Educational Reform and the Contradictions of Economic Life.* New York: Basic, 1976.

Bracey, Gerald W. "Research Oozes into Practice: The Case of Class Size." *Phi Delta Kappan,* September 1995: 89–90.

———. "International Comparisons and the Condition of American Education." *Educational Researcher,* January–February 1996a: 5–11.

———. "Asian and American Schools Again." *Phi Delta Kappan,* May 1996b: 641–42.

———. *Setting the Record Straight: Responses to Misconceptions About Public Education in the United States.* Alexandria, Va.: Association for Supervision and Curriculum Development, 1997.

———. "High Stakes Testing Comes a Cropper?" *Phi Delta Kappan,* April 1998a: 630.

———. "TIMSS, Rhymes with 'Dims,' as in 'Witted.' " *Phi Delta Kappan,* May 1998b: 686–87.

Bradley, Ann. "Muddle in the Middle." *Education Week,* 15 April 1998: 38–42.

Bredderman, Ted. "Effects of Activity-Based Elementary Science on Student Outcomes: A Quantitative Synthesis." *Review of Educational Research* 53 (1983): 499–518.

Brinkley, Ellen H. "What's Religion Got to Do with Attacks on Whole Language?" In *In Defense of Good Teaching: What Teachers Need to Know About the "Reading Wars,"* edited by Kenneth S. Goodman. York, Me.: Stenhouse, 1998.

Brodinsky, Ben. "Back to the Basics: The Movement and Its Meaning." *Phi Delta Kappan,* March 1977: 522–27.

Bronner, Ethan. "Better Schools Is Battle Cry for Fall Elections." *New York Times,* 20 September 1998a: A1, A32.

———. "Long a Leader, U.S. Now Lags in High School Graduate Rate." *New York Times,* 24 November 1998b: A1, A18.

Brooks, Jacqueline Grennon, and Martin G. Brooks. *In Search of Understanding: The Case for Constructivist Classrooms.* Alexandria, Va.: Association for Supervision and Curriculum Development, 1993.

Brown, Ann L. "The Advancement of Learning." *Educational Researcher,* November 1994: 4–12.

Brown, John Seely, Allan Collins, and Paul Duguid. "Situated Cognition and the Culture of Learning." *Educational Researcher,* January–February 1989: 32–42.

Brownell, William A. *The Development of Children's Number Ideas in the Primary Grades.* Chicago: University of Chicago, 1928.

———. "Psychological Considerations in the Learning and the Teaching of Arithmetic." In *The Teaching of Arithmetic,* the Tenth Yearbook of the National Council of Teachers of Mathematics. New York: Teachers College, 1935.

Bruner, Jerome. "The Act of Discovery." *Harvard Educational Review* 31 (1961): 21–32.
———. *Toward a Theory of Instruction.* Cambridge, Mass.: Harvard University Press, 1966.
———. *The Process of Education.* Cambridge, Mass.: Harvard University Press, 1977.
Bryant, Adam. "All for One, One for All and Every Man for Himself." *New York Times,* 22 February 1998: 4:1.
Burke, Daniel L. "Multi-Year Teacher / Student Relationships Are a Long-Overdue Arrangement." *Phi Delta Kappan,* January 1996: 360–61.
Bushweller, Kevin. "Teaching to the Test." *American School Board Journal,* September 1997: 20–25.
Business Roundtable. *A Business Leader's Guide to Setting Academic Standards.* Washington, D.C.: Business Roundtable, 1996.
Business Task Force on Student Standards. *The Challenge of Change: Standards to Make Education Work for All Our Children.* Washington, D.C.: National Alliance of Business, 1995.
Butkowsky, Irwin S., and Dale M. Willows. "Cognitive-Motivational Characteristics of Children Varying in Reading Ability: Evidence for Learned Helplessness in Poor Readers." *Journal of Educational Psychology* 72 (1980): 408–22.
Butler, Ruth. "Task-Involving and Ego-Involving Properties of Evaluation: Effects of Different Feedback Conditions on Motivational Perceptions, Interest, and Performance." *Journal of Educational Psychology* 79 (1987): 474–82.
———. "Enhancing and Undermining Intrinsic Motivation: The Effects of Task-Involving and Ego-Involving Evaluation on Interest and Performance." *British Journal of Educational Psychology* 58 (1988): 1–14.
———. "What Young People Want to Know When: Effects of Mastery and Ability Goals on Interest in Different Kinds of Social Comparisons." *Journal of Personality and Social Psychology* 62 (1992): 934–43.
Butler, Ruth, and Mordecai Nisan. "Effects of No Feedback, Task-Related Comments, and Grades on Intrinsic Motivation and Performance." *Journal of Educational Psychology* 78 (1986): 210–16.
Calkins, Lucy, Kate Montgomery, and Donna Santman. *A Teacher's Guide to Standardized Reading Tests: Knowledge Is Power.* Portsmouth, N.H.: Heinemann, 1998.
Campbell, David. "The Coriolanus Syndrome." *Phi Delta Kappan,* April 1997: 640–43.
Campbell, Patricia. "Empowering Children and Teachers in the Elementary Mathematics Classrooms of Urban Schools." *Urban Education* 30 (1996): 449–75.
Campione, Joseph C., Ann L. Brown, and Michael L. Connell. "Metacognition: On the Importance of Understanding What You Are Doing." In *The Teaching and Assessing of Mathematical Problem Solving,* vol. 3, edited by Randall I. Charles and Edward A. Silver. Washington, D.C.: National Council of Teachers of Mathematics, 1988.
Canady, Robert Lynn, and Phyllis Riley Hotchkiss. "It's a Good Score! Just a Bad Grade." *Phi Delta Kappan,* September 1989: 68–71.
Carpenter, Thomas P., Elizabeth Fennema, Penelope L. Peterson, Chi-Pang Chiang, and Megan Loef. "Using Knowledge of Children's Mathematics Thinking in Classroom Teaching: An Experimental Study." *American Educational Research Journal* 26 (1989): 499–531.
Carter, Glenda, and M. Gail Jones. "Relationship Between Ability-Paired Interac-

tions and the Development of Fifth Graders' Concepts of Balance." *Journal of Research in Science Teaching* 31 (1994): 847–56.

Central Park East Secondary School. "CPESS Graduation Handbook." Unpublished document. New York, N.Y., 1993.

Cenziper, Debbie. "Teachers Denounce ABCs Testing, Poll Says." *Charlotte* [N.C.] *Observer,* 12 August 1998: 1C, 7C.

Charlesworth, Rosalind, Craig H. Hart, Diane C. Burts, and Michele DeWolf. "The LSU Studies: Building a Research Base for Developmentally Appropriate Practice." In *Advances in Early Education and Day Care: Perspectives on Developmentally Appropriate Practice,* vol. 5, edited by Stuart Reifel. Greenwich, Conn.: JAI Press, 1993.

Checkley, Kathy. "Assessment That Serves Instruction." *ASCD* [Association for Supervision and Curriculum Development] *Education Update,* June 1997a: 1, 4–6.

———. "Problem-Based Learning: The Search for Solutions to Life's Messy Problems." *ASCD* [Association for Supervision and Curriculum Development] *Curriculum Update,* Summer 1997b: 1–8.

Chira, Susan. "Made in America: Asia's School Success." *New York Times,* 26 April 1992: E5.

Christensen, Linda. " 'High-Stakes' Harm." *Rethinking Schools,* Spring 1999: 14–18.

Cizek, Gregory J. "There's No Such Thing as Grade Inflation." *Education Week,* 17 April 1996: 32, 22.

Clark, D. Cecil. "Competition for Grades and Graduate-Student Performance." *Journal of Educational Research* 62 (1969): 351–54.

Clarke, Linda K. "Invented Versus Traditional Spelling in First Graders' Writings: Effects on Learning to Spell and Read." *Research in the Teaching of English* 22 (1988): 281–309.

Clinton, Bill. "State of the Union Message to Congress." Transcribed in the *New York Times,* 5 February 1997: A20.

Cobb, Paul, Terry Wood, Erna Yackel, John Nicholls, Grayson Wheatley, Beatriz Trigatti, and Marcella Perlwitz. "Assessment of a Problem-Centered Second-Grade Mathematics Project." *Journal for Research in Mathematics Education* 22 (1991): 3–29.

Cobb, Paul, Terry Wood, Erna Yackel, and Marcella Perlwitz. "A Follow-Up Assessment of a Second-Grade Problem-Centered Mathematics Project." *Educational Studies in Mathematics* 23 (1992): 483–504.

Cobb, Paul, Erna Yackel, and Terry Wood. "Young Children's Emotional Acts While Engaged in Mathematical Problem Solving." In *Affect and Mathematical Problem Solving: A New Perspective,* edited by D. B. McLeod and V. M. Adams. New York: Springer-Verlag, 1989.

Coe, Carol. "Turning Over Classroom Decision Making: A Teacher's Experience Over Time." *Active Learner: A Foxfire Journal for Teachers,* August 1997: 7–9, 38.

Cohen, David K. "A Revolution in One Classroom: The Case of Mrs. Oublier." *Educational Evaluation and Policy Analysis* 12 (1990): 311–29.

Cohen, David K., and Carol A. Barnes. "Pedagogy and Policy." In *Teaching for Understanding: Challenges for Policy and Practice,* edited by David K. Cohen, Milbrey W. McLaughlin, and Joan E. Talbert. San Francisco: Jossey-Bass, 1993a.

———. "Conclusion: A New Pedagogy for Policy?" In *Teaching for Understanding: Challenges for Policy and Practice,* edited by David K. Cohen, Milbrey W. McLaughlin, and Joan E. Talbert. San Francisco: Jossey-Bass, 1993b.

Cohen, Elizabeth G. "Restructuring the Classroom: Conditions for Productive Small Groups." *Review of Educational Research* 64 (1994): 1–35.

Coles, Jane. "Enough Was Enough: The Teachers' Boycott of National Curriculum Testing." *Changing English* (published by the University of London's Institute of Education) 1, 2 (1994): 16–31.

"College Admissions Test Scores by Family Income." *FairTest Examiner,* Spring 1998: 12.

Cooper, Harris M. *Homework.* White Plains, N.Y.: Longman, 1989.

Cooper, Harris, James J. Lindsay, Barbara Nye, and Scott Greathouse. "Relationships Among Attitudes About Homework, Amount of Homework Assigned and Completed, and Student Achievement." *Journal of Educational Psychology* 90 (1998): 70–83.

Corno, Lyn. "Homework Is a Complicated Thing." *Educational Researcher,* November 1996: 27–30.

Covington, Martin V. *Making the Grade: A Self-Worth Perspective on Motivation and School Reform.* Cambridge, England: Cambridge University Press, 1992.

———. "The Myth of Intensification." *Educational Researcher,* November 1996: 24–27.

Craig, Richard. "Don't Know Much About History." *New York Times,* 8 December 1997: A31.

Crooks, A. Duryee. "Marks and Marking Systems: A Digest." *Journal of Educational Research* 27 (1933): 259–72.

Cuban, Larry. *How Teachers Taught: Constancy and Change in American Classrooms, 1890–1980.* New York: Longman, 1984.

———. "A Fundamental Puzzle of School Reform." *Phi Delta Kappan,* January 1988: 341–44.

Cullen, Francis T., Jr., John B. Cullen, Van L. Hayhow, and John T. Plouffe. "The Effects of the Use of Grades as an Incentive." *Journal of Educational Research* 68 (1975): 277–79.

Cuoco, Al, and Faye Ruopp. "Math Exam Rationale Doesn't Add Up." *Boston Globe,* 24 May 1998: D3.

Daley, Beth, and Jordana Hart. "State Tests Worry Parents, Teachers." *Boston Globe,* 26 February 1998: A23.

Damon, William. *Greater Expectations.* New York: Free Press, 1995.

Daniels, Harvey. "Whole Language: What's the Fuss?" *Rethinking Schools,* Winter 1993: 4–7.

———. "Is Whole Language Doomed?" *Rethinking Schools,* Winter 1995: 1, 5.

———. "The Best Practice Project: Building Parent Partnerships in Chicago." *Educational Leadership,* April 1996: 38–43.

Daniels, Harvey, Steven Zemelman, and Marilyn Bizar. "Teacher Alert!: Phonics Fads Sweep Nation's Schools." *Rethinking Schools,* Summer 1998: 3, 13.

———. "The Research Behind Whole Language." *Educational Leadership,* in press.

Danner, Fred W., and Edward Lonky. "A Cognitive-Developmental Approach to the Effects of Rewards on Intrinsic Motivation." *Child Development* 52 (1981): 1043–52.

Darling-Hammond, Linda. *The Right to Learn: A Blueprint for Creating Schools That Work.* San Francisco: Jossey-Bass, 1997.

Darling-Hammond, Linda, and Beverly Falk. "Using Standards and Assessments to Support Student Learning." *Phi Delta Kappan,* November 1997: 190–99.

Davidson, Robert C., and Ernest L. Lewis. "Affirmative Action and Other Special Consideration Admissions at the University of California, Davis, School of Medicine." *Journal of the American Medical Association* 278 (1997): 1153–58.

de Charms, Richard. "Personal Causation Training in the Schools." *Journal of Applied Social Psychology* 2 (1972): 95–113.

Deci, Edward L., and Richard M. Ryan. *Intrinsic Motivation and Self-Determination in Human Behavior*. New York: Plenum, 1985.

Deci, Edward L., Richard M. Ryan, and Geoffrey C. Williams. "Need Satisfaction and the Self-Regulation of Learning." *Learning and Individual Differences* 8 (1996): 165–83.

Deci, Edward L., Nancy H. Spiegel, Richard M. Ryan, Richard Koestner, and Manette Kauffman. "Effects of Performance Standards on Teaching Styles: Behavior of Controlling Teachers." *Journal of Educational Psychology* 74 (1982): 852–59.

Delisle, James R. "How Proficiency Tests Fall Short (Let Me Count the Ways)." *Education Week*, 2 April 1997: 41, 44.

Delisle, Robert. *How to Use Problem-Based Learning in the Classroom*. Alexandria, Va.: Association for Supervision and Curriculum Development, 1997.

Delpit, Lisa. "Teachers, Culture, and Power." *Rethinking Schools*, Fall/Winter 1992.

Deppe, Roberta K., and Judith M. Harackiewicz. "Self-Handicapping and Intrinsic Motivation: Buffering Intrinsic Motivation from the Threat of Failure." *Journal of Personality and Social Psychology* 70 (1996): 868–76.

DeVries, Rheta. "Piaget's Social Theory." *Educational Researcher*, March 1997: 4–17.

DeVries, Rheta, and Betty Zan. *Moral Classrooms, Moral Children: Creating a Constructivist Atmosphere in Early Education*. New York: Teachers College Press, 1994.

Dewey, John. *School and Society* [originally published 1899] and *The Child and the Curriculum* [originally published 1902]. Chicago: University of Chicago Press, 1990.

――――. *Interest and Effort in Education*. Boston: Houghton Mifflin, 1913.

――――. *Democracy and Education*. New York: Free Press, 1916 / 1966.

――――. *Experience and Education*. New York: Collier, 1938 / 1963.

――――. Introduction to *The Use of Resources in Education* by Elsie Ripley Clapp. 1952. Reprinted in *Dewey on Education*, edited by Martin S. Dworkin. New York: Teachers College Press, 1959.

De Zouche, Dorothy. " 'The Wound *Is* Mortal': Marks, Honors, Unsound Activities." *Clearing House* 19 (1945): 339–44.

Dickinson, Alyce M. "The Detrimental Effects of Extrinsic Reinforcement on 'Intrinsic Motivation.' " *Behavior Analyst* 12 (1989): 1–15.

Dickinson, David K., and Lori Lyman DiGisi. "The Many Rewards of a Literacy-Rich Classroom." *Educational Leadership*, March 1998: 23–26.

Diegmueller, Karen. "A New Order." *Teacher Magazine*, August 1994: 12–13.

Diener, Carol I., and Carol S. Dweck. "An Analysis of Learned Helplessness: II. The Processing of Success." *Journal of Personality and Social Psychology* 39 (1980): 940–52.

Dorn, Sherman. "The Political Legacy of School Accountability Systems." *Education Policy Analysis Archives* 6, 1 (1998): 1–34. Available at http://olam.ed.asu.edu/epaa/v6n1.html.

Dossey, John A., Ina V. S. Mullis, Mary M. Lindquist, and Donald L. Chambers. *The Mathematics Report Card: Are We Measuring Up?—Trends and Achievement Based on the 1986 National Assessment*. Princeton, N.J.: Educational Testing Service, 1988.

Dougherty, Chrys. "Assessment of Student Reading Skills in the Early Grades." Unpublished manuscript. Austin, Tex.: Just for the Kids, 1998.

Driscoll, Marcy P. "The Relationship Between Grading Standards and Achievement: A New Perspective." *Journal of Research and Development in Education* 19 (1986): 13–17.

Duckworth, Eleanor. *"The Having of Wonderful Ideas" and Other Essays on Teaching and Learning.* New York: Teachers College Press, 1987.

Durkheim, Émile. *The Rules of Sociological Method.* New York: Free Press, 1938.

Dweck, Carol. "Motivational Processes Affecting Learning." *American Psychologist* 41 (1986): 1040–48.

Dweck, Carol, William Davidson, Sharon Nelson, and Bradley Enna. "Sex Differences in Learned Helplessness." *Developmental Psychology* 14 (1978): 268–76.

Dweck, Carol S., and Ellen L. Leggett. "A Social-Cognitive Approach to Motivation and Personality." *Psychological Review* 95 (1988): 256–73.

Dykstra, Dewey I., Jr. "Teaching Introductory Physics to College Students." In *Constructivism: Theory, Perspectives, and Practice,* edited by Catherine Twomey Fosnot. New York: Teachers College Press, 1996.

Edwards, Carolyn. "Partner, Nurturer, and Guide: The Roles of the Reggio Teacher in Action." In *The Hundred Languages of Children: The Reggio Emilia Approach to Early Childhood Education,* edited by Carolyn Edwards, Lella Gandini, and George Forman. Norwood, N.J.: Ablex, 1993.

Edwards, Carolyn, Lella Gandini, and George Forman. "Introduction." In *The Hundred Languages of Children: The Reggio Emilia Approach to Early Childhood Education,* edited by Carolyn Edwards, Lella Gandini, and George Forman. Norwood, N.J.: Ablex, 1993.

Eisner, Elliot W. "Standards for American Schools: Help or Hindrance?" *Phi Delta Kappan,* June 1995: 758–64.

Eldredge, [J.] Lloyd. "An Experiment with a Modified Whole Language Approach in First-Grade Classrooms." *Reading Research and Instruction* 30 (1991): 21–38.

Eldredge, J. Lloyd, and Dennie Butterfield. "Alternatives to Traditional Reading Instruction." *Reading Teacher* 40 (1986): 32–37.

Elley, Warwick B. *How in the World Do Students Read?* The Hague, The Netherlands: International Association for the Evaluation of Educational Achievement, 1992.

Elley, W. B., I. H. Barham, H. Lamb, and M. Wyllie. "The Role of Grammar in a Secondary School English Curriculum." *Research in the Teaching of English* 10 (1976): 5–21. Originally appeared in the *New Zealand Journal of Educational Studies* 10 (1975): 26–42.

Elliot, Andrew J., and Marcy A. Church. "A Hierarchical Model of Approach and Avoidance Achievement Motivation." *Journal of Personality and Social Psychology* 72 (1997): 218–32.

Elliot, Andrew J., and Judith M. Harackiewicz. "Approach and Avoidance Achievement Goals and Intrinsic Motivation: A Mediational Analysis." *Journal of Personality and Social Psychology* 70 (1996): 461–75.

Elliott, Elaine S., and Carol S. Dweck. "Goals: An Approach to Motivation and Achievement." *Journal of Personality and Social Psychology* 54 (1988): 5–12.

Farnham-Diggory, Sylvia. *Schooling.* Cambridge, Mass.: Harvard University Press, 1990.

Farr, Roger, and Beth Greene. "Improving Reading Assessments: Understanding the

Social and Political Agenda for Testing." *Educational Horizons,* Fall 1993: 20–27.

Feinberg, Walter. "Educational Manifestos and the New Fundamentalism." *Educational Researcher,* November 1997: 27–35.

Ferri, Daniel. "Education by the Numbers." *Harper's Magazine,* July 1998: 20–23.

Fielding, Linda G., and P. David Pearson. "Reading Comprehension: What Works." *Educational Leadership,* February 1994: 62–68.

Flink, Cheryl, Ann K. Boggiano, and Marty Barrett. "Controlling Teacher Strategies: Undermining Children's Self-Determination and Performance." *Journal of Personality and Social Psychology* 59 (1990): 916–24.

Flink, Cheryl, Ann K. Boggiano, Deborah S. Main, Marty Barrett, and Phyllis A. Katz. "Children's Achievement-Related Behaviors: The Role of Extrinsic and Intrinsic Motivational Orientations." In *Achievement and Motivation: A Social-Developmental Perspective,* edited by Ann K. Boggiano and Thane S. Pittman. Cambridge, England: Cambridge University Press, 1992.

Foorman, Barbara R., David J. Francis, Jack M. Fletcher, Christopher Schatschneider, and Para Mehta. "The Role of Instruction in Learning to Read: Preventing Reading Failure in At-Risk Children." *Journal of Educational Psychology* 90 (1998): 37–55.

Fosnot, Catherine Twomey. "Constructivism: A Psychological Theory of Learning." In *Constructivism: Theory, Perspectives, and Practice,* edited by Catherine Twomey Fosnot. New York: Teachers College Press, 1996.

Frederiksen, Norman. "The Real Test Bias: Influences of Testing on Teaching and Learning." *American Psychologist* 39 (1984): 193–202.

Freedman, Sarah Warshauer. "Linking Large-Scale Testing and Classroom Portfolio Assessments of Student Writing." *Educational Assessment* 1 (1993): 27–52.

———. "Exam-Based Reform Stifles Student Writing in the U.K." *Educational Leadership,* March 1995: 26–29.

Freeman, David, and Yvonne S. Freeman. "California Reading: The Pendulum Swings." In *In Defense of Good Teaching: What Teachers Need to Know About the "Reading Wars,"* edited by Kenneth S. Goodman. York, Me.: Stenhouse, 1998.

Freire, Paulo. *Pedagogy of the Oppressed.* New York: Continuum, 1970.

Freppon, Penny A. "Children's Concepts of the Nature and Purpose of Reading in Different Instructional Settings." *Journal of Reading Behavior* 23 (1991): 139–63.

Freppon, Penny A., Ellen McIntyre, and Karin L. Dahl. "A Comparison of Young Children's Writing Products in Skills-Based and Whole Language Classrooms." *Reading Horizons* 36 (1995): 150–65.

Fromm, Erich. Foreword to *Summerhill* by A. S. Neill. New York: Hart, 1960.

Fry, P. S., and K. J. Coe. "Interaction Among Dimensions of Academic Motivation and Classroom Social Climate: A Study of the Perceptions of Junior High and High School Pupils." *British Journal of Educational Psychology* 50 (1980): 33–42.

Fullan, Michael. *The Meaning of Educational Change.* New York: Teachers College Press, 1982.

Fyfe, Brenda. "A Conversation with James V. Wertsch: Part II." *Constructivist,* Spring 1997: 4–8.

Gallimore, Ronald, and Claude N. Goldenberg. "Tracking the Developmental Path of Teachers and Learners: A Vygotskian Perspective." In *Effective and Responsible Teaching: The New Synthesis,* edited by Fritz K. Oser, Andreas Dick, and Jean-Luc Patry. San Francisco: Jossey-Bass, 1992.

Gardner, Howard. *Frames of Mind: The Theory of Multiple Intelligences.* New York: Basic, 1983.

———. *The Unschooled Mind: How Children Think and How Schools Should Teach.* New York: Basic, 1991.

Gelberg, Denise. *The "Business" of Reforming American Schools.* Albany: State University of New York Press, 1997.

Gersten, Russell, and Thomas Keating. "Long-Term Benefits from Direct Instruction." *Educational Leadership,* March 1987: 28–31.

Ginsburg, Golda S., and Phyllis Bronstein. "Family Factors Related to Children's Intrinsic/Extrinsic Motivational Orientation and Academic Performance." *Child Development* 64 (1993): 1461–74.

Glaser, Robert. "Instructional Technology and the Measurement of Learning Outcomes: Some Questions." *American Psychologist* 18 (1963): 519–21.

Glovin, David. "Low-Paid Part-Timers Judge N.J. Students." *The Record* [of Hackensack, N.J.], 29 November 1998.

Gluck, Carol. "A Dose of Old-Fashioned 'How To.' " *Education Week,* 20 September 1995: 40, 33.

Gold, Richard M., Anne Reilly, Robert Silberman, and Robert Lehr. "Academic Achievement Declines Under Pass-Fail Grading." *Journal of Experimental Education* 39 (1971): 17–21.

Goldberg, Lewis R. "Grades as Motivants." *Psychology in the Schools* 2 (1965): 17–24.

Goldin, Davidson. "In a Change of Policy, and Heart, Colleges Join Fight Against Inflated Grades." *New York Times,* 4 July 1995: 8.

Goldstein, Amy. "Finding a New Gauge of Knowledge." *Washington Post,* 20 May 1990: A20.

———. "The Secret Behind the Scores." *Washington Post,* 20 May 1990: A1, A20.

Goodlad, John I. *A Place Called School: Prospects for the Future.* New York: McGraw-Hill, 1984.

———. "Flow, Eros, and Ethos in Educational Renewal." *Phi Delta Kappan,* April 1999: 571–78.

Goodman, Jesse. *Elementary Schooling for Critical Democracy.* Albany: State University of New York Press, 1992.

Goodman, Kenneth S. "Basal Readers: A Call for Action." *Language Arts* 63 (1986): 358–63.

———, ed. *In Defense of Good Teaching: What Teachers Need to Know About the "Reading Wars."* York, Me.: Stenhouse, 1998.

Gottfried, Adele Eskeles, James S. Fleming, and Allen W. Gottfried. "Role of Parental Motivational Practices in Children's Academic Intrinsic Motivation and Achievement." *Journal of Educational Psychology* 86 (1994): 104–13.

Green, Joan, and John Myers. "Conversations: Observations on the Implementation of Interactive Learning." In *Perspectives on Small Group Learning: Theory and Practice,* edited by Mark Brubacher, Ryder Payne, and Kemp Rickett. Oakville, Ont.: Rubicon, 1990.

Green, Lena, and Don Foster. "Classroom Intrinsic Motivation: Effects of Scholastic Level, Teacher Orientation, and Gender." *Journal of Educational Research* 80 (1986): 34–39.

Grolnick, Wendy S., and Richard M. Ryan. "Autonomy in Children's Learning: An Experimental and Individual Difference Investigation." *Journal of Personality and Social Psychology* 52 (1987): 890–98.

Gursky, Daniel. "After the Reign of Dick and Jane." *Teacher Magazine,* August 1991: 22–29.

Hall, Cathy W., Larry M. Bolen, and Robert H. Gupton, Jr. "Predictive Validity of the Study Process Questionnaire for Undergraduate Students." *College Student Journal* 29 (1995): 234–39.

Hamilton, V. Lee, Phyllis C. Blumenfeld, Hiroshi Akoh, and Kanae Miura. "Japanese and American Children's Reasons for the Things They Do in School." *American Educational Research Journal* 26 (1989): 545–71.

Hammill, Donald D., Stephen Larsen, and Gaye McNutt. "The Effects of Spelling Instruction: A Preliminary Study." *Elementary School Journal* 78 (1977): 67–72.

Harackiewicz, Judith M., Kenneth E. Barron, Suzanne M. Carter, Alan T. Lehto, and Andrew J. Elliot. "Predictors and Consequences of Achievement Goals in the College Classroom: Maintaining Interest and Making the Grade." *Journal of Personality and Social Psychology* 73 (1997): 1284–95.

Harackiewicz, Judith M., George Manderlink, and Carol Sansone. "Rewarding Pinball Wizardry: Effects of Evaluation and Cue Value on Intrinsic Interest." *Journal of Personality and Social Psychology* 47 (1984): 287–300.

Harp, Lonnie. "Wis. Governor Calls for Local High School Exit Exams." *Education Week,* 7 February 1996: 12.

Hart, Craig H., Diane C. Burts, and Rosalind Charlesworth. "Integrated Developmentally Appropriate Curriculum." In *Integrated Curriculum and Developmentally Appropriate Practice: Birth to Age Eight,* edited by Craig H. Hart, Diane C. Burts, and Rosalind Charlesworth. Albany: State University of New York Press, 1997.

Harter, Susan. "Pleasure Derived from Challenge and the Effects of Receiving Grades on Children's Difficulty Level Choices." *Child Development* 49 (1978): 788–99.

———. "The Relationship Between Perceived Competence, Affect, and Motivational Orientation Within the Classroom: Processes and Patterns of Change." In *Achievement and Motivation: A Social-Developmental Perspective,* edited by Ann K. Boggiano and Thane S. Pittman. Cambridge, England: Cambridge University Press, 1992.

Harter, Susan, and Bradley K. Jackson. "Trait vs. Nontrait Conceptualizations of Intrinsic/Extrinsic Motivational Orientation." *Motivation and Emotion* 16 (1992): 209–30.

Hartocollis, Anemona. "New State Test Sets Schools to Cramming." *New York Times,* 11 January 1999: A19.

Harwayne, Shelley. "Whole Language: Now More Than Ever." In *Whole Language: The Debate.* Bloomington, Ind.: ERIC Clearinghouse on Reading, English, and Communication, 1994.

Hauser, Robert M. "What If We Ended Social Promotion?" *Education Week,* 7 April 1999: 64, 37.

Hawkins, David. *The Informed Vision: Essays on Learning and Human Nature.* New York: Agathon Press, 1974.

———. "Defining and Bridging the Gap." In *Science Education: A Minds-On Approach for the Elementary Years,* edited by Eleanor Duckworth, Jack Easley, David Hawkins, and Androula Henriques. Hillsdale, N.J.: Erlbaum, 1990.

Hedges, Larry V., Richard D. Laine, and Rob Greenwald. "Does Money Matter?: A Meta-Analysis of Studies of the Effects of Differential School Inputs on Student Outcomes." *Educational Researcher,* April 1994: 5–14.

Henderson, Valanne L., and Carol S. Dweck. "Motivation and Achievement." In *At the Threshold: The Developing Adolescent,* edited by S. Shirley Feldman and Glen R. Elliott. Cambridge, Mass.: Harvard University Press, 1990.

Heyman, Gail D., and Carol S. Dweck. "Achievement Goals and Intrinsic Motivation: Their Relation and Their Role in Adaptive Motivation." *Motivation and Emotion* 16 (1992): 231–47.

Hiebert, James, and Diana Wearne. "Instructional Tasks, Classroom Discourse, and Students' Learning in Second-Grade Arithmetic." *American Educational Research Journal* 30 (1993): 393–425.

"High Stakes Tests Do Not Improve Learning." *FairTest Examiner,* Winter 1997–98: 1, 4–5.

Hill, David. "Shanker Stands Test of Time." *Education Week,* 21 February 1996: 31.

Hillocks, George, Jr., and Michael W. Smith. "Grammar and Usage." In *Handbook of Research on Teaching the English Language Arts,* edited by James Flood, Julie M. Jensen, Diane Lapp, and James R. Squire. New York: Macmillan, 1991.

Hiroto, Donald S., and Martin E. P. Seligman. "Generality of Learned Helplessness in Man." *Journal of Personality and Social Psychology* 31 (1975): 311–27.

Hirsch, E. D., Jr. *The Schools We Need: And Why We Don't Have Them.* New York: Doubleday, 1996.

———. "Response to Prof. Feinberg." *Educational Researcher,* March 1998: 38–39.

Hoff, David J. "U.S. Graduation Rates Starting to Fall Behind." *Education Week,* 25 November 1998a: 1, 11.

———. "Venerable National Honor Society Catching flak from Some Quarters." *Education Week,* 25 November 1998b: 1, 12.

Holloway, Susan D. "Concepts of Ability and Effort in Japan and the United States." *Review of Educational Research* 58 (1988): 327–45.

Holt, John. *How Children Fail.* Rev. ed. New York: Delta, 1982.

Horwitz, Robert A. "Psychological Effects of the 'Open Classroom.'" *Review of Educational Research* 49 (1979): 71–86.

House, Ernest R. "Policy Implications of Retention Research." In *Flunking Grades: Research and Policies on Retention,* edited by Lorrie A. Shepard and Mary Lee Smith. London: Falmer Press, 1989.

House, Ernest R., Gene V. Glass, Leslie D. McLean, and Decker F. Walker. "No Simple Answer: Critique of the Follow Through Evaluation." *Harvard Educational Review* 48 (1978): 128–60.

Howe, Harold, II. "Uncle Sam Is in the Classroom!" *Phi Delta Kappan,* January 1995: 374–77.

Howe, Kenneth R. "Standards, Assessment, and Equality of Educational Opportunity." *Educational Researcher,* November 1994: 27–33.

Hughes, Billie, Howard J. Sullivan, and Mary Lou Mosley. "External Evaluation, Task Difficulty, and Continuing Motivation." *Journal of Educational Research* 78 (1985): 210–15.

Hunt, James B., Jr. "Education for Economic Growth." *Phi Delta Kappan,* April 1984.

Irwin, Kathy. "The Eight Year Study." In *Progressive Education for the 1990s,* edited by Kathe Jervis and Carol Montag. New York: Teachers College Press, 1991.

Jackson, Allyn. "The Math Wars: California Battles It Out over Mathematics Education Reform." *Notices of the AMS* [American Mathematics Society], June/July and August 1997.

316 · *References*

Jackson, Philip W. *Life in Classrooms.* 1968. Reprint. New York: Teachers College Press, 1990.

Jacobson, Linda. " 'Looping' Catches On as a Way to Build Strong Ties." *Education Week,* 15 October 1997: 1, 18–19.

Jervis, Kathe, and Joseph McDonald. "Standards: The Philosophical Monster in the Classroom." *Phi Delta Kappan,* April 1996: 563–69.

Johnson, David W., and Roger T. Johnson. *Cooperation and Competition: Theory and Research.* Edina, Minn.: Interaction Book Co., 1989.

———. *Learning Together and Alone: Cooperative, Competitive, and Individualistic Learning.* Boston: Allyn and Bacon, 1994.

Johnson, Dirk. "Study Says Small Schools Are Key to Learning." *New York Times,* 21 September 1994: B12.

———. "Many Schools Putting an End to Child's Play." *New York Times,* 7 April 1998: A1, A18.

Johnson, Katie. "Context Is Everything." *Educational Leadership,* November 1992: 95.

Johnston, James M., and George O'Neill. "The Analysis of Performance Criteria Defining Course Grades as a Determinant of College Student Academic Performance." *Journal of Applied Behavior Analysis* 6 (1973): 261–68.

Johnston, Robert C. "Just Saying No: Mich. Sorts Out What Went Wrong as Parents Opt Children Out of Test." *Education Week,* 9 April 1997: 1, 26–27.

———. "In Texas, the Arrival of Spring Means the Focus Is on Testing." *Education Week,* 29 April 1998: 1, 20–21.

Jones, Ken. "Teacher Accountability: High Resolution, Not High Stakes." *Mathematics Education Dialogues* [published by the National Council of Teachers of Mathematics], May/June 1998: 10.

Jones, Ken, and Betty Lou Whitford. "Kentucky's Conflicting Reform Principles: High-Stakes School Accountability and Student Performance Assessment." *Phi Delta Kappan,* December 1997: 276–81.

Julyan, Candace, and Eleanor Duckworth. "A Constructivist Perspective on Teaching and Learning Science." In *Constructivism: Theory, Perspectives, and Practice,* edited by Catherine Twomey Fosnot. New York: Teachers College Press, 1996.

Kage, Masaharu. "The Effects of Evaluation on Intrinsic Motivation." Paper presented at the meeting of the Japan Association of Educational Psychology, Joetsu, Japan, 1991.

Kahramanidis, Jane. "Winning by Losing" (letter to the editor). *New York Times,* 6 March 1998: A24.

Kamii, Constance. "Leading Primary Education Toward Excellence: Beyond Worksheets and Drill." *Young Children,* September 1985a: 3–9.

———. *Young Children Reinvent Arithmetic: Implications of Piaget's Theory.* New York: Teachers College Press, 1985b.

———. *Young Children Continue to Reinvent Arithmetic—2nd Grade: Implications of Piaget's Theory.* New York: Teachers College Press, 1989.

———. *Young Children Continue to Reinvent Arithmetic—3rd Grade: Implications of Piaget's Theory.* New York: Teachers College Press, 1994.

Kamii, Constance, Faye B. Clark, and Ann Dominick. "The Six National Goals: A Road to Disappointment." *Phi Delta Kappan,* May 1994: 672–77.

Kanter, Rosabeth Moss. *Men and Women of the Corporation.* New York: Basic Books, 1977.

Kantrowitz, Barbara, and Pat Wingert. "How Kids Learn." *Newsweek,* 17 April 1989: 50–56.

Karnes, Merle B., Allan M. Shwedel, and Mark B. Williams. "A Comparison of Five Approaches for Educating Young Children from Low-Income Homes." In *As the Twig Is Bent . . . : Lasting Effects of Preschool Programs,* edited by the Consortium for Longitudinal Studies. Hillsdale, N.J.: Erlbaum, 1983.

Karweit, Nancy. "Time-on-Task Reconsidered: Synthesis of Research on Time and Learning." *Educational Leadership,* May 1984: 32–35.

Kasser, Tim, and Richard M. Ryan. "A Dark Side of the American Dream: Correlates of Financial Success as a Central Life Aspiration." *Journal of Personality and Social Psychology* 65 (1993): 410–22.

———. "Further Examining the American Dream: Differential Correlates of Intrinsic and Extrinsic Goals." *Personality and Social Psychology Bulletin* 22 (1996): 280–87.

Kasten, Wendy C., and Barbara K. Clarke. "Reading/Writing Readiness for Preschool and Kindergarten Children: A Whole Language Approach." 1989. Available as ERIC Document 312041.

Katz, Lilian. "The Disposition to Learn." *Principal,* May 1988: 14–17.

———. "What Can We Learn from Reggio Emilia?" In *The Hundred Languages of Children: The Reggio Emilia Approach to Early Childhood Education,* edited by Carolyn Edwards, Lella Gandini, and George Forman. Norwood, N.J.: Ablex, 1993.

———. "A Developmental Approach to Assessment of Young Children." *ERIC Digest,* April 1997. Publication number EDO-PS-97-18.

———. "Affirming Children's Minds." *Montessori Life,* Winter 1998: 33–36.

Katz, Lilian G., and Sylvia C. Chard. *Engaging Children's Minds: The Project Approach.* Norwood, N.J.: Ablex, 1989.

Katz, Lilian G., Demetra Evangelou, and Jeanette Allison Hartman. *The Case for Mixed-Age Grouping in Early Education.* Washington, D.C.: National Association for the Education of Young Children, 1990.

Keinan, Giora, and Moshe Zeidner. "Effects of Decisional Control on State Anxiety and Achievement." *Personality and Individual Differences* 8 (1987): 973–75.

Kellaghan, Thomas, George F. Madaus, and Anastasia Raczek. *The Use of External Examinations to Improve Student Motivation.* Washington, D.C.: American Educational Research Association, 1996.

Keller, Bess. "In Age of Accountability, Principals Feel the Heat." *Education Week,* 20 May 1998: 1, 16.

Kilpatrick, William H. "The Project Method." *Teachers College Record* 19 (1918): 319–35.

Kirschenbaum, Howard, Sidney B. Simon, and Rodney W. Napier. *Wad-Ja-Get? The Grading Game in American Education.* New York: Hart, 1971.

Kirst, Michael W., and Christopher Mazzeo. "The Rise, Fall, and Rise of State Assessment in California: 1993–96. *Phi Delta Kappan,* December 1996: 319–23.

Klaczynski, Paul A., and Joseph S. Laipple. "Rule of Content Domain, Logic Training, and IQ in Rule Acquisition and Transfer." *Journal of Experimental Psychology: Learning, Memory, and Cognition* 19 (1993): 653–72.

Klesius, Janell P., Priscilla L. Griffith, and Paula Zielonka. "A Whole Language and Traditional Instruction Comparison: Overall Effectiveness and Development of the Alphabetic Principle." *Reading Research and Instruction* 30 (1991): 47–61.

Knapp, Michael S., Patrick M. Shields, and Brenda J. Turnbull. *Academic Challenge for the Children of Poverty.* Summary Report of the Study of Academic Instruction for Disadvantaged Students. Washington, D.C.: U.S. Department of Education, 1992.

Kohlberg, Lawrence, and Rochelle Mayer. "Development as the Aim of Education." *Harvard Educational Review* 42 (1972): 449–96.

Kohn, Alfie. "Group Grade Grubbing Versus Cooperative *Learning*." *Educational Leadership,* March 1991: 83–87. (Reprinted in Kohn, 1998b.)

———. *No Contest: The Case Against Competition.* Rev. ed. Boston: Houghton Mifflin, 1992a.

———. "Resistance to Cooperative Learning: Making Sense of Its Deletion and Dilution." *Journal of Education* 174, 2 (1992b): 38–56. (Reprinted in Kohn, 1998b.)

———. *Punished by Rewards: The Trouble with Gold Stars, Incentive Plans, A's, Praise, and Other Bribes.* Boston: Houghton Mifflin, 1993a.

———. "Choices for Children: Why and How to Let Students Decide." *Phi Delta Kappan,* September 1993b: 8–20. (Reprinted in Kohn, 1998b.)

———. "The Truth About Self-Esteem." *Phi Delta Kappan,* December 1994: 272–83. (Reprinted in Kohn, 1998b.)

———. *Beyond Discipline: From Compliance to Community.* Alexandria, Va.: Association for Supervision and Curriculum Development, 1996a.

———. "What to Look for in a Classroom." *Educational Leadership,* September 1996b: 54–55. (Reprinted in Kohn, 1998b.)

———, ed. *Education, Inc.: Turning Learning into a Business.* Arlington Heights, Ill.: IRI/Skylight, 1997a.

———. "Students Don't 'Work'—They Learn: Our Use of Workplace Metaphors May Compromise the Essence of Schooling." *Education Week,* 3 September 1997b: 60, 43. (Reprinted in Kohn, 1998b.)

———. "Only for My Kid: How Privileged Parents Undermine School Reform." *Phi Delta Kappan,* April 1998a: 569–77. (Reprinted in Kohn, 1998b.)

———. *What to Look for in a Classroom . . . and Other Essays.* San Francisco: Jossey-Bass, 1998b.

———. "In Pursuit of Affluence, at a High Price." *New York Times,* 2 February 1999.

Kolker, Claudia. "Texas Offers Hard Lessons on School Accountability." *Los Angeles Times,* April 14, 1999.

Kosmoski, Georgia J., Geneva Gay, and Edward L. Vockell. "Cultural Literacy and Academic Achievement." *Journal of Experimental Education* 58 (1990): 265–72.

Kozol, Jonathan. *Savage Inequalities: Children in America's Schools.* New York: HarperCollins, 1992.

Krashen, Stephen. "The Effect of Training in Phonemic Awareness: Greatest in Tests with the Least Amount of Meaning." Unpublished ms. University of Southern California, 1998.

Krumboltz, John D., and Christine J. Yeh. "Competitive Grading Sabotages Good Teaching." *Phi Delta Kappan,* December 1996: 324–26.

Kuhl, Julius, and Virginia Blankenship. "Behavioral Change in a Constant Environment: Shift to More Difficult Tasks with Constant Probability of Success." *Journal of Personality and Social Psychology* 37 (1979): 551–63.

Kunen, James S. "The Test of Their Lives." *Time,* 16 June 1997: 62–63.

Labaree, David F. "Are Students 'Consumers'?: The Rise of Public Education as a Private Good." *Education Week,* 17 September 1997a: 48, 38.

———. *How to Succeed in School Without Really Learning: The Credentials Race in American Education.* New Haven: Yale University Press, 1997b.

Labinowicz, Ed. "Children's Right to Be Wrong." *Arithmetic Teacher,* December 1987: 2, 20.

Lampert, Magdalene. "Knowing, Doing, and Teaching Multiplication." *Cognition and Instruction* 3 (1986): 305–42.

Lapham, Lewis H. "Achievement Test." *Harper's,* July 1991: 10–13.

Lawton, Millicent. "New Images of Teaching." *Education Week,* 9 April 1997: 20–23.

———. "Calif. Education Officials Approve Back-to-Basics Standards in Math." *Education Week,* 14 January 1998: 6.

Le Countryman, Lyn, and Merrie Schroeder. "When Students Lead Parent-Teacher Conferences." *Educational Leadership,* April 1996: 64–68.

Lemann, Nicholas. "The Reading Wars." *Atlantic Monthly,* November 1997: 128–34.

———. "Ready, Read!" *Atlantic Monthly,* November 1998: 92–104.

Lepper, Mark R., Sheena Sethi, Dania Dialdin, and Michael Drake. "Intrinsic and Extrinsic Motivation: A Developmental Perspective." In *Developmental Psychopathology: Perspectives on Adjustment, Risk, and Disorder,* edited by S. S. Luthar, J. A. Burack, D. Dicchetti, and J. R. Weisz. Cambridge, Eng.: Cambridge University Press, 1997.

Lester, Jill Bodner. "Is the Algorithm All There Is?" In *Constructivism: Theory, Perspectives, and Practice,* edited by Catherine Twomey Fosnot. New York: Teachers College Press, 1996.

Levin, Henry M. "Clocking Instruction: A Reform Whose Time Has Come?" *IFG Policy Perspectives* [newsletter of the Institute for Research on Educational Finance and Governance at Stanford University's School of Education], Spring 1984: 1–4.

Levy, Jack, and Patricia Riordan. *Rank-in-Class, Grade Point Average, and College Admission.* Reston, Va.: NASSP, 1994. (Available as ERIC Document 370988.)

Lewis, Catherine C. *Educating Hearts and Minds: Reflections on Japanese Preschool and Elementary Education.* Cambridge, Eng.: Cambridge University Press, 1995.

Lewis, Catherine C., and Ineko Tsuchida. "The Basics in Japan: The Three C's." *Educational Leadership,* March 1998: 32–37.

Linder, Ivan H. "Is There a Substitute for Teachers' Grades?" *School Board Journal,* July 1940: 25–26, 79.

Lindsay, Drew. "In States, G.O.P. Stymied in Push to Revamp Policy." *Education Week,* 21 June 1995: 1, 14.

MacGyvers, Valanne L., and Carol S. Dweck. "Responses to the Early Adolescent Transition: A Test of a Theoretical Model of Motivation." Unpublished ms. 1994.

Mackenzie, Andrew A., and Richard T. White. "Fieldwork in Geography and Long-term Memory Structures." *American Educational Research Journal* 19 (1982): 623–32.

Madaus, George F., Mary Maxwell West, Maryellen C. Harmon, Richard G. Lomax, and Katherine A. Viator. *The Influence of Testing on Teaching Math and Science in Grades 4–12: Executive Summary.* Boston: Center for the Study of Testing, Evaluation, and Educational Policy, 1992.

Madell, Rob. "Children's Natural Processes." *Arithmetic Teacher,* March 1985: 20–22.

Maehr, Martin L., and Carol Midgley. "Enhancing Student Motivation: A Schoolwide Approach." *Educational Psychologist* 26 (1991): 399–427.

———. *Transforming School Cultures.* Boulder, Col.: Westview, 1996.

Maehr, Martin L., and William M. Stallings. "Freedom from External Evaluation." *Child Development* 43 (1972): 177–85.

Manegold, Catherine S. "Study Says Schools Must Stress Academics." *New York Times*, 23 September 1994: A22.

Manning, Maryann, Gary Manning, and Roberta Long. "Effects of a Whole Language and a Skills-Oriented Program on the Literacy Development of Inner City Primary Children." Paper presented at the annual meeting of the Mid-South Educational Research Association, New Orleans, November 1989. Available as ERIC Document 324642.

Manno, Bruno V. "The New School Wars: Battles Over Outcome-Based Education." *Phi Delta Kappan*, May 1995: 720–26.

"Many Fail New Nevada Tests." *Education Week*, 27 May 1998: 4.

Manzo, Kathleen Kennedy. "Limitations on Approved Topics for Reading Sessions Rile Teacher Trainers." *Education Week*, 5 November 1997: 18.

———. "NRC Panel Urges End to Reading Wars." *Education Week*, 25 March 1998a.

———. "More States Moving to Make Phonics the Law." *Education Week*, 29 April 1998b: 24.

———. "Drilling in Texas: Teachers in Houston Are Marching in Lockstep to Fulfill District Orders that Basic Skills Make Up the Core of Their Reading Instruction." *Education Week*, 10 June 1998c: 32–37.

———. "Trickling Down." *Education Week*, 18 November 1998d: 22-27.

———. "Board Oks Math, Language Arts Frameworks." *Education Week*, 16 December 1998e: 22.

Marcon, Rebecca A. "Doing the Right Thing for Children: Linking Research and Policy Reform in the District of Columbia Public Schools." *Young Children*, November 1994: 8–20.

Marlowe, Bruce A., and Marilyn L. Page. *Creating and Sustaining the Constructivist Classroom*. Thousand Oaks, Calif.: Corwin, 1998.

Marshall, Hermine H. "Children's Understanding of Academic Tasks: Work, Play, or Learning." *Journal of Research in Childhood Education* 9 (1994): 35–46.

———. "Beyond the Workplace Metaphor: The Classroom as a Learning Setting." *Theory into Practice* 29 (1990): 94–101. Reprinted in *Education, Inc.: Turning Learning into a Business*, edited by Alfie Kohn. Arlington Heights, Ill.: IRI/Skylight, 1997.

Marzano, Robert J., John S. Kendall, and Barbara B. Gaddy. "Deciding on 'Essential Knowledge.' " *Education Week*, 21 April 1999: 68, 49.

Mathews, Jay. *Class Struggle*. New York: Times Books, 1998a.

———. "Study Links Lower Grades to Computer Use." *Washington Post*, 30 September 1998b: A3.

Mathews, Jay, and Victoria Benning. "97 Percent of Schools in Va. Fail New Exam." *Washington Post*, 9 January 1999: A1.

Matson, Barbara. "Whole Language or Phonics? Teachers and Researchers Find the Middle Ground Most Fertile." *Harvard Education Letter*, March/April 1996: 1–5.

McClellan, Diane E., and Susan Kinsey. "Children's Social Behavior in Relationship to Participation in Mixed-Age or Same-Age Classrooms." *Early Childhood Research and Practice* 1,1 (1999). Available at http://ecrp.vivc.edu/v1n1/v1n1.html.

McGill-Franzen, Anne, and Richard L. Allington. "Flunk 'em or Get Them Classified: The Contamination of Primary Grade Accountability Data." *Educational Researcher*, January–February 1993: 19–22.

McGuire, Margit. "Taking a Storypath into History." *Educational Leadership*, March 1997: 70–72.

McKenna, Michael C., Beverly D. Stratton, Martha C. Grindler, and Stephen J.

Jenkins. "Differential Effects of Whole Language and Traditional Instruction on Reading Attitudes." *Journal of Reading Behavior* 27 (1995): 19–44.

McLaughlin, Milbrey W. "What Matters Most in Teachers' Workplace Context?" In *Teachers' Work: Individuals, Colleagues, and Context,* edited by Judith Warren Little and Milbrey W. McLaughlin. New York: Teachers College Press, 1993.

McNeil, Linda M. *Contradictions of Control: School Structure and School Knowledge.* New York: Routledge & Kegan Paul, 1986.

McQuillan, Jeff. "The Effects of Incentives on Reading." *Reading Research and Instruction* 36 (1997): 111–25.

———. *The Literacy Crisis: False Claims, Real Solutions.* Portsmouth, N.H.: Heinemann, 1998.

Meece, Judith L., Phyllis C. Blumenfeld, and Rick H. Hoyle. "Students' Goal Orientations and Cognitive Engagement in Classroom Activities." *Journal of Educational Psychology* 80 (1988): 514–23.

Meier, Deborah. "Why Reading Tests Don't Test Reading." *Dissent,* Fall 1981: 457–66.

———. "How Our Schools Could Be." *Phi Delta Kappan,* January 1995a: 369–73.

———. *The Power of Their Ideas: Lessons for America from a Small School in Harlem.* Boston: Beacon, 1995b.

———. "The Big Benefits of Smallness." *Educational Leadership,* September 1996a: 12–15.

———. "Supposing That . . ." *Phi Delta Kappan,* December 1996b: 271–76.

Meier, Deborah, and Alfie Kohn. "The MCAS Test: It's Difficult and Destructive." *Boston Globe,* 8 June 1998.

Meisels, Samuel J. "Remaking Classroom Assessment with the Work Sampling System." *Young Children,* July 1993: 34–40.

Middleton, Michael J., and Carol Midgley. "Avoiding the Demonstration of Lack of Ability: An Underexplored Aspect of Goal Theory." *Journal of Educational Psychology* 89 (1997): 710–18.

Midgley, Carol. "Motivation and Middle Level Schools." In *Advances in Motivation and Achievement,* vol. 8: *Motivation and Adolescent Development,* edited by Paul R. Pintrich and Martin L. Maehr. Greenwich, Conn.: JAI Press, 1993.

Milligan, Jerry L., and Herbert Berg. "The Effect of Whole Language on the Comprehending Ability of First Grade Children." *Reading Improvement* 29 (1992): 146–54.

Milton, Ohmer, Howard R. Pollio, and James A. Eison. *Making Sense of College Grades.* San Francisco: Jossey-Bass, 1986.

Miserandino, Marianne. "Children Who Do Well in School: Individual Differences in Perceived Competence and Autonomy in Above-Average Children." *Journal of Educational Psychology* 88 (1996): 203–14.

Mitchell, Joyce Slayton. "SATs Don't Get You In." *Education Week,* 27 May 1998: 33.

Mitchell, Ruth. *Testing for Learning: How New Approaches to Evaluation Can Improve American Schools.* New York: Free Press, 1992.

Moeller, Aleidine J., and Claus Reschke. "A Second Look at Grading and Classroom Performance: Report of a Research Study." *Modern Language Journal* 77 (1993): 163–69.

"A Moment of Truth." *Boston Globe,* 6 January 1998: A14.

Montaigne. *The Complete Essays of Montaigne,* translated by Donald M. Frame. Stanford, Calif.: Stanford University Press, 1958.

Morgan, George W. *The Human Predicament: Dissolution and Wholeness.* New York: Delta, 1970.

Morrow, Lesley Mandel. "The Impact of a Literature-Based Program on Literacy

Achievement, Use of Literature, and Attitudes of Children from Minority Backgrounds." *Reading Research Quarterly* 27 (1992): 251–75.

Morrow, Lesley Mandel, Ellen M. O'Connor, and Jeffrey K. Smith. "Effects of a Story Reading Program on the Literacy Development of *At-Risk* Kindergarten Children." *Journal of Reading Behavior* 22 (1990): 255–75.

Mosle, Sara. "The Answer Is National Standards." *New York Times Magazine,* 27 October 1996: 45–47, 56, 68.

Mueller, Claudia M., and Carol S. Dweck. "Praise for Intelligence Can Undermine Children's Motivation and Performance." *Journal of Personality and Social Psychology* 75 (1998): 33–52.

National Center for Education Statistics. "Understanding the Performance of U.S. Students on International Assessments." ERIC Document 370979. 1994. (Available at http://www.uncg.edu/edu/ericcass/achieve/docs/ed370979.htm.)

National Forum on Assessment. *Principles and Indicators for Student Assessment Systems.* Cambridge, Mass.: National Center for Fair and Open Testing (FairTest), 1995.

Natriello, Gary. "Failing Grades for Retention." *School Administrator,* August 1998: 14–17.

Neill, Monty. *Testing Our Children: A Report Card on State Assessment Systems.* Cambridge, Mass.: National Center for Fair and Open Testing, 1997.

Neill, Monty, Phyllis Bursh, Bob Schaeffer, Carolyn Thall, Marilyn Yohe, and Pamela Zappardino. *Implementing Performance Assessments: A Guide to Classroom, School and System Reform.* Cambridge, Mass.: FairTest, 1995.

Neill, D. Monty, and Noe J. Medina. "Standardized Testing: Harmful to Educational Health." *Phi Delta Kappan,* May 1989: 688–97.

Newman, Richard S., and Mahna T. Schwager. "Students' Help Seeking During Problem Solving: Effects of Grade, Goal, and Prior Achievement." *American Educational Research Journal* 32 (1995): 352–76.

Newmann, Fred M. "Conclusion." In *Student Engagement and Achievement in American Secondary Schools,* edited by Fred M. Newmann. New York: Teachers College Press, 1992a.

———. "Higher-Order Thinking and Prospects for Classroom Thoughtfulness." In *Student Engagement and Achievement in American Secondary Schools,* edited by Fred M. Newmann. New York: Teachers College Press, 1992b.

———. "Introduction." In *Student Engagement and Achievement in American Secondary Schools,* edited by Fred M. Newmann. New York: Teachers College Press, 1992c.

Newmann, Fred M., Helen M. Marks, and Adam Gamoran. "Authentic Pedagogy and Student Performance." *American Journal of Education* 104 (1996): 280–312.

Nicholls, John G. *The Competitive Ethos and Democratic Education.* Cambridge, Mass.: Harvard University Press, 1989.

———. "Students as Educational Theorists." In *Student Perceptions in the Classroom,* edited by Dale H. Schunk and Judith L. Meece. Hillsdale, N.J.: Erlbaum, 1992.

Nicholls, John G., and Susan P. Hazzard. *Education as Adventure: Lessons from the Second Grade.* New York: Teachers College Press, 1993.

Noble, Audrey J., and Mary Lee Smith. "Old and New Beliefs About Measurement-Driven Reform: 'The More Things Change, the More They Stay the Same.' " CSE Technical Report 373. Los Angeles: National Center for Research on Evaluation, Standards, and Student Testing (CRESST), 1994. (Available at http://cresst96.cse.ucla.edu/Reports/TECH373.PDF.)

Noddings, Nel. *The Challenge to Care in Schools: An Alternative Approach to Education.* New York: Teachers College Press, 1992.

Nolen, Susan Bobbitt. "Reasons for Studying: Motivational Orientations and Study Strategies." *Cognition and Instruction* 5 (1988): 269–87.

Novak, Joseph D. "How Do We Learn Our Lesson?" *Science Teacher*, March 1993: 50–55.

Oakes, Jeannie. *Keeping Track: How Schools Structure Inequality.* New Haven, Conn.: Yale University Press, 1985.

Office of Education. *Follow Through: Lessons Learned from Its Evaluation and Need to Improve Its Administration.* (Report to the Congress by the Comptroller General of the United States.) Washington, D.C.: U.S. General Accounting Office, 1975.

Ogle, Donna M. "K-W-L: A Teaching Model That Develops Active Reading of Expository Text." *Reading Teacher* 39 (1986): 564–70.

Ohanian, Susan. "Call Me Teacher." In *Whole Language: The Debate.* Bloomington, Ind.: ERIC Clearinghouse on Reading, English, and Communication, 1994.

———. *Ask Ms. Class.* York, Me.: Stenhouse, 1996a.

———. "Is That Penguin Stuffed or Real?" *Phi Delta Kappan,* December 1996b: 277–84.

Olson, Lynn. "The Push for Accountability Gathers Steam." *Education Week,* 11 February 1998: 1.

Otto, Beverly White. "Signs of Emergent Literacy Among Inner-City Kindergartners in a Storybook Reading Program." *Reading and Writing Quarterly* 9 (1993): 151–62.

Owings, William A., and Susan Magliaro. "Grade Retention: A History of Failure." *Educational Leadership,* September 1998: 86–88.

Paris, David C. "Schools, Scapegoats, and Skills: Educational Reform and the Economy." Originally published in *Policy Studies Journal,* 1994. Excerpted in *Education, Inc.: Turning Learning into a Business,* edited by Alfie Kohn. Arlington Heights, Ill.: IRI/Skylight, 1997.

Paris, Scott G., Theresa A. Lawton, Julianne C. Turner, and Jodie L. Roth. "A Developmental Perspective on Standardized Achievement Testing." *Educational Researcher,* June–July 1991: 12–20.

Parsons, Jacquelynne E., and Diane N. Ruble. "The Development of Achievement-Related Expectancies." *Child Development* 48 (1977): 1075–79.

Pascarella, Ernest T., Herbert J. Walberg, Linda K. Junker, and Geneva D. Haertel. "Continuing Motivation in Science for Early and Late Adolescents." *American Educational Research Journal* 18 (1981): 439–52.

Paterson, Frances R. A. "The Christian Right and the Prophonics Movement." Paper presented at the annual meeting of the American Educational Research Association, San Diego, April 1998.

Paul, Richard, A. J. A. Binker, Douglas Martin, Chris Vetrano, and Heidi Kreklau. *Critical Thinking Handbook: 6th–9th Grades.* Rohnert Park, Calif.: Center for Critical Thinking, Sonoma State University, 1989.

Pavan, Barbara Nelson. "The Benefits of Nongraded Schools." *Educational Leadership,* October 1992: 22–25.

Pear, Robert. "Modest Gains Reported in National Reading Tests." *New York Times,* 11 February 1999: A21.

Pearlman, Charles. "The Effects of Level of Effectance Motivation, IQ, and a Penalty/Reward Contingency on the Choice of Problem Difficulty." *Child Development* 55 (1984): 537–42.

Peck, Donald M., Stanley M. Jencks, and Michael L. Connell. "Improving Instruction Through Brief Interviews." *Arithmetic Teacher,* November 1989: 15–17.

Pentony, Joseph F. "Cultural Literacy: A Concurrent Validation." *Educational and Psychological Measurement* 52 (1992): 967–72.

Perkins, David. *Smart Schools: Better Thinking and Learning for Every Child.* New York: Free Press, 1992.

Perrone, Vito. "How to Engage Students in Learning." *Educational Leadership,* February 1994: 11–13.

———. "Why Do We Need a Pedagogy of Understanding?" In *Teaching for Understanding,* edited by Martha Stone Wiske. San Francisco: Jossey-Bass, 1998.

Piaget, Jean. *To Understand Is To Invent: The Future of Education.* Originally published 1948. New York: Grossman, 1973.

Pines, Burton Yale. *Back to Basics.* New York: Morrow, 1982.

Popham, W. James. "Performance Tests of Teaching Proficiency: Rationale, Development, and Validation." *American Educational Research Journal* 8 (1971): 105–17.

———. *Educational Evaluation.* 3rd ed. Boston: Allyn & Bacon, 1993.

———. "Farewell, Curriculum." *Phi Delta Kappan,* January 1998: 380–84.

———. "Why Standardized Tests Don't Measure Educational Quality." *Educational Leadership,* March 1999: 8–15.

Porter, Andrew. "A Curriculum Out of Balance: The Case of Elementary School Mathematics." *Educational Researcher,* June–July 1989: 9–15.

Powell, Robert W. "Grades, Learning, and Student Evaluation of Instruction." *Research in Higher Education* 7 (1977): 193–205.

Powers, John. "Feeling Good (for Nothing)." *Boston Globe Magazine,* 24 January 1993: 8.

Prawat, Richard S. "Teaching for Understanding: Three Key Attributes." *Teaching and Teacher Education* 5 (1989): 315–28.

Pritchard, Ivor. "Judging Standards in Standards-Based Reform." *Perspective* (publication of the Council for Basic Education), Summer 1996: 1–20.

Purcell-Gates, Victoria, Ellen McIntyre, and Penny A. Freppon. "Learning Written Storybook Language in School: A Comparison of Low-SES Children in Skills-Based and Whole Language Classrooms." *American Educational Research Journal* 32 (1995): 659–85.

Putnam, Ralph T., Magdalene Lampert, and Penelope L. Peterson. "Alternative Perspectives on Knowing Mathematics in Elementary Schools." In *Review of Research in Education,* vol. 16, edited by Courtney B. Cazden. Washington, D.C.: American Educational Research Association, 1990.

Queen, J. Allen, and Kimberly A. Gaskey. "Steps for Improving School Climate in Block Scheduling." *Phi Delta Kappan,* October 1997: 158–61.

Rainey, Robert G. "The Effects of Directed versus Non-Directed Laboratory Work on High School Chemistry Achievement." *Journal of Research in Science Teaching* 3 (1965): 286–92.

Rasmussen, Karen. "Looping—Discovering the Benefits of Multiyear Teaching." *ASCD* [Association for Supervision and Curriculum Development] *Education Update,* March 1998: 1, 3–4.

Rawl, Ruth K., and Frances S. O'Tuel. "A Comparison of Three Prereading Approaches for Kindergarten Students." *Reading Improvement* 19 (1982): 205–11.

Ray, Carol Axtell, and Roslyn Arlin Mickelson. "Restructing Students for Restructured Work: The Economy, School Reform, and Non-College-Bound Youths." Originally published in *Sociology of Education,* 1993. Excerpted in *Education, Inc.: Turning Learning into a Business,* edited by Alfie Kohn. Arlington Heights, Ill.: IRI/Skylight, 1997.

Raywid, Mary Anne. "Small Schools: A Reform That Works." *Educational Leadership,* December 1997/January 1998: 34–39.

Reigeluth, Charles M. "Educational Standards: To Standardize or to Customize Learning?" *Phi Delta Kappan,* November 1997: 202–6.

Resnick, Lauren B. *Education and Learning to Think.* Washington, D.C.: National Academy Press, 1987.

Resnick, Lauren B., and Leopold E. Klopfer. "Toward the Thinking Curriculum: An Overview." In *Toward the Thinking Curriculum: Current Cognitive Research,* edited by Lauren B. Resnick and Leopold E. Klopfer. Alexandria, Va.: Association for Supervision and Curriculum Development, 1989.

Resnick, Lauren B., and Katherine J. Nolan. "Standards for Education." In *Debating the Future of American Education: Do We Need National Standards and Assessments?,* edited by Diane Ravitch. Washington, D.C.: Brookings Institution, 1995.

Resnick, Lauren B., and Daniel P. Resnick. "Tests as Standards of Achievement in Schools." In *The Uses of Standardized Tests in American Education: Proceedings of the 1989 ETS Invitational Conference.* Princeton, N.J.: Educational Testing Service, 1990.

Reutzel, D. Ray, and Robert B. Cooter. "Whole Language: Comparative Effects on First-Grade Reading Achievement." *Journal of Educational Research* 83 (1990): 252–57.

Reynolds, Arthur, Judy Temple, and Ann McCoy. "Grade Retention Doesn't Work." *Education Week,* 17 September 1997: 36.

Reynolds, Sherrie, and Kathleen Martin. "Reframing Is a Way of Teaching." *The Constructivist,* Fall 1996: 15–19.

Ribowsky, Helene. "The Effects of a Code Emphasis Approach and a Whole Language Approach upon Emergent Literacy of Kindergarten Children." 1985. Available as ERIC Document 269720.

Riggs, Janet Morgan. "Self-Handicapping and Achievement." In *Achievement and Motivation: A Social-Developmental Perspective,* edited by Ann K. Boggiano and Thane S. Pittman. Cambridge, Eng.: Cambridge University Press, 1992.

Ritchie, Charles C. "The Eight-Year Study: Can We Afford to Ignore It?" *Educational Leadership,* February 1971: 484–86.

Ross, Sharon H. "Parts, Wholes, and Place Value: A Developmental View." *Arithmetic Teacher,* February 1989: 47–51.

Rossi, Rosalind. "Schools Testing the Limits." *Chicago Sun-Times,* 22 March 1999.

Rotberg, Iris C. "Interpretation of International Test Score Comparisons." *Science,* 15 May 1998a: 1030–31.

———. "The Trouble with Ranking." *American School Board Journal,* June 1998b: 26–28.

Rothenberg, James. "The Open Classroom Reconsidered." *Elementary School Journal* 90 (1989): 69–86.

Rothman, Robert. *Measuring Up: Standards, Assessment, and School Reform.* San Francisco: Jossey-Bass, 1995.

Rothstein, Richard. *The Way We Were?: The Myths and Realities of America's Student Achievement.* New York: Century Foundation Press, 1998.

Routman, Regie. *Invitations: Changing as Teachers and Learners K–12.* Portsmouth, N.H.: Heinemann, 1991.

———. *Literacy at the Crossroads: Crucial Talk About Reading, Writing, and Other Teaching Dilemmas.* Portsmouth, N.H.: Heinemann, 1996.

Ryan, Allison M., and Paul R. Pintrich. " 'Should I Ask for Help?': The Role of Motivation and Attitudes in Adolescents' Help Seeking in Math Class." *Journal of Educational Psychology* 89 (1997): 329–41.

Ryan, Richard M., James P. Connell, and Wendy S. Grolnick. "When Achievement Is *Not* Intrinsically Motivated: A Theory of Internalization and Self-Regulation in

School." In *Achievement and Motivation: A Social-Developmental Perspective,* edited by Ann K. Boggiano and Thane S. Pittman. Cambridge, Eng.: Cambridge University Press, 1992.

Ryan, Richard M., James P. Connell, and Robert W. Plant. "Emotions in Nondirected Text Learning." *Learning and Individual Differences* 2 (1990): 1–17.

Ryan, Richard M., and Wendy S. Grolnick. "Origins and Pawns in the Classroom: Self-Report and Projective Assessments of Individual Differences in Children's Perceptions." *Journal of Personality and Social Psychology* 50 (1986): 550–58.

Ryan, Richard M., Richard Koestner, and Edward L. Deci. "Ego-Involved Persistence: When Free-Choice Behavior Is Not Intrinsically Motivated." *Motivation and Emotion* 15 (1991): 185–205.

Sacks, Colin H., and John R. Mergendoller. "The Relationship Between Teachers' Theoretical Orientation Toward Reading and Student Outcomes in Kindergarten Children with Different Initial Reading Abilities." *American Educational Research Journal* 34 (1997): 721–39.

Sacks, Peter. "Standardized Testing: Meritocracy's Crooked Yardstick." *Change,* March/April 1997: 25–31.

Sadler, Philip M., and Robert H. Tai. "Success in College Physics: The Role of High School Preparation." Unpublished ms. Cambridge, Mass.: Harvard Smithsonian Center for Astrophysics and Harvard Graduate School of Education, 1997.

Salili, Farideh, Martin L. Maehr, Richard L. Sorensen, and Leslie J. Fyans, Jr. "A Further Consideration of the Effects of Evaluation on Motivation." *American Educational Research Journal* 13 (1976): 85–102.

Samson, Gordon E., M. Elizabeth Graue, Thomas Weinstein, and Herbert J. Walberg. "Academic and Occupational Performance: A Quantitative Synthesis." *American Educational Research Journal* 21 (1984): 311–21.

Sapon-Shevin, Mara, and Nancy Schniedewind. "If Cooperative Learning's the Answer, What Are the Questions?" *Journal of Education* 174, 2 (1992): 11–37.

Sarason, Seymour B. "Some Reactions to What We Have Learned." *Phi Delta Kappan,* September 1995: 84–85.

Schiefele, Ulrich. "Topic Interest, Text Representation, and Quality of Experience." *Contemporary Educational Psychology* 21 (1996): 3–18.

Schifter, Deborah. "A Constructivist Perspective on Teaching and Learning Mathematics." In *Constructivism: Theory, Perspectives, and Practice,* edited by Catherine Twomey Fosnot. New York: Teachers College Press, 1996.

Schmidt, William H., et al. *Facing the Consequences: Using TIMSS for a Closer Look at United States Mathematics and Science Education.* Dordrecht, Neth.: Kluwer, in press.

Schoen, Harold L., James T. Fey, Christian R. Hirsch, and Arthur F. Coxford. "Issues and Options in the Math Wars." *Phi Delta Kappan,* February 1999: 444–53.

Schoenfeld, Alan H. "When Good Teaching Leads to Bad Results: The Disasters of 'Well-Taught' Mathematics Courses." *Educational Psychologist* 23 (1988): 145–66.

Scholtes, Peter R. *The Leader's Handbook.* New York: McGraw-Hill, 1998.

"School Haze." *New Republic,* 16 December 1991: 7–8.

Schraw, Gregory, Terri Flowerday, and Marcy F. Reisetter. "The Role of Choice in Reader Engagement." *Journal of Educational Psychology* 90 (1998): 705–14.

Schuster, Edgar H. "Reforming English Language Arts." *Phi Delta Kappan,* March 1999: 518–24.

Schweinhart, Lawrence J., and Charles F. Hohmann. "The High/Scope K–3 Curriculum: A New Approach." *Principal,* May 1992: 16–19.
Schweinhart, Lawrence J., and David P. Weikart. "The High/Scope Preschool Curriculum Comparison Study Through Age 23." *Early Childhood Research Quarterly* 12 (1997): 117–43.
Schweinhart, Lawrence J., David P. Weikart, and Mary B. Larner. "Consequences of Three Preschool Curriculum Models Through Age 15." *Early Childhood Research Quarterly* 1 (1986): 15–45.
"Science Leader Criticizes Tests." *FairTest Examiner,* Spring 1998: 8.
Searfoss, Lyndon W., and Billie J. Enz. "Can Teacher Evaluation Reflect Holistic Instruction?" *Educational Leadership,* March 1996: 38–41.
Semb, George. "The Effects of Mastery Criteria and Assignment Length on College-Student Test Performance." *Journal of Applied Behavior Analysis* 7 (1974): 61–69.
Sengupta, Somini. "Are Teachers of Teachers Out of Touch?: A Gulf Is Seen in Education Professors' View on Fundamentals." *New York Times,* 22 October 1997: A28.
Sergiovanni, Thomas J. *Leadership for the Schoolhouse.* San Francisco: Jossey-Bass, 1996.
Shanker, Albert. "Business Makes Sense." Opinion column published as advertisement by the American Federation of Teachers. *New York Times,* 25 September 1994: E9.
———. "Why Schools Need Standards and Innovation." *Education Week,* 6 December 1995: 48, 37.
Sharan, Shlomo. "The Group Investigation Approach to Cooperative Learning: Theoretical Foundations." In *Perspectives on Small Group Learning: Theory and Practice,* edited by Mark Brubacher, Ryder Payne, and Kemp Rickett. Oakville, Ont.: Rubicon, 1990a.
———. "Cooperative Learning: A Perspective on Research and Practice." In *Cooperative Learning: Theory and Research,* edited by Shlomo Sharan. New York: Praeger, 1990b.
Sharan, Yael, and Shlomo Sharan. *Expanding Cooperative Learning Through Group Investigation.* New York: Teachers College Press, 1992.
Shepard, Lorrie A., and Carribeth L. Bliem. "Parent Opinions About Standardized Tests, Teacher's Information and Performance Assessments: A Case Study of the Effects of Alternative Assessment in Instruction, Student Learning and Accountability Practices." CSE Technical Report 367. Los Angeles: National Center for Research on Evaluation, Standards, and Student Testing (CRESST), 1993. (Available at http://cresst96.cse.ucla.edu/Reports/TECH367.PDF.)
Shepard, Lorrie A., and Mary Lee Smith. "Introduction and Overview." In *Flunking Grades: Research and Policies on Retention,* edited by Lorrie A. Shepard and Mary Lee Smith. London: Falmer Press, 1989.
Silberman, Charles E. *Crisis in the Classroom: The Remaking of American Education.* New York: Random House, 1970.
Simmons, Tim. "Schools Find Value, Vexation in ABCs Program." [Raleigh, N.C.] *News and Observer,* 26 October 1997.
Simon, Martin A., and Deborah Schifter. "Toward a Constructivist Perspective: The Impact of a Mathematics Teacher Inservice Program on Students." *Educational Studies in Mathematics* 25 (1993): 331–40.
Singham, Mano. "The Canary in the Mine: The Achievement Gap Between Black and White Students." *Phi Delta Kappan,* September 1998: 9–15.

Sizer, Theodore R. *Horace's Compromise: The Dilemma of the American High School.* Boston: Houghton Mifflin, 1984.

———. *Horace's School: Redesigning the American High School.* Boston: Houghton Mifflin, 1992.

Skaalvik, Einar M. "Self-Enhancing and Self-Defeating Ego Orientation: Relations with Task and Avoidance Orientation, Achievement, Self-Perceptions, and Anxiety." *Journal of Educational Psychology* 89 (1997): 71–81.

Skinner, Ellen A., James G. Wellborn, and James P. Connell. "What It Takes to Do Well in School and Whether I've Got It: A Process Model of Perceived Control and Children's Engagement and Achievement in School." *Journal of Educational Psychology* 82 (1990): 22–32.

Smith, Frank. "Learning to Read: The Never-Ending Debate." *Phi Delta Kappan,* February 1992: 432–41.

Smith, Hilton. "Foxfire Teachers' Networks." In *Democratic Teacher Education: Programs, Processes, Problems, and Prospects,* edited by John M. Novak. Albany: State University of New York Press, 1994.

Smith, Julia B., BetsAnn Smith, and Anthony S. Bryk. "Six Reasons Why Instruction Slows Down." In *Setting the Pace: Opportunities to Learn in Chicago's Elementary Schools.* Chicago: Consortium on Chicago School Research, November 1998.

Smith, Mary Lee. "Put to the Test: The Effects of External Testing on Teachers." *Educational Researcher,* June–July 1991: 8–11.

Smith, Teresa. "Standardized Tests Are Irrelevant" (letter to the editor). *Boston Globe,* 4 January 1999: A14.

Sommerfeld, Meg. "Research Spans Spectrum on Block Scheduling." *Education Week,* 22 May 1996: 15.

Sontag, Deborah. "Teachers' Leader Calls for a Return to Tradition." *New York Times,* 23 March 1992: B7.

Stahl, Steven A. "Is Whole Language 'The Real Thing'?" In *Whole Language: The Debate.* Bloomington, Ind.: ERIC Clearinghouse on Reading, English, and Communication, 1994.

Stebbins, Linda B., Robert G. St. Pierre, Richard B. Anderson, and Thomas R. Cerva. *Education as Experimentation: A Planned Variation Model.* Volume IV-A: *An Evaluation of Follow Through.* Cambridge, Mass.: Abt Associates, 1977.

Steinberg, Jacques. "Clashing Over Education's One True Faith." *New York Times,* 14 December 1997: 14.

———. "Stress Test." *New York Times Education Life,* 3 January 1999: 18.

Stevenson, Harold W. "A Study of Three Cultures: Germany, Japan, and the United States—An Overview of the TIMSS Case Study Project." *Phi Delta Kappan,* March 1998: 524–29.

Stiggins, Richard J. *Student-Centered Classroom Assessment.* New York: Macmillan, 1994.

Stigler, James W., and James Hiebert. "Understanding and Improving Classroom Mathematics Instruction: An Overview of the TIMSS Video Study." *Phi Delta Kappan,* September 1997: 14–21.

Stigler, James W., and Harold W. Stevenson. "How Asian Teachers Polish Each Lesson to Perfection." *American Educator,* Spring 1991: 12–20, 43–47.

Stipek, Deborah J. *Motivation to Learn: From Theory to Practice.* 2d ed. Boston: Allyn and Bacon, 1993.

Stipek, Deborah, Rachelle Feilder, Denise Daniels, and Sharon Milburn. "Effects of Different Instructional Approaches on Young Children's Achievement and Motivation." *Child Development* 66 (1995): 209–223.

Stipek, Deborah J., and Joel M. Hoffman. "Children's Achievement-Related Expectancies as a Function of Academic Performance Histories and Sex." *Journal of Educational Psychology* 72 (1980): 861–65.

Stipek, Deborah J., and John R. Weisz. "Perceived Academic Control and Academic Achievement." *Review of Educational Research* 51 (1981): 101–37.

Stolberg, Sheryl. "Students Sabotage School on State Test." *Los Angeles Times,* 27 April 1989: II, 1, 8.

Strickland, Dorothy S. "What's Basic in Beginning Reading?: Finding Common Ground." *Educational Leadership,* March 1998: 6–10.

Sulzby, Elizabeth, Chica McCabe Branz, and Roberta Buhle. "Repeated Readings of Literature and Low Socioeconomic Status Black Kindergartners and First Graders." *Reading and Writing Quarterly* 9 (1993): 183–96.

Sweet, Anne P., and John T. Guthrie. "How Children's Motivations Relate to Literacy Development and Instruction." *Reading Teacher* 49 (1996): 660–62.

Talbert, Joan E., and Milbrey W. McLaughlin. "Understanding Teaching in Context." In *Teaching for Understanding: Challenges for Policy and Practice,* edited by David K. Cohen, Milbrey W. McLaughlin, and Joan E. Talbert. San Francisco: Jossey-Bass, 1993.

Taylor, Kathe, and Sherry Walton. *Children at the Center: A Workshop Approach to Standardized Test Preparation, K–8.* Portsmouth, N.H.: Heinemann, 1988.

Tchudi, Stephen. "Slogans Indeed: A Reply to Hirsch." *Educational Leadership,* December 1987/January 1988: 72–74.

"Testing Boycott in Denver." *FairTest Examiner,* Spring 1992: 7.

" 'Test Score Optional' Admissions Enhance Equity & Excellence." *FairTest Examiner,* Fall 1998: 1,8.

"Text of Policy Statement Issued at National Summit." *Education Week,* 3 April 1996: 13.

Traver, Rob. "What Is a Good Guiding Question?" *Educational Leadership,* March 1998: 70–73.

Tunnell, Michael O., and James S. Jacobs. "Using 'Real' Books: Research Findings on Literature Based Reading Instruction." *Reading Teacher* 42 (1989): 470–77.

Urdan, Tim, Carol Midgley, and Eric M. Anderman. "The Role of Classroom Goal Structure in Students' Use of Self-Handicapping Strategies." *American Educational Research Journal* 35 (1998): 101–22.

Utman, Christopher H. "Performance Effects of Motivational State: A Meta-Analysis." *Personality and Social Psychology Review* 1 (1997): 170–82.

Van Moorlehem, Tracy. "Students, Parents Rebel Against State Test." *Detroit Free Press,* 29 April 1998: 1-A.

Van Moorlehem, Tracy, and Tamara Audi. "Most High School Students Meet Challenge of Revised State Tests." *Detroit Free Press,* 30 October 1998: 8-B.

Varble, Mary Ellen. "Analysis of Writing Samples of Students Taught by Teachers Using Whole Language and Traditional Approaches." *Journal of Educational Research* 83 (1990): 245–51.

Vasta, Ross, and Robert F. Sarmiento. "Liberal Grading Improves Evaluations But Not Performance." *Journal of Educational Psychology* 71 (1979): 207–11.

———. "Less Is More." *Education Week,* 12 July 1995: 33–35.

Viadero, Debra. "Mixed Blessings." *Education Week,* 8 May 1996: 31–33.

———. "Tenn. Class-Size Study Finds Long-Term Benefits." *Education Week,* 5 May 1999: 5.

Vigue, Doreen Iudica, and Beth Daley. "Some Students' MCAS Strategy: Refuse It." *Boston Globe,* 27 April 1999: B1, B8.

Vygotsky, L. S. *Mind in Society: The Development of Higher Psychological Processes*. Cambridge, Mass.: Harvard University Press, 1978.

Wagner, Tony. "Change as Collaborative Inquiry." *Phi Delta Kappan*, March 1998: 512–17.

Wainer, Howard. "Does Spending Money on Education Help?" *Educational Researcher*, December 1993: 22–24.

Wakefield, Alice P. "Supporting Math Thinking." *Phi Delta Kappan*, November 1997: 233–36.

Walberg, Herbert J. "Improving the Productivity of America's Schools." *Educational Leadership*, May 1984: 19–27.

Walsh, Mark. "Colo. Officials Couldn't Be Happier with Low Scores." *Education Week*, 26 November 1997: 14.

Wang, Margaret C., and Billie Stiles. "An Investigation of Children's Concept of Self-Responsibility for Their School Learning." *American Educational Research Journal* 13 (1976): 159–79.

Watson, Dorothy J. "Defining and Describing Whole Language." *Elementary School Journal* 90 (1989): 129–41.

Watts, Heidi. "Only by Living Them." In *Democratic Teacher Education: Programs, Processes, Problems, and Prospects,* edited by John M. Novak. Albany: State University of New York Press, 1994.

Watzlawick, Paul, ed. *The Invented Reality: How Do We Know What We Believe We Know?* New York: Norton, 1984.

Weaver, Constance, and Ellen H. Brinkley. "Phonics, Whole Language, and the Religious and Political Right." In *In Defense of Good Teaching: What Teachers Need to Know About the "Reading Wars,"* edited by Kenneth S. Goodman. York, Me.: Stenhouse, 1998.

Weaver, Constance, Lorraine Gillmeister-Krause, and Grace Vento-Zogby. *Creating Support for Effective Literacy Education*. Portsmouth, N.H.: Heinemann, 1996.

Webb, Noreen M. "Student Interaction and Learning in Small Groups." In *Learning to Cooperate, Cooperating to Learn,* edited by Robert Slavin, et al. New York: Plenum, 1985.

Weiner, Bernard. "A Theory of Motivation for Some Classroom Experiences." *Journal of Educational Psychology* 71 (1979): 3–25.

Welsh, Patrick. "Why Our Students Keep Snoozing Through Science." *Washington Post*, 20 May 1990: B1, B3.

White, Richard T. "Raising the Quality of Learning: Principles from Long-Term Action Research." In *Effective and Responsible Teaching: The New Synthesis,* edited by Fritz K. Oser, Andreas Dick, and Jean-Luc Patry. San Francisco: Jossey-Bass, 1992.

Whitehead, Alfred North. *The Aims of Education and Other Essays*. Originally published 1929. New York: Free Press, 1967.

Wigfield, Allan. "Children's Attributions for Success and Failure: Effects of Age and Attentional Focus." *Journal of Educational Psychology* 80 (1988): 76–81.

Wiggins, Grant P. *Assessing Student Performance: Exploring the Purpose and Limits of Testing*. San Francisco: Jossey-Bass, 1993.

Willis, Scott. "Breaking the Lockstep: Educators Explore Alternatives to Whole-Class Instruction." *ASCD* [Association for Supervision and Curriculum Development] *Curriculum Update,* September 1994: 1, 6.

———. "Reinventing Science Education." *ASCD* [Association for Supervision and Curriculum Development] *Curriculum Update,* Summer 1995a: 1–8.

———. "Whole Language: Finding the Surest Way to Literacy." *ASCD* [Association for Supervision and Curriculum Development] *Curriculum Update,* Fall 1995b: 1–8.

Willis, Scott, and Kathy Checkley. "Bringing Mathematics to Life." *ASCD* [Association for Supervision and Curriculum Development] *Curriculum Update,* Summer 1996: 1–8.

Wilson, Suzanne M. "Deeply Rooted Change: A Tale of Learning to Teach Adventurously." In *Teaching for Understanding: Challenges for Policy and Practice,* edited by David K. Cohen, Milbrey W. McLaughlin, and Joan E. Talbert. San Francisco: Jossey-Bass, 1993.

Winerip, Michael. "Schools for Sale." *New York Times Magazine,* 14 June 1998.

———. "Homework Bound." *New York Times Education Life,* 3 January 1999: 28–31, 40.

Wirth, Arthur G. *Productive Work—In Industry and Schools.* Lanham, Md.: Univ. Press of America, 1983.

Wiske, Martha Stone. "How Teaching for Understanding Changes the Rules in the Classroom." *Educational Leadership,* February 1994: 19–21.

———. "What Is Teaching for Understanding?" In *Teaching for Understanding,* edited by Martha Stone Wiske. San Francisco: Jossey-Bass, 1998.

Wolf, Dennie, Janet Bixby, John Glenn III, and Howard Gardner. "To Use Their Minds Well: Investigating New Forms of Student Assessment." *Review of Research in Education,* vol. 17, edited by Gerald Grant. Washington, D.C.: American Educational Research Association, 1991.

Wolk, Steven. "Project-Based Learning: Pursuits with a Purpose." *Educational Leadership,* November 1994: 42–45.

———. *A Democratic Classroom.* Portsmouth, N.H.: Heinemann, 1998.

Wood, George. *Schools That Work: America's Most Innovative Public Education Programs.* New York: Plume, 1992.

———. "Democracy and the Curriculum." In *The Curriculum: Problems, Politics, and Possibilities,* edited by Landon E. Beyer and Michael W. Apple. Albany: State University of New York Press, 1988.

Wood, Terry. "Events in Learning Mathematics: Insights from Research in Classrooms." *Educational Studies in Mathematics* 30 (1996): 85–105.

Wood, Terry, Paul Cobb, and Erna Yackel. "Change in Teaching Mathematics: A Case Study." *American Educational Research Journal* 28 (1991): 587–616.

Wood, Terry, and Patricia Sellers. "Assessment of a Problem-Centered Mathematics Program: Third Grade." *Journal for Research in Mathematics Education* 27 (1996): 337–53.

———. "Deepening the Analysis: Longitudinal Assessment of a Problem-Centered Mathematics Program." *Journal for Research in Mathematics Education* 28 (1997): 163–86.

Worthen, Blaine R. "Discovery and Expository Task Presentation in Elementary Mathematics." *Journal of Educational Psychology: Monograph Supplement* 59 (1968): 1–13.

Yackel, Erna, Paul Cobb, and Terry Wood. "Small-Group Interactions as a Source of Learning Opportunities in Second-Grade Mathematics." *Journal of Research in Mathematics Education* 22 (1991): 390–408.

Yager, Robert E. "The Constructivist Learning Model." *Science Teacher,* September 1991: 52–57.

Yarborough, Betty H., and Roger A. Johnson. "Research That Questions the Traditional Elementary School Marking System." *Phi Delta Kappan,* April 1980: 527–28.

Zahorik, John A. "Encouraging — and Challenging — Students' Understandings." *Educational Leadership*, March 1997: 30–32.

Zehr, Mary Ann. "Manufacturers Endorse National Tests, Vouchers." *Education Week*, 14 January 1998: 14.

Zemelman, Steven, Harvey Daniels, and Arthur Hyde. *Best Practice: New Standards for Teaching and Learning in America's Schools*. 2d ed. Portsmouth, N.H.: Heinemann, 1998.

Zuckerman, Miron, Joseph Porac, Drew Lathin, Raymond Smith, and Edward L. Deci. "On the Importance of Self-Determination for Intrinsically Motivated Behavior." *Personality and Social Psychology Bulletin* 4 (1978): 443–46.

# ACKNOWLEDGMENTS

The anthropologist Lionel Tiger once told a story about a professor who was carrying his granddaughter on his shoulders one day and happened to meet a friend. The other man looked up at the girl and commented on how tall she was, to which she replied, "Not all of this is me."

The same is quite obviously true of what you have just read. While I can't possibly list everyone whose theories, research, and practice have contributed to my thinking, I can (and will) thank those people who read and commented on pieces of this book. Their suggestions ranged from "I'd recommend that you insert a comma over here" to "I'd recommend that you write about something else." Helpful comments and criticisms pertaining to their respective areas of expertise were offered by Monty Neill, Carol Dweck, Carol Midgley, Terry Wood, Dorothy Watson, Larry Schweinhart, Laurel Robertson, Catherine Lewis, and Jerry Bracey. Huge chunks of the manuscript, meanwhile, were read by four individuals to whom I am especially indebted: Alisa Kohn (relation), Bill Greene, Smokey Daniels, and Eric Schaps. The more changes I made that were suggested by all these people, the better the book became. That it came to be at all is due to my agent, Kim Witherspoon, and to a cadre of wonderful folks at Houghton Mifflin, notably Anton Mueller, all of whom have my gratitude.

A final word: I came to this project as a former student, dissatisfied with what I was made to do, and as a former teacher, uneasy (in retrospect) with what I unthinkingly made others do. I am also a teacher of teachers and a reader of research, but the role that I am thinking about at the moment is being a parent. Nothing brings those clichés about "the next generation" down to earth faster than having a representative of that generation right in your house. I am parental enough to insist that my daughter deserves an education that is less traditional and more meaningful than the one I had. I also hope that I am reasonable enough to insist that what my child deserves is what everyone's child deserves.

# INDEX

ability
 differences in, among children,
  251–52n53
 as explanation for achievement,
  34–36
 as fixed vs. improvable, 250n37
 grouping students by, 70, 107
 types of, as differentially valued,
  251–52n53
Accelerated Reader, 171
accountability
 as applied to alternative
  assessments, 203
 standardized testing as unnecessary
  for, 201
 as supporting traditional practices,
  16, 104, 128
 of teachers for practices dictated to
  them, 268n9
 valid vs. invalid versions of, 95,
  104, 128, 268–69n11
 vs. collecting information, as
  purpose of testing, 197
achievement
 as byproduct of interest in learning,
  127–30
 causes of overemphasis on, 21, 26,
  123–24
 definitions of, 31–32, 41, 211–12
 effects of overemphasizing, 21,
  25–40, 196–97
  on ability vs. effort attribution,
   34–36
  on interest in learning, 28
  on preference for challenge,
   29–31, 272–73n38
  on quality of learning, 31–33

 on reaction to failure, 28–29
 importance of, at different grade
  levels, 27
 significance of students'
  explanations for, 34
 and Tougher Standards movement,
  21, 26
 of U.S. students, 16–21, 226–27
Advanced Placement (AP) courses,
 89
African-American students. *See*
 Students of color
age. *See* Grade levels
Allington, Richard, 222, 223
alternative education. *See*
 Nontraditional education
American Federation of Teachers
 (AFT), 16
Antonucci, Robert V., 87
assessment. *See also* Grades;
 Standardized testing
 alternative forms of, 9, 192–93,
  198–204
 class tests not required for,
  191–93
 and curriculum, 192, 204, 254n82
 harms of overemphasizing, 124,
  196–97, 203, 275n25
 high-stakes version of alternative
  forms of, 203
 purposes of, 191
 of schools, 200–204
 student involvement in, 291n35
 use of sampling for, 202
at-risk students. *See* Low-achieving
 students
Ayers, Bill, 63, 82